POVERTY, LAW, AND DIVINE JUSTICE
IN PERSIAN AND HELLENISTIC JUDAH

Find this bk
frustrating —
bc he reads behind
tight text which
are not true Persian
era + ignores those
that are, as well as
admin/archival
texts!

no kent,
no Brant...

ANCIENT ISRAEL AND ITS LITERATURE

Thomas C. Römer, General Editor

Number 32

POVERTY, LAW, AND DIVINE JUSTICE
IN PERSIAN AND HELLENISTIC JUDAH

Johannes Unsok Ro

SBL PRESS

Atlanta

Copyright © 2018 by Johannes Unsok Ro

Library of Congress Cataloging-in-Publication Data

Names: Ro, Johannes Unsok, author.
Title: Poverty, law, and divine justice in Persian and Hellenistic Judah / by Johannes Unsok Ro.
Description: Atlanta : SBL Press, 2018. | Series: Ancient Israel and its literature ; Number 32 | Includes bibliographical references and index.
Identifiers: LCCN 2017060322 (print) | LCCN 2018001454 (ebook) | ISBN 9780884142850 (ebk.) | ISBN 9781628372069 (pbk. : alk. paper) | ISBN 9780884142867 (hbk. : alk. paper)
Subjects: LCSH: Bible. Old Testament—Criticism, interpretation, etc. | Jews—Economic conditions—History—586 B.C.–70 A.D. | Punishment—Biblical teaching. | Poor—Biblical teaching. | Qumran community. | Jewish law.
Classification: LCC BS1171.3 (ebook) | LCC BS1171.3 .R625 2018 (print) | DDC 221.6/7—dc23
LC record available at https://lccn.loc.gov/2017060322

Printed on acid-free paper.

לאקוקו ויושין

CONTENTS

PREFACE

This volume is a work that has grown organically. I have been interested in socioeconomic and theological issues in Judah in the Persian and Hellenistic periods for more than a decade. I started with the issue of the piety of the poor (*die Armenfrömmigkeit*). Then my interest developed, and my attention turned to the biblical law codes and the question of divine justice. This book is an attempt to bridge and connect these developmental theses to each other and to build a synthesis thereupon. I hope this work presents at least a first step toward this goal.

I owe a debt of sincere gratitude to my teachers, who have inspired, encouraged, and brought me to reevaluate many particulars throughout my journey through biblical studies. From the bottom of my heart, I herewith express my deep gratitude to Emeritus Professor Karl-Friedrich Pohlmann, the late Emeritus Professor Otto Kaiser, and Emeritus Professor Namiki Koichi.

Heartfelt thanks are due also to Professor Thomas Römer, who accepted this work into the Ancient Israel and Its Literature series. His insightful advice has enhanced the value of the final product. I also thank the copyeditors and other people from the SBL Press team who carefully produced this volume.

Professor Diana Edelman in Oslo, Professor Wolfgang Zwickel in Mainz, and Professor Jörg Rüpke in Erfurt have kindly read an earlier version of this volume and provided me with useful and substantial comments. I would like to express gratitude to each of them for their help.

The present volume has benefited from the generous support of the Japan Society for the Promotion of Science (JSPS) through the KAKENHI research grant (15K02061).

Last but by no means least, I also wish to express deep appreciation to my wife Ikuko and my son Yushin. My wife has supported me for better as well as for worse throughout the time I spent researching and creating this volume. My son has given me his wonderful smiles, which have also made me smile. I dedicate this volume to Ikuko and Yushin.

Parts of this monograph were published in earlier forms as follows, and I am grateful to the respective publishers for permission to include them in this book: chapter 2 from "Socioeconomic Context of Post-exilic Community and Literacy," *ZAW* 120 (2008): 597–611; chapter 3 from "The Portrayal of Judean Communities in Persian Era Palestine through the Lens of the Covenant Code," *Semitica* 56 (2014): 249–89; chapter 5 from "The Theological Concept of YHWH's Punitive Justice in the Hebrew Bible: Historical Development in the Context of the Judean Community in the Persian Period," *VT* 61 (2011): 406–25; *From Judah to Judaea: Socioeconomic Structures and Processes in the Persian Period*, ed. Johannes Unsok Ro, HBM 43 (Sheffield: Sheffield Phoenix, 2013), 87–107; chapter 6, "3.3 Die Armenpsalmen," in *Die sogenannte "Armenfröm-migkeit" im nachexilischen Israel*, BZAW 322 (Berlin: de Gruyter, 2002), 113–99; and chapter 7, "2. Armenfrömmigkeit in der Qumrangemeinde," in *Die sogenannte "Armenfrömmigkeit" im nachexilischen Israel*, BZAW 322 (Berlin: de Gruyter, 2002), 9–34; "The Piety of the Poor in the Community of Qumran and Its Historical Origins," in *From Judah to Judaea: Socioeconomic Structures and Processes in the Persian Period*, ed. Johannes Unsok Ro, HBM 43 (Sheffield: Sheffield Phoenix, 2013), 54–86.

ABBREVIATIONS

1 En.	1 Enoch
2ms	second-person masculine singular
AB	Anchor Bible
ABD	Freedman, David Noel, ed. *Anchor Bible Dictionary*. 6 vols. New York: Doubleday, 1992.
ABRL	Anchor Bible Reference Library
ABS	Archaeology and Biblical Studies
AchH	Achaemenid History
AcT	*Acta Theologica*
AET	Abhandlungen zur Evangelischen Theologie
AIL	Ancient Israel and Its Literature
AM.T	Athenäums Monografien, Theologie
AnBib	Analecta Biblica
ASR	*American Sociological Review*
ASTI	*Annual of the Swedish Theological Institute*
ATD	Das Alte Testament Deutsch
ATDan	Acta theologica Danica
ATSAT	Arbeiten zu Text und Sprache im Alten Testament
BA	*Biblical Archaeologist*
BASOR	*Bulletin of the American Schools of Oriental Research*
BBB	Bonner biblische Beiträge
BCT	*Bible and Critical Theory*
BETL	Bibliotheca Ephemeridum Theologicarum Lovaniensium
Bib	*Biblica*
BHS	Biblia Hebraica Stuttgartensia
BibInt	*Biblical Interpretation*
BibInt	Biblical Interpretation Series
BiE	Biblische Enzyklopädie
BKAT	Biblischer Kommentar, Altes Testament
BN	*Biblische Notizen*

BThSt	Biblisch-theologische Studien
BVB	Beiträge zum Verstehen der Bibel
BWANT	Beiträge zur Wissenschaft vom Alten und Neuen Testament
BZABR	Beihefte zur Zeitschrift für Altorientalische und Biblische Rechtsgeschichte
BZAW	Beihefte zur Zeitschrift für die alttestamentliche Wissenschaft
CBC	Cambridge Bible Commentary
CBQ	*Catholic Biblical Quarterly*
CC	Covenant Code
CHJ	Davies, William D., and Louis Finkelstein, eds. *The Cambridge History of Judaism*. 4 vols. Cambridge: Cambridge University Press, 1984–2006.
CThM.BW	Calwer theologische Monographien Bibelwissenschaft
CurBR	*Currents in Biblical Research*
DC	Deuteronomic Code
DMOA	Documenta et monumenta Orientis antiqui
DtrH	Deuteronomistic History
EBib	Etudes bibliques
ECC	Eerdmans Critical Commentary
EdF	Erträge der Forschung
EHPhR	Etudes d'histoire et de philosophie religieuses
ETL	*Ephemerides Theologicae Lovanienses*
EV	English verse number
EvT	*Evangelische Theologie*
FAT	Forschungen zum Alten Testament
FB	Forschung zur Bibel
FO	*Folia Orientalia*
FRLANT	Forschungen zur Religion und Literatur des Alten und Neuen Testaments
GAT	Grundrisse zum Alten Testament
HAT	Handbuch zum Alten Testament
HBAI	*Hebrew Bible and Ancient Israel*
HBM	Hebrew Bible Monographs
HBS	Herders Biblische Studien
HBT	*Horizons in Biblical Theology*
HC	Holiness Code
HKAT	Handkommentar zum Alten Testament

HThKAT	Herders theologischer Kommentar zum Alten Testament
HUCA	*Hebrew Union College Annual*
IBC	Interpretation: A Bible Commentary for Teaching and Preaching
ICC	International Critical Commentary
IRT	Issues in Religion and Theology
JBL	*Journal of Biblical Literature*
JBS	Jerusalem Biblical Studies
JETS	*Journal of the Evangelical Theological Society*
JJS	*Journal of Jewish Studies*
JQR	*Jewish Quarterly Review*
JPSTC	Jewish Publication Society Torah Commentary
JRASup	Journal of Roman Archaeology Supplement Series
JSHRZ	Jüdische Schriften aus hellenistisch-römischer Zeit
JSJ	*Journal for the Study of Judaism*
JSJSup	Supplements to the Journal for the Study of Judaism
JSOT	*Journal for the Study of the Old Testament*
JSOTSup	Journal for the Study of the Old Testament Supplement Series
JSS	*Journal of Semitic Studies*
KAT	Kommentar zum Alten Testament
KD	Deuteronomistic composition as postulated by Blum, among others
KHAb	Kölner historische Abhandlungen
KHC	Kurzer Hand-Commentar zum Alten Testament
KStTh	Kohlhammer Studienbücher Theologie
LAI	Library of Ancient Israel
LH	Laws of Hammurabi
LHBOTS	Library of Hebrew Bible/Old Testament Studies
LSTS	Library of Second Temple Studies
LXX	Septuagint
NCB	New Century Bible Commentary: Based on the Revised Standard Version
NCBiC	New Cambridge Bible Commentary
NEchtB	Neue Echter Bibel
NICOT	New International Commentary on the Old Testament
NSKAT	Neuer Stuttgarter Kommentar: Altes Testament
NStB	Neukirchener Studienbücher
NTOA	Novum Testamentum et Orbis Antiquus

OBO	Orbis Biblicus et Orientalis
OTE	*Old Testament Essays*
OTL	Old Testament Library
OTS	Old Testament Studies
OtSt	*Oudtestamentische Studiën*
PEQ	*Palestine Exploration Quarterly*
PNAS	*Proceedings of the National Academy of Sciences of the United States of America*
RB	*Revue Biblique*
RBS	Resources for Biblical Study
RBL	*Review of Biblical Literature*
RelSRev	*Religious Studies Review*
RevQ	*Revue de Qumran*
Saec	*Saeculum*
SANT	Studien zum Alten und Neuen Testament
SAT	Schriften des Alten Testaments
SBS	Stuttgarter Bibelstudien
SBLDS	Society of Biblical Literature Dissertation Series
SBLSP	Society of Biblical Literature Seminar Papers
SemeiaSt	Semeia Studies
SFSHJ	South Florida Studies in the History of Judaism
sg.	singular
SHANE	Studies in the History of the Ancient Near East
SHBC	Smyth & Helwys Bible Commentary
SJOT	*Scandinavian Journal of the Old Testament*
SNVAO.HF	Skrifter utgitt av det Norske Videnskaps-Akademi—Historisk-Filosofisk Klasse
STAR	Studies in Theology and Religion
STDJ	Studies on the Texts of the Desert of Judah
StudBib	Studia Biblica
STW	Suhrkamp Taschenbuch Wissenschaft
SUNT	Studien zur Umwelt des Neuen Testaments
SymS	Symposium Series
Syr.	Syriac
TB	Theologische Bucherei
TBN	Themes in Biblical Narrative
TeDi	Témoins de Dieu
tg.	targum
ThA	Theologische Arbeiten

ThSt	Theologische Studien
ThW	Theologische Wissenschaft
ThWAT	Botterweck, G. Johannes, and Helmer Ringgren, eds. *Theologisches Wörterbuch zum Alten Testament*. Stuttgart: Kohlhammer. 1970–2000.
TRE	Krause, Gerhard, and Gerhard Müller, eds. *Theologische Realenzyklopedie*. Berlin: de Gruyter, 1977–2004.
TU	Texte und Untersuchungen zur Geschichte der Altchristlichen Literatur,
TWNT	Kittel, Gerhard, and Gerhard Friedrich, eds. *Theologisches Wörterbuch zum Neuen Testament*. Stuttgart: Kohlhammer, 1932–1979.
TZ	*Theologische Zeitschrift*
UF	*Ugarit Forschungen*
UTB	Uni-Taschenbücher
WBC	Word Biblical Commentary
WdF	Wege der Forschung
WMANT	Wissenschaftliche Monographien zum Alten und Neuen Testament
WUNT	Wissenschaftliche Untersuchungen zum Neuen Testament
VWGTh	Veröffentlichungen der Wissenschaftlichen Gesellschaft für Theologie
VT	*Vetus Testamentum*
VTSup	Supplements to Vetus Testamentum
ZABR	*Zeitschrift für altorientalische und biblische Rechtgeschichte*
ZAW	*Zeitschrift für die alttestamentliche Wissenschaft*
ZBK	Zürcher Bibelkommentare
ZDPV	*Zeitschrift des Deutschen Palästina-Vereins*
ZKT	*Zeitschrift für katholische Theologie*
ZTK	*Zeitschrift für Theologie und Kirche*

1

CHALLENGES AND RESPONSES
OF THE SECOND TEMPLE PERIOD

The aim of this study is to understand the Judean communities in Persian- and Hellenistic-era Palestine (and, in the case of ch. 7, partially thereafter) as reflected in the Hebrew Bible. This study does not intend to develop a single thesis but to highlight some major issues in Persian- and Hellenistic-era Palestine. Thus, this book addresses some of the core themes in the study of the Judean community, including: the relationship between the shaping of the canon and literacy in the Judean community; "strangers" in the biblical law codes; the socioeconomic structures of Judean communities reflected in the biblical law codes; the development of the theological concept of divine punitive justice; the piety of the poor in certain psalms; and the concept of poverty in the Dead Sea Scrolls. These topics indicate that the Judean communities in Persian- and Hellenistic-era Palestine are crucially important for understanding the background of the formation of the Hebrew Bible. The scriptural scope of this book includes the Pentateuch, the Deuteronomistic History (hereafter DtrH), the prophetic literature, the Psalms, and the Dead Sea Scrolls.[1]

Although this book deals with such a wide array of scriptural texts and thematic issues, I have attempted to maintain focus so that every chapter raises particular and specialized questions, develops logical arguments, and gives clear answers to the issues. It is the reader's task to judge whether my intention, namely, portraying Yehud from various angles through theological as well as socioeconomic lenses, succeeds. I hope that through this book not just one, but rather a series of compelling portrayals

---

1. Regarding the biblical text, I will employ the NRSV throughout this volume unless I provide my own translation; all translations from modern languages are mine unless otherwise specified.

of the Judean community in the Persian and Hellenistic periods emerges
that may bring us one step closer to illuminating this tremendously influential community.

Numerous biblical scholars approach ancient Israelite society through
the socioeconomic lens of the Hebrew Bible.[2] Four major socioeconomic
models have been employed in order to explain the structure of ancient
Israelite society (frequently including Judean communities in Persian- and
Hellenistic-era Palestine): (1) rent capitalism, (2) ancient class society, (3)
the tributary mode of production, and (4) the patronage system.[3]

Many scholars have a tendency to elevate a socioeconomic framework or even a mode of production to an all-encompassing key to explain
crucial characteristics of ancient Israelite or Judean society. However, the
ancient economy was not an independent entity isolated from other areas
of human life. It was deeply embedded in "the sacred."[4]

In his recent monograph *The Sacred Economy of Ancient Israel* (2015),
Roland Boer rejects a one-dimensional framework for ancient Southwest
Asia including ancient Israel. He proposes instead "the sacred economy,"
which is a highly theorized model capable of coping with various socioeconomic situations in ancient Southwest Asia from the Bronze Age to the
end of the Persian period. An axiological Marxian viewpoint that all socioeconomic circumstances are crisis-embedded and unstable informs Boer's
model. If there was stability for a while, it was an abnormality and there-

---

2. The literature that discusses socioeconomic issues in ancient Israelite society is extensive. A few selected monographs since 1980 would be enough to give a
general picture of current scholarship: Gottwald 1980, 2001; Ste. Croix 1981; Silver
1983; Garnsey, Hopkins, and Whittaker 1983; Lang 1985a; Epsztein 1986; Lemche
1985; M. Smith 1987; Dearman 1988; Fleischer 1989; Mosala 1989; Whybray 1990;
Archer 1990; Albertz 1992; Crüsemann 1992; Weinberg 1992; R. Kessler 1992; Hamilton 1992; Chirichigno 1993; Fager 1993; Gorringe 1994; Washington 1994; Weinfeld
1995; Bendor 1996; Malchow 1996; Hudson and Levine 1996, 1999; Jaruzelska 1998;
Carter 1999; McNutt 1999; Sneed 1999; Fox 2000; Pleins 2001; Ro 2002; Grabbe 2004;
Nurmi 2004; Liverani 2005; Sandoval 2006; Stevens 2006; Domeris 2007; Houston
2008; Baker 2009; Nam 2012; Dunn 2012; Olyan 2012; Guillaume 2014; Boer 2015;
and Bremer 2016.

3. For brief sketches of each of the four models, see Houston 2008, 26–51. For
(1): Wolf 1966, 50–57; Coote 1981, 29–31; Lang 1985b, 86. For (2): Kippenberg 1977,
34–36; 1978, 56–58. For (3): Gottwald 1993, 5–9; Chaney 1986, 53–76; 1993, 250–63;
Mosala 1989, 103–18; Banaji 2010, 1–44; Boer 2015, 146–92. For (4): Simkins 1999,
123–44; 2004, 1–17; Lemche 1994, 119–32; 1996, 106–20; Boer 2015, 105–8

4. Boer 2015, 8.

fore requires careful exposition, which is provided by regulation theory focusing on "how specific economic systems stabilize crises in order to gain some continuity for certain periods."[5] Instead of assuming capitalistic *homo economicus* acting in a free market, Boer attempts to revitalize Soviet-era Marxian theory. He claims that the whole socioeconomic history of ancient Southwest Asia, including ancient Israel, can be inferred from a single system that he terms the "sacred economy." According to Boer, in ancient Southwest Asia, including ancient Israel, the mode of regulation was "sacred" in the sense that "the sacred saturated daily life."[6] This supposition is highly insightful for the current study, and his many other hypotheses are also very enlightening. Careful readers may discern that the current study benefits considerably from and is stimulated by many aspects of Boer's study. However, there are in our view several serious flaws in his approach.

First, the time and space for the sacred economy are too broad and general. Addressing such a large expanse of time and space inescapably means that one cannot investigate deeply the details of particular features. As a result, the resolution of the heuristic model for understanding ancient socioeconomic life unavoidably becomes obscure.[7] Is it really true that "ancient Israel was no different from any other part of ancient Southwest Asia"?[8] The current study derives from the recognition that the Second Temple period was significantly different from any other era of ancient Israel.

Second, Boer's analysis and treatment of biblical texts is frequently minimal. Most of the biblical texts appearing in his volume remain in the footnotes and are not analyzed in detail.[9] Thus Boer mainly proceeds deductively, since the overarching theory and thesis go before (and often simply depart from) the concrete and detailed biblical evidence. As a biblical scholar, I regard this feature as problematic.

---

5. Ibid., 32.

6. Ibid., 8.

7. Chaney criticizes appropriately Boer's presupposition of "homogeneity" and "continuity" in relation to "ancient Southwest Asia" (Chaney 2016, 140). According to Chaney, due to this feature Boer's analysis fails to catch the population pressure on arable land in Iron II Palestine. On this issue, see §3.7, below.

8. Boer 2015, 8.

9. Ch. 5 is an exception where the nature of trade in the relevant biblical texts is discussed.

Third, Boer's views of human beings can be evaluated as too narrowly conceived. Of course, Boer's articulation and criticism in relation to the anachronistic analysis of free markets as well as the overcapitalistic notion of *homo economicus* have their own valid right in biblical studies. However, at least some characteristics of human beings as well as of the ancient world can be persuasively explained by those seemingly anachronistic aspects and elements.[10] In any human society, even in the modern era, *homo economicus* does not completely exclude *homo religiosus*. The two aspects of human nature are inseparably intertwined and appear in their combined form in various areas of human life. It was more so in ancient society, including ancient Israel.

Due to the above-mentioned points that mar the achievement of drawing appropriate portrayals of Yehud, I have decided to deploy a hybrid model instead of following Boer's otherwise solid framework of the sacred economy. Thus I have adopted a new term *religionness* that will be briefly clarified as this: I suggest that there was a nexus of core values and meanings that was an essential part of the religious world of Judean society in the Persian and Hellenistic periods. Since this concept can hardly be fully captured and expressed by the existing nouns *religiousness* or *religiosity*, I have coined here a new term, *religionness*, to indicate this part or aspect of the religious world of ancient Israel. Religionness is intended to connote a network of beliefs and values shared by various ancient Israelites, in particular Judean communities in the Persian and Hellenistic periods.

Strictly speaking, applying the term *religion* to ancient society is itself quite anachronistic because the concept of religion, which can be distinguished from other areas of human life such as economics, politics, and morals was absent in ancient society. The Hebrew Bible sometimes makes it evident that religious thought and the socioeconomic framework are so closely intertwined that one cannot clearly differentiate cause from effect, as some of the following chapters will indicate. Furthermore, the word religion was used with different meanings and connotations depending on the times. Therefore, modern biblical scholars are advised to be careful in utilizing and applying words such as *religion, faith,* or *belief,* which are categories of Christian dogmatics, directly to ancient Israel.[11] In order to remind ourselves of this risk of anachronism, it will be useful to utilize

---

10. See Nam 2016, 343, who illustrates a biblical example (2 Kgs 4:1–7) that seems to contradict Boer's articulation.

11. See Rüpke 2007, 73.

the new term religionness throughout this volume.[12] By doing so, I intend a kind of *Verfremdungseffekt* (distancing effect). Therefore, the portrayals that this volume attempts to delineate are not about the "religion of ancient Israel," but about the "religionness of Judean communities" within a certain historical time frame, namely, in the Persian and Hellenistic periods. In the religionness of Judean communities in the Persian and Hellenistic periods, *homo religiosus* not only dynamically interacts with *homo economicus*, but both are also merged and fused into one. Here relentless materiality and relentless spirituality are two sides of one coin.

It is one of the main assertions of the present study that "status inconsistency" played a crucial role in certain facets of the religionness of the Judean communities in the Persian and Hellenistic periods.[13] An outline of status inconsistency will be delineated below. A feature of Max Weber's class theory is that it is based on a multidimensional view of social stratification, in sharp contrast to the one-dimensional view of Karl Marx.[14] Weber's class theory describes the process through which inequality is born and established by three key elements: class, status, and party.[15] According to Weber, while class is primarily assigned within an economic order of rank, status emerges within a social order of rank and is related to the distribution of honor.[16] Correspondingly, party is an element in the pursuit of social and political power.[17] One aspect that must not be forgotten here is that these three components are interrelated

---

12. Von Rad's remark is highly insightful in this context: "There never was such a thing as a 'religion of the people of Israel,' i.e., an integrated abstract complex of all her ideas about the relationship between God and man" (von Rad 1965, 368).

13. The issue of status inconsistency has been hotly debated in sociology. The bibliography on this issue is quite extensive. Only a few selected works can be mentioned here: Lenski 1966, 86–88; 1967, 298–301; Goffman 1957, 275–81; Jackson 1962, 469–80; Randall and Strasser, 1976, 43–119; Segal and Knoke 1980, 149–66; Whitney 1980, 138–41; Hortmann, 1986, 52–67; Kimberly, 1986, 83–102; Bailey, 1986, 118–29; Bornschier, 1986, 204–20; Zaborowski, 1986, 262–74; Grimshaw, 1986, 307–20; Singh, 1986, 368–81; Hartman, 1986, 537–51; Faught, 1986, 592–605; Slomczynski and Mach 1997, 93–117; Strasser and Hodge 1993, 3–36; Stryker 1993, 70–82; Kreckel 1993, 248–69; Fuerstenberg 1993, 270–82; Meulemann 1993, 283–98; and Barnett 2004, 177–81. This concept was often applied to ancient societies related to early Christianity (see Stegemann and Stegemann 1999, 60–88; and Meeks 1983, 55).

14. Barnett 2004, 177.

15. Weber 1957, 180–95.

16. Ibid., 194–95.

17. Ibid.

and occasionally work in conjunction with each other. However, there is no certainty that the order of rank of status groups is proportional to the order of rank of economic classes. In this way, Weber presents a pioneering insight that can be used to explain the mechanism of status inconsistency. This insight by Weber is elaborated upon in the social theories of Gerhard Lenski.[18] According to Lenski's theory, a distributive system is necessarily present in a given society.[19] This distributive system is a structure used to determine the social status of each member in a society through the three elements of power, privilege, and prestige.[20]

When we further define power, privilege, and prestige, the three elements of the distributive system, they can be exchanged for the concept of multiple class systems. That is, the distributive system of a given society is constructed out of multiple class systems.[21] In Lenski's theoretical structure, a class system is a midlevel framework that connects the microlevel (a class) to the macrolevel (the distributive system).[22] Therefore, a class system is a hierarchy of classes ranked in terms of some single criterion.[23]

There are multiple class systems present in advanced agrarian societies.[24] For example, a political class system, an economic class system, an occupational class system, an educational class system, and an ethnic class system can be assumed. These can be employed as factors in deter-

18. Lenski 1954, 405–13; 1966, 80–88, 288–89; 1967, 298–301.
19. Lenski 1966, 79–82.
20. Ibid., 44–46. Weber defines power (*Macht*) as "the probability that one actor within a social relationship will be in a position to carry out his own will despite resistance, regardless of the basis on which this probability rests" (1947, 152). With Weber's definition in mind, Lenksi (1966, 44–46) asserts that power is the most important variable among the aforementioned three elements, as it is the variable that most crucially determines the distribution of surplus produced by a given society.
21. Lenski 1966, 79–82.
22. Ibid., 79.
23. Ibid., 79–80. The degree of inequality in the distributive system changes according to the size of the surplus its society produces (ibid., 85). In Lenski's view, the most important variable that can change the amount of surplus is the technological level that a society has reached. This is because a high level of technology has the power to transform the level of production and the size of the surplus in a given society. If a society's level of production and size of its surplus changes, the population of that society will change; and if the population changes, the social and economic systems for governing that population will change along with that society's form and type (ibid., 90).
24. For details on advanced agrarian societies, see chs. 2 and 8, below.

mining an individual's social status in Persian- and Hellenistic-era Palestine.[25] In this way, the distribution systems of Judean communities in Persian- and Hellenistic-era Palestine can be determined by multidimensional and multilayered factors within pluralistic class systems.

It is at this point that Lenski introduces the concept of status inconsistency.[26] Status inconsistency refers to a social phenomenon that emerges when an individual's resources within various social class systems become inconsistent. Lenski's theory is based on his assumption that humans strive to maximize their satisfaction even, if necessary, at the expense of others.[27] Lenski argues that, "where important decisions are involved, most human action is motivated either by self-interest or by partisan group interests."[28] For example, a person with strong economic power but weak political power would think of himself or herself in terms of his or her highest ranked status, namely, his or her position within the economic class system. A person of low rank in the occupational class who nevertheless had a high level of education would behave or think in a similar way. However, others in society who interacted with him or her would have a vested interest in treating the person in an opposite way, namely, in terms of that person's lowest ranked status.[29] In other words, an individual tends to define his or her social status in terms of the status that holds the most resources within his or her multidimensional class system, while others who come in contact with this individual will determine his or her status in terms of the status that holds the least resources. Because of this, a large gap emerges between both parties' expectations of social interrelations and how they actually treat each other. Lenski asserts that status inconsistency can be a cause of tension and conflict in a society.[30] According to Lenski, the individual who experiences social disadvantage derived from such status inconsistency tends to resist the political and economic system that the existing status quo legitimates and validates.[31] This phenomenon provides a logical answer to the intriguing question of why a select portion

---

25. Ibid., 80–81.
26. Ibid., 86–88.
27. Barnett 2004, 179.
28. Lenski 1966, 44.
29. Ibid., 86–88; and Barnett 2004, 179.
30. Lenski 1966, 86–88.
31. Ibid., 87.

of a society's upper and middle classes contributes to radical social and political movements.

According to Lenski, this type of social phenomenon is quantitatively small: it is rather an exceptional phenomenon.[32] However, there are cases throughout human history where the social phenomenon of political and economic radicalization of the upper and middle classes brought about by status inconsistency has produced qualitatively significant impacts and influences. The major force of movements to rapidly revolutionize the political and economic system of a society mostly derives from the desire and will of the lower stratum. However, it is extremely difficult for the lower stratum to execute such a radical movement and finally succeed without the support and direction of the upper and middle strata.[33] The social phenomenon of political and economic radicalization of the upper and middle strata deriving from status inconsistency explains why a large number of radical social movements throughout human history, including revolution, have succeeded with the active participation and dedication of the upper and middle strata.

In our view, some Judean communities in the exilic and postexilic periods experienced radical transformations of the distributive systems and accordingly dramatic amplifications of status inconsistency. For example, an elite individual of the kingdom of Judah such as a high-ranking priest exiled to Babylon must have suffered from extreme status inconsistency.[34] Until this tragic national disaster, no one would have questioned his high standing as an elite priest within his political, economic, occupational, educational, ethnic, and other class systems. But as soon as he became a captive, his former status would have been treated within all the class systems in the Babylonian Empire as though it were nonexistent. It is not difficult to imagine such status inconsistency causing acute discomfort and severe stress within this individual's mind.

Furthermore, in the Persian period the returnees from the Babylonian exile surely experienced a different type of status inconsistency, synchronic

---

32. Ibid., 88.

33. Ibid.

34. This type of status inconsistency can be regarded as "diachronic status inconsistency" while the former example in the previous paragraph (i.e., a person with a high rank in the economic class system and a low rank in the political class system) can be called "synchronic status inconsistency." I posit that both types of status inconsistency are serious factors in stress and of conflict.

status inconsistency. The citizen-temple community gradually took form in Yehud after the completion of the Second Temple.[35] This community was composed solely of returnees from the Babylonian exile and was separate from the central administration of the Persian Empire.[36] A large number of returnees from the Babylonian exile had neither a social base nor an economic foundation in Palestine.[37] Rather, it is safe to assume that socioeconomic power in Yehud at this time was held by the descendants of

---

35. Weinberg's hypothesis, which he terms the "Bürger-Tempel-Gemeinde" (citizen-temple community), has strongly influenced the history of research on the socioeconomic structure of the province of Yehud in the Persian period. Weinberg's theory argues that Yehud in the Persian period is most properly evaluated in the context of a general pattern of urbanization and economic growth as a form of "pre-Hellenism" (1992, 17–33).

The demographic situation in the exilic as well as the postexilic Judean communities in Palestine is a hotly discussed issue (on this, see §3.3, below). This study does not accept all of the assumptions of Weinberg's citizen-temple community theory. Scholars have put forth a number of valid criticisms regarding the concept of the citizen-temple community (Grabbe 2004, 143–45; Carter 1999, 297–307; Cataldo 2003, 240–52; Bedford 2001, 207–30). In particular, Weinberg's exaggerated population estimate for the citizen-temple community requires reevaluation. According to Weinberg (1992, 43), before 458/457 BCE the population of the citizen-temple community was around 42,360 and constituted about 20 percent of the population of Persian Yehud. Although it is beyond the scope of this study to pursue the issue of the demography of Yehud in detail, it can be said that compared with the estimated population at the end of the preexilic period, there was a considerable reduction in settlement and population in Persian-era Palestine (see Carter 1999, 190–213; Lipschits 2003, 323–76; 2006, 19–40; Finkelstein 2010, 39–54; Faust 2013, 108–26; Guillaume 2014, 227–30). However, the demographic sparsity in Persian-era Palestine should not be taken to imply that the land of Yehud was empty when the exiles returned to Jerusalem. There is clear textual evidence in the book of Jeremiah of tension and conflict between the *golah* community on the one hand and those who remained in Palestine on the other (see, e.g., Pohlmann 1978, 183–207). If we avoid extreme positions regarding demographic conditions in the exilic as well as the postexilic Judean communities in Palestine, the seemingly contradictory models of the postcollapse society and the citizen-temple community can be employed diachronically for the analysis of Yehud/Judah in the Persian and Hellenistic era. In other words, with the Babylonian exile ancient Judean society radically changed to a postcollapse society and then, with the establishment of the Second Temple, Yehud started to gradually develop as a citizen-temple community within its socioeconomic framework as an advanced agrarian society.

36. See §3.3, below.

37. See §3.3, below.

those who had not been exiled.[38] It is probable that the descendants of דלת
הארץ were outside the network of the citizen-temple community. That is,
at least early on, the members of the citizen-temple community held a disadvantaged position in the economic class system of Judean society in Persian-era Palestine. However, the members of the citizen-temple community had a high opinion of their status within the religious class system, the
ethnic class system, and the occupational class system. In most of recent
discussions related to Persian and Hellenistic Judah, the concept of status
inconsistency has been ignored and the socioeconomic strata have been
regarded as consistent throughout the hierarchy of Judean society. Therefore, it is frequently presupposed that from the beginning the members of
the *golah* community enjoyed consistent hegemony over the descendants
of those who had not been exiled throughout the multiple class systems
within Persian Judah. However, the socioeconomic position of the *golah*
could have been much more ambivalent, at least at the initial stage.

It is no coincidence that we find a desire and a passion for a radically new, ideal society in the Deuteronomic Code (DC) and the Holiness
Code (HC).[39] DC and HC have such a revolutionary character because
they were shaped and formed by returnees experiencing status inconsistency. Steck claims that the Deuteronomistic literature of postexilic Judean
society derived from eschatological theology.[40] Considered sociologically,
it could be said that the eschatological character of Deuteronomistic literature was stimulated by the status inconsistency experienced by the
nonpriestly returnees who composed such literature.[41] In this way, status
inconsistency offers an indispensable key to understanding postexilic biblical texts and their theologies, which were influenced by the socioeconomic structure of postexilic Judean society.

As far as religionness in Yehud is concerned, several intriguing questions emerge. As the formation of the Pentateuch clearly indicates, it is
obvious that Yahwism played a crucial role in the emergence of the iden-

---

38. See §3.6, below.

39. See §3.6, below. Of course, it is also true that there is a restorative and conservative tendency in the P material, as evidenced in Num 15:22–31 and 16:1–35. The
writers of these texts attempt to restore the preexilic concept of the flawless "cosmos"
(see §5.4, below). These contradicting tendencies within the P material are intriguing
research topics that might demonstrate the literary heterogeneity of the P source.

40. Steck 1982, 311–15.

41. See §3.6, below.

tity of the Judean communities in the Persian and Hellenistic eras. In our view, the central questions are as follows: Was religionness limited and conditioned by literacy? How did the socioeconomic and demographic circumstances influence the development and transformation of Yahwistic religionness and vice versa? Which theological perspectives participated in the composition and editing of the prophetic books (e.g., the book of Jeremiah) and the Psalms (e.g., the psalms of the poor)? How were their theological thoughts and religious worldviews inherited and transmitted by subsequent generations? These and other questions will be dealt with from various angles in the present study. It is the author's sincere hope that, taken together, these eight chapters represent an array of studies that reveal new perspectives on the Judean communities in Persian- and Hellenistic-era Palestine and provide some implications for further research.

LITERACY AND THE SOCIOECONOMIC CONTEXT OF THE JUDEAN POSTEXILIC COMMUNITIES

2.1. Introduction

The main body of this volume focuses on the issue of the relationship between the socioeconomic context of Yehud, on the one hand, and literacy, on the other. I demonstrate in this chapter that examining literacy is one of the most efficient methods for analyzing the socioeconomic stratification of the Judean communities in Persian- and Hellenistic-era Palestine. According to many scholars, considerable portions of prophetic and psalmic texts were written by an impoverished group to consolidate their identity and to retaliate against the power elite in Jerusalem at that time.[1] These scholars advance the notion of a "piety of the poor" (*Armenfrömmigkeit*) in exilic and postexilic Israel. According to Rainer Albertz's thesis, the authorial group consisted of poor peasants, shepherds, laborers, and others "who had been robbed of their rights and trampled."[2] They were the "margin of society, despised, forgotten and at best noticed as the recipients of alms."[3] Albertz writes:

> Here the lower-class circles gave an amazingly clear-sighted analysis of the reasons for their impoverishment: the harsh Persian policy of taxation was impoverishing the land and their own selfish leaders were not

---

1. See, e.g., Albertz 1992, 543–75; Hossfeld and Zenger 1993, 14–15; Berges 1998, 227–29; 1999, 153–77; 2000, 153–78; Scholl 2000, 286–87; and Bremer 2016, 317–471, 479–84. Albertz (1994, 503–7, 518–22) ascribes authorship of a number of passages to the material proletariats in the postexilic period; e.g., Pss 9–10; 12; 14; 35; 40; 69; 70; 75; 82; 109; 140; Isa 29:17–24; 56:9–57:21; Mal 2:17; 3:5, 13–21.
2. Albertz 1994, 521.
3. Ibid., 522.

doing anything about it. In Isa 57.3–5 there are again accusations against leaders who among other things are polemically entitled "children of transgression" and "offspring of deceit."... In still leveling against them the old accusation of worship on the high places and "child sacrifice," the lower-class circle were probably wanting to point out their lustful, homicidal godlessness.... The third text, Isa 29.17–24, clearly comes from a lower-class circle with a prophetic orientation (v.19), but it goes one step further than Isa 56.9ff., as the social fronts have visibly hardened further.[4]

This is an interesting theory with considerable appeal. But does it not oversimplify the socioeconomic strata of the period, and do poor people have the time and ability to write such texts?[5] Albertz bases his theory mainly on the uncritical assumption of a simple dichotomy between the upper stratum and the lower stratum.[6] However, can the complexities of the Judean communities in Persian- and Hellenistic-era Palestine be persuasively explained by his dichotomous model? Have we ever experienced such a utopian period in human history as Albertz depicts in which peasants, shepherds, craftsmen, and artisans actively participated in the theological and philosophical discourses surrounding the composition of high literacy texts?

These questions are the points we will now address. Employing several sociological theories, we will challenge the cogency of the above-mentioned assumptions. This chapter also explores the theological and ethical implications of the theology of the poor for our postmodern and postcolonial era, questioning the validity of the current socioeconomic status quo in which religion still seems to be limited and conditioned by literacy, which symbolizes power and wealth.

---

4. Ibid., 504–5.

5. For the socioeconomic situations of the Judean communities in Persian and Hellenistic era Palestine, see §6.7, below. See also Ro 2002, 187–99; Plöger 1968, 129–42; Grabbe 2004, 132–261; Edelman 2005, 34–78; Sivertsev 2005, 59–78; Olyan 2004, 1–16; Cataldo 2003, 240–52; and Janzen 2002b, 490–510.

6. Guillaume (2014, 16) also criticizes the dichotomous tendency of Albertz's hypothesis saying, "Albertz has little to offer besides repeating the standard scenario of economic prosperity resulting in the impoverishment of traditional smallholders."

2.2. Advanced Agrarian Societies and Literacy[7]

Albertz correctly characterizes the socioeconomic status of postexilic Israel in the following manner:

> It goes without saying that the small farmers who increasingly found themselves caught in the vortex of indebtedness and dispossession experienced the social crisis in quite a different way from the two camps in the upper class. What for the rich was a profitable business or a problem of social ethics was for the poor a massive existential threat. The more it became clear to them that they had to pay the bill for collaboration with the Persians which their leading class had run up, the more the suspicion must have dawned on them that all their aristocrats were collaborators to whom the favour of the occupying forces and their own advantage were more important than the anxiety and distress of their poor fellow countrymen (Job 22.8).... So we can start from the assumption that the social crisis led to a feeling of deep alienation and hopelessness among the lower class who were affected by it.[8]

I fully agree with Albertz's vivid depiction of the socioeconomic circumstances of postexilic Israel. However, I reject the conclusion that Albertz draws from the supposition of the adverse socioeconomic environments. Albertz argues that the oppressed underclass (mainly small peasantry) began to form a "prophetic conventicle" to establish worship separate from the temple cult and to design a new theology that reflected their specific socioeconomic interests in dispute with the status-quo theology of the upper class.[9] But let us consider a brief sketch of social environments in advanced agrarian societies.[10]

---

7. For an overview on literacy in ancient Israelite society, see Young 1998, 239–53; Blenkinsopp 2001a, 40–41; Schniedewind 2000, 327–32; Schaper 2005, 324–42; and Rollston 2010, 85–144.

8. Albertz 1994, 503.

9. Ibid., 519–22.

10. Lenski's sociological model is a useful device for gaining a sense of the social stratification in the postexilic community in Palestine. In particular, the model of "agrarian societies" (Lenski 1966, 190–296) fits well with the socioeconomic status of postexilic Israel. Lenski correctly argues that the level of technology is the main aspect for the typology of social models. Advanced agrarian societies are characterized, according to his definition, by the technique of smelting iron, among other things. Although his description of advanced agrarian societies is mainly associated

It is commonly held in sociology that advanced agrarian societies, including the postexilic community in Palestine, distributed their goods highly inequitably and unjustly according to social stratification. Lenski writes:

> Normally, in agrarian societies, the economic surplus was carried to the ruling classes and their dependents. As a result, all of the more advanced agrarian societies resembled a tree or plant with a system of feeder roots spreading over a vast area, tapping the surplus and moving it, by stages, to the ultimate consumers, the urban population. At the outer limits of this system were thousands, even hundreds of thousands, of small peasant villages, each typically containing a few hundred residents.[11]

This inequality pulls agrarian societies into a desperate economic situation, which Lenski describes in detail:

> The great majority of peasant farmers throughout history had little more than the bare necessities of life.... Household furniture consisted of a few stools, a table, and a chest to hold the best clothes and other treasured possessions. Beds were uncommon and most peasants simply slept on earthen floors covered with straw. Other household possessions were apparently limited to cooking utensils. In some cases, the lot of the peasant was not even this good. On many occasions conditions became so oppressive that it was impossible to eke out a livelihood and the peasants were forced to flee the land.[12]

It is highly intriguing that Philippe Guillaume regards the escape of small farmers as "a viable option."[13] According to Guillaume, peasant helplessness is a myth because the small farmers in the biblical period as well as in the Islamic and Ottoman period had bargaining power and other survival

---

with the Greco-Roman world, due to the similar socioeconomic prerequisites, this model is also applicable to the Persian and Hellenistic periods in Palestine with critical adjustment and adaptation (for details on this issue, see ch. 8, below). Lenski divides advanced agrarian societies into nine levels of social strata: ruling class, governing class, retainer class, priestly class, peasant class, merchant class, artisan class, unclean and degraded class, and expendable class (Lenski 1966, 210–85; Lenski, Nolan, and Lenski 1995, 216–18).

11. Lenski 1966, 205–6.

12. Ibid., 271.

13. Guillaume 2014, 59.

techniques such as "various methods of family limitation," including "the sale of children, abortion, infanticide and exposure."[14] Furthermore, "in times of famine, the youngest and the oldest members of the family were left to starve to preserve the health of the active adults upon whose survival the future of the group depended. Occasional banditry ... would supply additional resources."[15] However, could and should we say that "in light of the various strategies to cope with adverse conditions, ancient farmers were not helpless victims of intractable higher powers"?[16] Even though I sometimes employ Marxian theories and terms for analytic convenience, I do not consider myself a Marxist. However, the above vivid examples that Guillaume himself proposed are for me nothing but illustrations of the Marxian notion of proletarian alienation, namely, expressions of the deep desperation of small farmers deriving from profound helplessness rather than rational and successful methods of coping with adverse conditions. As long as the above-mentioned survival techniques occurred, I would delineate the situations that forced small farmers to utilize these ruthless techniques as "oppressive" and those small farmers as "helpless."

The proportion of urban dwellers to the overall population in an agrarian state remained small. This clear distinction between urban and rural residents regarding social stratification is also found in Neh 11:1: "But the heads of the people [שרי העם] lived in Jerusalem; so the rest of the people drew lots to bring one out of ten to live in Jerusalem, the holy city, while nine-tenths remained in the [outlying] towns."[17] Jerusalem was a place where only leaders and selected compatriots were allowed to settle. The supremacy of cities was established politically, economically, religiously, and culturally.[18] As a result, wealth and power were centralized in the cities. The broad majority of the rural population in advanced agrarian societies lived on a thin line between hunger and subsistence while city dwellers enjoyed affluent surplus and luxuries.[19]

Throughout the history of these advanced agrarian societies, most peasants paid rents and taxes of 30 to 70 percent of their total production

---

14. Ibid.
15. Ibid., 54.
16. Ibid., 55.
17. Translation of Myers 1965, 181.
18. See Stegemann and Stegemann 1999, 12.
19. Ibid., 51.

to landowners and kings.[20] Another painful burden on the underclass was compulsory labor.[21] Forced labor was assigned to rural populations for public works and obligations to the military.[22] As the relevant texts in Ezra and Nehemiah (Ezra 3:8–4:6; 6:13–15; Neh 3:1–4:23; 6:15) clearly indicate, the amount of forced labor on the shoulder of the peasants in postexilic Israel was not less than that of French farmers in the eighteenth century.[23]

Further disadvantages suffered among the small peasantry were crop failures and famines. Stegemann and Stegemann write:

> Thus crop failures were the burden of the lessee. The catastrophic consequences of such crop failures are reported to us by Josephus. He describes situations in which people have neither clothing nor seed for the next year. Most of the famines attested by Josephus fall in the first century BCE, but there is also a report of a great famine under Claudius in the year 46–47 CE. Thus we can generalize that in years of crop failure, farm families starved. Yet we must also realize that not even good harvest years provided sufficient provisions, if we assume that a minimum field of seventeen acres was probably necessary to feed a peasant family of six to nine people.... Small farmers have left us no literary artifacts.[24]

Centralization of resources, forced labor and, on occasion, natural disaster in advanced agrarian societies intensified the poverty of the small peasantry.[25] Yet this list remains incomplete. In advanced agrarian societies,

---

20. Ibid., 267–68.

21. Ibid., 268–69: "For example, in eighteenth-century France peasants owed the king twelve days' labor a year in addition to the several days per week they owed their local lord."

22. Stegemann and Stegemann 1999, 49.

23. Lenski 1966, 268–69.

24. Stegemann and Stegemann 1999, 46–47.

25. According to Guillaume, crop failures did not force small farmers into debt since crop failures and debts affected large estates as much as small farms (Guillaume 2014, 97–99). Guillaume's effort to break with the conventional repetition of slogans in biblical studies based on the greedy rich versus the holy poor dichotomy is praiseworthy. However, in our view, he goes too far to the opposite extreme. Perhaps size does not guarantee profit, but it does guarantee safety. Therefore, it seems to be rational to induce that crop failures could bring, at least potentially, a much more serious financial blow to small farms than to large estates with accumulated reserves. Guillaume is right when he writes "the struggle for justice is too important a cause to benefit

literacy was one of the most significant tools the upper class used to distinguish itself from the lower strata. The invention of writing is a decisive turning point in the development of the socioeconomic structure of agrarian societies. It is worth recognizing that literacy becomes a device of socioeconomic hegemony and that literacy is therefore found more in the urban minority than the rural majority.[26]

In agrarian societies, literacy was a highly sophisticated skill and an extremely rare privilege that only a well-educated minority of 6 or 7 percent in an urban area was able to possess.[27] In other words, ancient literacy was different from modern literacy, particularly with respect to the casually indifferent attitude and policy of ancient governments toward mass literacy.[28] Ancient governments revealed the character of society at large. In ancient societies it was a norm that illiterates and those with restricted literacy were able to collaborate with literates in the marketplace, in the workshop, and in the home without any inconvenience. Necessary crafts and techniques were mostly attained through oral explanations or instructions, not through texts. We can therefore conclude that literacy in

---

from the repetition of slogans" (Guillaume 2014, 107). However, Guillaume's overly harmonizing stance based on an assumption of ancient "equilibrium" theory (Guillaume 2014, passim, particularly in "General Conclusion," 247–49), which keeps eyes shielded from the sweat and tears of small farmers in Israelite history, cannot be an appropriate remedy for the problem. Guillaume seems to define "small farmers" as persons who had some socioeconomic means. As Houston properly comments, "in every age, not least ours, there have been those who make money by lending to those just above destitution" (2013, 170). The real miseries and distresses are generated in every age among the strata around and beneath that milieu. For criticisms on this aspect of Guillaume's monograph, see also Boer 2013, 109–12.

26. Stegeman and Stegeman 1999, 13. See also Lenski 1966, 207–8: "Writing, like money, initially developed as a response to the increasingly complex economic problems faced by the urban classes in early agrarian societies.... Writing also served to widen the traditional gulf between the ruling classes and the common people by introducing a major cultural distinction between the literate minority and the illiterate majority. In agrarian societies limited literacy was the rule, a pattern setting these societies apart from both preliterate horticultural societies and largely literate industrial ones." Robert Pattison's statement eloquently summarizes this particular characteristic of literacy and especially of ancient literacy: "Not every society has chosen to use literacy in the same way, but literacy is always connected with power" (Pattison 1982, viii).

27. Lenski 1966, 207–66.

28. For this and what follows, see Hanson 1991, 162.

advanced agrarian societies is a significant division between the underclass in rural areas and the upper class in urban areas.[29]

Furthermore, there were other technical conditions in antiquity that
hindered mass literacy: the shortage of schools and the expense of writing materials. The institutional lacuna, above all the absence of subsidized
schools, retarded the development of mass literacy. In addition to this, for
most strata of the population, writing materials were too expensive to pur-
chase. Therefore, in ancient societies, even in their most advanced forms,
there was no mass literacy, and even the milieu that can be called copier's
literacy was achieved only in certain limited strata, and the majority of
people were always illiterate.[30]

Due to the lack of clearly verifiable historical sources, modern scholars who write on Yahwism in the late Persian period encounter a difficult
task in any effort to compose a reliable history. However, it is safe to say
that the same social conditions, including the institutional lacunae, the
shortage of subsidized schools, and the lack of inexpensive writing materials, were prevalent in the postexilic community in Palestine.[31]

---

29. For a detailed discussion of the functions of literacy in advanced agrarian
societies, see Harris 1989, 25–42.

30. Ibid., 13–15.

31. According to Young (1998, 249–53), the frequent references to writing in
Deuteronomy as well as DtrH (Deut 6:9; 11:20; 27:3, 8; 28:58, 61; 29:20, 26; 30:10;
31:9, 19, 22, 24; Josh 1:8; 8:31, 32, 34; 10:13; 18:9; 23:6; 24:26; Judg 8:14; 1 Sam 10:25; 2
Sam 1:18; 11:14–15; 1 Kgs 2:3; 11:41; 14:19, 29; 15:7, 23, 31; 16:5, 14, 20, 27; 21:8, 9, 11;
22:39, 46; 2 Kgs 1:18; 8:23; 10:1, 6, 34; 12:20; 13:8, 12; 14:6, 15, 18, 28; 15:6, 11, 15, 21,
26, 31, 36; 16:19; 17:37; 20:20; 21:17, 25; 22:13; 23:3, 21, 24, 28; 24:5) are not proof of
widespread literacy in exilic or postexilic Israel. He also clearly articulates that the epigraphic evidence cannot be regarded as a reliable witness for assessing ancient Israelite
literacy. "A large amount of written material can be produced by a very small number
of literate people" (240). See also Blenkinsopp 2001a, 40–41: "It is nevertheless safe
to assume that reading and writing were confined for the most part to professional
groups and their milieux: scribes, priests and some merchants and persons engaged
in specialist crafts. Nothing in either the biblical or epigraphic material available contradicts this conclusion.… The ability to scratch a few letters of the Hebrew alphabet
on pottery, jar handles, seals, or the high priest's rosette (qodeš laYHWH, Exod 39:30)
hardly amounts to evidence for literacy, and there is no evidence for institutions of
higher or even lower learning before the time of Ben Sira—even then, the evidence is
hardly overwhelming. The conditions required for widespread literacy outside of very
limited professional circles did not exist even in the developed cultures of Mesopotamia and Egypt, much less so in a backwater province like sixth century BCE Judah. We

Furthermore, literacy is not a basic skill but an intricate set of techniques applied to texts. In addition to the technical rigors of literacy there exist different skill divisions. Ancient literacy can basically be divided into three totally different areas: (1) reading; (2) copier's or craftsman's writing; and (3) composer's writing. These respective divisions were not compatible with each other.[32]

The literacy of professional scribes can be called craftsman's or copier's literacy. Composing or drafting a new text was a far more challenging task than copying and was assigned to the more experienced and talented to execute.[33] Therefore, it is reasonable to distinguish high literacy (composer's writing) from copier's literacy. The skill of reading scripture was a primary goal of education in Roman Judea, while writing was rare, not because it was thought insignificant, but because the production of religious texts was a highly sophisticated task.[34] Due to the aforementioned circumstances in the postexilic community in Palestine, it was evidently extremely difficult for the struggling lower class of postexilic Judea to learn even reading skills let alone to achieve the level of copier's literacy.

Because of these difficulties, should we not be skeptical of the notion that peasant farmers, shepherds, craftsmen, and so on in the postexilic period composed such theological texts as Mal 2:17; 3:5, 13–21; Isa 29:17–24; 56:9–57:21; and Pss 9–10; 12; 14; 35; 40; 69; 70; 75; 82; 109; 140, all of which presuppose a high level of literacy? The literary milieux of the aforementioned texts express a complexity far beyond craftsman's or copier's literacy. In short, one may assume that the poorest farm or craftsman's shop was not a suitable place to achieve this high level of literary composition.

---

can therefore be sure that, given the lack of the means of reproduction and dissemination of written material and the absence of the ability and the motivation to read on the part of the vast majority of the population, whether in Judah or in the diaspora, but particularly in Judah, none of the prophetic writings from the period in question was written for a mass audience." Moreover, Rollston (2010, 133) writes, "The fact of the matter is that an alphabetic writing system in a society does not necessarily raise the literacy rates among the populace. Moreover, the Old Hebrew and epigraphic data are reflective of rigorous formal education.... I would contend that the Hebrew Bible was primarily a corpus written by elites to elites. That is, it would be difficult to suggest that statements in the Hebrew Bible could be used as a basis for assuming the literacy of non-elites."

32. Goodman 1994, 99–108.

33. Hanson 1991, 176.

34. Goodman 1994, 99–100.

At this juncture, it will be helpful to note how the lower classes in an advanced agrarian society, including peasantry and artisans, were evaluated by their contemporaries. For example, Ben Sira writes:

> The scribe's profession increases wisdom; whoever is free from toil can become wise. How can one become wise who guides the plow, who thrills in wielding the goad like a lance, who guides the ox and urges on the bullock, and whose concern is for cattle? His determination is to plow furrows, and he is careful to fatten the livestock. So with every engraver and designer who, laboring night and day.... So with the smith sitting by the anvil.... So with the potter sitting at his work.... But they are not sought out for the council of the people, nor are they prominent in the assembly. (Sir 38:24–33 [translation follows Skehan 1987, 445–46])

According to Ben Sira's point of view, only one who is completely free of all physical toil can become a student of scripture and act as judge, counselor, and interpreter of scripture. Farmers, shepherds, and craftsmen are not suited for the above-mentioned tasks.[35]

If this statement represents the common viewpoint of postexilic Israel concerning the religious teacher or interpreter (γραμματεύς: a person learned in the Mosaic law and in the sacred writings), we can get some sense of the postexilic context that thoroughly denied the lower class, including peasants, access to academic and literary activities.[36] In this kind of atmosphere it would hardly be conceivable for a peasant to devote himself to a reshaping or a creation of theology and its record. Furthermore, Biblical Hebrew in the postexilic period was not the language in common use. As Ernst Axel Knauf clearly indicates, "Biblical Hebrew was the language of literature and education in the Persian era, during which the people probably already spoke an early form of Middle Hebrew."[37] Thus, the use of Biblical Hebrew in the Persian period is comparable with the use of Latin in medieval Europe.[38]

---

35. Stegemann and Stegemann 1999, 26.

36. See also Matt 2:4; 5:20; 7:29; 8:19; 15:1; Mark 1:22; 2:6; 3:22; 7:1; Luke 5:21; 6:7; 11:44; 19:47; John 8:3; Acts 23:9; and 1 Cor 1:20.

37. Knauf 1994, 206; see also Rendsburg 2002, 23–46; Hurvitz 2000, 143–60; 1997, 301–15; Bergey 1988, 161–68; and Würthwein 1988, 90.

38. According to Faigenbaum-Golovin et al. 2016, 1–6, an educational infrastructure that could enable the composition of literary texts in Judah existed already around 600 BCE. A similar milieu of literacy is found again around 200 BCE. It means

2.3. The Socioeconomic Contexts of Postexilic Society

There is a general consensus among biblical scholars that from an economic perspective the exilic and early postexilic periods were the darkest times in the history of Israel.[39] Herbert Donner points out the possibility that those Israelites who were left on the land during the exilic period had to pay indirect taxes to and labor for the local officials, who were usually identified with the traitors who devoted themselves to work for the foreign superpower.[40] The miserable situation in exilic and postexilic Israel, not only economically, but also ideologically, is depicted in the book of Lamentations (among other passages, see Lam 1:3, 5–6, 18; 2:15, 20–21; 4:10; 5:2, 5, 10–12, 18).[41]

The screaming people in the book of Nehemiah deserve mention as well:

> We must pawn [עֹרְבִים following the suggestion of BHS] our sons and our daughters to get grain and to eat so that we may stay alive.... We are having to mortgage our fields, our vineyards, and our houses in order to get grain during the famine.... We had to borrow money for the

---

that there was a gap of about four hundred years during which a homogeneous educational infrastructure for literacy was not present.

39. See, e.g., Donner 1995, 387; Faust 2003, 37–53; 2013, 119–25; Zwickel 2015, 222–37; J. Wright 2006, 67–89; Carter 1999, 190–213; and J. Kessler 2002, 90–96. For an opposing position related to this issue, cf. Guillaume 2014, 225–26, 247–49.

40. Donner 1995, 388.

41. The historical background as well as the authorship of Lamentations have been much discussed (Boecker 1985, 13–15; Westermann 1990, 32–60; Kaiser 1992b, 103–10; Berges 2002, 64–72). The composition of Lamentations has been variously dated among scholars across a wide spectrum between 597 BCE and the Maccabean period. For many researchers Lam 2, 4, and 5 are the oldest, and Lam 1 and 3 are later additions. It must also be recognized that not all of the depictions of Lamentations related to the miserable situation reflect historical reality. Some should be regarded as standard expressions or typical tropes deriving from the wide cultural as well as literary contexts of the ancient Near Eastern genres (Berges 2002, 46–52). On the other hand, a wide consensus has developed among researchers that in Lam 2 and 4 in particular the horrible events were so vividly and visibly described with so many details that it is hard to imagine that decades or even centuries later the writer could have been psychically so close to and mentally affected by the events that occurred. Therefore, it is reasonable to assume that at least the oldest portion of Lamentations reflects the historical core that was linked to the catastrophe in 587 BCE.

king's tribute [מדת המלך] on our fields and our vineyards. (Neh 5:2–4;
author's translation)

This clearly shows the miserable plight of poverty and despair in the
postexilic era.[42] What is meant by the "king's tribute" in the previous quotation is a tax or rent for the king of the Persian Empire. "Economic collapse was on the horizon for all of the empire's colonies, and Yehud was no
exception."[43] Jon Berquist interprets Neh 5:2–4 as even implying a slave
trade which "at times sold off Judean children" to Greece and other areas.[44]

In this social context, it seems reasonable that postexilic peasants
became suspicious and contemptuous concerning the pertinence of the
heavy tribute and the authority of the upper class, which devoted itself
to gathering tribute for the Persian king. The national pride of postexilic
Israel was in a serious crisis because of its servile economy.

Thus, the postexilic culture in Palestine created a new upper class,
whose ideal was subservient devotion to the foreign superpower without
any consideration for whether their own brothers and sisters were exploited
by the colonial economic system. Their priority was not to support the
whole society with their power and wealth but rather, under the influence of the Persian government, to exploit the peasantry. The exploitative
disregard by the newly ruling postexilic elite warrants harsh denounce-
ment. This elite should be more sharply denounced than the preexilic
elite because they did the bidding of a foreign superpower and exploited
the economic and social misfortunes of their own people. When viewed
through the lens of a certain theological group which experienced how

---

42. Guillaume assumes that the above biblical text describes no more than a "bargaining process" between local taxpayers and local administrators (Guillaume 2014,
174). Even though the amount of tribute was fixed at the level of the larger fiscal unit
and therefore allowed for a certain degree of flexibility regarding the amount paid by
each subunit according to the actual local harvest (Guillaume 2014, 172), it would not
be illogical to infer that due to limited socioeconomic resources small farmers could
not always have been the winners in this bargaining process against local administrators. In our view, the distress of the screaming people in the book of Nehemiah can
be more appropriately understood when it is assumed that they were the returned
exiles (see §3.6, below) and therefore suffered not only from economic plight, but also
from "status inconsistency." Here *homo economicus* and *homo religiosus* appear again
in their merged form.
43. Berquist 1995, 109.
44. Ibid.

the peasantry fell into unprecedented miserable poverty and was pressed into debt-slavery, the rich and the new ruling elite seem emblematic of the traditional image of the sinner (רשע).

Thus, the members of the group who stood in opposition to the ruling class apparently considered themselves as the "poor." In their terms, the poor became associated with the traditional image of the righteous (צדיק). This theological circle left a significant trace during the formation of the Hebrew Bible, composing and editing the texts concerned with the so-called piety of the poor.[45] However, as discussed above, it is a historical question whether or not this theological circle belonged in the socioeconomic sense to the penniless lower class that included small peasants and craftsmen. Who were the people that created, edited and transmitted the theological texts relating to the piety of the poor?

Because I have reviewed elsewhere the evidence against Albertz's assumption, I will not repeat the details, except for certain key examples.[46] Based on traditio-historical as well as form-historical evidence (e.g., Pss 25; 34; 37; 62; 73), which attests to highly accomplished literary as well as theological education, "the author is a very sophisticated writer."[47] The relevant textual material "was written as communicative object."[48]

> One has to assume a very sophisticated audience; i.e., one able to understand the systems of cross references, ambiguities, puns on words, ongoing heightening of messages through consecutive versets and the like.... Thus, unless one assumes that all Israelites including the poorest peasant achieved the same high level of literacy (which, of course, is highly unlikely), one has to conclude that certain social locations are more likely than others.[49]

Among the nine social strata of Lenski's model (ruling class, governing class, retainer class, priestly class, peasant class, merchant class, artisan class, unclean and degraded class, and expendable class), which one would be the "more likely" social location for the high level of theological literacy?

The ideal candidate group must satisfy at least the following requirements:

---

45. See the biblical texts in §§4.4 and 6.5, below.
46. For the details, see Ro 2002, 194–99.
47. Ben-Zvi 1991, 353.
48. Ibid.
49. Ibid.

1. The authorial group did not belong to the ruling class or the governing class, both of which represented the status quo. As will be discussed in detail below (ch. 6.5.2), the relevant group of "poverty" texts is strongly eschatological, which is not compatible with preserving the status quo.[50]
2. The authorial group did not belong to the underclass, which lived with the constant concern of achieving the means of survival.
3. The authorial group possessed knowledge and skills to create the highest level of theological literacy in Classical Hebrew.

In view of these criteria, a priestly class such as the Levites (Ezra 2:40; 3:9–12; 6:16; 8:30; Neh 3:17; 7:43; 8:11; 10:28) or the forerunner of the group that was later called Hasidim (1 Macc 2:42; 7:13; 2 Macc 14:6) naturally attracts our attention because this group reflects a socioeconomic stratum that fulfills the aforementioned requirements.[51] For example, Levites and Hasidim did not belong to the upper class because they were lower-ranking priests in comparison to the כהנים (Ezra 2:36; 3:2; 6:9; Neh 3:22; 5:12; 7:64; 12:41).[52]

---

50. See Ro 2002, 49–75, 97–112, 182–203.

51. For the discussions in relation to the Levites, see, e.g., Weyde 2015, 238–53; Avioz 2014, 441–51; Moster 2015, 721–30; 2014, 729–37; Samuel 2014, passim; Winkler 2014, 3–22; Berner 2012, 3–28; van der Toorn 2007, 104–108. According to van der Toorn, the Levitical scribes belonged to the upper middle stratum (van der Toorn 2007, 105): "They could apparently afford to pay for the education of their children; for them, a tuition fee consisting of 'a large sum of silver' (Sir 51:28) was not prohibitive." (ibid.). The discussion on the Hasidim goes on interminably. For a survey on the issue, see Nodet, 2007, 63–87; Blenkinsopp, 2007, 394–402; van Grol 2011, 93–115; Ro 2002, 34, 193. Nodet claims that the members of the Hasidim (Hasidæans or Assideans) were proto-Pharisees and descendants of returned exiles from Babylon (2007, 81–82). Blenkinsopp supposes that the Hasidim derive from the Judean sectarianism that is witnessed in the memoirs of Ezra and Nehemiah (2007, 394–402). According to Albertz (1994, 539), the circle of the Hasidim was a Judean religious faction that consisted of "temple scribes" ("*Tempelschreiber*"). He correctly argues that in postexilic Judea the Levites and the Hasidim were very closely associated and that as social entities both groups almost overlapped (1992, 598–620).

52. "A circumstance that is particular to the position of the Levitical scribes from the Second Temple is the rivalry between scribes and priests. In the temple hierarchy, the Levites were subordinate to the priests.... For a long time, however, the scribes of the Second Temple had an uneasy relationship with the servants of the altar" (van der Toorn 2007, 107).

On the other hand, they were excellent theologians who were able to satisfy the criterion of the highest level of theological literacy.[53] Lenski writes:

> The priestly class [in advanced agrarian society] also performed other functions of great value to the political elite, and sometimes also to society at large. In societies where limited literacy was the rule, the clergy were often called upon to perform those administrative tasks which required a mastery of the art of writing.[54]

However, the merits and demerits of priestly contributions to "society at large" need to be examined more precisely. The priests were often unsuccessful in realizing the ideals they professed and contributed to the status quo of inequality by legitimizing and supporting the ruling class.[55] Nevertheless, in many cases, especially in the Judeo-Christian tradition, the priestly class challenged tyranny and injustice, upholding the interests of the underclass.[56] In particular, lower-ranking priests such as Levites often came into conflict with higher-ranking priests, the כהנים (e.g., Num 16:1–11; 18:1–7) [57]

In conclusion, the authorial group of the relevant texts was not itself materially poor, but belonged to a wealthier class that felt excluded and disenfranchised by those actually in power.[58] Those who developed the

---

53. See Pohlmann 2004, 488. Pohlmann correctly assumes that there is a layer of composition or edition of the book of Nehemiah that was used by Levites themselves or by a prolevitical circle: "The high priesthood is tarnished by intermarriages (Neh 13:28ff.); because the priesthood is obviously not capable of or willing to purify itself, the layman Nehemiah must intervene. He is also the one who has to redress the injustices tolerated by the priests in the Temple (13:4ff.) and strengthen the position of the Levites (13:10ff.). Certain anticlerical and at the same time pro-Levitical tendencies are discernable in Neh 9, because here—unlike the priest Ezra in Ezra 9—'the Levites appear as active participants'…, and in Neh 9:1 as well as 12:22, where the Levites outrank the priests." The Levitical scribes were not only professional writers, but also scholars committed to the transmission, interpretation, and divulgation of the tradition they had received (van der Toorn 2007, 90–96). It is also often argued that Levites composed the book of Chronicles (Zenger et al. 2016, 325–27; van der Toorn 2007, 301–2 n. 56).

54. Lenski 1966, 260.

55. Ibid.

56. Ibid., 263.

57. See, e.g., Cody 1969, 146–74; Nurmela 1998, 107–39; and Pohlmann 2004, 487–97.

58. As Karl Christ (1980, 216–17) has persuasively argued, a middle class does

theology of the poor, but who were not materially poor, also identified themselves to some extent with the materially poor and spoke for them. The socioeconomic situation of postexilic Judean society was severely overshadowed by the tributary mode of production and its extreme oppression as well as the inhumane exploitation of the underclass by the ruling and governing class.[59] The motivation of lower-ranking priests to take the side of the materially poor can be variously explained. It could have derived from the theological rivalry between higher-ranking priests and lower-ranking priests. It could have been the extreme misery of the materially poor that offended the conscience of the lower-ranking priests. It could have been that the situation of the materially poor resonated with the priests' sense of disenfranchisement. It could have resulted from the "status inconsistency" of the lower-ranking priests.[60] Or it could have derived from all of the above. I would suggest that the lower-ranking priests' alignment with the poor had theological as well as economic roots.

The authorial circle was also speaking for itself, under the self-designation of poverty, using the term in an almost metaphorical and anthropological way (e.g., poor in front of God, poor in spirituality, poor in social power).[61] The authorial group can be historically identified with lower-ranking priests, such as the Levites or forerunners of the Hasidim.[62]

---

exist within an advanced agrarian society. The Levites and the forerunners of the Hasidim belonged to the middle stratum of Judean society in the Persian period. According to van der Toorn, the Levitical scribes could have been on a par with financially protected civil servants (2007, 105).

59. "Tributary mode of production" is a modified form of Marx's Asiatic mode of production. For details and characteristics of this mode of production, see, e.g., Gottwald 1993, 5–9; Melotti 1977, 54–62; Houston 2008, 35–43; Boer 2003, 92–100; 2015, 38–39. In particular, for the discussions related to the question of the modes of production (especially regarding the Asiatic mode of production) in biblical studies as well as in other academic contexts, see Boer 2003, 229–46.

60. The concept of status inconsistency has been extensively researched and widely employed in sociology (see, e.g., Lenski 1966, 86–88; 1967, 298–301; Goffman 1957, 275–81; Jackson 1962, 469–80; Segal and Knoke 1980, 149–66; Whitney 1980, 138–41; Slomczynski and Mach 1997, 93–117; and Barnett 2004, 177–81). Status inconsistency means a social phenomenon that appears when an individual's resources and status are not congruent according to heterogeneous class systems. For details on this issue, see ch. 1, above.

61. For the pessimistic anthropology that seems to have profoundly influenced the theology of the poor, see Ro 2002, 17–21.

62. Regarding the identification of the authorial group responsible for the theol-

2.4. Conclusion

All theory is somewhat speculative, but some speculations fit the known facts better, requiring fewer amendments and adjustments to explain the extant historical data. In the case of postexilic Israel, the lack of clearly verifiable historical sources for this period makes scholarly speculation based on the few known facts, including the words of the biblical texts, unavoidable. In light of the lack of scholarly consensus on the social stratification of the postexilic community, Albertz's theories prove unsatisfactory in that they do not fit the facts well and contain certain contradictions.[63] My thesis endeavors humbly and simply to create clarity from this confusion.

Of course, people in poverty can and do speak for themselves. People everywhere, in all social strata, are equidistant from the ultimate questions

---

ogy of the poor, Bremer's view is ambiguous and vague (2016, 426–29, 436–37, 442–43, 446, 470–71). On the one hand, he claims that there are no explicit statements in Pss 9/10, 25, 31, and 40/41 associated with material poverty, although it should not be completely rejected that the suppliant was materially poor (428–29). According to Bremer, the authors of Pss 42–72, including the relevant psalms of the poor, belonged to a theological circle that was close to the materially poor and economically marginalized (436–37). On the other hand, he concludes that the authors themselves were not poor in a socioeconomic sense (484). In particular, it is confusing what Bremer means by a "*wesentlich Elenden und Bedürftigen nahestehenden kultkritischen Trägerkreis*" ["a cult-critical circle of tradents that was closely associated with the materially poor and economically marginalized"] (437). Were the members of the circle materially poor or not? How were they "associated" ("*nahestehend*") with the poor? Did they belong to an economically lower stratum in Yehud or not? Finding an authorial group within an ancient agrarian society that was closely associated with the materially marginalized but was not poor itself seems to be almost impossible. Thus, it is no wonder that Bremer eventually gives up on clarifying the socioeconomic and historical identification of the authorial group of the psalms of the poor, claiming that such an identification cannot be expected in a study that is intended only to outline the socioeconomic conditions of Judean society in Persian-era Palestine (471). In this way, without proposing his own hypothesis concerning the authorship of the psalms of the poor, Bremer criticizes my theory that lower-ranking priests created the theology of the poor, taking the side of the materially poor (Bremer, 471). However, all of his contentions related to the theology of the poor except the aforementioned vague points are very close to mine, e.g., his conclusions that the authorial group responsible for the psalms of the poor was not socioeconomically poor itself (484) and that the theology of the poor derives in large part from the suppliant's consciousness of sin (428). On the suppliant's confession and consciousness of sin, see §6.4.2, below.

63. See §2.2, "Advanced Agrarian Societies and Literacy," above.

of life. All people, regardless of class, gender, and ethnicity, are concerned with existential questions, and everyone is capable of dealing with these questions significantly through a confrontation with their ultimate concern.[64] I do not deny this. My explanation, however, addresses the issue of "amazement" when Albertz writes, "here the lower-class circles gave an *amazingly* clear-sighted analysis of the reasons for their impoverishment."[65] This amazement calls for clarification. I am attempting such clarification by suggesting that perhaps the lower classes, who lacked the time and finances to formulate theologies, *did not* record the theology of the poor.

An issue that is worthy of note here is the relationship between written and oral traditions in ancient Judaism. Interestingly, in postbiblical Judean history, literacy did become the norm even for poor (male) Jews; but this relates to developments in rabbinic Judaism, and we can reasonably assume that this does not apply to postexilic biblical Judeans.[66]

Would the absence of literacy among the very poor have meant that they lacked the categories to formulate, orally, a kind of theology of liberation? I do not think so. Could a theology of the poor have materialized orally among the very poor, and have found written expression among a wealthier class? I would say: Yes, it is possible. Here I make it clear that my assumption of limitation on the part of the underclass focuses strictly on the literacy issues and not intellectual or spiritual capacity.[67]

----

64. Tillich 1951, 11–12: "The ultimate concern is unconditional, independent of any conditions of character, desire, or circumstance. The unconditional concern is total: no part of ourselves or of our world is excluded from it; there is no 'place' to flee from it. The total concern is infinite: no moment of relaxation and rest is possible in the face of a religious concern which is ultimate, unconditional, total, and infinite."

65. Albertz 1994, 504, emphasis added.

66. See Goodman 1994, 99–107; Schaper 2005, 328; and Knauf 1994, 206.

67. Gerstenberger charges me with ignoring the theological capacity of the underclass in postexilic Israel because I do not attribute the literal authorship of the texts concerning the piety of the poor to the postexilic underclass. He writes: "Finally, the alleged political and spiritual incompetence of impoverished segments of a given population to defend itself [*sic*] (normally with the help of gifted leaders, be they members of whatever social stratum) is an illusion of theoreticians of the Scriptures who apparently are living a long way from the social reality of any time or period.... How can anyone deny the force of impoverished parts of society, reducing effective opposition to well-to-do and optimally educated layers of that same society?... To ignore strong evidence for close ties between language and the reality of poverty in those periods is reckless at best" (Gerstenberger 2003, 214).

[handwritten marginalia: very much echoing... present realities]

It is true that we are still living in a world where "no voice is resounding except that of the rulers."[68] Bertolt Brecht's poem has not yet lost its currency. In these socioeconomic circumstances, do we really acknowledge the dignity of the poor and encourage a more equitable distribution of wealth and opportunity in our society when we credit the disempowered with powers (for example, literacy) that unjust circumstances have kept from them? If we keep shielding our eyes from the misery of poor people in a manner that dramatizes and glorifies their poverty, this constitutes for a conscientious scholar nothing but "intellectual self-satisfaction" and frivolous "triumphalism" that bring no real change.[69]

To avoid such a misleading dramatization, it is worth attempting to identify more carefully the circles of tradents responsible for relevant biblical texts in their socioeconomic and theological location. Therefore, it will be part of the investigation in the next chapter to search for

---

68. Original: "keine Stimme ertönt außer der Stimme der Herrschenden" (Brecht 1988, 237).

69. Gutierrez 1988, 174. Recent UNESCO statistics show that as of 2016 the number of illiterates who do not possess even basic reading skill exceeds 750 million globally (UIS 2017, 3). It should be noted here that the regions of the globe with large numbers of illiterates overlap the regions with high infant mortality rates due to famine (FAO 2017, 58). There is a growing tendency in biblical studies to draw "too rigid a line between now and then with regard both to modes of production and the meanings of the biblical texts" (Hankins 2016, 134). For example, Guillaume articulates that biblical prophets are misunderstood as being fair social critics by some biblical scholars who attempt to apply these ethical principles to our own times, and this misunderstanding is responsible for systematic misinterpretation of biblical texts (Guillaume 2014, 14–15, passim). Boer shares this feature with Guillaume since he declines to regard the biblical message as directly relevant to our contemporary situation because this document was shaped in a society with a qualitatively different mode of production (2015, 41–52, 218–20). Of course, due attention should be paid to "the qualitative difference between modes of production." However, Hankins fittingly cites W. Benjamin: "history is …'time filled by the presence of the now' [Jetztzeit]" (Hankins 2016, 134–35). Brueggemann also says: "The intention of such prayer, I suggest, would be not unlike the prayers of Martin Luther King at the Pettis Bridge before the long march. It is real prayer addressed to God; it is at the same time, real petition, addressed to the sheriff and to the press. We need not choose between these two addressees. Both belong there, because prayer is not an innocent or isolated religious act" (Brueggemann 2016, 182). In our view, there are in history glaring "continuities" in the midst of "discontinuities."

the authorial groups behind the biblical law codes such as the Covenant Code (CC), the Deuteronomic Code (DC), and the Holiness Code (HC).

3

THE PORTRAYAL OF JUDEAN COMMUNITIES
IN PERSIAN-ERA PALESTINE: THROUGH THE LENS
OF THE COVENANT CODE

3.1. Introduction

In the previous chapter, after analyzing the relationship between literacy and the piety of the poor within the Judean society of the Persian period, we have confirmed that with regard to understanding the formation history of the Hebrew Bible, it is crucially important to identify carefully the authorial groups behind the biblical law codes such as the Covenant Code (CC), the Deuteronomic Code (DC), and the Holiness Code (HC) in their socioeconomic and theological location. Furthermore, attentive investigation of the contents of a society's law codes is helpful for understanding the microstructure of that society. These are the reasons why this chapter deals with the historical relationship between biblical law codes.

The dating and the historical background of CC are still much debated.[1] CC has often been regarded as the oldest law code in Israelite history.[2] According to Julius Wellhausen, CC is older than DC, and DC depends literarily on CC because the altar law (Exod 20:24–26) and the cultic laws (23:10–19) reflect a developmental stage in Israelite religionness that is

---

1. For a detailed history of research, see, e.g., Zenger 1971, 13–45; Schwienhorst-Schönberger 1990, 3–22; and Van Seters 2003, 8–46.

2. Among the majority of the scholars, see Noth, 1966, 175; Paul 1970, 44; Boecker 1984, 122; Hyatt 1980, 218; Crüsemann 1992, 132; Albertz 1992, 182–83; 2015, 78–130; Zehnder 2005, 315–23; Stackert 2007, 113–64; Fried 2007, 180; Achenbach 2011, 29–43; Nihan 2011, 131–33; Markl and Ezechukwu 2015, 225; Awabdy 2014, 169–226.

earlier than the altar laws in DC.[3] According to Wellhausen, the literal dependence of DC on CC also explains the lack of logical consistency and literary unity in DC.[4] His theory has been accepted by most scholars, many of whom contend that the laws repeated in DC and HC should be considered as revised or expanded versions of the earlier CC.[5] These laws are often regarded as evidence of an evolutionary development in Israelite law brought about by the socioeconomic transformation of the period.

However, legitimate doubt is expressed in recent research concerning the older sources.[6] I believe that it would be more appropriate, therefore, to refrain from using labels such as J, E, and JE for the characterization of the prepriestly Tetrateuch and, accordingly, reconsider the dating and historical background of CC.[7] In this chapter, the author investigates and defends the possibility that the final composition of CC is to be attributed to the Judean society of Persian-era Palestine. A comparative study among CC, HC, and DC leads to the conclusion that CC (Exod 20:24–23:19) was chiastically structured around the *mishpatim* (21:12–22:19*) in the Persian era. The author believes that CC was not included out of archival interest, but that it, along with HC and DC, indicates the contested positions of the subgroups in Yehud. In other words, the historical relationship between

---

3. Wellhausen 1957, 33: "As the Book of the Covenant, and the whole Jehovistic writing in general, reflects the first pre-prophetic period in the history of the cultus, so Deuteronomy is the legal expression of the second period of struggle and transition. The historical order is all the more certain because the literary dependence of Deuteronomy on the Jehovistic laws and narratives can be demonstrated independently, and is an admitted fact." See also Wellhausen 1957, 29–30; and 1963, 203: "Deuteronomy 12 polemicizes the state sanctioned by Exod 20:24 and provides no clues concerning the tabernacle as the sole basis of the cult since the covenant at Sinai." This view has been challenged by Van Seters (2003, 62–67), who argues that the relevant texts in CC presuppose the Deuteronomistic theology of cult centralization.

4. Wellhausen 1963, 193–94.

5. E.g., Levinson 1997, passim; 2004, 272–325; Stackert 2007, passim.

6. See, e.g., Kaiser 1984, 101; 1992a, 51–58; H. Schmid 1976, 83–118; and Van Seters, 1975, 309–12; 1994, 457–68; Rendtorff 1990, 101–36; Römer 2006b, 9–27; 2009a, 129; 2014, 65–93; Blum 2002, 119–56; 2006, 89–106; K. Schmid 1999, passim; 2006, 29–50; Gertz 2000, 357–96; 2006, 73–87; 2009, 260–85; de Pury 2006, 51–73; Kratz 2015, 95–98.

7. On refraining from using labels, see, e.g., Römer 2006b, 9–27; 2009a, 129; 2014, 65–93; Blum 1990, passim; 2006, 89–106; K. Schmid 1999, passim; 2006, 29–50; Gertz 2000, 357–96; 2006, 73–87; 2009, 260–85; de Pury 2006, 51–72; Kratz 2015, 95–98. On reconsidering the dating, see, e.g., Van Seters 2003, 172–75; and Knight 2009, 97–116.

CC, HC, and DC is not linear but rather simultaneous and reciprocal. In our view, the three biblical law codes clearly reflect the respective theological and ideological values of postexilic subgroups based in an agrarian society. The main purpose of this chapter is to indicate several pieces of evidence that support this hypothesis.   what

3.2. Literary Analysis of the Covenant Code

Indubitably, the diverse literary patterns and styles in CC suggest a diachronic history of composition. However, it would be misguided to assume a direct, one-to-one relationship between a particular literary form and a social circumstance that is assumed as its *Sitz im Leben*. Such an approach would necessitate a theory that incorporates redactional operations for the literary combination of the diverse laws together with their independent background.[8] Therefore, in this chapter, we will not focus on the form-critical approach.

The composition of CC is of a concentric nature with compositional frames around one core collection (Exod 21:12–22:19*).[9] With the exception of Exod 21:13–14, 23 (ונתתה); 22:17 (תחיה), Exod 21:12–22:19* can be regarded as a homogeneous unit.[10] In this chapter, Exod 21:12–22:19* will be called the *mishpatim* and the remaining portion of CC will be called the *debarim*. There are several contrasts between the two parts of CC: (1) the *mishpatim* contain no references to the narrative context, while the *debarim* indicate many points of contact.[11] (2) The *mishpatim* do not employ first person divine speech, while many texts written in the first person are found in the *debarim* (e.g., Exod 20:22–24; 22:26).[12] Furthermore, God does not refer to Moses or the Israelites as "you" in

---

8. For similar opinions, see Van Seters 2003, 9–29 and Levinson 2004, 277.

9. According to Otto (1988, 9–11), CC consists of two law collections, namely, Exod 21:2–22:26 and 22:28–23:12. However, Schwienhorst-Schönberger (1990, 21–37) argues that CC cannot be viewed as a redactional combination of two originally independent law collections. In our view, CC is rather concentrically structured.

10. Exodus 21:13–14, 23; 22:17 seem to be modifications by the later author who completed and inserted CC into its current location.

11. E.g., the motif of being slaves or strangers in Egypt (Exod 22:20, 23:9; cf. Exod 1:8–14), the divine hearing of human shouting in crisis (Exod 22:22, 26; cf. Exod 3:7, 9) and the feast of unleavened bread (Exod 23:15; cf. Exod 12:15–20).

12. Exod 21:13–14 is an exception and seems to be a later addition to CC.

the *mishpatim*.[13] However, in the *debarim* Moses and the Israelites are addressed in the second person throughout.[14] (3) It is also significant that, in sharp contrast to the *debarim*, the *mishpatim* contain, with only a few exceptions, fully formulated casuistic regulations.[15]

The literary structure can be set out as follows:[16]

---

13. Exod 21:13–14, 23 (ונתתה); 22:17 (תחיה) are exceptions and seem to be later insertions within CC.

14. In earlier research, CC was considered as originally divine law that was later transformed by a body of profane laws (see, e.g., Halbe 1975, 506–7). However, in more recent research—and for good reason—a more common view is that CC is a collection of originally profane laws that were increasingly theologized into divine law (see, e.g., Schwienhorst-Schönberger 1990, 415–17). According to Schwienhorst-Schönberger (ibid., 415), Exod 21:12–22:16* is the oldest portion of CC. On the other hand, Houtman (1997, 15) regards the text in Exod 21:1–22:16 with the exception of Exod 21:12–17 as the original part of CC. However, (1) Exod 21:1–11 seems to be torn out of its original context; (2) these verses seem to be intentionally set as counterparts of Exod 22:20–23:9* as well as of Exod 23:10–12 within the chiastic structure of CC; and (3) a new element, namely, "pseudo-casuistic" law (e.g., כי תקנה in Exod 21:2), is found that is almost entirely absent in the *mishpatim*. Thus, it is more probable that Exod 21:1–11 does not belong to the original part of CC.

15. In our view, the מות יומת-laws in Exod 21:12, 15–17; 22:17–19 cannot be considered as exceptions to the *mishpatim* because the מות יומת-laws do not belong to the category of apodictic laws. Schwienhorst-Schönberger (1990, 227–28) properly regards this type of law as substantially homogeneous with the casuistic law. The מות יומת-laws in Exod 21:12, 15–17 feature prohibitions beginning with a participle and ending with capital punishment using the formula מות יומת that basically correspond with the syntactic structure of casuistic law. The regulations in Exod 22:17–19 demonstrate a more obvious flexibility in form; capital punishment is stated in diverse ways without the phrase מות יומת. However, the regulations can be viewed as related to the מות יומת-laws in a wider sense. In other words, the מות יומת-laws are of a casuistic nature and were inserted in order to frame the primary section of casuistic laws.

16. D. Wright (2009b, 171–81) similarly regards CC as chiastically structured even though he differs in detail from the position presented in this study. He insists that, "in the case of CC, any estimate of chiastic formulation must be weighed against the use and influence of LH [the Laws of Hammurabi] as a source text" (181). Regardless of the validity of the hypothesis that CC primarily and directly depends on LH for its entire composition (see D. Wright 2009a, 29–359), Wright's dating of CC to the Neo-Assyrian period between 740–640 BCE seems to require more solid evidence (see Van Seters 2007, 18–21).

> A. Exod 20:22–26 Cultic law[17]
>> B. Exod 21:1–6 Release of slaves (six-seven structure)[18]
>>> C. Exod 21:7–11 Social and humanitarian commandments[19]
>>>> D. Exod 21:12–22:19* *mishpatim* (starting and ending with the מות יומת laws)
>>> C′. Exod 22:20–23:9* Social and humanitarian commandments [with the exception of Exod 22:28–30][20]
>> B′. Exod 23:10–12 Sabbath year and Sabbath day (six-seven structure)
> A′. Exod 23:13–19* Cultic law[21]

---

17. Noth (1966, 176) comments on the homogeneity of the two sections (Exod 20:24–26 and 23:10–19) in the following manner: "The law of the altar (20:24–26), which immediately follows, stands, remarkably, before the superscription 21:1 which, as no further superscriptions follow in the Book of the Covenant, may once have introduced the whole law book, even if it originally belonged perhaps only to one subsection of the book. The law of the altar may therefore have been put at the beginning of the book at a later date. In fact it would best fit in with the cultic regulations of the Book of the Covenant in 23:10–19." In our view, it is more probable to regard Exod 23:10–12 as an intended counterpart of Exod 21:1–6 in the aforementioned chiastic structure. The obvious analogy of the six-seven structure between Exod 21:1–6 and 23:10–12 confirms this assumption. Thus, Exod 20:22–26 and 23:13–19 suitably match as counterparts.

18. The introductory formula in Exod 21:1 marks the beginning of a new section, but not a different redactional layer, since it presupposes the narrative circumstance of the dialogue between God and Moses, which fits perfectly with the preceding texts (see Van Seters 2007, 6; against C. Levin 2000, 123).

19. Most scholars regard Exod 21:7–11 as unified with the preceding regulations of Exod 21:1–6. However, Exod 21:7–11 distinguishes itself from the preceding regulations because it has nothing to do with the Sabbath release nor (in sharp contrast to Exod 21:1–6) with the six-seven structure corresponding to Exod 23:10–12. While the regulations of Exod 21:1–6 describe the conditions of service and release of male slaves, the texts of Exod 21:7–11 delineate the legal rights of female slave brides (cf. Dozeman 2009, 526–27). Thus, considering the entire chiastic structure of CC, Exod 21:7–11 is basically of a protective as well as humanitarian nature, and most suitably corresponds with the social and humanitarian commandments in Exod 22:20–23:9*. This conclusion is further supported by the observation that both text sections (Exod 21:7–11 and 22:20–23:9*) are thematically and lexically linked to each other (cf. עם נכרי in 21:7 with גרים/גר in 22:20; בתו in 21:7 with יתום in 22:21; and כסותה in 21:10 with כסותה in 22:26).

20. In our view, Exod 22:28–30 seems to be a later insertion which interrupts the purely chiastic literary structure in the previous compositional stage of CC.

21. Exod 20:22–26 and 23:13–19* are chiastic counterparts. Both sections articu-

To sum up, CC is a chiastically structured text centering on (D) Exod 21:12–22:19*. There are three mutually corresponding layers in this chiastic structure: (A) 20:22–26 and (A′) 23:13–19*; (B) 21:1–6 and (B′) 23:10–12; and (C) 21:7–11 and (C′) 22:20–23:9*.

3.3. The Stranger (גר)

There is a general tendency to view the core part of CC as being derived from the monarchic period between the ninth and seventh centuries BCE.[22] For example, Ludger Schwienhorst-Schönberger argues that the decisive "*gottesrechtliche*" redaction derives from the time period between Hosea and Deuteronomy.[23] Following Yuichi Osumi's literary analysis, Frank Crüsemann contends that CC was mainly composed between the

---

late the regulations relating to cultic rituals and display a similar structure. Likewise, both sections begin with the prohibition against idolatry (cf. 20:22–23 and 23:13), which is followed by the cultic laws (cf. 20:24–26 and 23:14–19*). This structural parallelism makes the hypothesis that the phrase ובכל אשר אמרתי signals the original end of CC superfluous. It can be understood as the author's rhetorical reemphasis of the theological significance of the relevant regulations (as opposed to Albertz, 1992, 284–85). Furthermore, Exod 23:13–19 is a parallel text to Exod 34. There are multiple arguments both for and against the early date of Exod 34 (see Carr 2001, 108–12). According to Blum (1996, 366), the so-called "privilege law" ("*Privilegrecht*") in Exod 34 does not derive from an early stage in the Torah's formation but rather from a late period. If Exod 34 is not viewed as the earliest of the sources (J), there is no compelling reason to consider its parallel in Exod 23:13–19 as Elohistic. As Carr (2001, 109–11) correctly observes, Exod 23:13–19 seems to be earlier than its parallel in Exod 34:11–26, since (1) 34:18 is an expansion of 23:15; (2) 23:17 is simpler than 34:23; and (3) 34:25 is more specific than its parallel in 23:18.

22. See Schwienhorst-Schönberger 1990, 284–86; Crüsemann 1992, 230; Albertz 1992, 183; 2011, 53–70; Zehnder 2005, 315–23; Stackert 2007, 113–64; Fried 2007, 180; Achenbach 2011, 29–43; Nihan 2011, 131–33; Markl and Ezechukwu 2015, 225. On the other hand, Ebach asserts that Exod 22:20b and 23:9b are Deuteronomistic additions from the Persian period since גר is considered as the subject of protection and is connected with the memory of slavery in Egypt in the above-mentioned references (2014, 58–59 n. 192).

23. Schwienhorst-Schönberger 1990, 284–86. According to Schwienhorst-Schönberger, the most basic material in CC (Exod 21:12, 18–22:14*) was edited through the following text of the "*gottesrechtliche*" (proto-Deuteronomic) redaction: Exod 20:24–26*; 21:2–11*, 13–17, 20–21, 22aβbβ, 23–24, 26–27, 30; 22:1–2, 9*–10*, 15–16, 17–19a, 20aα, 22b, 24a*, 25–26 (ibid., 284). A further layer of Deuteronomistic redaction was added to this stage of CC, which includes the following verses: Exod 20:23,

eighth and seventh centuries BCE and that the document was probably finalized after 722 BCE.[24] The argument mainly derives from the fact that CC pays special attention to the protection of the stranger (Exod 22:20; 23:9), which could be a reaction to the increasingly serious refugee problem that Judah faced after the fall of Samaria.[25] Thus, Crüsemann and Albertz share the view that CC derives from the time period in which the Northern Kingdom was destroyed. However, we have to ask at this point whether the fall of Samaria was the exclusive historical context leading to concern for the stranger.[26]

Commandments concerning the widow and orphan in Exod 22:21 come after the provisions for the גר in Exod 22:20. An argument against exploitation and for the protection of these three marginalized groups (stranger, widow, and orphan) is found in the following references: Deut 10:18; 14:29; 16:11, 14; 24:17, 19, 20, 21; 26:12, 13; 27:19; Ps 146:9; Jer 7:6; 22:3; Ezek 22:7; Zech 7:10; and Mal 3:5. It is striking that the texts in Isa

----

24aβ; 21:1, 2aα*, 6aβγ, 8b, 25; 22:19b, 20aβb, 21, 22a, 23, 24aα*b, 30; 23:8–9, 13, 15aα*, 20–33* (ibid., 286).

24. Crüsemann 1992, 230, based on Osumi 1991, 219–20. Furthermore, see, e.g., Albertz 1992, 183; 2011, 53–69; Zehnder 2005, 315–23; Fried 2007, 180; Achenbach 2011, 29–43; Nihan 2011, 131–33; Markl and Ezechukwu 2015, 225.

25. Crüsemann 1992, 229–30; Albertz 1992, 183; 2011, 53–69. For Hezekiah's reform as the historical background for Exod 20:22–26; 34:11–26, see also Phillips 1984, 42–52.

26. Na'aman argues that the hypothesis that mass migration of Israelite refugees accounted for the growth of Jerusalem and Judah in the eighth century BCE is misleading (2014, 1–14). Based on systematic investigation of the textual as well as archaeological evidence available, he concludes that the growth of Judah and Jerusalem was gradual and that no theory of a flood of Israelite refugees is necessary to explain that growth. The issue of the migration of Israelites into Judah after 720 BCE has been hotly debated. Even if one would accept the migration theory, the fact still remains valid that the fall of Samaria is not the only and exclusive historical event resulting in concern for the stranger. For various positions related to this issue, see van der Toorn 1996, 339–72; Finkelstein and Silberman 2001, 243–45; Finkelstein 2015, 188–206; Schniedewind 2005, 68–95; Faust 2005, 97–118; Knauf 2006, 293–94; P. Davies 2007, 93–112; Guillaume 2008, 195–211. For criticisms concerning Crüsemann's as well as Schwienhorst-Schönberger's thesis related to the stranger, see Bultmann 1992, 166–69. According to Bultmann, the regulations in Exod 22:20–23; 23:1–3, 6–9 are generalizing protection laws (*generalisierende Schutzgebote*) that are late Deuteronomistic and therefore presuppose Deut 24:17, 27:19, among others. Bultmann dates the relevant texts in CC to the second half of the sixth century BCE or even later. For detailed arguments on this dating, see Bultmann 1992, 166–74.

1:17, 23; 10:2 speak only about the protection of orphans and widows but do not address the problem of the גר at all.[27] In other words, the issue of the גר was not on the agenda of prophets in the eighth century. Even if the texts of Jer 7:6; 22:3 derive from the prophet himself, the issue appears, at the earliest, in the late monarchic period.[28] This fact implies that it is unnecessary to connect the problem of the גר with the fall of Samaria as Crüsemann and Albertz assume.[29]

Furthermore, the concerns of the three biblical law codes (CC, HC, and DC) for the stranger (גר) are also intriguing. The term גר occurs frequently within the three law codes.[30] In other words, the subject of the stranger was a burning problem not only in CC, but also in HC and DC. The authors of the three law codes share the same awareness of the seriousness of the issue even though there is a slight variation in tone.[31] The difference seems to be more related to the respective authors' internal perspectives on the stranger than to external socioeconomic changes. In CC, the term for stranger (גר) is used as a synonym for the poor (עני, אביון: Exod 22:24; 23:6, 11), widows (אלמנה: Exod 22:21–22) and orphans (יתום: Exod 22:21–22). In HC (Lev 19:10), the stranger (גר) is also juxtaposed with the poor person (עני). The social status of the stranger in DC is not drastically changed. The stranger is considered as equal to orphans (יתום), widows (אלמנה), hired servants (שכיר), and Levites (לוי) in Deut 14:29; 16:11, 14; 24:14, 17, 19–21; 26:12–13.[32] Most of the regulations relating to

---

27. Osumi 1991, 178.

28. Deut 10:18 is a postexilic text (Otto 2012, 1037–43). In our view, the lexeme גר in Deut 14:29; 16:11, 14; 24:17, 19, 20, 21; 26:12, 13; 27:19 is basically a postexilic extrapolation (for the historical background of the theme of the "stranger" in DC, see below). Psalm 146 derives from a period between the third and second centuries BCE (Hossfeld and Zenger 2008, 809–22).

29. Van Seters 2003, 131; Na'aman 2014, 1–14.

30. גר ("stranger") is found in the following biblical references: Exod 22:20 (2x), 23:9 (2x), 12; Lev 17:8, 10, 12, 13, 15; 18:26; 19:10, 33, 34 (2x); 20:2; 22:18; 23:22; 24:16, 22; 25:23, 35, 47 (2x); Deut 14:21, 29; 16:11, 14; 23:8; 24:14, 17, 19, 20, 21; 26:11, 12, 13.

31. As opposed to Albertz (2011, 53–70), who attempts to explain the differences of the biblical law codes regarding the stranger in diachronic terms. Markl and Ezechukwu recognize that redactions of the Pentateuch in the Persian period tried to allow for a relatively consistent and synchronic reading of the law codes (2015, 225).

32. Of course, it is striking that in DC there are no instances in which the Hebrew words for "poor" (אביון, עני, דל, etc.) are linked with the collocation "stranger, fatherless, and widow." According to Lohfink (1990b, 27–40), the implication of this phenomenon is that the author of the relevant texts in Deuteronomy attempts to claim

the stranger in the three law codes have to do with protection.[33] If CC is regarded as originating during the monarchic period between the ninth and seventh centuries because of the stranger-motif, should we not also date HC and DC shortly after 722 BCE for the same reason?

It is beyond the scope of this chapter to delve deeply into the chronological order of CC, HC, and DC. However, this similarity among the biblical law codes seems to provide a clue regarding their common historical background. Albertz differentiates the biblical law codes diachronically, assuming that CC derives from the eighth–seventh centuries BCE, DC from the late seventh–sixth centuries BCE, and HC from the postexilic period.[34] However, we are then forced to ask why the topic of the stranger appears more frequently in DC than in CC. Was there a more dramatic historical incident in the late seventh–sixth centuries than the fall of

---

that the strangers, widows, and fatherless cannot be surmised to belong to the same category as the poor in the socioeconomic stratification of Judean society. Lohfink contends that this concept is absent in CC, which is older. This points, therefore, to a diachronic gap between CC and DC. However, his opinion is highly speculative at this point, because the discrepancy between CC and DC can be also explained synchronically. In our view, this phenomenon seems to reveal the authors' internal biases rather than the external shifts in socioeconomic circumstances.

33. Lev 17:10; 20:2; 25:47; and Deut 14:21 are particularly intriguing. Throughout the ancient Near Eastern culture it was a widespread custom to consume animal blood. This custom is rigorously prohibited for both the Israelites and the strangers in Lev 17:10 (see also Lev 3:17; 7:26–27; 19:26). The author of Lev 17:10 emphasizes the universal validity of this prohibition. The law in Lev 20:2 also forbids offering children to Molek for both Israelites and strangers. This regulation, which was originally valid only for Israelites, became universalized by the author of Lev 20:2. The author of Lev 17:10 and 20:2 tries to facilitate the religious integration of the strangers. Lev 25:47 seems to exhibit the socioeconomic situation of Judean society in Persian-era Palestine in which the descendants of those who remained in Palestine during the exilic period assumed socioeconomic power in Judean society. The author of Deut 14:21 seems to have tied the law related to land animals (Deut 14:3–20) with the law concerning the annual and triennial tithes (Deut 14:22–29). Holiness in Deut 14:21 is based on the divine election for Israel that locates the cultic burden on the shoulders of the Israelites (Weinfeld 1972, 232). Stressing the particular theological position of his own community, the author seems to have critically revised the law in Lev 17:15 that regulates eating from any animal found dead or mauled. For a different position, see Awabdy (2014, 179–80, 220–26), who claims that there is no intertextual correlation between Lev 17:15–16 and Deut 14:21.

34. Albertz 2011, 53–69. Moreover, see, e.g., Zehnder 2005, 315–23; Fried 2007, 180; Achenbach 2011, 29–43; Nihan 2011, 131–33.

Samaria that necessitated the greater inflow of refugees into the Southern Kingdom? If not, did the authors of DC blindly imitate CC even though the stranger was not a real social issue for them?

The fact that the socioeconomic settings of the three law codes relating to the stranger are similar seems to render improbable the assumption that there are century-long chronological gaps between the respective law codes.[35] In our view, the theme of the stranger in the biblical law codes should be understood synchronically. It must have been an urgent problem for the Judean communities in Persian-era Palestine because of the massive number of returnees from the Babylonian exile.

It is worth noting that the term גר connotes an outsider of some type and is often described as a resident stranger, sojourner, or immigrant who occupies an intermediate social position between the native and the real foreigner (נכרי, Exod 21:8).[36] The term נכרי was used in the Pentateuch for

---

35. Albertz (2011, 56) contends that the increased social obligation of DC stems from the fact that the socioeconomic condition of the stranger in the late preexilic period became even worse than in the time of CC. According to Albertz (2011, 56–63), in sharp contrast to CC and DC, the texts of HC show diachronic developments of socioeconomic circumstances in which the multiethnic and multireligious situation challenged Judean society in Persian-era Palestine. However, his arguments are rather weak, since the increased social obligation of DC can be well explained by the hopeful passion of the Deuteronomistic author in the early postexilic period for the rebuilding of the ideal Israelite society. Furthermore, the examples of HC Albertz proposes seem to have more to do with internal Judean competition and tension concerning the building of the social infrastructure based on בית אבות rather than with the multiethnic and multireligious environment. Thus, the discontinuity of HC in comparison to CC and DC regarding the topic of the stranger probably stems from a difference in the legislator's definition and view of the גר rather than from external social changes arising out of diachronic gaps of several centuries.

According to Hölscher, the social vision of Deuteronomy is only understandable when based on the historical background related to the return of the *golah* (1922, 247). In light of several other features of Deuteronomy, including its ideological character, he concludes that Deuteronomy, including DC, was composed around 500 BCE. As Hölscher (233–46) correctly observes, it is striking that the oldest layers in the books of Jeremiah, Ezekiel, Haggai, and Zechariah do not show any awareness of Deuteronomy. On the other hand, in our view, the possibility cannot be entirely negated that DC was not completely shaped anew and formed ex nihilo around 500 BCE but had older parts that had been transmitted from the preexilic period. At any rate, the final form of DC seems to have eventually been conclusively molded in the Persian period, primarily as a reflection of the situation of Judean society in Persian-era Palestine.

36. Marshall 1993, 148.

men who were nonresident foreigners as distinct from the גר.[37] The term
גרים in Lev 19:33–34 seems to include many Judeans who had left their
original livelihood for whatever reason in the postexilic period.[38]

It is probable that, depending on the contexts, the texts relating to the
גר in the biblical law codes target the returnees from the Babylonian exile
as well as the descendants of the דלת הארץ in the Persian period. From
the perspective of the descendants of the דלת הארץ, the returned exiles
are strangers (גרים) and vice versa. Early Persian-era Palestine was a place
where multiple Judean communities coexisted side by side, and this social
environment necessarily caused most Judeans belonging to different communities to be strangers to each other.[39]

At this point it is intriguing to observe the threat of an unknown people
or strangers possessing the lands and fields of Judeans in Deuteronomy:

A people whom you do not know [עם אשר לא־ידעת] shall eat up the fruit
of your ground and of all your labors; you shall be continually abused
and crushed. (Deut 28:33)

Aliens [הגר] residing among you shall ascend above you higher and
higher, while you shall descend lower and lower. They shall lend to you
but you shall not lend to them; they shall be the head and you shall be
the tail. (Deut 28:43–44)

The unknown people and stranger in the aforementioned cases seem to
indicate another postexilic Judean group, who are to be identified with
the עם הארץ.[40] In our view, the above passages are a postexilic reflection
of what happened when the divine voice was not obeyed. The texts can be
interpreted as a lament of the returned exiles, which regards the practical
possession of the best arable land by the descendants of the דלת הארץ as a
divine punishment because of the transgressions of their ancestors.

---

37. Achenbach 2011, 43–45; Wuench 2014, 1139–48; Ebach 2014, 62–4; Douglas
2002, 7; Lang and Ringgren 1986, 456–60.

38. D. Smith 1991, 93–96; and Grabbe 1998, 94.

39. Weinberg (1992, 105–26) hypothesizes that the self-governing community of
the *golah* and the central administration with its local organs coexisted side by side
within the territory of Yehud. It is reasonable to assume that the descendants of those
who remained in Palestine during the exilic period were members of a community
that was distinct from the *golah* community in the early postexilic period (see Oswald
1998, 183).

40. D. Smith 1991, 93.

Generally speaking, at the beginning of the fifth century BCE the descendants of the דלת הארץ tended to be in a much more solid position than the returnees who had recently changed the location of their livelihood.[41] In the initial stages, the returned exiles were socioeconomically in a weaker position. However, they dared to build a community based on an ideological kinship system, the בית אבות.[42] For Joel Weinberg, the concept of the בית אבות acts as the operative infrastructure for the returned exiles in Persian-era Palestine.[43]

---

41. As opposed to Blenkinsopp 1991, 44–51. Among others, Y. Levin (2003, 237–41) argues that the returned exiles constituted a socially and economically privileged class distinct from the common people in the subprovince. However, this assumption is incomprehensible given the current situation of the *aliyah* in Israel. It is reasonable to assume that the Judeans in the Babylonian diaspora who belonged to the upper stratum tended to stay with the solid and safe bases of their various livelihoods. There is another intriguing question here about the status of those who remained in the land during the Babylonian exile. Were they prisoners of war who were stripped of land and only worked estate land owned by the Neo-Babylonian crown? Or would they have been assigned land plots so that the Neo-Babylonians could also demand tributes, corvée, and military service from them? These obligations were not usually assessed against the landless. Since the latter option was far more profitable for the Neo-Babylonians from a socioeconomic point of view, it is highly probable that the conquerors assigned and endowed land plots to those who remained in the land (see 2 Kgs 25:12; Jer 39:10). On this issue, see §3.6, below.

42. Weinberg's socioeconomic model of the citizen-temple community (1992, 17–104) is a fitting explanatory social theory for the Judean communities in Persian-era Palestine even though many parts of the theory could be critically adjusted and adapted (see, e.g., Grabbe 2004, 143; Cataldo 2003, 241–42; Janzen 2002b, 490–97; and Carter 1999, 294–96). Weinberg's theory presumes that membership in the citizen-temple community is restricted to the priesthood and members of agnatic groups that are economically connected with the temple (1992, 17–33). Although the validity of Weinberg's theory has been challenged in many respects (e.g., Horsley 1991, 165–66; Grabbe 2004, 144–45; Carter 1999, 297–307; Cataldo 2003, 240–52; Bedford 2001, 207–30; and Y. Levin 2003, 237–40; 2004, 603–5), Weinberg's view regarding the concept of the בית אבות is still fitting.

43. Weinberg 1992, 49–61. Weinberg defines the בית אבות as an "agnatic band which came into existence in the peculiar situation of the exile and repatriation" (61). According to Weinberg, while the preexilic concept of the בית אב may have been based on a literal lineage, the subsequent development of the concept of the בית אבות reflects a postexilic shift in realities, which cast the plausibility of the earlier concept of the בית אב into question (ibid., 49–61). Dyck also assumes that the term בית אבות indicates a socioeconomic structure that essentially differs from the preexilic בית אב (1998, 188–203). In this context, Mowinckel's engaging hypothesis is that during the

It is probable that the returned exiles gradually formed a self-governing community within the territory of Yehud, a subprovince controlled by the Persian central administration. The two structures, the subprovince and the local community, were not identical.[44] The former was a territorial entity of the Persian Empire, while the latter was a (real as well as fictive) kinship community.[45] This implies that the returned exiles and the descendants of the דלת הארץ dwelled side by side within the same territorial area but belonged to different communities based on different preconditions of membership.[46] Therefore, in our view, *Judean community* is a less accurate term than *Judean communities* to describe the internal social or demographic situation of Judean society in Persian-era Palestine.[47] Judean society in Persian-era Palestine was heterogeneous and diverse. The self-governing community of the *golah* was only one aspect of this society.[48] These communities were not separated so much geographically as psychologically, since the members of the respective communities had to inhabit the same territory.[49] In this sense, perhaps *communal network* would be a proper characterization of this type of community.[50] It is likely that the members of the respective communities had to interact daily with each

---

Babylonian exile most Judeans lived in ghetto-like settlements with their own local authorities (1964, 75–77). Comprising the structural pyramid of these Judean settlements was the "head" (ראש) and then the "elders" (זקנים), who gradually formed a kind of community council. It is no wonder that the members of such Judean settlements came to regard each other as "kinsmen." They felt like "sons" of their leaders, who assumed responsibility during the communal crisis. The basis of the feeling of kinship was communal living in exile (ibid., 76). This feeling of kinship became the foundation of the major socioeconomic system called the בית אבות. In our view, Mowinckel is correct in his observation that the concept of the בית אבות does not always reflect a genuine kinship connection but more often a hypothetical or an ideological construction for the purpose of establishing a structure and a sense of identity.

44. See, e.g., Weinberg 1992, 105–7; Blenkinsopp 1991, 50–51; Edelman 2007, 64; and Gerstenberger 2005, 89–93.

45. E.g., Oswald 1998, 182–83.

46. Ibid., 183.

47. See, e.g., Rom-Shiloni 2013, 265–76.

48. See, e.g., Y. Levin 2003, 239–41.

49. See Rom-Shiloni 2013, 13–29 with further bibliography.

50. Of course, this is inseparably intertwined with the difficult question of whether the returned exiles were free to settle anywhere or assigned to certain plots of land. On this issue, see §3.6, below.

other in order to survive and prosper.[51] This was done by employing and being employed as well as providing and receiving compensation.

The demographic and economic situation in the exilic as well as the postexilic Judean communities in Palestine has been much debated.[52] According to Charles Carter, the population of Persian I (539–450 BCE) was 13,350 and the population of Persian II (450–333 BCE) was 20,650.[53] Carter states that, "Jerusalem during this period was inhabited by a maximum of 1500 people at any given time."[54] Lipschits's estimate is a bit higher than Carter's (a population of 30,125 for Yehud).[55] According to Lipschits, Jerusalem was uninhabited during the Neo-Babylonian period after the destruction and was only partially resettled in the Persian period.[56] Even though Lipschits and Carter arrived at slightly different results, their counting methodologies in general seem to be quite similar. Finkelstein's number is about half of that calculated by Lipschits and Carter.[57] Israel Finkelstein argues that the population of the entire province of Yehud in the Persian

---

51. See Grabbe 2015, 302–3; Oswald 1998, 159–67. On this, see §3.6, below. The relationships between the three groups (the descendants of the דלת הארץ, including Samaritans, the lay returnees, and the priestly returnees) were not completely adversarial or hostile to each other (for details, see §3.6, below). As discussed above, there are many provisions and regulations protecting strangers (גר) in the three law codes. This indicates that the reciprocal viewpoints of the members of the three groups were not always antagonistic or in opposition but often largely collaborative even though the members of the three groups sometimes competed with each other.

52. See, e.g., Janssen 1956, 39–42; Weinberg 1992, 43–48; Ben-Zvi 1997, 194–209; Carter 1999, 190–213; Albertz 2001, 97–116; 2003, 1–17; J. Kessler 2002, 90–96; Barstad 2003, 3–14; 2008, 90–159; Faust 2003, 37–53; 2007, 23–50; 2013, 119–25; Becking 2006, 3–13; Lipschits 2003, 323–76; 2006, 19–40; Lipschits and Tal 2007, 33–48; Lipschits and Vanderhooft 2007, 75–94; Knowles 2008, 23; Finkelstein 2010, 39–54; Guillaume 2014, 227–30. For the position articulating the sparse population in Jerusalem and Yehud during the Babylonian and early Persian periods, see, e.g., Ben-Zvi 1997, 194–209; Carter 1999, 190–213; J. Kessler 2002, 90–96; Faust 2003, 37–53; 2007, 23–51; 2013, 119–25; Lipschits 2003, 323–76; 2006, 19–40; Finkelstein 2010, 39–54; Guillaume 2014, 227–30; for the contrasting position, see, e.g., Janssen 1956, 39–42; Weinberg 1992, 43–48; and Barstad 2003, 3–14; 2008, 90–159.

53. Carter 1999, 201–2.

54. Ibid., 201.

55. Lipschits 2003, 360–64. Grabbe seems to follow the middle way between Carter and Lipschits, suggesting that the population of Judah in the Persian period was 20,000 to 30,000 at its height (2015, 295).

56. Lipschits 2005, 211–18.

57. Finkelstein 2010, 44–45.

period was ca. 12,000.[58] On the other hand, Weinberg claims that before 458/457 BCE the population of the citizen-temple-community was around 42,360, and this was about 20 percent of the population of Persian Yehud.[59] It is beyond the scope of this study to present a detailed research analysis on the issue of the demography of Yehud. Nevertheless, we can say that compared with the estimated population at the end of the preexilic period, there was a considerable decline in settlement and population in Persian-era Palestine. The archaeological remains obviously indicate that the territory of Yehud was substantially smaller than in the time period before the Babylonian exile.[60] On the other hand, the demographic sparsity in Persian-era Palestine should not be exaggerated to the point where the land of Yehud was empty when the exiles returned to Jerusalem. There are obvious textual vestiges in Jer 37–42* of tension and conflict between the *golah* community, on the one hand, and those who remained in Palestine, on the other hand.[61]

The fact that the stranger issue is so frequently mentioned in CC, HC, and DC likely reflects the contemporary *Zeitgeist* of postexilic Judean communities that can be characterized "with strong external boundaries that remained in some anxiety over whether they were truly strong enough."[62]

3.4. The So-Called Deuteronomistic Redactor

The *mishpatim* presuppose a village society and seem to derive from a society that was primarily local and agrarian. There is no mention of a king.[63]

---

58. Ibid., 54.

59. Weinberg 1992, 43.

60. Lipschits 2003, 326–57; Finkelstein 2010, 40–46; and Faust 2013, 108–26.

61. See, e.g., Pohlmann 1978, 183–207; Oswald 1998, 159–67.

62. Janzen 2002a, 114. Janzen contends that the poor peasants in Neh 5 are those who were refused entry into the assembly as they remained in the land during the exile (92–93). However, in our view, it is more probable that the peasants belonged to a community of returnees who had recently come to Yehud.

63. Conforming to Alt's form-critical viewpoint of the literary genre, Noth insists that CC (Exod 20:22–23:33) was originally a separate block of laws and was placed into the book of Exodus as an independent unit. Regarding the historical background of CC, he asserts that there is no reference in CC to institutions of kingship, so that one may assume that it was compiled before Israel became a state (Noth 1966, 175). The נשיא of Exod 22:28 was the tribal representative of the twelve tribes in premonarchic Israel. For a similar argument for the dating of CC, see, e.g., Paul 1970, 44; Boecker 1984, 122; and Hyatt 1980, 218. However, the absence of kingship particularly in the

The people in the *mishpatim* raise oxen (שור: Exod 21:28, 29, 33, 35, 36, 37; 22:8, 9), sheep (שה: Exod 21:37; 22:3, 8, 9), and donkeys (חמור: Exod 21:33; 22:3, 8, 9), but there are no references to camels (גמל) or horses (סוס). Slavery existed (Exod 21:32). There was trade and a limited money economy, based on weighed pieces of silver, not minted coins (Exod 21:32).[64] The regulations in Exod 21:32 presuppose an economic framework which maintains a monetary system capable of supporting a loan system.[65] Jay Marshall assumes "even a standardized measure of silver."[66] On the other hand, he argues that any monetary system reflected in the *mishpatim* was rudimentary, because no mention is made of weights or measures in the marketplace, nor of a merchant class or specialized labor.[67] However, based on the current form of CC, it is not clear whether the monetary system presupposed by Exod 21:32 consisted of the rudimentary use of silver or the employment of a more sophisticated ("reformed") measure of silver.[68] The weighing of metal in Palestine is clearly witnessed in silver hoards which are dated as early as MB II, according to finds from Shechem, Nahariya, and Megiddo.[69] From the mid-fifth century BCE there is a transition in the means of payment from the use of weighed metal to that of foreign coinage and, subsequently, of local coinage.[70] In other words, the monetary system that Exod 21:32 reflects could have been valid for the lengthy time period from the Middle Bronze Age until at least the mid-fifth century BCE Persian period. Even after the production and circulation of local coinage, the traditional means of payment using weighed metal continued.[71] The transition from barter economy to monetary economy in Palestine was a

---

debarim can be understood as evidence of its exilic or postexilic origin. In this context, it is illuminating that the lexeme נשיא (Exod 22:27) is predominantly found in the book of Ezekiel and other exilic or postexilic priestly literature in the Hebrew Bible (for the biblical books in which the lexeme is found, see Schwienhorst-Schönberger 1990, 362).

64. For coin production and circulation in ancient Palestine, see Avigad 1976, 28–29; Stern 1982, 224–27; 2001, 565–69; Rappaport 1984, 25–29; Betlyon 1986, 633–42; Hübner 1994, 119–45; 2014, 159–83; Machinist 1994, 365–80; Mildenberg 1996, 119–46; 1998, 67–76; Meshorer 1998, 33–50; 2001, 1–18; Meshorer et al. 2013, 237–41.

65. Marshall 1993, 143–46.

66. Ibid., 143.

67. Ibid., 172.

68. Kletter 1998, 93–107, 139–46.

69. Gitler and Tal 2006, 9.

70. Ibid.

71. Hübner 2014, 182.

long and gradual process and, accordingly, various methods of payment were not exclusive, but rather complementary and supplementary to each other during the transition.

The people in the *mishpatim* cultivated vineyards (כרם: Exod 22:4) and grain fields (שדה: Exod 22:4, 5) but not olive trees (זית). The olive tree (זית) appears only once throughout the entire CC (Exod 23:11, in the *debarim*). Vineyards (כרם) and olive trees (זית) are found together ten times, as a pair of terms for fertility and food supply, almost exclusively in late (exilic/postexilic) texts such as Deut 6:11; Josh 24:13; Judg 15:5; 1 Sam 8:14; 2 Kgs 5:26; 18:32; Amos 4:9; and Neh 5:11; 9:25.

There is a broad consensus among scholars that CC is not an essential part of the tradition of the Sinai theophany and was included in its current position as a self-contained entity by a Deuteronomistic editor.[72] According to many scholars, Exod 20:22–23 is a redactional layer. For example, Martin Noth argues that Exod 20:22–23 derives from a Deuteronomistic redaction. From this, Noth concludes that one may suppose the incorporation of CC into the pentateuchal narrative in the period after Deuteronomy.[73] In other words, not primarily linked to the Sinai tradition, CC was later incorporated as a separate unit into the post-Dtr Pentateuch. This means that the text of CC is early in its origin but late in its insertion into the Pentateuch. Among the majority of scholars, these conclusions from Noth's analysis still remain as an axiom for the research on CC.

Brevard Childs, Ernest Nicholson, Erich Zenger, Eckart Otto, and Ludger Schwienhorst-Schönberger, among others, also assign Exod 20:22–23 to a "Deuteronomistic redactor."[74] Childs postulates that the

---

72. See, e.g., Noth 1966, 173–74; Perlitt 1969, 156–237; Childs 1974, 465; Zenger 1971, 68–70; Otto 1988, 4–8; Schwienhorst-Schönberger 1990, 410–12; and Crüsemann 1992, 74. Regarding the insertion of CC into the pentateuchal narratives, Noth (1966, 174) contends that the addition (Exod 23:20–33) is evidently secondary to CC (Exod 20:22–23:19) and may already have been in existence before the time of the insertion. His reasoning is as follows: it is the only explanation about the discussion concerning the question of the presence and activity of God in the impending conquest at such an early stage. For recent research on the origin and features of CC, see, e.g., Otto 2010, 1–26; Oswald 2012, 35–51; 2014, 169–92; Ausloos, 2014, 17–29; D. Wright 2014, 220–44; Wells 2015, 234–66. These studies presuppose that CC was added in its current position at a late stage.

73. Noth 1966, 174.

74. Childs 1974, 465; Nicholson 1977, 429–32; Zenger 1971, 68–70; Otto 1988, 4–5; and Schwienhorst-Schönberger 1990, 410–12.

"Deuteronomistic redactor" integrated CC into the Sinai theophany: "Verse 22 gives every sign of being a redactional link, perhaps from the Deuteronomist, which served to join the Book of the Covenant to the Sinai theophany.... The reference to Yahweh's speaking from heaven, which is missing from the Exodus account of the theophany, represents the subsequent deuteronomic reflection on the event."[75] Nicholson also asserts that it is hard to understand the reference to God speaking from heaven in Exod 20:22 and the connection of this divine action to the prohibition against making divine images without the dependence of Exod 20:22 upon Deut 4:36 and the entire theology of Deut 4.[76]

It seems probable the author of Exod 20:22–23 was influenced by Deut 4:36 because of (1) the sudden change from "thunder, lightning, shofar, and smoke" in Exod 20:18 to the "speaking from heaven" in Exod 20:22 and (2) the unexplained link between the "speaking from heaven" on the one hand and the prohibition against idolatry on the other in Exod 20:22.[77] However, whether or not we can call the author of Exod 20:22 (as well as of Exod 23:11) "Deuteronomistic" based upon the foregoing observations is another issue, since "being influenced" by some minor imagery traditions does not guarantee a wholehearted reception of the entire theology.

In this context, it is interesting that, within the narrative framework, Exod 20:22–23 and 19:3b–8; 24:3–8 seem to belong to the same literary layer that inserted CC into the Sinai pericope.[78] Many scholars suppose that the literary layer is purely redactional and has nothing to do with the composition of CC. However, there is no persuasive reason to separate the aforementioned units from the *debarim*-portion of CC.[79] It is more natural

75. Childs 1974, 465.

76. Nicholson 1977, 424–32. In recent research, Deut 4 is often regarded as one of the latest texts of Deuteronomy (e.g., Blum 2011, 61, 67; Wissmann 2011, 248; Römer 2005, 124; Otto 2000, 168–172). Feder argues that the aniconic tradition in Deut 4 is dependent on the cultic law of CC (2013, 263–66). However, due to the above-mentioned observations this study employs the view that the reverse direction is the more appropriate one.

77. Van Seters 2003, 51.

78. For the lexical and philological linkages among Exod 19:3b–8; 20:22–23; and 24:3–8, see Patrick 1977, 145–46; and Oswald 1998, 90.

79. As opposed to Patrick (1977, 156), who insists that there is nothing in CC that proves a link with the narrative framework because Exod 20:22–33 is formulated with the plural form of address, while the following altar laws in Exod 20:24–26 are singular. However, his argument is not compelling because the change from plural to

to regard the literary layer as having been created as part of the formation of CC.[80] Further, there are close links between the *debarim*-portion of CC and the wider narrative context in Exodus, including the experience of slavery or of being strangers in Egypt (Exod 22:20, 23:9; cf. 1:8–14), the divine hearing of human shouting in crisis (Exod 22:22, 26; cf. 3:7, 9), and the feast of unleavened bread (Exod 23:15; cf. 12:15–20). In addition, as already mentioned above, the framework text of Exod 20:22–23 simultaneously functions as an element in the chiastic structure of CC. The independence of the *mishpatim* (21:12–22:19*) as a base text of CC can be accepted. However, if we are freed from the presupposition of the so-called Deuteronomistic redactor inserting the older CC into its current position in the Sinai pericope, there is no compelling argument to assume that the *debarim*-portion of CC was also a self-contained unity which was originally separated from the narrative framework. In our view, the *debarim*-portion of CC was composed by the same author who was responsible for Exod 19:3b–8; 20:22–23; and 24:3–8.[81] That author was partly influenced by Deuteronomistic thought and theology but was not the Deuteronomistic redactor, since there are clear contradictions between CC and Deuteronomy.[82] At this point, it suffices to present two pieces of evidence.[83]

---

singular is of a stylistic nature, so that the significant theological commandment in Exod 23:13 is articulated concomitantly in both the plural (תזכירו; תשמרו; אליכם) and the singular forms (פיך) (see Albertz 1992, 182–83). This combination of plural and singular forms indicates an intentional rhetorical emphasis addressing both the community and the individual (ibid., 183).

80. Van Seters (2007, 13) rightly notes the "epistemological error" of many scholars, although he goes too far in arguing that the entire Sinai pericope is a coherent composition by a single author called J with a few later P insertions (2003, 53–54).

81. For the socioeconomic location of the author in question, see §3.6, below.

82. Concerning the influence, cf. the aforementioned literary dependence of Exod 20:22–23 on Deut 4:36 as well as the aforementioned Deuteronomistic imagery of vineyards (כרם) and olive trees (זית) as symbols of fertility and food supply. According to Blum (1990, 199–200), the author responsible for the Deuteronomistic composition (KD), advocating for the class of landowning farmers in the postexilic period simply juxtaposed CC and DC in spite of the obvious conflicting elements between the two law codes; this is because he was "positively interested" in the content of CC (ibid.). CC and DC are identified as one and the same in the compositional logic and structure in KD. Both law codes were understood by the author responsible for KD as the same manifestation of divine will in their respective wholeness. However, Blum overemphasizes the homogeneity of CC and DC, which in fact contain glaring differences.

83. For other evidence, see Van Seters 1999, 161–69; 2003, 54–55.

First, the usage of לחץ "to oppress" reveals an unconcealable tension between CC and DC. Exodus 22:20 states: "You shall not defraud [לא תונה] a stranger or oppress [ולא תלחצנו] him, for you were strangers in the land of Egypt." The commandment is repeated with almost the same wording in Exod 23:9: "You shall not oppress [לא תלחץ] a stranger, since you your-selves know the mind of a stranger, for you also were strangers in the land of Egypt." This verb לחץ "to oppress" is frequently found in Deuteronomistic or Deuteronomistically influenced texts such as Deut 26:7; Judg 2:18; 4:3; 6:9; 10:12; 1 Sam 10:18; 2 Kgs 13:4, 22; Ps 106:42; and Jer 30:20.[84] However, in the Deuteronomistic texts, the verb is employed to refer to strangers oppressing Israelites.[85] On the other hand, the term is used in Exod 22:20 and 23:9 such that it now refers to Israelites oppressing strangers. It points out the fact that the author of Exod 22:20 and 23:9 attempts to keep a theological distance from the usual usage of the verb לחץ among Deuteronomistic circles.

Second, Exod 20:24 and Deut 12:14 clearly differ fundamentally regarding the centralization of the cult: "In *every* place where I cause my name to be remembered, I will come to you and bless you" (בכל המקום אשר אזכיר את שמי אבוא אליך וברכתיך) (Exod 20:24). An altar "in *every* place" is precisely the opposition against which the Deuteronomistic movement fervently fought.[86] Thus the above text would be the last thing a Deuter-onomistic author could endure.[87]

Eckart Otto and Bernard Levinson share the view that the regulation of the cult centralization in Deut 12 is a theological development and legal innovation based on Exod 20:24.[88] Otto believes, as do many others,

---

84. Reindl 1984, 551.

85. Van Houten 1991, 52.

86. As opposed to Van Seters (2003, 62), who argues that "it is better to interpret verse 24b as an act of worship apart from the sacrificial cult." For detailed reasoning that refutes this hypothesis, see Levinson 2004, 297–315.

87. C. Levin 2000, 122–28: "The formulation of the cult in the Covenant Code completely contradicts the aims of the Deuteronomic formulation of cult centraliza-tion. The Covenant Code is post-Deuteronomic" (125). According to Levin, CC clearly indicates an anti-Deuteronomistic orientation; contrary to Otto (1993, 260–78) and Levinson (1997, 30–36), who regard Deut 12:13–15 as a Deuteronomic innovation to Exod 20:24. In this context, the probable authorial circle of the *debarim*-portions of CC can be found in the descendants of the דלת הארץ and the Samaritans. Both groups would have shared the same concern regarding the centralization of the cult. For details on this issue, see §3.6, below.

88. Otto 1993, 260–78; 1994a, 24; 1994b, 192–95; and Levinson 1997, 30–36.

that Exod 20:23 and 21:1 derive from a later Deuteronomistic editor who sought to exclude the disturbing altar law in Exod 20:24 from the core portion of CC.[89] However, as argued above, the cultic law in Exod 20:22–26 should be regarded as a coherent unit which is designed as the chiastic counterpart to Exod 23:13–19.[90] Furthermore, the cultic law in Exod 20:22–26 as a whole should be dated as exilic at the earliest, because there is no preexilic text outside the Pentateuch that articulates this kind of concern regarding the making of divine images.[91] If this is the case, there is no compelling reason to assume the diachronic priority of Exod 20:24 over Deut 12:14. In our view, Exod 20:24 seems rather to polemicize against Deut 12:14, changing במקום אשר יבחר יהוה into בכל המקום אשר אזכיר את שמי and תעלה עלתיך into את עלתיך עליו זבחת. According to Levinson, the Deuteronomic authors dexterously break up and reforge the phrasing of the older altar law in Exodus.[92] In our view, however, it is more probable that the diachronic development occurred in the opposite direction. The author of Exod 20:24 masterfully summarized, revised,

---

Levinson (1997, 33–34) argues that since the altar law in Exod 20:24 enjoyed a high standing in ancient Israelite society, the law could not be bypassed by the later authors of Deuteronomy. The authors reworked and transformed the altar law in Exod 20:24 "to command the distinctive innovations of Deuteronomy—both cultic centralization and local, secular slaughter" (1997, 32). Otto (1994b, 192–96) goes one step further, claiming that almost all the laws of CC were reworked in Deuteronomy in light of cult centralization. He argues that the Deuteronomic/pre-Deuteronomistic Deuteronomy of the Josianic period is structured along the lines of CC. The pre-Dtr Deuteronomy includes the principal laws in Deut 12:13–28*; 13:2–18 and the social laws of God's privilege in Deut 14:22–15:18; 26:2–13*, which bracket the festival system (Deut 15:19–16:17), the order of courts (Deut 16:18–18:8*) and the system of ethical rules (Deut 19:2–25:12*) (ibid., 193).

89. Otto 1994a, 24; 1994b, 186–88; see also Hossfeld 1982, 181–83; and Schwienhorst-Schönberger 1990, 286. According to Otto, in this way the direction of literary influence between CC and DC turns out to be mutual and reciprocal, as the later Deuteronomistic editor exercised an influence upon the final shape of CC. However, in our view, the tradents of CC and DC were heterogeneous Judean groups in Persian-era Palestine. For the homogeneous character of the texts in Exod 20:23–24 and 21:1, see the entire chiastic structure of the *debarim*-portions of CC in §3.2, above.

90. See §3.2, above.

91. Van Seters 2003, 60. Van Seters correctly concludes that Isa 2:8, 18, 20; 2 Kgs 17:29; 19:18; and Jer 16:20 are exilic or postexilic. For corresponding archeological finds regarding cultic figurines during the Persian period, see Stern 2006, 199–205.

92. Levinson 1997, 32–34.

and transformed the various regulations of Deut 12:13–28 according to his own theological orientation.[93]

3.5. The Critique of Kingship

Based upon the relevant narrative context of CC (Exod 19:3b–8, 20:22–23:19, 24:3–8), the divine endowment of CC signifies the establishment of a covenant community.[94] CC obviously seeks to regulate and organize the life of this covenant community. The fact that such a significant theological foundation (CC) is localized in the Mosaic period by the relevant author should be regarded as a drastic criticism of the traditional monarchical system of the Israelite state.[95] Wolfgang Oswald is assuredly correct when he asserts:

> If the king has nothing to do with the legislation, nor with the juris-diction, nor with the cult, then he is simply unnecessary. If in the beginning—established and viewed as good by Yhwh—Israel gets along without a king, then any later king is only disfigured, or at best a deco-rative addition, definitely something secondary and therefore already inherently not regal.[96]

Such an extreme and radical criticism of the Sinai pericope against the entire paradigm of the monarchy cannot be located in the monarchic period. Furthermore, the other two law codes (HC and DC) do not men-tion any kings of Israel except for brief regulations in Deut 17:14–20.[97] If we consider the significance of kingship as a political institution of ancient

---

93. For instance, the lexeme עלה in the plural form with the 2ms suffix appears in Exod 20:24; Deut 12:13, 14, 27; Ps 50:8; and Isa 43:23. In particular, the combination of את עלתיך with the verb זכר is only found in Exod 20:24 throughout the Hebrew Bible. It is worth noting that the verbs זבחת in Exod 20:24 and יזבחו in Exod 24:5 appear to be associated with one another, as they are employed in a similar manner. In the former, זבחת commands the democratization of the cultic place, while in the latter, יזבחו stipulates the democratization of the cultic personnel. The compositional inten-tions of these references indicate their theological homogeneity. For the theological as well as socioeconomic orientations of the tradent of CC, see §3.6, below.

94. Oswald 1998, 128.

95. Ibid.

96. Ibid.

97. Deut 17:14–20 has recently been regarded as post-Deuteronomistic; see Achenbach 2009, 216–33; Römer 2015, 95–97; and Rückl 2016, 295–318.

Israel and Judah, it is remarkable that only this one passage (Deut 17:14–20) deals with the features and roles of the position within the biblical law codes. It is also worth noting that this passage indicates a frank skepticism regarding the monarchy that seems to reflect Israel's experience, because the aim of the passage is the restriction of royal power, which poses a serious threat if left unchecked.[98] As Gustav Hölscher correctly observes, the passage seems to presuppose the experience of exile.[99]

Based on the foregoing evidence, it can be concluded that the current position of CC within the broader compositional structure of the Sinai pericope seems to indicate that CC attained its final shape during the postexilic period. The *mishpatim* appear to have originally been transmitted without the surrounding narrative framework. This block of text should be considered as the base text of CC. It is probable that these *mishpatim* had been followed in some villages of Palestine since the monarchic or even the premonarchic period before they became part of their current literary context in the postexilic period.[100] The *mishpatim* must have been useful for governing Judean society in Persian-era Palestine and thus worth preservation according to the judgment of the later author of the *debarim*. It is also possible that the later author of the *debarim* selected the usable portions from the preexilic customary law collection and made these the core of his own law code. He seems to have composed his law

---

98. Biddle 2003, 287–88. Niesiolowski-Spano also appropriately expresses skepticism concerning the conventional view that associates most of DC with Josianic reform by saying: "what sources do we really have, despite 2 Kings, to reconstruct the reform taking away from the king every royal competence, including military leadership, justice, luxury, and taxes (horses and numerous wives are banned, all others are attributed to the priests)? There is no Near-Eastern analogy for such an anti-royal reform conducted by the king, which makes an important obstacle in itself" (Niesiolowski-Spano 2017, 6).

99. Hölscher 1922, 199–201; for a different position, see Nicholson 2006, 46–61, who argues that the "foreigner" in Deut 17:15b indicates the king of Assyria.

100. Knight 2009, 113. I will not pursue here the issue of the time period in which the *mishpatim*-portion of CC was formed and completed. Because of the obvious influence of the laws of Hammurabi on Exod 21:23–25, the *mishpatim* would seem to be the oldest part of CC. Regarding the dating of this section, there is a wide spectrum of scholarly hypotheses ranging between the premonarchic and the exilic periods (e.g., Schwienhorst-Schönberger 1990, 3–22; Van Seters 2003, 8–46; and Levinson 2004, 288–97). For the positive as well as subversive reception of the laws of Hammurabi in CC, see Otto 2010, 1–22.

collection chiastically, centering it on the existing *mishpatim* and combining the *debarim* with the narrative framework.

3.6. The Juxtaposition of the Covenant Code, the Holiness Code, and the Deuteronomic Code in the Pentateuch

At this point, a question should be raised about why such contradictory law codes as CC, HC, and DC were simply juxtaposed in the Pentateuch with a minimal effort to create a harmonious synthesis. Regarding this inquiry, many scholars share the viewpoint that CC was the oldest text and that it filled a solely archival function throughout the formation history of the Pentateuch.[101] This supposition implies that the later redactor felt it necessary to integrate law material as old and outdated as CC, which significantly contradicts other biblical law codes, into the Sinai pericope only for the purpose of preservation, even though it was nothing but the informal literature of the opposition group (Crüsemann) or the legal foundation for an ultimately failed preexilic reform movement (Albertz). This hypothesis is hard to justify. It is highly improbable that the integration of CC in its current location took place because a later redactor intended to preserve CC out of archival interest or to use CC as a kind of placeholder for Deuteronomy.[102]

It is legitimate to ask how and why such law materials as CC, DC, and HC were compiled if the biblical law codes were not intended to regulate and control the Judean communities of Persian-era Palestine. In the biblical texts of the Persian period (Ezra, Nehemiah, 1 and 2 Chronicles), certain decisions were made based on authoritative written regulations (2 Chr 23:18; 25:4; 30:5, 18; 31:3; 35:12, 26; Ezra 3:2, 4; Neh 8:15; 10:35, 37). It is widely accepted that the authors of relevant texts in the books of Ezra

---

101. See, e.g., Crüsemann 1992, 229–30; Albertz 1992, 183; and Zenger et al. 2016, 125–31.

102. Oswald 1998, 138. Oswald's argument against the placeholder theory is compelling: "Whatsoever reason do the editors of Deut 5 have to devise their bold construction (Moses initially receives the law personally in order to then convey it 40 years later!) if they are not forced to subsequently transform the structure of Exod 20–21 to the structure of Moab which is given to them in Deuteronomy?" (137). Thus, it is reasonable to presume that Exod 20:22–23 depends literarily on Deut 4:36, but that Deut 5 presupposes the juxtaposition of the Decalogue and CC in Exod 20–23*. In our view, this phenomenon indicates the complex and reciprocal relationship between CC and Deuteronomy.

and Nehemiah were familiar with what are now known as DC and HC and considered them normative.[103] The biblical text holds that biblical law codes are regulations that are authoritative and binding because the laws are presented as divine revelations; more binding even than secular law.[104]

Moreover, the narrative framework in Exod 19:8; 24:3, 7 implicitly solicits the readers' acceptance regarding the current validity of CC. The wholehearted consent of Israel in the narrative framework (Exod 19:8; 24:3, 7) is deliberately inserted to motivate and to demand Judean readers in the Persian period to unequivocally follow the regulations of CC.[105] If CC and the narrative framework were integrated in the current position at a time period in which the adherence to and observance of CC would not have been desirable, because different provisions would have been valid, then the demanding tone of the narrative framework for complete observance (Exod 19:8; 24:3, 7) would have been unnecessary.

In our view, it is more reasonable that CC (particularly the *debarim*) and its narrative framework were composed and placed in their current position in the Sinai pericope in order to regulate the Judean communities in Persian-era Palestine. There were basically three heterogeneous types of inhabitants in Palestine in the fifth century BCE: (1) the descendants of the דלת הארץ including Samaritans, (2) the lay returnees, and (3) the priestly returnees.[106] The best arable land was already occupied by the descendants of the דלת הארץ.[107]

---

103. Blenkinsopp 2001b, 57–58 and Blum 1990, 351–52.

104. Marshall 1993, 24.

105. Oswald 1998, 138.

106. For the demographic and economic situation in the exilic and the postexilic Judean communities, see §3.3, above. It is intriguing that there is a growing tendency to argue that the Samaritan community played a significant role in the Pentateuch formation process. According to Pummer, "Given the shared culture and the long-standing substantial contacts, then, there is no reason that the interactions between the two communities should not have included participation in the development of some of the narrative and legal traditions that came to constitute the Pentateuch.... Included in this common legacy were the Jacob traditions connected with Shechem and Bethel" (2007, 263–64). Nihan also articulates that "the various passages in Deuteronomy and Joshua describing a covenant ceremony in or near Shechem do not represent an ancient Northern tradition, as was usually assumed during the 20th century, but correspond to several attempts to acknowledge Samaria's religious and political role at the time of the Torah's composition" (2007b, 223). In his view, the Pentateuch was never composed only for the Judean community but was intended to be accepted by both the Judean and the Samaritan communities (ibid). Furthermore, Hensel argues

There have recently been voices that increasingly deny any kind of socioeconomic or theological conflict between the descendants of the דלת הארץ and the returned exiles.[108] According to these voices, the returned exiles did not meet with any resistance from those on the land, since they were assigned plots of arable land by the official Persian administration. However, we have to reflect on what we really know and can presuppose as historical fact regarding Persian imperial policy on the arable land of Yehud. Did the Persian official administration attempt to increase land productivity by gathering returned exiles to cultivate the land? Did the officials allow the returned exiles to claim possession of any uncultivated land? Did they randomly allocate land parcels they had identified as available? Or did the officials assign the returned exiles to available land close to any ancestral properties they still remembered? Or, more basically, were the land shares periodically allocated and reallocated by lot? These questions are deeply related to the legal relationship, on which we have only very fragmentary knowledge, between Persian imperial ownership of land and local possession of land in Levantine agrarian societies. Basically, we cannot be certain about what kind of imperial policy was established regarding the arable land in Yehud. Biblical references are also too vague on this particular.[109] Thus, some arguments are based on the

---

that the formation of the Pentateuch was a common project of the Judean and the Samaritan communities (2016, 170–93). In our view, their claims are legitimate. See Oswald 1998, 184ff.; of course, this tripartite distinction cannot be established without a process of simplification regarding the socioeconomic reality of Judean society in Persian-era Palestine. Thus, the classification attempted in this study should be understood as an "ideal type." According to Weber (1949, 90), an ideal type is indispensable for heuristic as well as expository purposes. It is not meant to correspond to all of the characteristics of reality, but is rather formed by the accentuation of one or more points of view and by the synthesis of a great many diffuse, discrete, more or less present, and occasionally absent concrete individual phenomena, which are arranged according to those emphasized viewpoints into a unified analytical construct ("*Gedankenbild*").

107. D. Smith 1991, 96 and Oswald 1998, 160.

108. Guillaume 2014, 14–15; Hoglund 1992, 58–59, among others.

109. E.g., נחלה, אחוזה, and חלק השדה. On this, see Guillaume 2014, 18–21; Boer 2013, 109–110. Guillaume rejects "inalienable property" as a meaning of נחלה based on his own exegesis of the story of Naboth's vineyard in 1 Kgs 21 (Guillaume 2014, 20, 67–75). However, Guillaume's interpretation of 1 Kgs 21 is so biased that his only focus and interest seems to be downplaying and underestimating every clue that could possibly lead to "inalienable property" as the meaning of the lexeme, conclud-

Murasu archive from Nippur, which attests to a Judean existence there in the Persian period.[110] Others are based on illustrations of Ottoman or pre-Islamic land categories.[111] These attempts are heuristically valid to a certain extent, and their results are sometimes quite illuminating. However, in an epistemological sense, to piece together the limited analogies from elsewhere in the Persian Empire or from later time periods in the same area, to apply them directly to Yehud, and then to claim that Yehud was the same cannot be fully legitimized.[112] For example, Guillaume's attempt to apply a template from the Islamic period to the biblical material and to make it the foundation of his central thesis are at least questionable moves.

Even though the value of relevant biblical texts as a historical source is questionable, some provide at least a glimmering of clues for clarifying the above-mentioned issues. According to Jer 39:10, after the destruction of Jerusalem, Nebuzaradan, the captain of the guard, left some of the poor people (הדלים אשר אין־להם מאומה) in the land of Judah. Vineyards and fields (כרמים ויגבים) seem to have been distributed to the landless people at that time. In other words, the land was endowed to the poor people who had been workers without any ability to possess land. It is probable that they were legally invested with their own vineyards and fields by the Baby-

---

ing: "Hence, it is doubtful that a serious case for the inalienability of the *naḥalah* can be built from the Bible" (Guillaume 2014, 72). For example, he asserts that the author of 1 Kgs 21 does not quote any law, tradition, or practice related to the inalienability of the *naḥalah*, since there was none to quote (Guillaume 2014, 73). But to be fair, I think we need to raise the possibility that the author of 1 Kgs 21 was able to presuppose such a law, tradition, or practice as common sense, well known to his audience and contemporaries, and therefore that he did not feel a need to quote anything. In this way, if the lexeme נחלה could designate "inalienable property" as opposed to Guillaume's interpretation, his whole theory related to periodic allocation and reallocation of land based on Deut 19:14, 27:17, Josh 14:1–2, 18:2, Hos 5:10, among others, (Guillaume 2014, 49–53) becomes untenable.

110. On Judeans at Nippur, see Zadok 2002, 61–63; Bedford 2001, 47–49; Pearce 2015, 8–20, among others.

111. See Guillaume 2014, 21–27.

112. See Guillaume 2014, 21: "Yet, the hope that neat categories may be drawn from the Bible is illusory since the semantic field of terms is likely to have fluctuated across the centuries during which the texts were produced. If vocabulary is too ambiguous to serve as a firm basis of analysis, some help can be gained from Islamic land categories as they were used in the Ottoman tenure system." This position is severely criticized by Boer 2013, 111.

lonian administration.[113] In Ezek 33:24 a clear textual witness is found on a quarrel related to the land between those who remained in Palestine and the exiles. Relevant texts in Gen 12–25, Isa 51:1–2, 63:16, and Jer 24, 32, among others, also indicate the tense relationships between the two groups.[114] In particular, Jer 32:44 is enlightening since it witnesses that fields (שדות) could be sold (יקנו) with money (בכסף) and by deed (בספר) at least among some Judeans in Persian-Hellenistic periods.[115]

This textual evidence can be complemented by some archaeological findings. The settlements in Yehud seem to have consisted mainly of unwalled farmsteads or hamlets with a small number of towns and villages.[116] The settlement pattern changed considerably in comparison to the Late Iron Age, and there were many new settlements on virgin land.[117] According to Edelman's investigation, the returned exiles may have been allowed to settle freely on fields in Yehud, which were then administered within the system of the בית אבות.[118] Some returned exiles may have succeeded in resettling on their ancestral land.[119] If so, it is also highly probable that some of the returned exiles were not able to achieve the same goal, since descendants of the דלת הארץ had in practice possessed their ancestral land. Persian authorities would not have confiscated the ancestral land in question from the descendants of the דלת הארץ to give it to the relevant returned exiles; such a policy would have caused serious conflict situations

---

113. See Edelman 2005, 326.

114. See Pohlmann 1978, 183–207; Schmid 1999, 117–20; Ska 2009, 23–45, among others. In conjunction with de Pury's view, Schmid attributed the patriarchal narrative to those who remained in Palestine during the exile (see Schmid 1999, 119 for further bibliography related to this thesis). Ska developed this thesis further by articulating that in Gen 12–25 the returned exiles edited the text related to Abraham, which was influential among those who remained in Palestine, in such a way that the ancestor of Israel was remodeled as the symbolic figure of the Golah (Ska 2009, 45). By doing so, the returned exiles deprived the people who remained on the land of a significant theological foundation: "Abraham was in fact more the father of the returning exiles than of those who had stayed in the country" (Ska, 2009, 43).

115. See Deist 2000, 144.

116. Edelman 2005, 311; 2007, 53; Zwickel et al. 2013, 203.

117. See Edelman 2005, 281–331; 2007, 52–64; Zwickel et al. 2013, 203; Zwickel 2015, 223–30, among others. Edelman suggests that 23 percent of the total settlements currently identified in Yehud were newly created farmsteads that were unknown in the Late Iron Age.

118. Edelman 2005, 281–331; 2007, 52–64.

119. Edelman 2007, 64.

in Yehud.[120] Even though the relevant returned exiles could have settled on a plot of land connected to an abandoned or newly created farmstead,[121] this would not have removed the enmity or envy of the returned exiles toward those who actually possessed and controlled their ancestral land or the more fertile land.[122]

The conflict among these three subgroups was deeply associated with the completion of the Pentateuch in the postexilic environment.[123] In our view, CC seems to reflect the interests of the descendants of those דלת הארץ who were left behind during the exilic period, while DC attempts to materialize the benefits of the lay returnees.[124] Consequently, the priestly returnees are the most promising candidates to have decisively shaped the form and content of HC.[125]

There is growing scholarly agreement that the relationship of CC, HC and DC cannot be described as unilateral but rather as simultaneous and reciprocal.[126] At least in the final phase of their compositions, the biblical

---

120. On the related issues of the arable land in Yehud, see also §3.7, below.

121. Edelman articulates that the sites established in Yehud on previously unoccupied land were allocated to nonnative soldiers as *ḫatru*-estates. On the other hand, however, she properly recognizes that different interpretive frameworks are certainly possible (Edelman 2007, 64).

122. See D. Smith 1991, 93–96; Y. Levin 2003, 237–40, with further bibliography.

123. Oswald 1998, 184.

124. M. Smith claims that the descendants of those דלת הארץ and the returnees embody mutually opposing religious directions. The descendants of those who remained in Palestine followed the direction of "the syncretistic cult of Yahweh" while the returnees belonged to the "Yahweh-alone party" (1987, 98–102). In our view, his assumption should be adjusted and revised according to the aforementioned delineation.

125. I will not pursue here issues such as the composition history of HC or the relationship of HC to other P materials. For a detailed history of research on the book of Leviticus or HC, see, e.g., Nihan 2007a, 1–19, 562–575; Grünwaldt 1999, 5–22 and Ruwe 1999, 5–35. For HC within the framework of the Penta- or Hexateuch, see D. Wright 2016, 71–101; Wells 2015, 234–66; Otto 2007, 175, 183; Nihan 2007b, 189, 219. In this context, Bettenzoli's thesis (1984, 385–98) that DC and HC reciprocally influenced to each other is particularly insightful. However, in our view, not only DC and HC, but also CC were involved in this process of mutual influence.

126. E.g., Crüsemann (1992, 63) describes a scenario of "coexistence, mutuality, and contradiction between Deuteronomistic and Priestly theology." In our view, not only DC and HC, but also CC (and its narrative framework) deserve to be regarded as independent catalysts within this simultaneous, mutual, and reciprocal relationship among the biblical law codes.

law codes seem to have been subject to addition, revision, and reinterpretation in relation to each other. This implies that the returned exiles and the descendants of the דלת הארץ dwelled side by side within the same territorial area but belonged to different communal networks connected to the respective law codes. In the early postexilic period, there was no community in Palestine that was in a powerful enough position to force their own law code on another community. Thus, the three biblical law codes reflect the various, sometimes contrasting, interests among different sociopolitical communities in Persian-era Palestine.[127] CC evidently expresses the socioeconomic bias for the descendants of the דלת הארץ.

The critical attitude toward the monarchy (Exod 19:3b–8), the freedom to sacrifice everywhere (Exod 20:24–25), and the antihierarchical (anticlerical) stance (Exod 19:6; 24:5) all seem to serve to the advantage of those who remained in Palestine. According to the author of CC, not only the returned priesthood, but the entire Israelite population would be a holy people (Exod 19:6).[128] Therefore, the offering of sacrifices is not the exclusive privilege of the priesthood, but the general right of the "young men" of the Israelites in Exod 24:5.[129]

On the other hand, in sharp contrast to HC and DC, it is obvious that CC indicates a conservative orientation deriving from those who seek to maintain the economic status quo (Exod 21:21, 26–27, 32; 22:27; 23:3), in that there is no vestige of hope or vision for the revival and renewal of Judean society. The stance of CC within the narrative framework can be summarized as economic conservatism in conjunction with cultic radi-

---

127. At this point, Ska's hypothesis related to the authorship of Gen 2–3 is highly intriguing. He regards the account of the creation in Gen 2–3 as deriving from "the people of the land" who remained in Palestine during the exile (Ska 2008, 21–23). Genesis 2–3 is a vision of the world that reflects the concern and interest of "the people of the land" in opposition and juxtaposition to the account in Gen 1 elaborated by the priestly returnees. Therefore, the text of Gen 2–3 delineates a theology in which God created a farmer in a garden who was the ancestor of "the people of the land," relativizing the theology as well as the ideology reflected in Gen 1. If this is the case, we can perhaps discern the texts formed and shaped by those who remained in the land of Judah during the exile or their descendants beyond CC throughout relevant narratives in the Pentateuch.

128. Oswald 1998, 165–66.

129. As already mentioned above, the *debarim*-portion of CC was formed and shaped by the same person who composed Exod 19:3b–8; 20:22–23; and 24:3–8 (see §3.4, above).

calism. This ambivalence could have derived from the inconsistent status of the descendants of the דלת הארץ. In other words, this came from the unique position of the descendants of the דלת הארץ, many of whom possessed vested rights to the best arable land.[130] The end of exile, therefore, could hardly have been welcomed as a fresh start for a new Judean society. Even though some degree of solidarity exists in the face of economic differences, such as extending social protection for marginalized groups including servants (Exod 21:2–11), strangers (Exod 22:20; 23:9), widows (Exod 22:21–22), orphans (Exod 22:21–22), and the poor (Exod 22:24–26), CC does not hide its main interest in maintaining the current socioeconomic state, especially the status and property of the land-possessing class (Exod 21:21, 32; 22:1–6). There is no jubilee year (Lev 25) or year of remission (Deut 15) in CC. The poor (דל) should not be privileged in their legal disputes (Exod 23:2–3). In addition, CC regards servants as their owner's property (Exod 21:21) and reinforces the existing economic stratification (Exod 21:26–27, 32; 22:27).[131] In sharp contrast, Lev 25 attempts to abolish the institution of slavery among the "Israelites," who can be identified with returned (priestly) exiles. The absence of the ear-boring ritual in HC is understandable in the light of the aim of its authors to eliminate the practice of slavery among the returnees.[132]

Furthermore, CC reflects the perspective of the creditor, using the verb לוה in the sense of "borrowing, lending, loaning," which is completely absent in HC and DC.[133] It is not improbable to imagine that the author

---

130. To be more precise, it is reasonable to assume that there was also a poor stratum among the descendants of the דלת הארץ that did not have this privilege.

131. Marshall 1993, 140.

132. This radical and revolutionary stance of the priestly authors of HC can be partially explained by the concept of status inconsistency. It is not accidental that we find a desire and passion for a radically new idealized society in DC and HC. In our view, DC and HC reflect such revolutionary aspects because they were composed by returnees experiencing status inconsistency. On the concept of status inconsistency and its various applications, see, e.g., Lenski 1966, 86–88; 1967, 298–301; Goffman 1957, 275–81; Jackson 1962, 469–80; Segal and Knoke 1980, 149–66; Whitney 1980, 138–41; Slomczynski and Mach 1997, 93–117; and Barnett 2004, 177–81. For details on this concept, see ch. 1, above.

133. The term לוה reflects the perspective of the creditor, so that the "borrowing" is described in a value-neutral context (Isa 24:2) or occasionally as socially desirable (Ps 112:5 and Prov 19:17). In sharp contrast to the verb לוה, the term נשא/נשה emphasizes the viewpoint of the debtor so that the exploitation associated with loan-

of CC derives from the wealthier circle among the descendants of the דלת הארץ, whose interest was mostly in maintaining the economic status quo, attempting to invalidate the cultic priority of the priestly hierarchy at the same time. Perhaps the placement of the *mishpatim* at the heart of CC reflects the economic conservatism of the wealthier descendants of the דלת הארץ, since the *mishpatim* derive from a preexilic customary law collection whose inclusion emphasizes the continuity of Judean society in spite of the experience of exile.

The altar law (Exod 20:24–26), the appointment of a place of asylum (Exod 21:13–14), and the cultic laws related to the three pilgrimage feasts (Exod 23:14–18) clearly indicate the geographical orientation of CC toward Palestine.[134] In our view, the aforementioned regulations would have been particularly significant for those who (1) possessed land in Palestine, (2) had a guaranteed life in Palestine, (3) remained in an inessential or marginal position in a cultic or clerical area, and (4) were critical concerning the project to rebuild the Jerusalem temple and/or the Deuteronomistic theology of cult centralization.[135]

---

ing at interest and subsequent pauperization are well attested in combination with this verb; see 1 Sam 22:2 (נשא); 2 Kgs 4:1 (הנשה); and Jer 15:10 (נשיתי/נשו) (Schäfer-Lichtenberger and Schotroff 2009, 509–10).

134. If the geographical origin of CC is to be identified with Palestine, then the exilic period is not the ideal candidate for the completion of CC, since up to the end of the sixth century BCE the demographic and economic conditions in Yehud would not have been sufficiently developed to sustain the significant literary activity necessary for legislation. Of course, it does not exclude the possibility that some portions of prophetic literature such as Jer 37–42* were composed by those who remained in Palestine during the exilic period in an attempt to find theological meaning in the national catastrophe of 587/586 BCE (Pohlmann 1978, 198). Legislative documents such as CC presuppose a much more solid communal foundation than the prophetic literature. Van Seters (2003, 175) attempts to defend his hypothesis regarding the Babylonian origin of CC by arguing that the relevant regulations are future-oriented. It sounds as if his "Yahwist" in the Babylonian exile already anticipated the impending victory and edict of Cyrus for the return of exiles. On this point, Van Seters' argument is not sufficiently compelling.

135. According to Ezra 4, the legitimate *Yehudim* are those descended from the returned exiles and no one else. Even the YHWH-worshipers who remained in the land during the exile were barred from the rebuilding project of the Jerusalemite temple (Ezra 4:1–3) (see Janzen 2002a, 90–92). It is reasonable to suppose that this kind of exclusive policy stimulated criticism on this matter from those who remained in the land. In this context, it is worth indicating that the Samaritan community could

It has long been recognized that the postexilic period, especially the Persian era, was a decisive time period during which the core parts of the Hebrew Bible came to be finalized in their present form. Adopting the thesis of "imperial authorization" regarding the final compilation of the Pentateuch, biblical scholars have noted that the Persian period was crucial to the history of the formation of the biblical law codes.[136] The pivotal foundation for the thesis of imperial authorization is the insight that the juxtaposition in the Pentateuch of mutually incompatible regulations of law and mutually irreconcilable viewpoints on law (especially D and P) is a result of compromises among different theological subgroups in the Judean communities in Persian-era Palestine in order to shape a common law code under imperial pressure.[137] This can be adequately explained through Lenski's theory, in which this kind of compromise takes place when subgroups within a society collaborate together to generate constitutional agreements in order to avoid social conflicts and to increase communal unity.[138]

---

have shared a common interest in this area with the descendants of the האר׳ץ דלת. As already mentioned above, there is a growing tendency to articulate that the Samaritans made their own contribution to the Pentateuch formation process (Pummer 2007, 263–64; Nihan 2007b, 223; Hensel 2016, 170–93). In our view, this perspective may provide some puzzling questions regarding the formation history of the Pentateuch with persuasive answers.

136. Zenger 1971, 164–205; Blum 1990, 333–60; Grabbe 2004, 173–83; Frei 2001, 11–17; Hoglund 1992, 230–36; Albertz 1992, 461–68; and Douglas 2002, 8–9.

137. See Blum 1990, 356–57 and Blenkinsopp 2001b, 60. Of course, the legitimacy of this theory has been increasingly challenged in many respects (see Fantalkin and Tal 2013, 172–98 with further bibliography). According to Fantalkin and Tal, rather than being a product of external imperial authorization, the canonization of the Pentateuch should be regarded as a conscious internal response by Judean circles to a new geopolitical reality (the rebellion of the Egyptian province, the establishment of a new buffer zone, and Achaemenid imperial investment and monitoring). Even though the theory of "imperial authorization" is preferred as a probable historical background in this chapter, it is not indispensable or even essential for the hypothesis proposed here, since the hypothesis can well corroborate other theories, such as that of Fantalkin and Tal. What is important is not whether the pressure was external or internal but whether there was a watershed moment in the Judean communities of Yehud when significant ideological rethinking and theological reorientation were required so that intensive attempts took place compiling, redacting, combining, and juxtaposing the various literary blocks out of different subgroups in order to form a document of consensus.

138. Lenski 1966, 67–68, 442.

It is reasonable to assume that the respective authors of the biblical law codes were addressing significant social issues faced by their respective communities in Persian-era Palestine. This explains why the biblical law codes contradict each other and do not cover all areas of life, since they were mainly designed to address only some of the major issues of their respective communities that had caused chronic local problems.[139] The particular theological profile and socioeconomic focus of CC, DC, and HC respectively vary from each other and presuppose different social circles for their tradents. Of course, this does not mean that CC, DC, and HC were *creatio ex nihilo* in the Persian period. In other words, these three law codes were not entirely newly composed from scratch around 500 BCE. As in the *mishpatim* in CC, it seems that DC and HC also had older cores that had been passed down from the preexilic period. The older parts were selected and edited in relation to the correlation between the three groups, complemented largely by new elements, and decisively and ultimately completed in the Persian period.

3.7. The Socioeconomic Context of the Covenant Code

It is highly probable that there were tensions and conflicts between these communities around land possession.[140] The sparsity of the population in

---

139. Kaiser (1984, 67–68) argues that there are two types of law collections, namely "*Rechtsbücher*" and "*Gesetzbücher*," and that CC is not a *Gesetzbuch* but rather a *Rechtsbuch*. On the unsystematic character of the content of CC, see also Douglas 2002, 8–9; Grabbe 2004, 173–83; Frei 2001, 11–17; Hoglund 1992, 230–36; and Albertz 1992, 461–68.

140. Guillaume sharply criticizes the concept of land ownership in ancient Israel as anachronistic. It would be appropriate to distinguish between "ownership" on the one hand and "possession" on the other. For discussions on land tenure and communal land in the biblical period as well as in the Islamic and Ottoman period, see Guillaume 2014, 9–55. Based on the theory of ruralization, Hoglund (1992, 59) opposes the theory of economic conflict between returned exiles and the עם הארץ related to the possession of arable land. However, there are some weak points in Hoglund's argument. First, as Hoglund himself acknowledges, there is no evidence that this rural settlement pattern was the result of intentional imperial policy (58). Second, given the difficulty in establishing Persian-period chronology, Hoglund's dating of the settlement activity seems to be arbitrary (Carter 1999, 43). Third, even though a deliberate decentralization of the population could have been imperial policy, it would not have eradicated the feeling of disapproval among the returned exiles (see Oswald 1998, 159–63). It is easy to imagine that there was significant economic as

the Judean communities in Persian-era Palestine did not mitigate competition for certain arable land since the fertility of the land became more important due to the lack of manpower. Guillaume underlines again and again the plenitude of fertile land on the one hand and the deficiency of manpower on the other.[141] Boer also shares this viewpoint with Guillaume saying that

> With the important matter of beer and wine under our belts, it is time to consider how the edible flora was itself produced. The risk in considering such production is that we impose assumptions from our own era, in which land is scarce and population heavy. Thus land becomes the primary focus. By contrast, in contexts in which land was plentiful and labor in short supply, the prime concerns were labor and usufruct.[142]

The common assumption made by Guillaume and Boer is that arable land was always plentiful while manpower was in chronically short supply throughout ancient Near Eastern regions, including ancient Israel and Judah, in all periods. [143] However, their staunch articulation pays little attention to recent historical demographic data. Based on the data from the research of Magen Broshi and Israel Finkelstein, Marvin Chaney (2016, 140) correctly indicates that the Iron II population in Palestine was more than double that of the Bronze Age or of Iron I.[144] The population of the highlands increased much faster than that of the lowlands and for the first time included half or more of the total population.[145] According to recent archaeological data, the Cisjordan highlands were the location of

---

well as ideological conflict between the returned exiles as former landlords and those דלת הארץ left behind (see D. Smith 1991, 93–96 and Y. Levin 2003, 237–40 with further bibliography).

141. Guillaume 2014, passim.

142. Boer 2015, 70.

143. For a further bibliography on the shortage of labor in ancient Near Eastern regions, see Boer 2015, 228–29.

144. Broshi and Finkelstein 1992, 47–60; "The combined population of the two kingdoms, therefore, reached ca. 460,000. This figure demonstrates their relative importance during the time of the Assyrian campaigns. By comparison, the combined population of the city-states of Philistia (Ashdod, Ashkelon, Ekron, and Gaza) was ca. 50,000 people (the subregions of Philistia and Gaza, and the western Shephelah), half the population of Judah." (54); Furthermore, see Herr 1997, 137, who places the population numbers in Israel alone for the eighth century between 250,000 and 300,000.

145. Ibid.

a demographic reality for Iron II in which population pressure on arable land may have been possible.[146] Of course, the population of Yehud in the Persian period had severely decreased.[147] However, this does not exclude the possibility that there was some kind of tension and conflict related to certain arable land among inhabitants in Yehud. Plenitude and fertility of land are relative concepts and it is easy to infer that some land must have been better or more fertile. This more fertile land was frequently limited and therefore precious. Approximately 8 ha of arable land was necessary for managing the basic livelihood of a family with four to five members (parents plus two to three children) throughout Israelite history, including the Persian and Hellenistic periods.[148] If the Judean society in Persian and Hellenistic Judah suffered from a chronic shortage of manpower, the significance of land fertility must have increased to a greater extent since, with a limited labor supply, the size of the harvest varied greatly depending on the fertility of the arable land. Therefore, the search and competition for the more fertile arable land among the inhabitants would not have been rare phenomena in Yehud.

Furthermore, land in the Judean communities was related to ancestral identity and religious legitimacy as reflected in relevant biblical texts (e.g., Gen 12:7; 13:15, 17; 31:3; Lev 20:24; 23:10; Num 34:13; Deut 1:8, 21; 4:40; 5:16; 26:3; Josh 1:13; 17:6).[149] It is not absurd to suppose that the most fertile and most significant land was already occupied by the descendants of the דלת הארץ when the exiles returned to Yehud. Likewise, it can be assumed that the returned exiles were met with serious resistance by the descendants of those who had moved onto the best arable lands of Judah following the destruction of Jerusalem. In other words, the returned exiles stood in sharp contrast to another socioeconomic community, which consisted of the עם הארץ. Ezra 4 indicates that the עם הארץ is equal to the צרי יהודה (the enemies of Judah).[150] Confronted with these socioeconomic

146. See, e.g., Faust 2007, 23–51; 2013, 106–32; Lipschits 2003, 323–76; 2006, 19–20.

147. For the population of Yehud in the Persian period, see §3.3, above with further bibliography there.

148. Zwickel 2010, 73–74.

149. Brett 2013, 114.

150. "As has often been suspected, it is likely that these 'adversaries' were simply the descendants of those who had not been deported in the first place and thus hardly foreigners" (Grabbe 1998, 94). See also D. Smith 1991, 90–96. For a different position, see Fried 2006, 123–41, who argues that the עם הארץ in Ezra 4:4 were the satrapal

environments, the new immigrants asserted their agnatic identity—the בית אבות—and based on this agnatic identity validated their claims of religious superiority and socioeconomic privilege vis-à-vis the people of the land (עם הארץ).

In this context, it is striking that DC and HC frequently use the term אח to describe the members of their respective communities (Lev 19:17; 25:14, 25, 35–36, 39, 46–47; Deut 15:2–3, 7, 9, 11–12, 17:15, 20; 18:2, 7, 15, 18; 19:18–19; 20:8; 22:1–4; 23:20–21; 24:7, 14; 25:3), while this term is completely absent in CC. This phenomenon supports the assumption that DC and HC presuppose the system of the בית אבות as the fundamental social infrastructure. The law codes represent the viewpoints of the insiders within the citizen-temple community based on the system of the בית אבות. In sharp contrast, CC seems to reflect the perspective of those outside the citizen-temple community who did not have such a kinship network.

The returnees claimed a link between agnatic identity and the possession of land. Constructing genealogical lineages was closely connected with legal and religious rights to claim possession of land. According to the books of Nehemiah and Ezra, the בית אבות often played a decisive role in building the new temple (Ezra 1:5) and performing the reconstruction of the walls of Jerusalem (Neh 3).[151] Every בית אבות was also obligated

---

officials who administered the government of Beyond-the-River. One should acknowledge that the term עם הארץ seems to vary in meaning according to context (Nicholson 1965, 59–66), so that the meaning of the term is also dubious in the narrative of Ezra 4. However, in our view, the expression עם הארץ in Ezra 4:4 includes YHWH-worshipers (cf. Ezra 4:2), some of whom are the descendants of the דלת הארץ and the Samaritans. Both communities could have had similar interests in many areas of life, in particular in the cultic area. In our view, the descendants of the דלת הארץ and the Samaritans played a significant role in the Pentateuch formation process (Pummer 2007, 263–64; Nihan 2007b, 223; Hensel 2016, 170–93). For recent developments in research on Samaritan history and literature, see Hjelm 2004, 9–59.

151. Of course, there is a chronological difference between the texts of Ezra 4:4–6:15 (sixth–fifth century BCE) and most other texts of Ezra-Nehemiah (fourth–third centuries BCE) (Zenger et al. 2016, 341–42, 346). It is reasonable to assume that the fundamental social structure of Judean society based on the בית אבות remained throughout the time period and the returned exiles ultimately established their hegemony over the descendants of those who remained on the land by the middle of the fourth century BCE. Even the single fact that the books of Nehemiah and Ezra were canonized confirm this assumption (Oswald 1998, 184; for the *golah*-oriented redaction in the book of Jeremiah, see Pohlmann 1978, 183–91).

to deliver the tributes due to the treasury of the Jerusalem temple.[152] The ראשי האבות (the chiefs of the בתי אבות) even had civil power to investigate the status of the interethnic couples within their בית אבות (Ezra 10:16). The positions of the chiefs were hereditary (Neh 11:4–5). The chiefs of the בתי אבות were identical with the שרים (Ezra 8:29; 10:5) who lived in Jerusalem (Neh 11:1; 12:31). Every בית אבות seems to have had some available land split into plots farmed by each family.[153] However, due to the limited amount of fertile arable land, it is plausible to presume that many families belonging to the בתי אבות were unable to gain or gave up access to highly productive arable land and had to labor as the poor (עני, אביון, דל), strangers (גר), hired workers (שכיר) or even to sell themselves or their family members as indentured servants (עבד, אמה). In sharp contrast to the recently popularized hypothesis claiming that fertile land was plentiful and manpower was deficient in ancient Israel, the aforementioned terms eloquently articulate that there were many marginalized strata that were excluded for whatsoever reason from even usufruct of arable land.[154] It is

---

152. Kippenberg 1978, 40; Blenkinsopp 1991, 48; Cataldo 2003, 247–48.
153. Blenkinsopp 1991, 48.
154. Guillaume 2014, passim; Boer 2015, 70 hypothesize plentiful fertile land. However, as already mentioned in a previous paragraph (68), plenitude and fertility of land are relative concepts. It should be remembered that approximately 8 ha of arable land was indispensable for fulfilling the essential material needs of a family with four to five members throughout the Persian and Hellenistic periods. It can be easily rationalized that the required area of land and necessary amount of labor to supply the minimal needs of a family would considerably increase if the fertility and productivity of the land was not high. Furthermore, farming in Palestine is heavily dependent on rain for irrigation. Even more fertile land would still have been at the mercy of adequate rainfall and without adequate rain would have yielded poor harvests in spite of its fertility. In such an environment and such capricious economic circumstances, people such as some small peasants or persons in marginalized strata with little or no economic accumulation would have preferred to labor as hired workers (שכיר) or indentured servants (עבד, אמה) for a powerful and rich household than to get the usufruct of less fertile arable land. In other words, for many people in marginalized strata who could not have gained access to highly productive arable land, particularly during an extended drought, there would have been no other option than to proffer themselves or their family members for sale as indentured servants, knowing that usufruct of a large unproductive plot of land could not provide them with the necessary economic foundation for supplying their minimal and fundamental needs for survival. We can reasonably infer that this kind of practical exclusion from usufruct would have been a widespread phenomenon in Persian-era Palestine. On this point, Hans G. Kippenberg's assumption related to בית אבות is insightful. According to Kip-

no wonder that the biblical law codes deal so extensively with the issues of the aforementioned groups.[155]

The portrayal of Yehud that has been drawn so far matches well with the socioeconomic model called "Foreign Tributary Mode of Production."

---

penberg, the replacement of the clan name with a genealogy of family heads is not a sign of the dissolution of the clans but an expression of a hierarchy within the clans (1978, 38–39). Kippenberg articulates that the kinship system of בית אבות in Yehud in the Persian period was not a literary fiction but a part of the social structure. It is probable that the kinship structure of בית אבות linked families to one another in a hierarchy based on the privileges of the stronger families over the weaker ones, at times creating relationships and necessitating regulations around such issues as enslavement or land sales (Kippenberg 1978, 41). The distribution of land within בית אבות could have followed fixed rules concerning inalienable property rights. Land could have been traded through various types of exchange, but not outside of the kinship system. This principle could have led to an accumulation of fertile land in the hands of rich and powerful families (Kippenberg 1978, 41). If the above-mentioned assumptions are correct, a communal system such as בית אבות would not have prevented the alienation of people from communal land, since the socioeconomic power of individual families within the kinship system was not equal but highly hierarchically structured. Thus, one should not simply or naively presuppose that the communal system of בית אבות in Yehud functioned on the basis of the redistribution of commonly held land possessed within the kinship system regardless of fertility or productivity. Weak members within the communal system do not seem to have been able to gain access to highly productive arable land and therefore would have been practically excluded for the above-mentioned reasons from even usufruct of arable land.

155. In the biblical law codes the following marginalized groups are ascertainable: אביון ("poor"): Exod 23:6, 11; Deut 15:4, 7 (2x), 9, 11 (2x); 24:14; עני ("poor"): Exod 22:24; Lev 19:10; 23:22; Deut 15:11; 24:12, 14, 15; דל ("poor"): Exod 23:3; Lev 19:15; גר ("stranger"): Exod 22:20 (2x), 23:9 (2x), 12; Lev 17:8, 10, 12, 13, 15; 18:26; 19:10, 33, 34 (2x); 20:2; 22:18; 23:22; 24:16, 22; 25:23, 35, 47 (2x); Deut 14:21, 29; 16:11, 14; 23:8; 24:14, 17, 19, 20, 21; 26:11, 12, 13; שכיר ("hired servants"): Exod 22:14; Lev 19:13; 22:10; 25:6, 40, 50, 53; Deut 15:18; 24:14 (it is significant that the term שכיר in Deut 24:14 is identified with עני ואביון); עבד ("male servants"): Exod 21:2, 5, 6, 7, 20, 26, 27, 32; Lev 25:6, 39, 42 (2x), 44 (2x), 55 (2x); 26:13; Deut 12:12, 18; 13:6, 11; 15:15, 17; 16:11, 12, 14; 23:16; 24:18, 22 (the laws in Exod 21:2–6 command that a male servant must be released after he serves for six years. This temporal state of being a slave implies that this law stipulates debt slavery rather than other types of servitude; see Marshall 1993, 116. The texts in Exod 21:7–11, Lev 25:39–46, and Deut 15:17 seem to indicate that the female slaves are also in debt slavery: אמה ("female servants"): Exod 21:7, 20, 26, 27, 32; 23:12; Lev 25:6, 44 (2x); Deut 12:12, 18; 15:17; 16:11, 14; אלמנה ("widow"): Exod 22:21, 23; Lev 21:14; 22:13; Deut 14:29; 16:11, 14; 24:17, 19, 20, 21; 26:12, 13; יתום ("fatherless"): Exod 22:21, 23; Deut 14:29; 16:11, 14; 24:17, 19, 20, 21; 26:12, 13.

The socioeconomic foundation of the system was a number of local agricultural communities. The means of production engaged small peasant
farmers who paid tribute to various layers of the ruling strata, at local as
well as imperial levels. Furthermore, the ruling strata of the respective
communities functioned simultaneously as subordinates of the Persian
Empire. The delineated characteristics of Foreign Tributary Mode of Production in Yehud are also compatible with Lenski's sociological model of
an Advanced Agrarian Society.[156] In our view, the Judean communities in
the Persian and Hellenistic periods can be viewed on two different levels,
namely, on a macro- and a micro-level. On the macro-level, in the context
of the Persian and Greek Empires as a whole, the general theoretical framework of Gottwald's Tributary Mode of Production or Lenski's Advanced
Agrarian Society can be utilized. However on the micro-level, in the context of the Judean communities in Persian- and Hellenistic-era Palestine,
a more specific theory is needed. In other words, the Judean communities
in the Persian and Hellenistic eras should be scrutinized on the micro-
level as a citizen-temple community with the particular attribute of status
inconsistency. The unique features of the Judean citizen-temple community distorted and twisted the distributive systems of advanced agrarian
communities. They contributed to the enlargement of status inconsistency
of social strata within the communities in Yehud and thus to the origins of
the unparalleled radicalism of certain biblical law codes in the Pentateuch.

3.8. Conclusion

The foregoing observations can be summarized as follows:

(1) CC (Exod 20:24–23:19) was composed and chiastically structured
around the *mishpatim* (Exod 21:12–22:19*) in Persian-era Palestine. The
person who structured CC in this way also composed the narrative framework (Exod 19:3b–8; 20:22–23; 24:3–8).

(2) CC was not generated from theoretical or archival interests. Like
DC and HC, it reflects the competing interests of the subgroups in postexilic Yehud. The relationship of CC, HC, and DC cannot be described as
unilateral but rather as simultaneous and reciprocal. The authors of the
biblical law codes had the obvious intention of practically regulating and
controlling their own respective communities in Persian-era Palestine,

---

156. Houston 2008, 36–37.

as well as addressing some major issues of their own time which caused local conflicts, such as those concerning strangers and poverty. Those who were not able to gain access to land had to struggle as the poor (אביון, דל, עני), strangers (גר), hired workers (שכיר) or even to offer themselves or their family members for sale as indentured servants (אמה, עבד). It is easily understandable that the biblical law codes deal so extensively with the issues of these groups.

(3) There were basically three types of inhabitants in Palestine in the early postexilic period: (1) the descendants of the דלת הארץ and Samaritans, (2) the lay returnees, and (3) the priestly returnees. The tension and balance among the three subgroups deeply influenced the production and completion of the Pentateuch in the postexilic period. CC seems to reflect the interests of the descendants of the דלת הארץ, while DC attempts to materialize the benefits of the lay returnees. The priestly returnees are those who decisively shaped the form and content of HC. Thus, the biblical laws (CC, HC, and DC) each reflect the specific perspectives of various communal networks in the Judean society of Persian-era Palestine. Since no subgroup in Palestine occupied an overpowering position, CC, DC, and HC were simply juxtaposed, under the political pressure of the Persian Empire, in order to shape a document of consensus.

4

The Postexilic Construction
of the Prophetic Figure of Jeremiah

4.1. Introduction

In the previous chapter the Judean communities were portrayed through the lens of the biblical law codes (CC, DC, and HC). Up to the previous chapter the focus of attention was the Pentateuch. Now we turn our attention to the prophetic literature, in particular to the book of Jeremiah, since it also reveals valuable information related to the Judean communities in the Persian and Hellenistic periods. This chapter will take a close look at the so-called Deuteronomistic editorial layer in the book of Jeremiah. It remains inconclusive whether a Deuteronomistic editorial layer exists in the book of Jeremiah, and this is a major research topic and a subject of continuing debate.[1] Bernhard Duhm is the originator of the hypothesis that there is a kind of Deuteronomistic revision in the book of Jeremiah. He divided the book of Jeremiah into three categories: (1) Jeremiah's poetry, (2) Baruch's texts, and (3) a multitude of secondary supplements. Part of the third category is Deuteronomistic.[2]

This hypothesis has been taken up by many scholars, including Sigmund Mowinckel. Mowinckel modified Duhm's supplementary theory into a source theory. In his view, the original book of Jeremiah (Jer 1–45) can be divided into the following four sources: (A) Jeremiah's poetic oracles in Jer 1–25, (B) the third-person narratives, (C) Jeremiah's prose ser-

---

1. For detailed reviews of research, see, e.g., Stipp 2015, 261–97; 2013, 487–517; Fischer 2007, 55–71; Willi-Plein 2007, 163–82; S. Herrmann 1990, 53–181; K. Schmid 1996, 12–43; Albertz 2001, 231–36; and C. Maier 2002, 14–41.

2. Duhm 1901, x.

mons, and (D) postexilic additions (Jer 30–31).[3] Mowinckel asserted that Jer 7:1–8:3; 11:1–5, 9–14; 18:1–12; 21:1–10; 25:1–11a; 32:1–2, 6–16, 24–44; 34:1–7, 8–22; 35:1–19; and 44:1–14 belong to the C source, meaning that these texts were written by a Deuteronomistic theologian around 400 BCE either in Babylon or in Palestine. Jeremiah 7 deserves recognition as the beginning of this Deuteronomistic text.[4] Mowinckel's theory was revised redaction-critically and further developed by subsequent generations of scholars such as J. Philip Hyatt, Wilhelm Rudolph, Moshe Weinfeld, Ernest Nicholson, and Winfried Thiel, to name a few.[5] Thiel in particular attempted to discern a single layer of Deuteronomistic redaction through-out the book of Jeremiah that could be dated to around 550 BCE.[6] Thiel's hypothesis has been accepted by many scholars, and it has come to be seen as a standard theory. However, there is a growing tendency to revise, chal-lenge, or even reject his hypothesis altogether nowadays.[7]

One of the most important concerns is whether the verses in the book of Jeremiah that have come to be regarded as a Deuteronomistic editorial layer are actually Deuteronomistic or not. Is it not the case that Jeremiah's authentic voice can be heard through these texts? Is it not also true that they contain other heterogeneous redactions distinct from the Deuterono-mistic layer? This chapter seeks to address these concerns by analyzing Jer 7. Some Deuteronomistic expressions are found in Jer 7:1–12, but in our view their Deuteronomistic spirit should be verified more carefully than has usually been done. I will demonstrate in this chapter that as criteria for determining whether or not a text is "Deuteronomistic" the theology, ideology, and worldview are more important factors than literary style or expressions.[8] On the other hand, Jer 7:1–12 and Jer 20:7–13 show a strik-ing analogy. In our view, there is a connection between some texts in Jer-

---

3. Mowinckel 1914, 20–55.

4. Ibid., 31.

5. Hyatt 1984, 249–50; Rudolph 1968, 44–46, 51–52; Weinfeld 1972, 325, 352; Nicholson 1970, 34, 68–69; and Win. Thiel 1973, 105–15. These scholars transformed Mowinckel's source-critical theory into a redaction-critical hypotheses.

6. Win. Thiel 1981, 114.

7. See, e.g., Pohlmann 1978, 184–85; Carroll 1986, passim; McKane 1986, 1996, passim; Wanke 1995, 11–17; K. Schmid 1996, 355–88; Römer 1999, 192–98; Albertz 2001, 236–60; C. Maier 2002, passim; W. Schmidt 2008, 36–41; Stipp 2015, 261–97.

8. K. Schmid 1996, 346–49: "Linguistic 'Deuteronomism' and factual 'Deuterono-mism' should be distinguished from each other" (349).

emiah's "confessions" (Jer 12:2, 20:7–13) and some portions of Jeremiah's prose sermons (Jer 7:1–12, 32:40–41).

4.2. Did Jeremiah 7:1–12 Derive from the Prophet Jeremiah?

Jeremiah 7 has come to be perceived by many scholars as an archetypal Deuteronomistic text.[9] On the other hand, however, there are predictably also voices that ask whether these verses can be called Deuteronomistic or not.[10] When was this text written, and by whom, and how did it become part of the book of Jeremiah? Were these verses—as Artur Weiser, Georg Fohrer, John Bright, Helga Weippert, William Holladay, Jack Lundbom, Douglas Jones, and others have claimed—written in a form reflective of the natural voice of the prophet Jeremiah himself?[11] According to Bright, Jer 7, together with Jer 26:2–6, provides evidence that the prophet Jeremiah preached at the temple of Jerusalem in the autumn of 609 BCE.[12] If this is so, then the

---

9. Compared to LXX, the MT of Jer 7:1–4 is strikingly long (on the details, see Bright 1965, 52–58; Weippert 1973, 27–28; and Holladay 1986, 235–36). E.g., the only expression in the Hebrew text of Jer 7:1–2 also present in LXX is "Hear the word of the LORD, all you people of Judah" (שמעו דבר יהוה כל יהודה). In Jer 7:4, "This is the temple of the LORD" (היכל יהוה) is repeated three times in the Hebrew text, but the corresponding passage in LXX stops at two. These differences have been interpreted by scholars in different ways (for details, see the works cited above). This study, excluding two portions (compared to the corresponding passages in LXX, הזה in Jer 7:10 and צבאות אלהי ישראל in Jer 7:21, which seem to be secondary additions), will essentially perform its analysis based on MT, which is thought to be closer overall to the original (see Fischer 2005a, 42–46, 288–89; see also Weiser 1956, 59–64 and Weippert 1973, 27–28) even though this is not necessarily the position of the majority of recent text-critical approaches (for various positions regarding the literary relationship between MT and LXX, see Fischer 2007, 31–53; Backhaus and Meyer 2016, 554–61; Stipp 1995a, 109–10). Those holding it as Deuteronomistic include: Mowinckel 1914, 31; Rudolph 1968, 51–52; Weinfeld 1972, 325, 352; Nicholson 1970, 34, 68–69; Win. Thiel 1973, 105–15; Hyatt 1984, 251–64; McKane 1986, 164–68; Wanke 1995, 87–91; Albertz 2001, 246; Römer 1999, 191–93; 2000, 407–16; W. Schmidt 2008, 176–80; and Stipp 2015, 334.

10. See, e.g., Weippert 1973, 26–48; Lundbom 1999, 454–59; C. Maier 2002, 34–42, 368–70; and Fischer 2005a, 120–22.

11. Weiser 1956, 61; Fohrer 1967, 194–98; Bright 1965, 58; Weippert 1973, 26–48; Holladay 1986, 240; Lundbom 1999, 454–71; Jones 1992, 142–46.

12. Bright 1965, 58; see also Weiser 1956, 61. According to Win. Thiel (1973, 114), the texts of Jer 7:4, 9a, 10a*, 11*, 12, 14* belong to the *ipsissimum verbum*. W. Schmidt (2008, 176–77) supports Thiel's position.

words of Jer 7:2–15 belong to the *ipsissima verba* of the prophet Jeremiah. Are the words and the deeds that Jer 7:1–15 describe really what the prophet Jeremiah spoke and did in the autumn of 609 BCE? In order to answer this question, it is first necessary to analyze Jer 7 redaction-critically.[13]

The text is mainly composed of a prophecy proclaimed by YHWH through Jeremiah to the people of Judah, but beginning in Jer 7:16 the literary style of the text changes. YHWH speaks directly to Jeremiah in the second person singular. Thus, a new literary unit seems to start with Jer 7:16. It can be supposed that Jer 7:1–15 is a separate text completed through a complicated editing process. For example, the word מקום appears five times in this section and is clearly used once as a synonym for the temple (7:12) while elsewhere it indicates the land of Judah (7:14). In the other instances, in Jer 7:3, 6, and 7, the word מקום can be interpreted as hinting at the temple or at the land of Judah. Such differences in meaning make it clear that this text was not composed in a single sitting. Rose postulates that the meaning of the Hebrew word מקום gradually expanded from "temple" to include "the land of Judah."[14]

It is significant that Jer 7:3–7 and 7:13–15 express different stances on God's judgment of the Judeans. Jeremiah 7:3–7 speaks from the viewpoint that the outcome of divine judgment is not yet finally determined, but in Jer 7:13–15 divine judgment is declared to already be irreversibly decided.[15] Based on the discrepancy between these views on divine judg-

---

13. Here it is worth noting the literary and stylistic similarity between Jer 7:1–15 and 26:2–6. Jeremiah 7:1–15 and 26:2–6 are so alike that one cannot help but think that one of these units depends literarily on the other. Whether Jer 7:1–15 or Jer 26:2–6 came first is a problem that has not been solved conclusively by the history of research and is still disputed (see, e.g., Mowinckel 1914, 25–26; Volz 1928, 87–99; Weippert 1973, 28–37; Win. Thiel 1973, 115–19; Holladay 1986, 240; Seidl 1995, 141–79; Fischer 2005b, 25–27; Willi-Plein 2007, 163–72; Stipp 2015, 334–47). E.g., Mowinckel thinks that the shorter unit 26:2–6 came first and that a C source writer in a later period wrote the longer unit 7:1–15, referencing 26:2–6. On the other hand, Weippert concludes that, since 7:1–15 is more logically consistent and uniform, 26:2–6 was a later summary of it. Since this problem is beyond the scope of this study, I will not seek to answer it further.

14. Rose 1975, 218.

15. Carroll (1986, 211–12) also takes note of the tense relationship between Jer 7:3–7 and 7:13–15: "The two sections, admonition and destruction, do not belong together" (211).

ment, we may assume that Jer 7:13–15 derives from a different author and accordingly that the paragraph originally ended at Jer 7:12.[16]

Here, I would like to bring attention to the phrase in Jer 7:1, "This is the word that came to Jeremiah from the LORD." This expression is frequently used as an introduction to the editorial layer in the book of Jeremiah (Jer 7:1; 11:1; 18:1; 21:1; 25:1; 30:1; 32:1; 34:1, 8; 35:1; 40:1; 44:1).[17] Thiel, who was influenced by Mowinckel, asserts that this expression is a typical literary style of the Deuteronomistic editorial layer.[18] However, the phrase in question, "This is the word that came to PN from the LORD," does not appear once in Deuteronomy or in DtrH.[19]

In any case, if we compare this introduction to others, its distinctive quality becomes apparent:

Jer 1:4   ויהי דבר יהוה אלי לאמר

Jer 7:1   הדבר אשר היה אל ירמיהו מאת יהוה לאמר

According to Mowinckel, Jer 1:4 belongs to the A source and Jer 7:1 to the C source.[20] It has been traditionally considered as a consensus among

---

16. However, האלה in Jer 7:13 seems to originate from the hand of the author of Jer 7:1–12. The author added this word in order to create a linkage between his own text and Jer 7:13–15. Holladay (1986, 236) also claims the literary unit ended at Jer 7:12.

17. Win. Thiel 1973, 106.

18. Of course, Thiel also radically transformed Mowinckel's approach. For Win. Thiel (1973, 103–19), C is not a source but rather a redactional layer and should be called D. That it is the typical literary style, see Thiel 1973, 106; see also Mowinckel 1914, 31–32. Win. Thiel (1973, 114–16) supposes that by removing the Deuteronomistic editorial layer from Jer 7:1–15, the prophet Jeremiah's original words can be reconstructed. According to Thiel (114), Jeremiah's *ipsissimum verbum* consists of Jer 7:4, 9a, 10a*, 11*, 12, and 14*. However, there is a logical problem with this methodology. First, determining which redaction in Jer 7:1–15 is Deuteronomistic is not, as Thiel supposes, self-evident. Second, there is no guarantee that all of the text remaining after removing those redactions would be Jeremiah's *ipsissimum verbum*. On this problem, see Seidl 1995, 151–52 and Hardmeier 1991, 174–76.

19. For details on this problem, see §4.3, below. For recent discussions and theories related to the concept of the Deuteronomistic History, see Römer 2005, 33–65; 2006a, 45–70. The term "Deuteronomistic History" (DtrH) as employed in this chapter is a somewhat simplified one, indicating the Dtr-influenced historical books of Joshua, Judges, Samuel, and Kings.

20. Mowinckel 1914, 20–21, 31.

scholars that Jer 1:4 is part of Jeremiah's *ipsissima verba*.[21] As Thiel points out, Jer 1:4 shows the dynamic character of the prophecy as an event by placing ויהי first, while Jer 7:1 places הדבר first and then employs היה as part of a relative clause. This means that the theological focus and the point of emphasis move from the event of the prophecy (Jer 1:4) to the contents of the prophecy (Jer 7:1).[22] Between Jer 1:4 and Jer 7:1, the mere existence of this heterogeneity hints at the possibility that each was composed by a different hand.

The expression that appears in Jer 7:3, "Reform your ways and your deeds" (היטיבו דרכיכם ומעלליכם), is also very intriguing. The combination of the verb היטיב and the noun דרך also appears in Jer 2:33.[23] However, even if the literary expression is identical, the contents are completely different. That is to say, Jer 7:3 was written while there still existed a possibility for the Judean people to repent and return to God, while in Jer 2:33 that possibility has been completely eliminated.[24] Each demonstrates a completely contrary stance regarding the possibility of salvation. It is difficult to understand how one writer could adopt such completely different stances concerning important theological problems depending on the occasion. Jeremiah 2:33 resembles Jer 7:13–15 in the irreversibility of divine judgment found therein. Therefore, the hopeless position regarding the repentance of the Judean people seen in Jer 2:33; 4:22; 7:13–15; 13:23, and so on, and the hopeful possibility of repentance in Jer 7:3; 18:11; 35:15, and so on, can only be judged as conflicting.[25] If Jer 2:33 is the closest thing to the prophet Jeremiah's authentic voice, we should conclude that the contradictory Jer 7:3 comes from a later redactor.

Moreover, an illuminating expression appears in Jer 7:6. This is the triple group of the alien (גר), the widow (אלמנה), and the orphan (יתום). The mention of these three groups suggests that Jer 7:1–12 does not come from Jeremiah himself but is a secondary text added to the book of Jer-

---

21. See, e.g., Mowinckel 1914, 20; Bright 1965, 6; Rudolph 1968, 4–5; Win. Thiel 1973, 63–64; Holladay 1986, 20–46; Wanke 1995, 28–30; Lundbom 1999, 230; and W. Schmidt 2008, 42–49.

22. Win. Thiel 1973, 106.

23. There is also a broad consensus that Jer 2:33 derives from the prophet himself; see Mowinckel 1914, 20; Bright 1965, 16–18; Rudolph 1968, 22–23; Win. Thiel 1973, 108; Holladay 1986, 109–10; and S. Herrmann 1990, 118–19.

24. Win. Thiel 1973, 108.

25. On the prophet's spirit in the book of Jeremiah, see Namiki 2014, 93–100 (on the interpretation of Jer 13:23, see esp. 97–98).

emiah. As discussed above in §3.3, "stranger" (גר) became an archetypal socially marginalized group subject to protection in Yehud beginning in the early Persian era. References to the aforementioned three groups appear in the following passages in the Hebrew Bible: Deut 10:18; 14:29; 16:11, 14; 24:17, 19, 20, 21; 26:12, 13; 27:19; Pss 94:6; 146:9; Jer 7:6; 22:3; Ezek 22:7; Zech 7:10; and Mal 3:5.

In our view, aside from the two verses in Jeremiah (Jer 7:6; 22:3), these verses were all written in the exilic period or thereafter.[26] As discussed in chapter 3, up until at least the eighth century BCE in the southern kingdom of Judah, serious social consideration had not yet been given to the alien (גר). Neither can we presume that there was a large social change connected to the problem of the alien (גר) in the time of the prophet Jeremiah (late seventh to early sixth century BCE). Thus, we can reasonably conclude that the reference to the alien (גר) in Jer 7:6 did not originate with the prophet Jeremiah in the preexilic period; rather, it is appropriate to suppose that a postexilic editor incorporated a topic relating to the people who began to return from the Babylonian exile.[27]

These three socially marginalized groups bring to mind the piety of the poor in the book of Jeremiah. The word "needy" (אביון) appears in Jer 20:13, which is part of the material referred to as Jeremiah's "confessions," and is used as a term indicating the prophet Jeremiah.[28] The aforementioned three groups and the "needy one" of Jer 20:13 all represent innocent and oppressed people suffering from unfair persecution. Therefore, we can recognize a theological continuity and similarity between Jer 7:6 and 20:13.[29]

In the history of the research, the question of the identity of the author of Jeremiah's confessions has long been disputed. Broadly speaking, two major hypotheses exist. The first group of researchers interprets the confessions as a sign of the exhausted Jeremiah's internal despair and spiritual anguish following the prophecy and proclamation concerning the

---

26. On this issue, see §3.3, above.

27. On this issue, see §3.3, above.

28. The group of Jeremiah's confessions is as follows: Jer 11:18–12:6, 15:10–21, 17:12–18, 18:19–23, 20:7–13. According to Mowinckel's analysis (1914, 20–21), most of this belongs to the A source.

29. For a discussion of the piety of the poor and its characteristics and effects, see ch. 6, esp. §§6.5.2, 6.6, and 6.7.

destruction of Jerusalem.[30] However, as Karl-Friedrich Pohlmann per-
tinently notes, it is difficult to assume that the confessions were written
by the prophet Jeremiah.[31] Perhaps the answers will become clear when
we ask how and by whom this exceedingly personal text—one that goes
so far as to express words of resentment against God—was recorded and
taken up by the next generation to eventually be conserved as part of the
book of Jeremiah. Why did the prophet Jeremiah feel the need to record
these extremely personal confessions, which were not a public message he
received from God? By minutely detailing his personal anguish, may he
have meant to leave behind proof of his personal spiritual growth? Or did
he record it as a model of reference for future generations who have internal struggles and spiritual doubts? However, this kind of individualistic
way of thinking would have been foreign to ancient Israelite society.[32] Not
only that, but we should not forget that there exists a close thematic and
lexical relationship between the confessions and the eschatological prophetic texts of the postexilic period.[33]

In light of the aforementioned problems, scholars who adopt the
second hypothesis argue that the confessions were written in the postexilic
period and were later incorporated into the book of Jeremiah. Researchers have recognized that within the first-person speech of Jeremiah the
confessions represent thematically and formally a secondary layer of tradition, since "nowhere else in the prophetic tradition are the form and
content so close to those psalms which are called 'lamentation of the
individual.'"[34] According to this hypothesis, the relevant editors, by incor-
porating the confessions, responded to questions about the way in which
Jeremiah harbored doubts concerning YHWH's difficult-to-comprehend
divine providence, and how he ultimately restored his religionness toward
YHWH.[35] Furthermore, the postexilic editors probably tried to express
theologically the way that Jeremiah, unlike his opponents, was saved by

30. See, e.g., Baumgartner 1917, 86–91; von Rad 1936, 265; Ittmann 1981, 4; and
Ahuis 1982, 3–8; Stipp 2009, 148–86.
31. Pohlmann 1989, 22–25. Recently Bezzel (2007, 53) has also reconfirmed this
position: "It should be assumed that there is a span of several centuries between the
base layer of 'confessions' and the historical Jeremiah."
32. On this point, see Pohlmann 1989, 22–25.
33. Ibid., 43–100.
34. Ibid., 3.
35. See Jer 20:11–13.

God at the time of destruction.[36] In this way, through the confessions, later editors reconstructed Jeremiah from an increasingly eschatological point of view to reflect their own religious ideals, focusing on the desirable order of the future brought about by YHWH and presumably aiming to solidify a worldview based on their own religionness and theology.[37]

Concerning the two hypotheses surrounding the origin of the confessions, the distinctiveness of this group of texts is more adequately explained by the latter hypothesis, and so we will adopt the viewpoint that the confessions do not stem from the prophet Jeremiah but rather were added by postexilic editors.[38]

In the final confession in Jer 20:7–13, Jeremiah is regarded as righteous (צדיק: Jer 20:12) and thus confesses to being persecuted. In the preceding passage (Jer 20:1–6), Jeremiah debates with a representative of the temple of Jerusalem, the high-ranking priest Pashhur. Upon hearing Jeremiah's prophecy, Pashhur beats Jeremiah and puts him in the stocks. Thus, in the following confession in Jer 20:7–13, Jeremiah clearly portrays himself as "needy" of which we should take note: "Sing to the LORD; praise the LORD! For he has delivered the life of the needy [אביון] from the hands of evildoers" (Jer 20:13).

As already stated, we should consider Jeremiah's confessions as a text that came into existence in the postexilic period. In the framework of the confessions, "Jeremiah" speaks from an eschatological worldview as a devout person attempting to rise up from persecution.[39] The author of Jer 20:7–13 tries to establish a parallel between his own situation and the situation of persecution faced by Jeremiah. He does this by tying together the immediately preceding text (Jer 20:1–6) and the text of the confessions. Like Jeremiah, the author faces a situation of persecution that derives from a discrepancy in theological viewpoints.[40] The author was also trying to show that the persecutors were located among the ruling class of the

---

36. Jeremiah 39 onward.

37. Pohlmann 1989, 101–11 and Bak 1990, 221–23.

38. The postexilic editors' self-identification with Jeremiah is not individualism, since it is not an autobiographical record like *Meditations* by Marcus Aurelius. It is a typical postexilic phenomenon of the idealization of the unjustly persecuted righteous (e.g., Pss 34; 37; 62; 73). For further arguments in support of the postexilic dating of confessions in the book of Jeremiah, see Bezzel 2007, passim, in particular 53–54.

39. Pohlmann 1989, 108–9.

40. On the theological discrepancy between the postexilic authors oriented toward the piety of the poor and their adversaries, see §§6.5.2, 6.6, and 6.7, below.

temple of Jerusalem.[41] Furthermore, he wanted to make clear that the
reason for opposing the ruling class of the temple of Jerusalem was their
false prophecies (נבאת להם בשקר, Jer 20:6).[42]

The theological structure of Jer 20:1–13 bears a surprising resemblance
to Jer 7:1–12. The analogy between the three groups—the alien (גר), the
widow (אלמנה), and the orphan (יתום)—in Jer 7:6, on the one hand, and
the "needy" (אביון) in Jer 20:13, on the other, has already been mentioned.
In addition, Jer 7:1–12 presents a critical and negative view of the temple
of Jerusalem and the priests in charge of that temple, as does Jer 20:1–13.[43]
Of course, it is difficult to answer the question of whether texts such as Jer
7:1–12 and 20:1–13 reflect a negative view of the temple itself or a criticism of a wrong attitude towards the temple.[44] At any rate, according to

---

41. On the theological tendency that is hostile to the temple of Jerusalem as well
as to its priestly leadership in the texts based on the piety of the poor, see §§6.5.2 and
7.1.2, below.

42. This reminds us of the emphasis on the correct verbal practice in some psalms
of the poor (e.g., Pss 34:14; 37:30; 40:5; and 62:5). On this issue, see §6.4.3.1, below.
Furthermore, the subject of "falsehood" (שקר) related to prophecy appears in the following verses in the book of Jeremiah: 5:31; 6:13; 7:4, 8, 9; 8:10; 14:14; 20:6; 23:14, 25,
26, 32; 27:10, 14, 15, 16; 28:15; 29:9, 31.

43. This is particularly striking because the temple of Jerusalem is a frequent topic
throughout the book of Jeremiah, and the temple itself is not usually judged negatively
in the book of Jeremiah in general. Aside from the aforementioned references in Jer
20:1–13 and Jer 7:1–12 (plus its parallel text of Jer 26:1–19), which reflect a critical
stance against the temple of Jerusalem as well as against its priestly leadership, the
temple of Jerusalem is found in the following references: היכל Jer 24:1; 50:28; 51:11;
בית יהוה Jer 17:26; 19:14; 23:11; 27:16, 18, 21; 28:1, 3, 5, 6; 29:26; 33:11; 35:2, 4; 36:5, 6,
8, 10; 38:14; 41:5; 51:51; 52:13, 17, 20; מקדש: Jer 17:12; 51:51. On the attitude toward
the temple of Jerusalem in the aforementioned references, see §4.3, below.

44. Many scholars claim that the passage in Jer 7:4 does not call into question
the temple but, rather, misguided expectations regarding the military safety offered
by YHWH's presence at the sanctuary (see, e.g., Carroll 1986, 209–10; Seidl 1995,
153–54; C. Maier 2002, 133–35). It should be acknowledged that Jer 7:4 is ambiguous on this point and thus can be interpreted in different ways. However, we tend to
assume that the two aspects (the temple itself and the expectation placed on it) in the
worldview of ancient Judeans cannot be so easily distinguished from each other. They
seem to be two sides of the same coin, so to speak. From where did the expectation
regarding military safety derive? High regard for the temple includes YHWH's special
protection for the temple and vice versa. One cannot take one side away from the
other. Why did the author of Jer 7:1–12 let Jeremiah call into question expectations
regarding the military safety offered by YHWH's presence at the sanctuary. This is

Jer 7:4 and 7:8, the Judean people believe the false prophecies (דברי השקר)
related to the temple of Jerusalem. In short, in both Jer 7:1–12 and 20:1–13
Jeremiah's criticism of the priestly leadership of the temple of Jerusalem is
due to the false prophecy (דברי השקר) that the priests preach.

We cannot dismiss this continuity and resemblance as a mere coincidence. Therefore, it should be assumed that the authors of Jer 7:1–12 and
20:1–13 were part of the same theological group or orientation, active in
the same way in the postexilic period. From the above observation, we
can conclude that Jer 7:1–12 did not originate with the prophet Jeremiah
himself, but is affiliated with an editor from a later period.

4.3. Does Jeremiah 7:1–12 Belong to a Deuteronomistic Editorial Layer?

It is oversimplistic to conclude that any text where Deuteronomistic literary style and expressions appear can be categorized as a Deuteronomistic
editorial layer. As Pohlmann points out, since the Deuteronomistic literary style and expressions are very easy to imitate, to conclude from these
alone that the text was written in a Deuteronomistic spirit and ideology is
too rash.[45] Accordingly, when determining whether an editorial layer is
"Deuteronomistic" or not, we should base our conclusion not only on literary style and expressions but also on theology, ideology, and worldview
in order to form a comprehensive standard.[46]

Bearing this in mind, let us reconsider Jer 7:1–12. What kind of theology and ideology does this redactional text reflect? As noted above,
many scholars claim that the text displays Deuteronomistic theology
and ideology.

Thiel claims that Jer 7:3 and 7:5, which include the *hiphil* form of יטב,
belong to a Deuteronomistic editorial layer.[47] According to Thiel, in order
to point out the sins of Judah, the prophet Jeremiah in Jer 2:33 paradoxi-
cally used the *hiphil* form of יטב, and the Deuteronomistic editor creatively
changed the usage of the word in Jer 7 to a warning for the sake of repen-

---

because his estimation of the temple itself did not correspond to expectations. The
attempt to separate two aspects, which are inseparable elements of the same religionness, could be estimated as too modern.

45. Pohlmann 1978, 16–18.

46. See K. Schmid 1996, 347–49; C. Maier 2002, 34–47; Kugler 1999, 127–44; and
Stipp 2015, 328–32.

47. Win. Thiel 1973, 108.

tance. As stated above, since a clear discontinuity does indeed exist in the meaning of the *hiphil* form of יטב between Jer 2:33 and Jer 7:3, 5, it can be concluded that each comes from a different hand. However, can we conclude from this that Jer 7:3, 5 is Deuteronomistic?

The *hiphil* form of יטב appears ten times in Deuteronomy (Deut 5:28; 8:16; 9:21; 13:15; 17:4; 18:17; 19:18; 27:8; 28:63; 30:5) as well as ten times in DtrH (Josh 24:20; Judg 17:13; 19:22; 1 Sam 2:32; 16:17; 20:13; 25:31; 1 Kgs 1:47; 2 Kgs 9:30; 11:18). However, not a single usage of the *hiphil* form of יטב in Deuteronomy or DtrH has the meaning that it does in Jer 7:3, 5 of "to reform/change (one's ways and deeds)."

Furthermore, the combination of the Hebrew words דרך "way" and מעלל "deed" used in Jer 7:3, 5 appears nowhere in Deuteronomy or DtrH except in Judg 2:19. The expression in Judg 2:19 is, in any case, quite distant from the expression in Jer 7:3, 5. First, in Jer 7:3, 5, the form is such that דרך comes first, followed by מעלל; but in Judg 2:19, this order is reversed. Further, in Judg 2:19, מעלל and דרך are combined with the preposition מן, but in the book of Jeremiah such wording is not found. Therefore, it is difficult to conclude that this expression is Deuteronomistic. In the book of Jeremiah, the combination of דרך and מעלל is frequently seen in poetic oracle passages such as Jer 4:18; 17:10; and 23:22, and this expression also often appears in the prose sermon passages such as Jer 7:3, 5; 18:11; 25:5; 26:3; and 35:15. Based on the considerations we have reviewed up to this point, it seems appropriate to conclude that the aforementioned expressions (the *hiphil* form of יטב, the combination of דרך and מעלל, etc.), rather than being a Deuteronomistic redaction, originated through reciprocal influences between editorial layers within the book of Jeremiah.[48] Here a prob-

---

48. It is also worth considering the *qal* form of נטע "to plant", which occurs thirteen times in the book of Jeremiah (Jer 2:21; 11:17; 12:2; 18:9; 24:6; 29:5, 28; 31:5, 28; 32:41; 35:7; 42:10; and 45:4). Of these occurrences, nine describe God as planting the Judean people (Jer 2:21; 11:17; 12:2; 18:9; 24:6; 31:28; 32:41; 42:10; and 45:4). On the other hand, the *qal* form of נטע appears seven times in Deuteronomy and DtrH (Deut 6:11; 16:21; 20:6; 28:30; Josh 24:13; 2 Sam 7:10; 2 Kgs 19:29). However, the only instance among these references in which this verb is used to describe God as planting the Judean people is in 2 Sam 7:10. Therefore, when the *qal* form of נטע is used with reference to God planting the people, rather than regarding it as Deuteronomistic, the correct conclusion would be to call it "Jeremianic" or "Deutero-Jeremianic." In particular, in Jer 12:2 (part of the confessions), after the phrase stating that the people have been planted (נטעתם) by God, a theological theme is found that God is near in the people's mouths but far from their hearts (רחוק מכליותיהם). Here, the motif of God planting the people

lem surrounding research concerning possible Deuteronomistic editing in
the book of Jeremiah comes to light. There is no consensus among scholars regarding what sort of standards should be used to determine whether
words and expressions are Deuteronomistic. For example, Louis Stulman
collects ninety-two Deuteronomistic expressions from the C source in the
book of Jeremiah and classifies them into four categories as follows:[49]

1.   C Diction documented more than once in DtrH
2.   C Diction documented once in DtrH
3.   C Diction undocumented in DtrH but documented in Deu-
     teronomy
4.   C Diction undocumented in DtrH and in Deuteronomy

According to the criteria Stulman establishes, Jer 7:1–12 contains thirteen typical Deuteronomistic phrases. However, when we consider these
expressions and phrases carefully, the ambiguity and vagueness of their
Deuteronomistic character become apparent. In particular, categories 2
and 4 are logically problematic. Phrases that are found more frequently
in the book of Jeremiah than in DtrH (category 2) cannot be considered as Deuteronomistic but should instead be considered as Jeremianic
or Deutero-Jeremianic.[50] If this is the case, then it goes without saying
that the expressions and phrases which do not appear at all in DtrH
or in Deuteronomy (category 4) cannot be regarded as Deuteronomistic either. In this way, categories 2 and 4 are located in the gray area

---

and the theme of the people's hearts are joined. This rare combination also appears in
Jer 32:40–41. These verses are usually regarded as Deuteronomistic, but just as in Jer
12:2, the combination of the motifs of the people's hearts and God planting people
appears. The word כליה in Jer 12:2 literally means "kidney" but figuratively expresses
the innermost domain of the human spirit. In the Hebrew Bible, it is frequently used
as a synonym for and juxtaposed against the words לב and לבב "heart" (e.g., Pss 7:10;
26:2; 73:21; Jer 11:20; 17:10; 20:12). On the other hand, as noted above, the only passage
in DtrH describing God planting the people using the *qal* form of נטע is 2 Sam 7:10.
However, there the combination of the theological motifs of the people's hearts and of
God planting people cannot be observed. Therefore, the use of the *qal* form of נטע in
Jer 32:40–41 (part of the prose sermons) is much closer to Jer 12:2, which is part of
Jeremiah's confessions, than to 2 Sam 7:10, which is a part of DtrH. It is also possible to
regard Jer 32:40–41 as a response to Jer 12:2.
    49. Stulman 1986, 33–44.
    50. Sharp 2003, 17–18.

between Deuteronomistic and Jeremianic and are therefore not persuasively Deuteronomistic.

Moreover, the logical presuppositions of categories 1 and 3 are also questionable. If words and expressions found in Deuteronomy or in DtrH also appear in the book of Jeremiah, are these texts necessarily Deuteronomistic? As already stated above, some words and expressions appear more frequently in the book of Jeremiah than in DtrH. Should these be called Deuteronomistic or Jeremianic? When words are used with completely different meanings in the book of Jeremiah and in DtrH, should the corresponding parts in the book of Jeremiah be called Deuteronomistic merely because they appear in both places? These questions have been overlooked by many researchers, but in truth they are questions fundamental to investigating the existence of Deuteronomistic editorial layers in the book of Jeremiah.[51]

The three groups of the alien (גר), the widow (אלמנה), and the orphan (יתום) in Jer 7:6 (no. 58 of Stulman's list; category 3) certainly also appear in Deuteronomy, yet, as already stated, it would be too hasty to conclude from this alone that the verse is Deuteronomistic.[52] These three groups appear eleven times in Deuteronomy but are not found once in DtrH.

Furthermore, if we compare the way these expressions are used in Deuteronomy to the way they are used in the book of Jeremiah, we can observe that the way the three groups are discussed in the book of Jeremiah does not correspond to the connotations of the same groups in Deuteronomy. In Deuteronomy, the existence of these three groups does not extend beyond socially weak and poor persons whose lives must be protected. However, as previously mentioned, the way the three groups are discussed in the book of Jeremiah (Jer 7:6 and 22:3) includes a sense of innocent people being unfairly persecuted by the wicked, such as in the mention of the "needy" (אביון) in Jer 20:13.[53] This can also be seen

51. Ibid., 14–16.

52. Jones 1992, 144.

53. This theological connotation of the three groups is also found in Pss 94:6 and 146:9. In Ps 94 the widow, the alien, and the fatherless are delineated as a part of God's people (עמך: Ps 94:5) and possession (נחלתך: Ps 94:5). In Ps 146:9, the three groups are juxtaposed as opposing terms to the wicked (רשעים). In sharp contrast, in Ps 68:6 the two groups (the fatherless and the widow, here the alien is not mentioned) are no more than the socially weak and economically poor. Furthermore, the fatherless in Ps 82:3 (here the widow and the alien are not mentioned) is nothing but an object of special protection as a marginalized group. On this issue, see §6.2, below.

in the expression "do not shed innocent blood" (ודם נקי אל תשפכו) in
Jer 7:6 and 22:3. In the Hebrew Bible, the expression "to shed innocent
blood"—in other words, the combination of the verb שפך and the noun
דם plus the adjective נקי (no. 13 of Stulman's list; category 1)—almost
always describes the victimhood of innocent people under unjust persecution. This combination appears three times throughout Deuteronomy
and DtrH (Deut 19:10; 2 Kgs 21:16; 24:4). However, the three groups of
the alien (גר), the widow (אלמנה), and the orphan (יתום) are never associated with the aforementioned phrase in Deuteronomy or DtrH. The theological connotations of the three groups in Deuteronomy and DtrH are
quite different from the corresponding groups in the book of Jeremiah.
Even though the adjective נקי is lacking, the combination of שפך and דם in
Ps 79:10, signifying the sacrifice of God's servants, is revealing. In Ps 9:13
also, the righteous "poor" (עניים) and their "blood" (דמים) are expressed
in combination (כי דרש דמים אותם זכר לא שכח צעקת עניים). This kind of
theological nuance cannot be seen at all in the three groups in Deuteronomy or DtrH. Therefore, we can conclude that the mention of the three
groups of the alien (גר), the widow (אלמנה), and the orphan (יתום) in Jer
7:6 is not particularly Deuteronomistic.

Notably, the phrase "to follow after other gods" (ואחרי אלהים אחרים
תלכו ...)[54] in Jer 7:6, 9 frequently appears in Deuteronomy and DtrH
(Deut 6:14; 8:19; 11:28; 13:3; 28:14; Judg 2:12; 19:1; 1 Kgs 11:10; 2 Kgs
17:15, etc.). However, this alone is insufficient for us to conclude from this
phrase that the relevant verses are Deuteronomistic. This is because similar phrases appear in the poetic oracles in the book of Jeremiah (Jer 2:5,
23; 5:19, etc.). As with the aforementioned combination of דרך and מעלל, it
is also possible to draw the conclusion that the expression "to follow after
other gods" (ואחרי אלהים אחרים ... תלכו) in Jer 7:6, 9 was formed through
internal influences among editorial layers within the book of Jeremiah.
However, as we cannot conclusively answer the question of whether or not
the verses in question are Deuteronomistic from this alone, the analysis
should proceed bearing in mind that the phrase itself is not able to give
the final answer.

Expression no. 4 in Stulman's list is as follows:[55] "the land/place/city/
inheritance that I gave to you/your fathers/your descendants" (Jer 7:7;

---

54. The phrase is no. 3 in category 1 of Stulman's list.
55. Stulman 1986, 33.

לך/לכם/לזרעך/לאבותיכם נתן/נתתי ... המקום/הארץ). This phrase appears very frequently (more than eighty times) in the Hebrew Bible and is also found outside Deuteronomy as well as DtrH.[56] Therefore, it cannot be considered as particularly Deuteronomistic but rather as belonging to the oldest layer of historical tradition within the framework of the Hebrew Bible.[57]

Now we turn to no. 67 of Stulman's list (category 3): "(the site that YHWH will choose) to make his name dwell there" (לשכן שמו שם). This expression appears in Jer 7:12. Although Stulman (1986, 42) concludes that this phrase is Deuteronomic, significant theological differences emerge when the expression in Jer 7:12 and the corresponding phrases in Deuteronomy (Deut 12:11; 14:23; 16:2, 6, 11; 26:2) are compared. The author of Jer 7:12 seems to have used a similar style and expression to the relevant texts of Deuteronomy, but the message which he wanted to communicate is fundamentally different in nature from that in Deuteronomy.

According to Jer 7:12, the place where God originally put his name is not the temple of Jerusalem but rather the holy place in Shiloh. Even the holy place in Shiloh was destroyed due to the sins of the Israelite people. Thus, it goes without saying that the temple of Jerusalem, as the successor to the sanctuary in Shiloh, is also exposed to the same serious danger. In other words, in Deuteronomy this expression is employed in order to emphasize the significance and value of the temple in Jerusalem, while in Jer 7:12 the phrase is used in order to downplay and relativize the importance of the Jerusalem temple.

As already mentioned, when determining whether or not a text is Deuteronomistic, it does not suffice to examine only the literary style or expressions of the text, for the most reliable criteria are located in the theology, ideology, and worldview of the text.[58] The theological viewpoint and evaluation of the temple in Jerusalem could fit such criteria. In the case of Jer 7:12, superficial words or phrases are similar to corresponding portions of Deuteronomy. However, the content and the worldview of the texts are fundamentally different. Jeremiah 7:12 relativizes the theological significance of the temple in Jerusalem, which the corresponding portions of Deuteronomy strongly emphasize. In fact, the author of Jer 7:12 attacks

56. E.g., Gen 15:7; 24:7; Exod 20:12; Lev 14:34; Num 14:8; Ezek 20:42.
57. Jones 1992, 144 views it as Deuteronomistic, whereas Holladay 1986, 243–44 regards it as part of the oldest layer.
58. K. Schmid 1996, 346–49.

the Deuteronomistic viewpoint concerning the temple of Jerusalem by using Deuteronomistic diction. The theological criticism of the Jerusalem temple in Jer 7:1–12 will be examined in more detail below.

The expression "this house, which is called by my name" (הבית הזה אשר נקרא שמי עליו) in Jer 7:10, 11, 14 does not appear once throughout Deuteronomy. A similar phrase is found only twice in DtrH (2 Sam 6:2; 1 Kgs 8:43). Furthermore, the name theology articulated in the aforementioned verses of the book of Jeremiah seems to be quite different from its theological sense in Deuteronomy.[59] Despite these arguments, Thiel declares these verses to be Deuteronomistic.[60] The main reason for his conclusion is that the same expression appears in verses such as Jer 32:34 and 34:15 that Thiel has determined belong to a Deuteronomistic editorial layer. However, as Carolyn Sharp has pointed out, this is nothing more than a circularly reasoned tautology.[61] Therefore, the phrase "this house, which is called by my name" (הבית הזה אשר נקרא שמי עליו) in Jer 7:10, 11, 14 should be designated as Deutero-Jeremianic rather than as Deuteronomistic.[62] To conclude our examination, it has been demonstrated that none of the aforementioned examples of Deuteronomistic phrases found in Jer 7:1–12 can be confidently established as Deuteronomistic.

The most compelling evidence for the non-Deuteronomistic character of Jer 7:1–12 is its central theological theme, namely, the false religionness of the Judean people in the temple of Jerusalem.[63] As previously

---

59. Jones 1992, 143.

60. Win. Thiel 1973, 111.

61. Sharp 2003, 22: "Instead of referring to the absence of the term as such in Deuteronomy and the DtrH, [Thiel] chooses to say it occurs without exception in D texts (in Jeremiah!). His assertion that 'die Formel ist charakteristisch für D' ['the formulation is characteristic of D'] is qualified only to the extent that he acknowledges it to be a unique coinage of D in Jeremiah."

62. Ibid., 17–18.

63. The observations so far do not imply that there is no Deuteronomistic editorial layer at all in the book of Jeremiah. Of course, there are some Deuteronomistic elements found in the book of Jeremiah. E.g., as Römer observes, there are strong stylistic and theological parallels between Jer 52 and 2 Kgs 24–25 and thus Jer 52 seems to be a Deuteronomistic text (Römer 2009b, 171–72). Römer's thesis that the book of Jeremiah was edited by Deuteronomistic redactors as a supplement to the existing Deuteronomistic "library" (ibid., 168–79) is insightful at many points. I would like to make it clear that the assertion of this essay regarding the lack of a Deuteronomistic layer is mainly focused on Jer 7:1–12. It seems probable that the current book of Jeremiah underwent at least three different redactions: a Deuteronomistic redaction, a

mentioned, Jer 7:1–12 passes extremely harsh judgment on the temple of Jerusalem and its priestly leadership.[64] As stated above, the temple of Jerusalem is a favorite theme throughout the book of Jeremiah.[65] It was concluded in the previous section that Jer 20:1–13 and Jer 7:1–12 (plus its parallel in Jer 26:1–19) indicate extremely critical views of the temple of Jerusalem. However, such a negative notion concerning the temple of Jerusalem is very rare in other references in the book of Jeremiah.[66]

For example, the lexeme היכל in Jer 24:1 is employed in order to set the spatial background of the vision. It reveals that the two baskets of figs are offerings consecrated to the temple. The lexeme is used in a theologically neutral sense and does not contain any negative connotations regarding the temple of Jerusalem. The same lexeme also appears in Jer 50:28 and 51:11:[67]

> Listen! Fugitives and refugees from the land of Babylon are coming to declare in Zion the vengeance of the LORD our God, vengeance for his temple [היכלו]. (Jer 50:28)

> Sharpen the arrows! Fill the quivers! The LORD has stirred up the spirit of the kings of the Medes, because his purpose concerning Babylon is to destroy it, for that is the vengeance of the LORD, vengeance for his temple [היכלו]. (Jer 51:11)

In these passages, YHWH is depicted as taking revenge on Babylon for the destruction of the temple in Jerusalem. In other words, YHWH highly

---

golah-oriented redaction, and a piety-of-the-poor-oriented redaction. The redaction-historical layers of the book of Jeremiah can be delineated as follows: The layer of Deuteronomistic redaction was incorporated between the end of sixth century BCE and the beginning of fifth century BCE. It includes Jer 1:1–6:11; 7:13–8:3; 11:1–14; 18:1–12; 25:1–11a; 34:1–22; 35:1–11, 16–19; 46:2–52:34*. Thereafter, the layer of *golah*-oriented redaction was inserted throughout the fifth century BCE including Jer 21:1–10; 24:1–10; 32:16–44; 37:1–44:30*. Around the fourth century BCE a piety-of-the-poor-oriented redaction was added (Jer 6:13–14; 7:1–12; 8:10; 11:18–12:6; 15:10–21; 17:12–18; 18:19–23; 20:1–13; 22:3–5; 26:1–19; 32:40–41).

64. On the antitemple and antisacerdotal theological tendency in the texts based on the piety of the poor, see chs. 6.5.2 and 7.1.2, below.

65. See §4.2, above.

66. On this issue, see note 43 above.

67. Scholars are divided over whether Jer 50–51 derived from the prophet Jeremiah himself or from later editors. For detailed arguments on both sides, see Keown et al. 1995, 357–64.

values the temple of Jerusalem and thus seeks revenge on Babylon for the sin of destroying it. Therefore, the theological perspective concerning the temple of Jerusalem in the passages above should be viewed as much more positive than the perspectives of Jer 7:1–12 and 20:1–13.

The phrase בית יהוה is also used with a theologically positive nuance in Jer 17:26. Furthermore, in most of the remaining references in the book of Jeremiah, the same wording is employed to indicate either a theologically neutral or a positive meaning.[68] The lexeme מקדש in Jer 17:12 and 51:51 also indicates a theologically positive connotation. The temple of Jerusalem in Jer 17:12 is portrayed as a sacred place of divine presence.[69] Although the same lexeme (מקדשי) in Jer 51:51 is used in order to refer to a kind of defilement of the temple by the entrance of strangers, the temple itself is regarded positively, as such a sacred place that no stranger is supposed to enter.

In the book of Jeremiah in general, Jerusalem and its inhabitants are very often severely criticized and sometimes even blamed, but the temple of Jerusalem itself is often evaluated much more positively.[70] Based on the observations made thus far, it can be concluded that the analogy between

---

68. For theologically neutral meanings (in other words, the temple of Jerusalem is mentioned merely as spatial background or in descriptive passages where there is no clear theological judgment on the temple), see Jer 19:14; 27:16, 18, 21; 28:1, 3, 5, 6; 29:26; 35:2, 4; 38:14; 41:5; 52:13, 17, 20. (Although the three references in Jer 52 mention the destruction of the temple, the temple itself is not criticized. The three references are factual rather than theological and thus can be judged as neutral.) For theologically positive meanings, see Jer 33:11 (thanksgiving offerings to the temple as a symbol of restoration); 36:5, 6, 8, 10 (the temple as the place for the proclamation of a divine message); 51:51 (the temple as a holy place: מקדשי בית יהוה). Jer 23:11 is an exception in which the temple and its priestly leadership are judged negatively (i.e., Hebrew terms such as חנפו and רעתם).

69. It is worth noting that Schmidt observes a contrast between Jer 7:4 on the one hand and Jer 17:12 on the other: "It is difficult to harmonize v. 12 with the temple sermon, which urges listeners not to trust in the Temple (7:4) and is consequently hardly Jeremianic. In particular, v. 13 changes Jeremiah's words. So v. 12f forms a counterweight to, if not a form of restriction of, Jeremiah's insights" (2008, 303). Based on the aforementioned observations, I disagree with Schmidt's position that the criticism of the temple (Jer 7:1–15) derives from the prophet Jeremiah himself. However, Schmidt's insight helps us understand that there are references in the book of Jeremiah that contradict Jer 7:4 in their views concerning the temple.

70. Jerusalem and its inhabitants are criticized in, e.g., Jer 2:2; 4:4, 14; 5:1; 6:1, 6; 7:17, 34; 8:5; 11:9, 12; 13:9, 27; 14:16; 19:7; 44:6; and 52:3.

Jer 7:1–12 and 20:1–13 regarding their views on the temple of Jerusalem is rather an exceptional phenomenon in the book of Jeremiah and thus deserves special attention.

In Jer 7:4, 8, Jeremiah declares that the people of Judah believe the false prophecies (דברי השקר) related to the temple of Jerusalem. Jeremiah 7:10 refers to the words of the Judean people, "we are saved." Here, the verb נצלנו is the *niphal* form of נצל, which appears fifteen times in the Hebrew Bible and often refers to a special kind of salvation from God.[71] Jeremiah 7:10 is the only place in the book of Jeremiah where the *niphal* form of נצל is used.[72]

The author of Jer 7:4, 10 harshly refutes the outlook of DtrH concerning the temple of Jerusalem. In DtrH, the editors reveal a strong theological interest in the temple of Jerusalem as well as in the Davidic dynasty and highly esteem their salvific value (1 Kgs 8:33–50). According to DtrH, the Judean kingdom was able to escape many dangers due to the divine promise to the Davidic dynasty and the temple of Jerusalem. This was so when the unified kingdom of the Davidic dynasty was exposed to the danger of ruin (1 Kgs 11:12–13, 32–39). The promise continued when the kingdom was divided and war broke out between the two resulting kingdoms (1 Kgs 15:4; 2 Kgs 8:19). Of course, DtrH ends with the destruction of the temple (2 Kgs 25:8–17). However, the destruction was described in a concise style without any theological comment. It hardly means a repudiation of the temple's theological value or salvific function. It only intends to delineate the outcome of Judah's grave sin as God's rigorous punishment.

The salvific function of the temple of Jerusalem is noted especially clearly in 2 Kgs 18–19. By the Assyrian king Sennacherib's command, the Rabshakeh (an Assyrian high official) went up from Lachish to attack Jerusalem with a large army.[73] When the Rabshakeh came to Jerusalem, he

---

71. On the *hiphil* form of נצל found in one of the psalms of the poor (Ps 34), see §6.3.2.3, below. The occurrences are: Gen 32:31; Deut 23:16; 2 Kgs 19:11; Pss 33:16, 69:15; Prov 6:3, 5; Isa 20:6, 37:11; Jer 7:10; Ezek 14:16, 18; Amos 3:12; Mic 4:10; and Hab 2:9. Exceptionally, in Deut 23:16; Prov 6:3, 5; and Isa 20:6, the *niphal* form of נצל does not refer to special salvation from God.

72. Seidl claims at this point that Jer 7:10 is Deuteronomistic, since the same *niphal* form of נצל appears there just as in Deut 23:16 and 2 Kgs 19:11 (156–57). However, this claim is based on a superficial observation. The *niphal* form of נצל in Jer 7:10 is employed in a completely different context than in Deut 23:16 and 2 Kgs 19:11. On this issue, see the observations below.

73. The Rabshakeh is the title of a high-ranking Assyrian official. However, the biblical passage seems to regard it as personal name.

tyrannically forced Jerusalem's delegation to surrender.[74] Thereafter, Sennacherib again sent messengers to Jerusalem to speak as follows:

> Thus shall ye speak to Hezekiah king of Judah, saying, Let not thy God in whom thou trustest deceive thee, saying, Jerusalem shall not be delivered into the hand of the king of Assyria. Behold, thou hast heard what the kings of Assyria have done to all lands, by destroying them utterly: and shalt thou be delivered [ואתה תנצל]? (2 Kgs 19:10–11 KJV)

Here the *niphal* form of נצל is used with an ironic tone to express the impossibility of salvation through God. However, according to DtrH, YHWH thereafter dispatched Isaiah to king Hezekiah and had him speak the following prophecy:

> This [is] the word that the LORD hath spoken concerning him;
> The virgin the daughter of Zion hath despised thee, [and] laughed thee to scorn;
> the daughter of Jerusalem hath shaken her head at thee.
> ...
> For out of Jerusalem shall go forth a remnant,
> and they that escape from mount Zion:
> the zeal of the LORD [of hosts] shall do this.' (2 Kgs 19:21, 31 KJV)

According to the Deuteronomistic presentation, on the night this prophecy was given God's messenger struck down one hundred eighty-five thousand soldiers in the Assyrian camp (2 Kgs 19:35). In the Deuteronomistic view, YHWH actualized the *niphal* form of נצל "to be delivered" and saved the people, contradicting Sennacherib's disparaging use of the word to his messengers. YHWH showed the sincerity of his promise to the temple

---

74. The speech of the Rabshakeh in 2 Kgs 18 is reminiscent of Jeremiah's preaching in Jer 7. E.g., the *qal* form of בטח (to trust) that appears in Jer 7:4, 8 is found six times in the Rabshakeh's speech (2 Kgs 18:19, 20, 21 [2x], 22, 24). According to Hardmeier (1990, 321–92), the Rabshakeh's speech was written by a Deuteronomistic editor who was hostile toward Jeremiah's theology (see also Stipp 1995b, 232–33). In other words, Hardmeier supposes that Rabshakeh's speech is a kind of parody of Jeremianic theology by a Deuteronomistic editor. It is clear that the pro-Babylonian position in Jer 7 and the anti-Assyrian perspective of 2 Kgs 18–19 are somewhat contradictory to each other. However, the question of which of the two texts (Jer 7:1–12 or 2 Kgs 18–19) was written first must be investigated more closely. In our view, it is possible that 2 Kgs 18–19 was composed earlier than Jer 7:1–12.

of Jerusalem and the Davidic dynasty. In this way, the Deuteronomistic editor consistently emphasizes the salvific effects of the temple of Jerusalem and expresses the view that a correctly practiced rite in the temple of Jerusalem is the only way to surmount the crises of the exilic period and to attain salvation from them. The temple of Jerusalem itself is the theological heart of DtrH, and we can also say that for the Deuteronomistic editor the temple of Jerusalem is the foundation for a new beginning.[75]

This theological focus and the value of the temple of Jerusalem for attaining divine salvation in DtrH are entirely negated in Jer 7:1–12 (particularly in Jer 7:4, 10). The aforementioned prophecy in 2 Kgs 19:21, 31 includes words that can be expected to have been spoken by the very priests that Jeremiah opposed. The author of Jer 7:1–12 seems to declare the aforementioned prophecy on the inviolability of the temple in 2 Kgs 19:21, 31 to be "deceptive words" (דברי השקר; cf. Jer 7:4). As far as the author of Jer 7:1–12 is concerned, the temple of Jerusalem is not a theological focal point, nor does it hold any efficacy for salvation. This author has Jeremiah say that it is a theological error to hold out hope for salvation through the temple of Jerusalem. Also, rather than religionness concerning the prophecy related to the temple of Jerusalem, the author of Jer 7:1–12 requests repentance and reform with regard to social ethics (Jer 7:3–7; 22:1–5). In our view, Jer 7:4 is a parody of the theology of DtrH articulated in 2 Kgs 19, written by a Deutero-Jeremianic editor in the postexilic period.

Rainer Albertz and Hermann-Josef Stipp assert that in spite of this kind of theological heterogeneity, due to the stylistic and ideological similarities between DtrH and the relevant editorial layer in the book of Jeremiah, they both belong to the theological group rooted in Deuteronomistic tradition and spirit.[76] Their views are that the theological heterogeneity of the two is nothing more than a clash of opinion within the Deuteronomistic school. However, regarding the theologically fundamental significance of the perspective on the temple of Jerusalem, it seems difficult to conclude that individuals of completely opposite opinions fell within the same theo-

---

75. Albertz 1989, 45.

76. Albertz 1989, 46–48; 2001, 242–60; Stipp 2015, 325–47. Albertz attempts to explain the various characteristics of the editorial layers in the book of Jeremiah with his hypothesis of three stages of Deuteronomistic redactions (2001, 242–60). However, in our view, it is more likely that some redactional layers in the book of Jeremiah should not be classified as Deuteronomistic. On this issue, see also Stipp 2015, 330–34.

logical group. It cannot be denied that a more multifaceted approach is required regarding research on the formation history of the book of Jeremiah.[77] In other words, careful consideration will lead researchers to the conclusion that heterogeneous editorial layers are present and that they are theologically incompatible with the Deuteronomistic editorial layers in the book of Jeremiah.

Stipp claims the Deuteronomistic nature of Jer 7, proceeding from the assumption that the Deuteronomists expanding the book of Jeremiah, represent a separate branch of their school and, accordingly, that certain differences in terminology and outlook are par for the course.[78] However, it is quite doubtful whether we modern scholars could or should label the polemically opposing groups with the same term Deuteronomistic.

Indeed, as Stipp himself acknowledges, Deuteronomistic is not a self description of biblical authors but a modern scientific delineation intended to contribute to a clearer formation of a differentiated field of conceptual orientations.[79] Thus, its usage is intended to aid collegial agreement and mutual understanding among biblical scholars. Accordingly, we dare to posit that for collegial agreement and mutual understanding scholars could and should label differently the authors of the two above-mentioned highly heterogeneous theological groups that are so diverse that they argue fiercely on fundamental issues. Did the members of the two groups have a feeling of homogeneity? In our view, they did not.

Stipp supposes that the theological differences between Jer 7:1–12 and 2 Kgs 18–19 are only "disagreement" within the same Deuteronomistic school.[80] However, in our view, one should wonder in which way they were mutually connected as "members of the Deuteronomistic school" when their communication was associated with fighting on every possible

---

77. See, e.g., Pohlmann 1978, 183–97; K. Schmid 1996, 201–304.

78. Stipp 2015, 269–70: "It is now certain that the Deuteronomistic authors who expanded the Joshian original of Deuteronomistic History during the exilic period deviated radically on a key point from the Deuteronomistic tradents of the book of Jeremiah: The latter honored Jeremiah, the former opposed him" (ibid., 267). "Consequently, in Jer 7 Deuteronomists polemicized against Deuteronomists (at least, among others). The gap between the two branches of the Deuteronomistic movement was as a consequence also documented by the Deuteronomistic author in the book of Jeremiah" (ibid, 269).

79. Ibid., 296.

80. Ibid., 267–70.

fundamental issue? It is not just a disagreement within the same school, but a struggle between two fiercely opposing groups.

In our view, Jer 7:1–12 derives from an author influenced by the piety of the poor opposing Deuteronomistic theology. The similarity between Jer 7:1–12 and 20:1–13 has already been indicated above.[81] Furthermore, it is intriguing that there is a resemblance between the confessions (Jer 11:18–12:6; 15:10–21; 17:12–18; 18:19–23 and 20:7–13) and some texts of the psalms of the poor (e.g., Pss 37; 73).[82]

Jeremiah 12:1 states: "You will be in the right, O Lord, when I lay charges against you; but let me put my case to you. Why does the way of the guilty prosper? Why do all who are treacherous thrive?" Formulated here as an introduction, the problem in 12:1–2—part of the first confession in Jer 11:18–12:6—is the very same one that is thrust on the speaker in Ps 37 and Ps 73. The suppliant introduced in Jer 12:1–2 turns to YHWH, irritated, because he cannot understand why the wicked and disloyal are so happy and successful. Furthermore, he complains that the latter are in a safe position (v. 2a) despite the fact that they appear to be believers of YHWH only outwardly and YHWH is far from their hearts.

Furthermore, we cannot disregard the fact that the confessions of Jeremiah present a similar characterization of the enemy as in Ps 37 and Ps 73.[83] However, the confessions make it clear that the tensions between the suppliant (and his group) and the opposing faction have increased in comparison to the tensions in Pss 37; 73, so that we can only assume an irreversible split within Judean society in late Persian or early Hellenistic-era Palestine.[84] This development, which is also evident in Ps 37 and Ps 73 as compared to Pss 25; 34; and 62, might have also resulted from the fact that the power structure within the community of YHWH had shifted so unfavorably against the righteous that even their socioeconomic situation was

---

81. For details, see §4.2, above.

82. For details of the psalms of the poor, see ch. 6, below.

83. See, e.g., the references to the prospering of adversaries in Ps 73:3–5 and Jer 12:1–2. Furthermore, in Ps 37:35 as in Jer 12:2 the well-being of the adversaries is compared to a magnificently growing plant. On the *qal* form of נטע "to plant," which is found in the piety-of-the-poor-oriented redaction of the book of Jeremiah, see §4.3, above.

84. E.g., the suppliant's radical desire for destruction articulated in Jer 12:3 ("Pull them out like sheep for the slaughter, and set them apart for the day of slaughter."); see also Jer 17:18; 18:21–23; and 20:11–12.

affected.[85] What actual effect it had in this regard that caused this circle of the believers of YHWH to feel more and more marginalized or neglected is, however, not clear.

Nevertheless, we could refer to Ps 37:16: "Better is a little that the righteous person has than the abundance of many wicked." However, this text does not mean a total impoverishment of the righteous, since Ps 37:21 indicates that the righteous continue to be in a position to help others freely and generously. Therefore, the claim in verse 16 is only an indication that the righteous possess less compared to their prospering adversaries.

The relevant terminology relating to the poor seeks to highlight a certain permanent attitude, namely humility before YHWH, that is, a theologically reflected awareness of lowliness that is derived from the typical pattern of orientation in the wisdom literature: "pride goes before a fall."[86] As to the question of why this terminology relating to the poor and the awareness of lowliness were seen as important, we can consider the following. As the people of the opposing group gained more power and wealth due to their selfish practices, some of the pious had to disqualify the opposing group from true piety toward YHWH. Therefore, the pious differentiated themselves from their adversaries by pointing to different attitudes toward YHWH, with the "righteous" on one side and the "wicked" on the other. It was necessary for the pious to explain to the public that they did not want to be identified with the selfish practices and material ambitions of their adversaries (e.g., Pss 37:1, 7, 8; 62:11; 73:6, 7) but instead understood themselves as poor compared to the opposing group. With the terminology relating to the poor as a self-depiction, therefore, the intention was to demonstrate "before the world" as well as "before God" that, unlike their prospering adversaries, the pious did not want to "go up the ladder." Depicting themselves as poor in this way was the religious trademark of this (not necessarily impoverished) pious group.

As already viewed above, the self-depiction "poor" as a religious marker is clearly the case in the last confession (Jer 20:7–13).[87] The confessions of Jeremiah and the text of Jer 7:1–12 seem to have been composed by the theological circle that was influenced by the piety of the poor in the late Persian or early Hellenistic period. "Jeremiah" plays a role in this, in coordination with the entire framework of the book of Jeremiah, as a figure

---

85. For the details of this development, see §6.6, below.

86. On this, see also §7.1.1, below.

87. On the continuity between Jer 20:7–13 and Jer 7:1–12, see §4.2, above.

of identification to which the eschatological group of the pious should be oriented in a situation of persecution.[88] With regard to Jer 20:7–13 and the preceding context, the assumption is that by situating this confession after Jer 20:1–6, its author seeks to show that his own persecution, just like that of Jeremiah, has to do with conflicting theological perspectives, and that the hostile persecutors are found among the leading circles of Jerusalem's temple.[89] Jeremiah 20:13 clearly demonstrates that the terminology relating to the poor (אביון) in the late Persian or early Hellenistic period was employed in the context of theological conflicts in order to underline a theological standpoint (awareness of lowliness). A situation of material poverty was not decisive for using the term since "Jeremiah" in the book of Jeremiah was not economically poor, as can be seen from the story of Jeremiah buying a field (Jer 32).

4.4. Conclusion

It is significant in Jer 7:1–12 to look at the unique phenomenon of intertextual debates by different theological groups in the postexilic period. In our view, Jer 7:1–12 is an intriguing witness to understand how various theological groups produced, interpreted, and recorded intertextual debates in Persian or Hellenistic Judean society.

Based on the above analyses and observations, the following conclusions can be drawn. First, Jer 7:1–12 and 20:7–13 show a surprising similarity when their theological structures are compared. Neither text seems to have originated from the prophet Jeremiah himself but rather may be deemed to have been written by postexilic editors. This indicates that there exists a theological continuity between some texts of Jeremiah's confessions (Jer 12:2; 20:7–13) and some portions of the prose sermons in the book of Jeremiah (Jer 7:1–12; 22:1–5; 26:2–6; 32:40–41). In our view, Jer 7:1–12 and 20:7–13 were probably both written by the same theological group in the postexilic period. It is also probable that the members of this theological group overlapped with the members of the piety-of-the-poor-movement.[90] The theological circle of the piety of the poor intended to correct the theological direction of the Deuteronomistic redaction in the book of Jeremiah. For example, Jer 7:4 can be regarded as a kind of parody

---

88. Pohlmann 1989, 108–9.
89. On this, see also §4.2, above.
90. On the piety of the poor, see chs. 6 and 7, below.

of the Deuteronomistic theology reflected in 2 Kgs 19, written by an editor of piety of the poor. Accordingly, the theological circle of the piety of the poor cannot be found in the lay returnees from the Babylonian exile or their descendants who were deeply influenced by the Deuteronomistic theology forming DC.[91] As already mentioned in chapter 2, the piety of the poor seems to have been shaped by a priestly class such as the Levites (Ezra 2:40; 3:9–12; 6:16; 8:30; Neh 3:17; 7:43; 8:11; 10:28). Levites do not seem to have been part of the upper stratum but rather part of the middle stratum, since they were priests who were ranked lower than the כהנים (Ezra 2:36; 3:2; 6:9; Neh 3:22; 5:12; 7:64; 12:41). This conclusion does not contradict the fact that the Levites appear frequently in Deuteronomy as a marginalized group deserving protection (Deut 12:12, 18, 19; 14:27, 29; 16:11, 14; 26:11, 12, 13) because the category of "Levites" includes a wide socioeconomic and theological spectrum. Therefore, it is no wonder that some Levites were favored by Deuteronomi(sti)c authors, but that some opposed the Deuteronomi(sti)c theology.

A few Deuteronomistic phrases can be found in Jer 7:1–12, but this does not necessarily mean that this unit is a Deuteronomistic editorial layer. If Jer 7:1–12 was not mainly formed from the prophet Jeremiah's words, it may also not have been mainly formed by the Deuteronomistic editor's hands. Redactions other than "Deuteronomistic" surely exist in the book of Jeremiah.[92] By freeing ourselves from the dead end of having to choose whether something is either from the prophet Jeremiah himself or from a Deuteronomistic editorial layer, we are able to recognize other editorial layers, such as the *golah*-oriented redaction and the piety-of-the-poor-oriented redaction. Thus, research into the formation process of the book of Jeremiah can become even more nuanced than it has traditionally been.

---

91. On this, see §3.6, above.
92. Pohlmann 1978, 183–97.

5

THE THEOLOGICAL CONCEPT OF YHWH'S PUNITIVE JUSTICE IN THE HEBREW BIBLE: HISTORICAL DEVELOPMENT IN THE CONTEXT OF THE JUDEAN COMMUNITY IN THE PERSIAN PERIOD

5.1. Introduction

In Marxist theory, the base determines the superstructure. Concerning the formation history of the Hebrew Bible, did mental or theological patterns have a deeper impact than material and economic conditions? Or vice versa? The previous chapters focused more on the first aspect; this chapter will demonstrate that the material situation and political as well as economic circumstances in the Judean communities of Persian- and Hellenistic-era Palestine significantly influenced the theological concepts and ideas present in the Hebrew Bible, in particular the theological concept of YHWH's punitive justice.[1] This chapter also widens the textual scope further by integrating the Pentateuch and the prophetic literature.

In the poem of Erra, written in Akkadian, the subject of divine justice as the equivalent of destructive punishment that does not distinguish the righteous from the wicked is a topic of serious discussion. In the poem, Isum, a lieutenant of Erra, accuses Erra of cruelty (tablet IV):

---

1. As opposed to Silverman 2013, who criticizes the earlier version of this chapter based on questionable criteria. Silverman claims that my essay "relies too much on complex philosophical and theological concepts (i.e., theory of justice) as dating criteria and moves too directly from an idea to a sociological context." However, what is wrong with considering "philosophical and theological concepts" as dating criteria? If "too much" is a problem, then the reviewer should have clarified why and from which aspect he judged my essay in this way. Neither does Silverman present any concrete argument as to why he felt my essay "moves too directly."

104   Hero Erra, you killed the righteous one [*kinamma*].
105   You killed the unrighteous one [*la kinamma*].
106   You killed the one who sinned against you.
107   You killed the one who did not sin against you.
108   You killed the priest eager to bring the offerings to the gods.
110   You killed the old men on the threshhold.
111   You killed the young girls in their chambers.

Accordingly, in the fifth tablet, Erra admits that he was too cruel: "Like one who ravages a country I made no distinction between good and bad: I slew them (alike)."[2] There are some places in the Hebrew Bible in which YHWH appears to be cruel in the same way as Erra.[3]

The issue of the relationship between the individual and the community, and the guilt and punishment arising from that relationship, is one of the most important topics throughout the Hebrew Bible.[4] Therefore, this chapter pursues the historical development of theological ideas concerning divine punitive justice. Some relevant texts touching upon the question of sin and its consequences for the righteous as well as for the wicked are carefully analyzed in this chapter. This analysis situates that inquiry, with a focus on Gen 18, within the larger context arising from pentateuchal as well as prophetic traditions. The dialogue between YHWH and Abraham in Gen 18 and its theological perspective provide a starting point for a consideration of the idea that God tolerates or endures the guilt of a community because of righteous individuals within that community. The following goals of this theological concept alluded to in the dialogue will be discussed: to encourage the Judeans who were confused by the delay of divine justice and to meet the practical needs of the socioeconomically weak Judean community in Persian-era Palestine. This concept of YHWH's punitive justice in the Hebrew Bible indicates historical development that reflects socioeconomic as well as demographic changes. The text of Gen 18:22b–33a is, in our view, clear evidence that socioeconomic and demographic conditions stimulated the development of a theological concept in the Judean communities of Persian-era Palestine.

---

2. Bodi 1991, 267.
3. For details, see Römer 2013, 46–70.
4. Matties 1990, 125.

5.2. Genesis 18:22b–33a

In this first example of the presentation of the dichotomy of guilt and punishment in the Hebrew Bible, the relevant text is located between the scenes of Gen 18:1–16a and 19:1–3, within a dialogue between YHWH and Abraham inserted between the departure of the men from Abraham's tent (18:16a) and their arrival at Sodom (19:1).[5] When the conversation is finished, YHWH departs (18:33a) and Abraham returns (18:33b). Gunkel divides Gen 18:16–33 into three parts:

1. 18:16, 20–22a, 33b: connecting section (*Zwischenstück*)
2. 18:17–19: YHWH's soliloquy[6]
3. 18:22b–33a: Abraham's intercession for Sodom

In the history of research, it has been recognized that the dialogue between YHWH and Abraham in Gen 18:23–32 reflects a theological point of view generated in the postexilic period. According to some scholars, the theological horizon, the main concern, and the literary style of the relevant text seem to be typically postexilic. Scholars such as J. Alberto Soggin, Reinhard Kratz, Christoph Levin, Lothar Ruppert, Edward Noort, Matthias Köckert, André Flury-Schölch, Walter Brueggemann, Diana Lipton, Urmas Nõmmik, and Roman Vielhauer assert that the relevant text of Gen 18 (the dialogue between YHWH and Abraham) is a secondary addition from the postexilic period.[7] For example, Soggin

---

5. Westermann 1985, 285.

6. Gunkel 1922, 202. According to Westermann, Gen 18:17–19 belongs to the dialogue between YHWH and Abraham and the dialogue in 18:17–32 is self-contained, because Abraham's query (vv. 23–32) presupposes YHWH's reflection in vv. 17–21 (1985, 285). Westermann asserts that v. 22 divides the text into two scenes: it merely serves to remove the three men so that Abraham can now converse alone with YHWH. The conversation consists of two parts: the announcement to Abraham of the destruction of Sodom (vv. 17–21) and Abraham's objection or query (vv. 23–32).

7. Soggin 1994, 214–18; Kratz 2000, 276; C. Levin 2001, 347–51; Ruppert 2002, 372–77; Noort 2004, 4–5; Köckert 2006, 126; Flury-Schölch 2007, 305; Brueggemann 2010, 162–76; Lipton 2012, 27–41; Nõmmik 2012, 195–208; Vielhauer 2013, 161–63. See, among the publications of previous generations, Wellhausen 1963, 25–36; Gunkel 1922, 203; Skinner 1930, 303; Westermann 1985, 286; Blum 1984, 400. According to Blenkinsopp, Gen 18:23–32 is a midrashic comment on the account of the destruction of the city (1982, 121). Ben Zvi also argues that Gen 18:23–32 is a theological text deal-

argues that the theological horizon of the relevant text reflects a typically exilic or postexilic theme, similar to Jer 31:29 or Ezek 18:2. Lipton also argues that both Gen 18 and 19 in their final form respond to Ezek 14.[8]

However, scholars have not been unanimous about the theory that the scene was generated in the postexilic period. For example, scholars including Gerhard von Rad, Martin Noth, Otto Eissfeldt, Rudolf Kilian, Nahum Sarna, and Gordon Wenham assigned the pericope to the J source or one of its subgroups.[9] Sarna claims that the Sodom narratives and the flood story belong to the earliest traditions of Israel and derive from a time before the doctrine of repentance had been developed because, in sharp contrast to the theological outlook of the prophetic literature, the religious teaching of repentance is not found in this text.[10] Wenham also posits that the textual block of Gen 18–19 constitutes a clear unit that contains many structural as well as verbal echoes of the flood story.[11]

However, the secondary character of Gen 18:22b–33a is indicated by several considerations. First, while there is no scene in which YHWH reveals his true identity as God in Gen 18:20–21, Abraham already perceives him as God in 18:23–25.[12] Moreover, in 18:20–21 the fate of Sodom remains undecided, while in 18:23–25 its destruction is regarded as already announced.[13] In 18:22a "the men" (i.e., all three) have moved away to Sodom. However, in 18:22b YHWH suddenly remains behind with Abraham. That YHWH was one of the three is certainly the view of the later editors.[14] Verse 18:33b would be equally appropriate after

---

ing with and reflecting the main concerns of the postmonarchic historical community in which it was written (1992, 33). L. Schmidt argues that Gen 18:23–32 reflects a postexilic milieu and was composed between 500 and 350 BCE (1976, 164).

8. Lipton 2012, 28 n. 5.

9. Von Rad 1976, 199; Noth 1972, 238; Eissfeldt 1965, 194; Kilian 1966, 96–189; Sarna 1989, 133; Wenham 1994, 40.

10. Sarna 1989, 133.

11. Wenham (1994, 40) regards Gen 18–19 as constituting a discrete unit with four main sections: (1) 18:1–15, Isaac's birth announced to Abraham and Sarah; (2) 18:16–33, Abraham pleads for Sodom; (3) 19:1–29, Lot and his family escape from Sodom; (4) 19:30–33, Lot's daughters commit incest with their father.

12. Gunkel 1922, 203.

13. Ibid. and Skinner 1930, 304.

14. Gunkel 1922, 203; "It therefore presupposes a section that is not an independently developed legend, but belongs to an artfully created frame." Furthermore, see Skinner 1930, 304.

18:22a. This observation leads us to the possibility that 18:22b–33a is a secondary addition that was inserted between 18:1–22a and 18:33b. Furthermore, the view of the "men" in 18:22b–33a is contradictory to that in 18:1–8. The men in 18:1–8 are so anthropomorphic that they eat cheese curds, milk, and roasted meat, while the transcendental aspect is strongly emphasized in 18:25, where Abraham calls one of the "men" the "judge of all the earth." In sharp contrast to older narratives in 18:1–16, the pericope does not describe any action by Abraham or God. In other words, while the older narratives relate events, this text articulates concepts in the form of a detailed dialogue. This different style of narrating a story indicates that the pericope was generated in a later time period.[15] Yet 18:17–19 also builds a self-contained unit whose compositional intention stands in tension with that of 18:22b–33a. The former attempts to clarify the scope of divine blessing, while the latter seeks to define the scope of divine punishment.[16] Moreover, the entire atmosphere of the passage indicates that it is a product of a more reflective age than that in which the ancient legends originated.[17] The text focuses on a very refined theological problem, which emerges especially in the postexilic period. The unique point of view articulated here seems very similar to passages such as Jonah 4:1–11; Jer 31:29–30, and Ezek 14:12–20. As Hermann Gunkel correctly observes: "It is also difficult to understand Abraham's intercession for Sodom from the cultural context of ancient Israel; in the ancient period it might have been that Abraham would intercede for his relative Lot; but ancient Israel would hardly have understood how a pious Israelite could pray for a godless people that barely concerns him."[18] Finally, the deeper issue of the text is the social function of the righteous few in the midst of a corrupt society. The theological reflection presented in 18:22b–33a contradicts some other pentateuchal traditions, which will be examined in more detail in the next chapter.

At this point, based on the foregoing observations, we can conclude that Gen 18:22b–33a constitutes a coherent textual unit that was secondarily added between Gen 18:1–22a and 18:33b. In sum, although there are some signs of textual unity in Gen 18–19, which is shown by Wenham

---

15. Gunkel 1922, 203.
16. Rendtorff 1990, 59.
17. Skinner 1930, 304.
18. Gunkel 1922, 203.

among others, we can conclude that these chapters are not completely consistent and therefore that 18:22b–33a is secondary.

5.3. Additional Examples of Pentateuchal Traditions

Ehud Ben-Zvi correctly observes that the place of the dialogue in Gen 18:22b–33a (i.e., preceded by 18:17–22 and between 18:1–10 and 19:1–29) indicates that the theological issues expressed in the dialogue contained significant community concerns.[19] Ben-Zvi writes:

> Within such a community, the image of Sodom probably evoked the image of monarchic Jerusalem just before the divine punishment (i.e. the destruction of the city) fell upon it. Accordingly, the text could have suggested to the community an image of their archetypal pious ancestor asking God to spare their City, which is also the city in which their actual ancestors were dwelling at the time of the divine destruction.[20]

The text raises the theological question of how and whether divine justice can be realized in the midst of total destruction. After noticing the fate of Sodom, Abraham discusses with God the theological significance as well as the salvific function of the righteous within a corrupt society and a wicked community. The main concern of the author of the dialogue is to assure his audience that God is righteous, which means that God will not punish the righteous with the wicked even in total destruction. In Gen 18:25, Abraham challenges God, asking: "Far be it from you to do such a thing, to slay the righteous with the wicked, so that the righteous fare as the wicked! Far be that from you! Shall not the Judge of all the earth do what is just?" This dialogue articulates at least three theological presuppositions. First, it is unfair and illegitimate to let the righteous perish with the wicked, such that the righteous and the wicked are treated the same, even if that kind of treatment is carried out by God. This concept can be interpreted as a phenomenon of "individualization" in Israelite society.[21]

---

19. Ben Zvi 1992, 30.

20. Ibid., 31.

21. According to Lindars (1965, 452–67), the individuals in the relevant texts in the book of Ezekiel are an allegory for the collective. Robinson (1980, 25–44) asserts a "corporate personality in ancient Israel," which means that individuals in the Hebrew Bible are never regarded as isolated from their social groups. It would be safe to say that the individualism of ancient Israelite society was not identical to the individual-

Second, even though a social entity is corrupt and wicked, there is still a possibility that a small portion of the social entity is righteous. If this is the case, it is theologically a more desirable divine action to be patient with the whole entity on behalf of the righteous minority than to destroy it on behalf of the wicked majority. Third, YHWH is not only the God of Israel, but the Judge of all the earth. The unique quality of these theological concepts expressed in the dialogue becomes more pronounced if we compare it with some other pentateuchal traditions.

In the Decalogue, the question of divine punishment is clearly articulated:

> I the LORD your God am a jealous God, punishing children for the iniquity of parents, to the third and the fourth generation of those who reject me, but showing steadfast love to the thousandth generation of those who love me and keep my commandments. (Exod 20:5b–6)

According to the author of Exod 20:5b–6, the concepts of sin and punishment are intergenerationally transmittable. This contradicts the "individualistic" approach of texts such as Gen 18:25–26; Jer 31:29–30; Ezek 14:12–20; 18:1–24.[22]

---

ism of modern society. However, it is also correct that the theological or ethical significance of individuals within a community or collective is clearly emphasized in some texts of the Hebrew Bible that seem to derive from the historical background of the exilic and the early postexilic periods (e.g., Deut 24:16; Jer 31:29–30; and Ezek 14:14; 18:1–24). On the dialectical relationship between the "individual" and the "collective" in the Hebrew Bible, see Namiki 2001, 170–75.

22. Wellhausen utilizes the "intergenerational" or the "individualistic" concept of punitive justice in order to diachronically arrange texts in Genesis: "We cannot regard it as fortuitous that in this point Gen. i. asserts the opposite of Gen. ii. iii.; the words spoken with such emphasis, and repeated in i. 27, v. 1, ix. 6, sound exactly like a protest against the view underlying Gen. ii. iii., a protest to be explained partly by the growth of moral and religious cultivation, but partly also no doubt due to the convulsive efforts of later Judaism to deny that most firmly established of all the lessons of history, that the sons suffer for the sins of the fathers" (Wellhausen 1957, 307). Levinson regards the texts of Ezek 18 as diachronically late in comparison to Exod 20:5b–6 (2008, 60–71). According to Levinson, the author of Ezek 18 rejects the Decalogue's principle of transgenerational punishment and suggests a corrective by articulating "the freedom of an individual to transform and renew his life, at every moment in his life, whatever the burden of his past (18:21–29)" (67).

It is also worth mentioning the cultic laws concerning offerings in Num 15:22–31, which relate to the atonement for unintentional transgression by a community or by an individual.[23] With regard to unintentional sin by a whole congregation:

> If this was done unintentionally, through the inadvertence of the community, the whole community shall present one bull of the herd as a burnt offering of pleasing odor to the LORD, with its grain offering and its drink offering, and one he-goat as a purification offering. (Num 15:24, my translation)

When an unintentional sin is committed by an individual, "he shall offer a she-goat in its first year as a purification offering" (Num 15:27). These two verses present differing ideas about how the community and the individual should engage in repentance. It is possible that the laws in Num 15 relating to individual sin (Num 15:27–31) with its illustration (Num 15:32–36) presuppose a later conceptual development concerning puni-

---

23. The laws contain the חטאת or "purification offering" (Milgrom 1990, 402–5; Ashley 1993, 284; Anderson 1992, 17). This text is almost unanimously recognized as P among scholars (see, e.g., Budd 1984, 172; E. Davies 1995, xlviii–l; and Seebass 2003, 136–37). While its present position in Num 15 seems to be quite late, the core elements of the law are often regarded as belonging to an earlier stratum in P (Budd 1984, 172–73), a view that derives from comparison with other parallel laws in Lev 4. The literary relationship between Num 15:22–31 and Lev 4 has been intensively discussed (see, e.g., Milgrom 1990, 402–5; E. Davies 1995, 156–57; and Ashley 1993, 284–86). On the one hand, some scholars argue that Num 15:22–31 depends on Lev 4, asserting that the priestly author of Numbers was familiar with Leviticus in its present form (Budd 1984, 172–73). These scholars also emphasize that the types of sacrifice to be presented are more differentiated in Num 15:22–31 than in Lev 4. The inadvertent sin is to be atoned by the dedication of a bull as a burnt offering and a he-goat as a purification offering, while in Lev 4 the bull is required as a purification offering and a burnt offering is not commanded (ibid.). On the other hand, some scholars assert that Lev 4 presupposes Num 15:22–31, since the laws in Lev 4 seem to be much more specific and elaborate overall than the laws in Num 15:22–31 (Binns 1927, 103; Rendtorff 1963, 14–17; and Sturdy 1976, 112). E. Davies (1995, 157) argues that the literary relationship between Num 15:22–31 and Lev 4 is not one-sided but rather mutual and reciprocal, since neither text can be viewed as a homogeneous unit. It is beyond the scope of this chapter to engage further with the literary relationship between Num 15:22–31 and Lev 4. However, in our view, it can be concluded that apart from a considerable amount of later additions, the core of Num 15:24–26 reflects an earlier phase of cultic regulations.

tive justice, since they have a much more individualistic orientation. The author of Num 15:22–26 views the concepts of sin and punishment as fundamentally collective in nature (i.e., the repeated verb in the second-person plural form: תשגו). Therefore, Num 15:27–36 could be regarded as a later addition to Num 15:22–26. However, we should not overexaggerate the disparity between Num 15:22–26 and Num 25:27–36, since "cult is by definition the religious expression of a group and not a feature of personal religion."[24] The individual in Num 15:27–36 seems to be inseparably embedded in the concept of communal purification as an intertwined part of the community. The focus of the laws is on the community as an almost flawless "cosmos." Therefore, it can be concluded that the diachronic gap between Num 15:22–26 and Num 25:27–36 is small, if it exists at all.

In Num 15:22–31, it should also be noted that the unintentional sins of a community are restorable and forgivable if they are within a permissible scope (to sin unintentionally: שגה) and correctly addressed through rituals and sacrifices. In sharp contrast, the individual transgression "with a high hand" (sinning intentionally or defiantly = sinning inexpiably: ביד רמה) has the prescribed consequence of excommunication from the community (Num 15:30–31).

According to the perspectives represented in the aforementioned texts, a community could be purified and restored through proper rituals and sacrifices as well as the elimination of the sinner. The social and ethical order of the cosmos can be maintained by excluding evil things and wicked persons, along with everything related to them, from the community, to which they are considered minor and peripheral. According to this concept, the social and ethical cosmos can be preserved when the sphere of guilt is repressed as a peripheral or minor phenomenon. In this way, the whole community could be viewed as good and sound. In the preexilic period, the religious laws and ethical commands provided ancient Israelites with the necessary criteria to verify the status of outsiders and insiders of this almost flawless cosmos.[25] Furthermore,

---

24. McKenzie 1974, 32.

25. Eliade describes the cosmos in the following way: "One of the outstanding characteristics of traditional societies is the opposition that they assume between their inhabited territory and the unknown and indeterminate space that surrounds it. The former is the world (more precisely, our world), the cosmos; everything outside it is no longer a cosmos but a sort of 'other world,' a foreign, chaotic space, peopled by ghosts, demons, 'foreigners' (who are assimilated to demons and the souls of the dead).... On

regulations regarding sacrifices and rituals offered the possibility of the recovery of status and purification for the community as a whole. Whosoever endangers the order of the cosmos should be dealt with accordingly to repair the damaged order. This could be accomplished either through rituals and sacrifices, which would lead to the reintegration of the sinner, or through his or her excommunication from the community.[26] This concept of a flawless cosmos interconnected with a cultic sacrificial system was by its nature group-oriented and transgenerational.[27] In cultic sacrificial systems, an individual in a family, a community, and a people was always regarded as a part of one living entity, not as a self-sustaining, independent personality.

The story of Korah's rebellion in Num 16 is significant regarding the issue of the relationship between individual guilt and collective responsibility. The present text of Num 16 is a composite text.[28] After Korah's rebellion, YHWH appears and says to Moses and Aaron: "Separate yourselves from

---

one side there is a cosmos, on the other a chaos. But we shall see that if every inhabited territory is a cosmos, this is precisely because it was first consecrated, because, in one way or another, it is the work of the gods or is in communication with the world of the gods.... The sacred reveals absolute reality and at the same time makes orientation possible; hence it founds the world in the sense that it fixes the limits and establishes the order of the world" (1959, 29–30). The worldview which Eliade delineates above can be regarded as a crucial element which is also constitutive of the religionness of ancient Israel.

26. Ezekiel 14:1–11 reflects a similar theological concept in which the cosmos was regarded as valid.

27. Wellhausen 1963, 85 n. 1: "Instead of the moral commandments which are the main issues in Exod 20, only sacrifice and festival laws appear in chapter 34; this is associated with the fact that in the former the individual and in the latter the entire people are addressed because cult is a matter for the whole community, [while] morals [are] for the individual."

28. Mirguet 2008, 311–330; Kellenberger 2008, 1–2; Kupfer 2012, 166–89, 197–200. According to Levine (1993, 405), the present text of Num 16 is a combination of JE and P. On the other hand, Jeon concludes that Num 16 is a rebellion narrative that is comprised of three different strands: a non-P story of Dathan and Abiram and two stories with a priestly flavor (Jeon 2015, 381–411). Römer articulates that the book of Numbers is a bridging book and that the texts of Num 16–17 were composed as a mediation between Priestly and Deuteronomistic traditions (Römer 2002, 215–31). A detailed literary analysis of Num 16 is beyond the scope of this chapter. It must suffice to say that the present text of Num 16 went through a complicated process of transmission, and the passages articulating transgenerational and collective punishment by YHWH reflects the priestly spirit and environment.

this congregation, so that I may consume them in a moment" (Num 16:21). Moses and Aaron fell upon their faces crying out "O God … shall one person sin and you become angry with the whole congregation?" (Num 16:22). YHWH accepts their request, which is like that of Abraham in Gen 18 in its distinguishing the innocent from the guilty.[29] According to Joseph Blenkinsopp, this is in the form of a rhetorical question of the kind used by Abraham at Sodom.[30] Blenkinsopp argues that there is thus some sort of link between Gen 18:23–32 and Num 16.

However, according to Num 16:32, the principle of group-oriented and transgenerational punishment is still valid, since "the earth opened its mouth and swallowed them up, along with their households—everyone who belonged to Korah and all their goods." In sharp contrast to, for example, Gen 18:22b–33a; Jer 31:29–30; and Ezek 18:1–24, in Num 16 not only the sinner (Korah) but also the men who are connected to him are destroyed. In other words, Num 16 is not as individualistic as Gen 18:22b–33a; Jer 31:29–30; and Ezek 14:12–20. The concept of divine punishment in Num 16 is in some degree still transgenerational and collective.[31] This significant difference seems to indicate that the theological concept concerning divine punitive justice found in Num 16 was developed earlier than that of Gen 18:22b–33a.[32]

5.4. Relevant Texts in the Prophetic Traditions

As mentioned earlier, the concepts of sin and punishment were based on religious laws and ethical commands, which offered Israelites a vantage point to examine those who belong to the flawless cosmos and those who do not. This cosmos could be maintained by purifying or eliminating sin, corruption, evil, and wickedness by offering sacrifices or performing rituals. When

---

29. Matties 1990, 127.

30. Blenkinsopp 1982, 126.

31. In this theological context, Num 26:11 seems to be a later amendment which was inserted to reconcile the contradiction between Num 16:32 and Num 26:58 as well as to mitigate the transgenerational and collective concept of punitive justice in the earlier version of Korah's story of Num 16.

32. The story of Achan (Josh 7) also reflects the transgenerational and collective concept of retribution "when Achan breaks the taboo on the spoil of Jericho, and involves the whole of Israel in defeat and, on discovery, the whole of his family in destruction" (Robinson 1980, 26). From this perspective, Josh 7 as well as Deut 13:12–16 and 2 Sam 21 can be regarded as earlier than Gen 18:22b–33a.

a sin or act of corruption or evil was too serious to be forgiven through such religious means, the sinner who committed the serious transgression and those associated with the sinner could expect to be cut off from the community. This rule was also valid for an entire community: in the event that the community was corrupt and wicked (as Sodom was), it was to be destroyed by God in order to preserve the divine cosmos.

As Gunkel correctly notes, it is not uncommon in the preexilic period that death and catastrophe destroy an entire community for the purpose of punishing the sin and wickedness of its inhabitants.[33] A similar theological position is found frequently in prophetic texts. For example:

> This is what the Lord GOD showed me—a basket of summer fruit. He said, "Amos, what do you see?" And I said, "A basket of summer fruit." Then the LORD said to me, "The end has come upon my people Israel; I will never again pass them by." (Amos 8:1–2)

Here we find that there is no distinction between the righteous and the wicked part of a people (i.e., Israel). A family, a community, a city, and even a people were considered to be a homogenous unit. On the same note, the old layer of the Sodom narrative explains that the city was destroyed by God because the people of Sodom were evil (Gen 13:13).

Gunkel writes, "In this time period the idea that in the accursed Sodom an individual citizen could have been righteous appeared completely egregious: How could that be possible!"[34] However, as a consequence of the massive disasters of the early sixth century BCE, the widespread religionness in the flawless cosmos concept was eradicated once and for all. The surviving Israelites were completely shocked and fell into deep despair; God's temple was demolished, leaving them without a place in which to orient themselves, offer sacrifices, perform rituals, or communicate with the divinity.[35] Thus, the foundational concern of exilic and early postexilic

---

33. Gunkel 1922, 204: "That death and destruction come upon a whole people to punish their sins is an idea which was accepted in ancient Israel without resistance."
34. Ibid.
35. "From all that has been said, it follows that the true world is always in the middle, at the Center, for it is here that there is a break in plane and hence communication among the three cosmic zones. Whatever the extent of the territory involved, the cosmos that it represents is always perfect. An entire country (e.g., Palestine), a city (Jerusalem), a sanctuary (the temple in Jerusalem), all equally well present an imago mundi.... Palestine, Jerusalem, and the temple severally and concurrently rep-

Israelites (until the establishment of the Second Temple) became how to experience forgiveness and recovery without being able to perform religious acts at the temple. By challenging the traditional concept of totality regarding the principle of retribution, Ezek 18:14–20 (together with the present version of Ezek 18:5–13) was directed at those who were driven to despair because of the annihilation of the divine cosmos concept. The author of Ezek 18:14–20 emphasized individual retribution because there was no longer a communal framework of religious rituals or a collective order of the divine cosmos in which individuals felt embedded as there was during the preexilic period. After 587 BCE the possibility of the concept of total retribution disappeared because there was no longer a communal basis or a collective foundation of Israelite religionness for a community, a city, a people, or even a nation. Therefore, without a cult, the only option that remained for the exilic/early postexilic community was to individualize the religious principle of retribution so as not to entirely lose their orientation.

Consequently, Ezek 18:14–20 clearly asserts that the old collective point of view has to be transformed:

> The person who sins shall die. A child shall not suffer for the iniquity of a parent, nor a parent suffer for the iniquity of a child; the righteousness of the righteous shall be his own, and the wickedness of the wicked shall be his own. (Ezek 18:20)

This obviously revokes the principle of transgenerational and collective retribution, which was so usual in the preexilic period. These theological features of Ezek 18 are shared in Ezek 14:12–20:

> The word of the LORD came to me: Mortal, when a land sins against me by acting faithlessly, and I stretch out my hand against it, and break its staff of bread and send famine upon it, and cut off from it human beings and animals, even if Noah, Daniel, and Job, these three, were in it, they

---

resent the image of the universe and the Center of the World.... It seems an inescapable conclusion that the religious man sought to live as near as possible to the Center of the World" (Eliade 1959, 42–43). In short, for Judeans who survived the Babylonian exile, the destruction of the temple of Jerusalem meant not simply the material collapse of a single building but also the destruction of their cosmos and the collapse of the religionness that Judeans cherished in their hearts as one of the crucial axes of their spiritual world.

would save only their own lives by their righteousness, says the Lord
GOD. (Ezek 14:12–14)

I. G. Matthews describes this development in the following manner:

> To the field of ethics, belongs his [Ezekiel's] contribution on individu-
> alism, which some have considered his chief message. While national
> solidarity had been the preaching of the earlier prophets, the query
> must often have arisen as to the justice of the saint suffering with the
> sinner. That the sins of the fathers should be visited on the children, to
> the fourth generation, was questionable justice. In national practice indi-
> viduals, not families, had been condemned (cf. 2 Kings 14:5, 6); and this
> had been written into the code of Deuteronomy as something new (Deut
> 24:16). But it was the destruction of the city that shattered group life,
> thereby shattering national solidarity that furnished an incentive for the
> new philosophy, individualism.[36]

However, it should be more carefully examined whether or not the relevant texts from the book of Ezekiel derived from the prophet himself.[37]
Blenkinsopp claims that there are some terminological, conceptual, and
theological connections between Gen 18:23–32 and the book of Ezekiel,
especially Ezek 18.[38]

It has long been recognized among scholars that the "individualistic"
concept of Gen 18:22b–33a ("Will you indeed sweep away the righteous
with the wicked?") is similar to that of Ezek 14:12–20 and Ezek 18. How-

---

36. Matthews 1939, xxiii–xxiv. Levinson also values highly the philosophical significance of the "individualistic" concept in Ezek 18: "Although widely heralded in
standard Old Testament theologies for its focus upon the individual, Ezekiel's formulation of freedom represents a largely unrecognized landmark in the history of
thought. Despite its religious terminology, it is essentially modern in its conceptual
structure. With its powerful critical engagement with existing assumptions, it amounts
to a theory of human action that rejects determinism, affirms individual responsibility for one's standing in the present, and mandates the importance of moral choice.
Within the history of philosophy, the comparable groundbreaking conceptualization
of moral freedom as independence from the burden of the past is associated with the
early-modern philosopher Immanuel Kant (1724–1804)" (Levinson 2008, 67).
37. With the term "Ezekiel," Levinson means "to designate the literary persona
represented in chapter 18 and [does] not mean to imply that the entire chapter represents a unified literary composition that derives from the historical prophet" (ibid.,
65). This viewpoint is very close to that of this study.
38. Blenkinsopp 1982, 124.

ever, if we compare the texts carefully, there are some clear differences regarding the theological concept. First, according to Ezek 14:12–20 and Ezek 18, if Noah, Daniel, and Job (or the righteous in Ezek 18) were there, they would not be able to save the lives of others (even though the others are their own children); only their own lives would be spared. They are the paradigmatic righteous ones and the text only concedes that their own lives can be saved, but they do not have any salvific function for others, even for their own offspring. In other words, the pericope focuses on the issue of whether God will take care of the righteous few and save them in the midst of the total destruction of the land. In sharp contrast, Gen 18:22b–33a deals more with the question of whether God would be patient with a corrupt community on behalf of the righteous. Do the righteous have a salvific function for an evil society before God? That is the central question the pericope raises. In the pericope, God finally replies to Abraham's repeated questions: "For the sake of ten I will not destroy it." The answer is yes. The few (ten) righteous have a salvific function for the entire city. God prefers to protect the lives of the righteous few rather than to destroy the wicked city. God's justice is no longer realized by bringing total destruction to a sinful society (as in Amos 8:1–2) or by assigning merely individual retribution (as in Ezek 14:12–20 and Ezek 18), but by being patient with a sinful society to protect the lives of a righteous few. This is a dramatic change in the theological paradigm of divine justice: the main concern is shifted from the punishment of the sinner to the protection of the righteous. In sharp contrast to Gen 18:22b–33a, Ezek 14:12–20 and Ezek 18 say nothing about the concept that the existence of a righteous few can have a positive effect on a wicked community. It is important for the author of Ezek 18 that righteous as well as wicked persons receive appropriate consequences for their actions and attitudes. However, this correct retribution is no longer an essential question for the author of Gen 18:22b–33a. The protection of a righteous and innocent few is much closer to the heart of the author.

Second, whereas in Ezek 14:12–20 and Ezek 18 the three righteous do not form a subgroup within a community, the author of Gen 18:22b–33a seems to regard the righteous few as a social entity.[39]

Third, both Ezek 14:12–20 and Ezek 18 are profoundly influenced by priestly style and theology in sharp contrast to Gen 18:22b–33a, which does

---

39. L. Schmidt 1976, 150–59.

not reflect any priestly characteristics.[40] Furthermore, the phrase השפט
כל הארץ is found only in Gen 18:25 in the Hebrew Bible. This expression
obviously presupposes the universal monotheistic theology of Deutero-
Isaiah (see, e.g., Isa 45:5–7), while the Ezek 14:12–20 and Ezek 18 suppose
only a local divinity (cf. ארץ in Ezek 14:13 and ישראל in Ezek 18:2). At this
point we can conclude that Gen 18:22b–33a reflects a later stage of theological development in comparison to Ezek 14:12–20 and Ezek 18.[41]

As previously mentioned, the annihilation of the flawless cosmos
concept generated a new concept, one of individual retribution (i.e., Ezek
14:12–20 and Ezek 18). However, the completion of the Second Temple led
to a new theological milieu and a recovery of the macro-aspect of theology. After the establishment of the Second Temple, the postexilic Judeans
gradually realized the potential danger of the individualized theology of
retribution: this individualistic approach impedes the conceptual path to
the God of history who controls and rules the destiny and fate of nations.
God, in the individual concept, shrank in importance to one who cares for
the petty troubles of individuals—he had lost the theological dimension of
the magnificent history of salvation.

Therefore, it is no wonder that besides the P writers attempting to
restore the preexilic concept of the flawless cosmos, there was a certain
theological circle of Judeans in the Persian period that generated a dualistic concept of eschatology that is aimed at complementing the weaknesses
of the concept of individual retribution.[42] At the same time, this new dualistic eschatological concept distinguished itself from the preexilic view of
total destruction (i.e., Amos 8:1–2):

> Then the offering of Judah and Jerusalem will be pleasing to YHWH, as
> in the days of old and as in former years. Then I will draw near to you for
> judgment; I will be swift to bear witness against the sorcerers, against the
> adulterers, against those who swear falsely, against those who oppress
> the wage earner in his wages, the widow and the fatherless, and against
> those who turn aside the stranger, and do not fear me, says YHWH of
> hosts. (Mal 3:4–5, my translation)

---

40. Ibid., 159.
41. L. Schmidt (ibid., 158) correctly notes that Gen 18:22b–33a presupposes Ezek
14:12–20 and Ezek 18 chronologically and theologically.
42. It is probable that this theological circle overlapped at least partially with the
tradent group of the piety of the poor. For the unique eschatology in the piety of the
poor, see §§6.5.2 and 6.6, below.

Hear the word of YHWH, you who tremble at his word: Your brothers [אחיכם] who hate you, who cast you out for my name's sake, have said, "Let YHWH be glorified [יכבד], that we may see your joy!" Yet they shall be ashamed. A voice of uproar from the city, a voice from the temple, the voice of YHWH who is rendering recompense to his enemies. (Isa 66:5–6, my translation)

Through this dual eschatology, the circle of authors tried to address two theological issues in the traditional concepts. From the principle of individual retribution, the group attempted to recover the historical-collective dimension of YHWH. As already mentioned, the building of the Second Temple was completed in this time period, so that the historical necessity of recovering the macro-aspect of theology, namely, YHWH as the lord of history, was fulfilled. Against the doctrine of total destruction, the group articulated that YHWH would sharply discriminate between the righteous and the wicked when judging a community. In sharp contrast to the preexilic collective worldview, the cosmos is no longer regarded as flawless according to this theological group's perspective. In the priestly worldview, society could be purified and restored by proper rituals and sacrifices, since evil was treated as an exceptional phenomenon. But now evil has become a major, central entity. Therefore, the whole community cannot be viewed as homogeneously good and sound. According to this "dual eschatology" theological group, the goodness and soundness of current society is partial and even exceptional, such that the cultic sacrifices and rituals can no longer provide recovery and purification for the community as a whole. Only radical divine intervention and judgment can restore and recover the desirable order of the sacred cosmos by bringing completely different rewards to the righteous minority and the wicked majority within a heterogeneous society.

If this is so, the author of Gen 18:22b–33a seems to take a theological position that opposes the expectation of dualistic eschatological judgment that is represented, for example, in Mal 3 and Isa 66, which was widespread in the Persian period.[43] Genesis 18:22b–33a assumes instead that a dramatic divine decision to punish the wicked is not necessary insofar as

---

43. Blenkinsopp 2007, 398–402; Reeder 2007, 703–9; Oswalt 1981, 299; and Preuss 1978, 302.

a righteous few remained.[44] Moreover, the aforementioned shift in focus might be connected with the particular historical background of Persian-era Palestine. Through this new doctrine regarding the salvific function of a righteous few for a social entity, the author of Gen 18:22b–33a might be trying to explain the delay of divine judgment, which embarrassed many pious Israelites during this time period.

The Judean community in Persian-era Palestine was a society torn apart by deep schisms. It was also severely affected by a shrunken population and a diminished material culture.[45] In other words, the province of Yehud demonstrated the typical features of a postcollapse society, which include depopulation, disruption of the social order, simplification of the social hierarchy, and territorial as well as political fragmentation.[46] These features are phenomena that can reasonably be assumed to have in fact occurred in exilic and postexilic Judean society. Not only Jerusalem, but also many other sites (about 65 percent) in the province were smaller than five dunams, with populations of less than 125.[47] According to Avraham

---

44. The author of Jonah 4:11 even suggests that YHWH is deeply concerned about the fate of animals.

45. On the demographic and socioeconomic situation of Persian-era Palestine, see §3.3, above. According to Lipschits, "There are no architectural or other finds that attest to Jerusalem as an urban center during the Persian period" (2006, 31).

46. Tainter (1988, 4) defines "collapse" as "a political process" which has consequences in such areas as economics, art, and literature but is fundamentally a sociopolitical phenomenon. A society has collapsed when it shows a rapid, significant loss of an established level of sociopolitical complexity. Tainter's model is applied to Yehud in the Persian period by Faust (2013, 123–26). According to Faust, almost all of the characteristics Tainter describes concerning postcollapse societies can be found in sixth-century BCE Judah. Based on regulation theory, Boer posits that crisis must be considered as the norm and stability as an exception calling for explanation. In his view, collapse may have been rather welcomed by the villages: "Yet from the perspective of the village communes, of the subsistence and estate laborers, of socially determining clan house-holds, a 'collapse' actually means a blessed relief from various means of extraction" (Boer 2015, 196). The fact that a collapse such as the Babylonian exile could have Janusian duality has been displayed in §3.3, above. Thanks to the Babylonian exile, at the beginning of the fifth century BCE the condition of the descendants of the דלת הארץ had grown stronger in comparison to the returnees. Crisis for a socioeconomic stratum could sometimes function as an opportunity for another even though it is not an invariable principle. See also Tainter 1999, 1021–26.

47. Carter 1999, 246. Furthermore, see, e.g., Faust 2003, 37–53; 2007, 23–51; 2013, 119–25; Lipschits 2003, 323–76; 2006, 19–40; Finkelstein 2010, 39–54.

Faust, "The demographic and settlement peak of the Persian period was (at most) about one-third of those of the late Iron Age and Hellenistic periods.... The entire Persian period should be viewed as one of postcollapse. All of Judean/Jewish society of the Persian period existed in the shadow of this collapse."[48] For a considerably large portion of the Persian era, urban life flourished only on the coastal provinces, and the major Judahite cities of the preexilic period played only a minor role in the life of the Judean community.[49] The lack of significant architectural remains can be interpreted as indicating that the Judean community in Persian-era Palestine was miserably poor, at least until a certain point during the Persian period.

Numismatic evidence also sheds light on the socioeconomic situation of the Judean community in the Persian period.[50] If we compare the number of coin-types in the coinage of the neighboring provinces (e.g., Philistia and Samaria) with that of Judah, the neighboring provinces had far more coin-types than Judah.[51] What can be said from a socioeconomic point of view about these differences in terms of the variety and amount of coinage? For example, the diversity of types and of motifs depicted on the coins of Philistia derived mainly from many minting authorities (i.e., Gaza, Ashdod, and Ashkelon).[52] However, one possible interpretation is that the Judean community in Persian-era Palestine in general was economically weaker than the surrounding regions. The small size of the community with its main concerns—which were mere survival and restoring the sociopolitical system—did not allow the Judean community in Persian-era Palestine to engage in a thriving trade economy. Such an economic system, in turn, would have necessitated more varied and abundant coinage. Several scholars argue that the major purpose of coinage in Judah was related to the maintenance of the Persian military and that the coins were mainly used for day wages for Persian soldiers in Yehud.[53]

---

48. Faust 2007, 49.

49. Ibid., 50.

50. For Judean coinage in the Persian (and Hellenistic) period, see Avigad 1976, 28–29; Stern 1982, 224–27; 2001, 565–69; Rappaport 1984, 25–29; Betlyon 1986, 633–42; Hübner 1994, 127–34; 2014, 165–68; Machinist 1994, 365–80; Mildenberg 1996, 119–46; 1998, 67–76; Meshorer 1998, 33–50; 2001, 1–18; Meshorer et al. 2013, 237–41. For archaic and Athenian coins in Palestine between the fifth and fourth centuries, see Gitler and Tal 2006, 13–30.

51. Carter 1999, 268–80; Stern 2001, 555–70; Hübner 1994, 127; 2014, 164.

52. Stern 2001, 562–65; Hübner 2014, 163.

53. Machinist 1994, 372–73; Carter 1999, 281; Stern 2001, 568.

Perhaps Abraham's intercession for Sodom in Gen 18 indicates that some members of the Judean community in Persian-era Palestine felt that they were fragile and inadequate. For the author of Gen 18:22b–33a, the focus is not on the punishment of the sinner but on the protection of the righteous, because the Judean community itself was struggling for survival at that time. From the author's perspective, the dualistic eschatological concept was not an acceptable theology for two reasons. First, it was not able to explain the delay of eschatological judgment and/or salvation, which discouraged many pious Judeans in Persian-era Palestine. Second, it did not reflect the desperate need of the reduced and weakened Judean community for survival during that time period. If the aforementioned relevant texts were differentiated according to conceptual pattern, this might yield further conclusions about the different groups of YHWH's punitive justice.

5.5. Conclusion

Since in Gen 18:22b–33a the issue of justice initiated after a catastrophe that YHWH controlled and enacted is treated differently than in other biblical texts, for example, in the book of Ezekiel (Ezek 14:12–20; Ezek 18), it is necessary to examine the historical and other connections between these important theological concepts. In Gen 18 Abraham tries to comprehend what value YHWH might give the righteous in a fully corrupt place such as Sodom. The main focus in this text is primarily to emphasize that, through divine justice, YHWH does not treat the righteous and the wicked in the same way in the midst of punitive judgment.

However, there seems to be a contrasting emphasis in Ezek 14:12–20 and Ezek 18, in which the author concentrates solely on the problem of whether and how God can treat the righteous and the wicked differently. On the other hand, Gen 18:22b–33a mainly focuses on whether and to what extent the fact that some righteous people inhabit an immoral society could prevent divine judgment for all (see 18:24–26): whether YHWH would be patient with the entire society in favor of the righteous, and suspend punitive destruction. In Gen 18:22b–33a the righteous serve a special salvific function for a community.

The texts discussed above can be arranged conceptually in different groups. Group 1 is represented by texts such as Exod 20:5b–6; Num 15–16; Deut 13:12–16; Josh 7; 2 Sam 21; and Amos 8:1–2, in which religionness in the flawless cosmos is valid. The notions of sin and punishment focused on religious laws and regulations, which provided Judeans with criteria to determine who were the insiders and outsiders of the flawless cosmos. This cosmos could only be preserved if sins and flaws were eliminated by offering sacrifices or performing rituals. If a sin or a flaw was too grave to be purified through such religious means, the person who committed the grave violation as well as everything that belonged to that person, were to be eliminated from society. This principle could also be applied to an entire community. If a society was completely degraded, it was to be destroyed by God in order to maintain the divine cosmos. In sum, the concept of divine punishment during this period was basically collective and transgenerational.

The exilic/early postexilic era may be classified as Group 2, and examples of this stage may be found in Deut 24:16; Jer 31:29–30; Ezek 14:12–20; and Ezek 18. In these texts, religionness in the divine cosmos was decisively broken as a result of the Babylonian conquest of 587 BCE. The surviving Judeans were shocked and disoriented. The eradication of the flawless cosmos concept gradually generated the individualization of retribution theology in the exilic/early postexilic period. During this period, an individualized theology of retribution was the primary approach to human sin and divine punishment. This tendency was more or less continued until the establishment of the Second Temple, which began to function as a focal point of communal cult and collective religionness, and recovered the macro-dimension of YHWH worship and therefore also to some degree the concept of divine cosmos. This recovery of the preexilic flawless cosmos was mainly attempted in the priestly milieu; however, there was also another theological current that tried to overcome the limits of the traditional concepts regarding divine punitive justice in the postexilic period.

The postexilic/Persian era, which may be termed Group 3, is exemplified in Gen 18:22b–33a; Mal 3; and Isa 66. In these passages, the completion of the Second Temple fulfilled the theological prerequisite for recovering the macro-aspect of theology, namely, YHWH as the lord of history. At least some portion of the divine cosmos was recuperated. According to the priestly worldview, this historical turning point enabled Judeans in Persian-era Palestine to regain criteria for determining the insiders and outsiders of this flawless cosmos. However, because this recovery of the macro-aspect of YHWH worship proceeded against the background of an individualized theology of retribution, the theological sensitivity of the Judean community regarding the relationship of YHWH's punitive justice to the individual and the collective increased considerably. This general tendency facilitated the development of a dualistic eschatology (Mal 3; Isa 66), which gave birth to its theological complement or antithesis, namely, the concept of the salvific function of the righteous few (Gen 18:22b–33a). This new concept in Gen 18 seems to reflect a postexilic author's struggle. This Persian-period author attempted to achieve two theological goals: (1) to encourage some religious Judeans who were severely confused by the delay of divine punitive justice, and (2) to meet the practical need of the Judean community in Persian-era Palestine, which was numerically reduced and socioeconomically weak. From the author's point of view, the historical situation of the Judean community in Persian-era Palestine required the protection of the righteous rather than the punishment of the wicked. These two concepts both complemented and competed with each other during this time period.

6

THE PSALMS OF THE POOR

6.1. Earlier Research Trends and Problems

In chapter 4, the piety-of-the-poor-oriented redaction in the book of Jeremiah was recognized and investigated. Thus far the Judean community in Persian- and Hellenistic-era Palestine in some selected portions of the Pentateuch and the prophetic literature has been examined and investigated. Now the focal point of inquiry turns to the role of the Writings, in particular to the Psalms. How is the Judean community in Persian- and Hellenistic-era Palestine portrayed through the lens of the psalms of the poor? This is the essential inquiry this chapter raises. Thus, in this chapter we will approach the piety of the poor in the Psalms and its historical background in more detail.

This chapter investigates the question of whether the group of psalms in which the suppliants call themselves "poor of God" (the psalms of the poor) is directed particularly at the poor. In this chapter, the author deals with several controversial questions: What is meant by "poverty" in the Psalms? To what extent can these texts illuminate the "piety of the poor"? What kinds of theological groups or perspectives were responsible for the composition and transmission of these psalms? What historical circumstances led to the piety of the poor?

Careful investigation of the piety of the poor provides evidence that the relevant terminology for poverty serves mainly as the self-expression of an authorial group to articulate its own incomplete and fragile nature. The members of the group oriented themselves to a unique type of piety using the language of poverty. They seem to have been confronted with a worsening conflict with the prominent priestly circle of the Second Temple in Jerusalem.

The words pertaining to the piety of the poor—אביונים/אביון "poor, miserable" (twenty-three times), עני/ענוים "poor, oppressed, humble" (thirty-eight times) and, דל "poor, low" (five times)—are used with unusual frequency in the Psalter. This fact has been treated in a variety of ways by previous researchers. Before we attempt to clarify in which psalms a type of piety of the poor is articulated that is markedly close to the viewpoints of some prophetic literature (cf. esp. Isa 66 and Zeph 3), it would be worthwhile to first briefly review earlier research trends and to analyze the problems encountered in earlier research on the so-called psalms of the poor.[1] By reviewing previous research, it is possible to trace the origin of the ambiguity surrounding the meaning of the term *poverty* in the psalms of the poor. It continues to be controversial whether and to what extent there are references to poverty or the piety of the poor and, furthermore, how such references can be situated within a broader theological as well as sociological context. For these reasons, the history of research on this theme will be outlined in the following section.[2]

6.1.1. Interpreting the Terminology Related to the Poor as a Group

Existing research shows that a significant number of exegetes have interpreted the terminology relating to the poor in the Psalms as pointing to a specific faction or group, in other words, a well-organized spiritual community of poor pious people who are the speakers in the relevant texts.[3] However, closer investigation of this "faction" or "orientation" may result in a completely different interpretation of its chronological, religious, and sociological location.[4]

---

1. On the details of the prophetic texts, see Ro 2002, 35–112. For the psalms of the poor, see Lohfink's list (1986, 153): Pss 9–10; 12; 14; 18; 22; 25; 31; 34; 35; 37; 40; 41; 44; 49; 52; 68; 69; 70; 72; 73; 74; 76; 82; 86; 88; 90; 94; 102; 103; 107; 109; 113; 116; 119; 129; 132; 140; 145; 146; 147; 149.

2. A detailed presentation of the research history is not necessary here (on this, see esp. Lohfink 1986, 153–76 and Bremer 2016, 21–42); the core questions disputed are of principal interest.

3. As assumed, e.g., by Graetz 1882, passim; Rahlfs 1892, passim; Causse 1922, passim; R. Kittel 1929b, passim; and Gunkel 1933, passim; see also Gelin 1953, passim.

4. Baudissin (1912, 219) rejected the term "party" in favor of the term "orientation" and was followed by Causse and R. Kittel.

Alfred Rahlfs prefers to classify the 'anawim as "a faction within the people" but not as "members of a particular social class"; they are "rather the pious and determined followers of Yahweh during their exile."[5]

Antonin Causse modifies this view by claiming to recognize the roots of the movement of the poor in the nomadic beginnings of Israel. Yet he then attributes the relevant psalms to the postexilic period. "Here, as in the preaching of the prophets, we hear the protest of the poor, the sorrowful sigh of the slave, the call to Yahweh of the rebels against social egotism."[6] Causse supposes that the עניים are a well-organized party-like community of poor pious people, a "community of the poor" who loved their poverty.[7] According to Causse, the psalms reflect a progression from a patiently borne suffering to a religionness of humility, characterized by patience, loyalty to the law, eschatological hope in YHWH, and, finally, action that would overturn the world order.[8]

In contrast to Causse, Rudolf Kittel believes that the piety of the poor only emerged during the exile, while the psalms of the poor appeared around the Hellenistic period, when it "becomes clear that they are concerned above all with an antithetical religious position. In the time since the return and since Ezra and Nehemiah, the religious antitheses intensified more and more."[9] The word עני had been applied to these conservatives as a title of respect even during the exile. Considering the sorrows and tribulations of the nation, this usage would now be affirmed through the social position of the pious, who feel themselves to be oppressed. Meanwhile, the pious core of the nation had stepped in to represent the nation as a whole. As with Hirsch Graetz, Kittel posits that material poverty and religious piety are inseparably bound together.

---

5. Rahlfs 1892, 83. Rahlfs seeks to situate the terminology relating to the poor, particularly the term עניים, primarily within the religious domain.

6. Causse 1922, 82.

7. Ibid., 104.

8. Other French researchers strongly influenced by Causse include esp. Gelin. The main difference between Causse and Gelin is that Gelin locates the origins of the piety of the poor in the messages of the prophet Zephaniah and the terminology relating to the poor in the book of Zephaniah. He regards it as being used with a religious and spiritual connotation even before the exilic period (Gelin 1953, 157–59). In his view, the terminology relating to the poor signals the desire for a humble existence in quietude, willingness to suffer for the sake of God, and joy in the temple and its cult mingled with eschatological expectation.

9. Kittel 1929b, 702–3.

Gunkel is no different. He understands the antithesis between the suppliants of the psalms of the poor and their adversaries primarily as one induced by socioeconomic circumstances.[10] At the same time, religious tensions were associated with it: "The poor one claims to be pious, and is convinced that the rich are evildoers; the poor are persecuted because of their religion."[11] For Gunkel, the relevant suppliants in the psalms of the poor primarily belong to the lower classes. Moreover, the enemies of the poor use their power to shamelessly exploit economically weak people.[12] Very often they are not described as individuals but rather as a type of person because they are seen as part of an undifferentiated whole: enemies and pious groups existing in juxtaposition.[13]

Similar views are expressed by Albertz, Zenger, Wolfram Herrmann, and Norbert Lohfink. Albertz agrees with Gunkel, arguing that we can find the piety of the poor "of the lower class in the relevant psalms."[14] The piety of the poor expressed the self-image of a certain lower class during the postexilic period as being truly pious, especially because of their economic misery, and helped to sustain their human dignity.[15] It was "not a religious transfiguration of poverty, but religious compensation for a social lack."[16] Pauperization was not an indication of being left out and despised by God but rather of being associated with God in a special way. To be seen as truly pious, especially in their misery, would have led to the

---

10. "They are separated from each other by a social contradiction" (Gunkel 1933, 209).

11. Ibid.

12. Ibid., 208–9.

13. Ibid., 209.

14. "Thus in lower-class circles, too, the question of God's righteousness arose, but from quite a different perspective from that of the pious upper-class group. Their members had no merits to which they could refer; they had only their wretched and oppressed existence, which they therefore never tired of presenting to God in order to touch him.... And for them a settlement with the wicked was not just a theoretical but a deeply existential problem. The wicked had to be annihilated, so that they could be freed and again be able to rejoice in God" (Albertz 1994, 519–20; see also Albertz's broader discussion of "The 'piety of the poor' in lower-class circles" (ibid., 518–22).

15. Regarding the preexilic history of the piety of the poor Albertz comments: "Already in the late monarchy Zephaniah could see the simple population of the land rather than the city aristocracy as those who were handing down true faith in Yahweh" (Albertz 1994, 506 n. 76).

16. Albertz 1994, 522.

fact "that the social concepts for 'poor' acquire a religious undertone in the piety of the poor."[17]

Zenger also promotes the idea that the terminology relating to the poor in the psalms of the poor primarily refers to a collective group.[18] For him, as for Albertz, the piety of the poor arose mainly as a result of socio-economic factors, although he speaks about a spiritualization of the piety of the poor emerging in the fifth–fourth centuries.[19] Zenger understands the אביונים in Ps 12:6 primarily to mean "people without landed property in different social circumstances, from the small craftsman to daily wage earners and beggars, whose commonality is that they can scrape out their existence only in economic dependence on the powerful or the rich."[20] According to Zenger, the piety of the poor decisively influenced the development and structure of David's Psalter, that is, Pss 3–41 (and Pss 2–89).[21]

Presenting a different perspective, Herrmann rejects the idea of a "well-knit faction-like organization." On the other hand, he argues that the poor were not isolated individuals:

The singularly established genitive linking of קהל חסידים in Ps 149:1 in parallel to ענוים in v. 4 allows us to conclude that those who feared

---

17. Ibid.

18. "In this late exilic/early postexilic compendium of 'Prayers of the Laity' the group awareness of the poor is articulated. The poor wish to live as the 'righteous'.... Their concern is to see among the suppliants of the psalms the typical poor ones as the representatives of the 'true Israel' who can resist the enemies of God's people on the basis of the mutual close relationship between YHWH and 'the righteous servants of YHWH' because they know that YHWH and his world order ... will prevail" (Hossfeld and Zenger 1993, 14–15).

19. Ibid.

20. Ibid., 95.

21. Ibid., 14–15. The results of Zenger's research seem to be associated methodologically with the recent trend toward synchronic readings of biblical texts (e.g., holistic interpretation and canonical approaches); on this, see Millard 1994, 2 (with further bibliography on this topic): "After isolated essays during the 1960s several studies have appeared since the mid-1970s on individual groups of psalms. Since the mid-1980s such writings have also been published with regard to the Psalter as a book. After the commentary on the Psalms by Delitzsch, the commentary on the Psalms by F.-L. Hossfeld and E. Zenger is the first to discuss in detail the correlation of the psalms in the Psalter. This new commentary on the Psalms is, therefore, part of a noticeable exegetical trend." On new developments in this method of research on the Psalms and its aims, see Zenger 2000, 416–35 (with further bibliography).

YHWH were aware of the fact that they were not alone. They knew about each other because they were there in many places, and they would not have remained without at least partial contact with each other until they met others during the cult practices in the temple.[22]

Unlike Albertz and Zenger, Herrmann sees the terminology relating to the poor as simply a religious concept.[23]

According to Lohfink, different perceptions of the piety of the poor can be seen in the Psalter:

> In it the cry of the exploited poor continues to sound from the early lamentations, to put it more concretely, yet without any theological approximation which we have found in the Hodayot. In it, at the same time, the ancient Near Eastern piety of the poor is reflected, which had flourished during the last millennium BCE, especially in the so-called 'personal piety' of Egypt.[24]

Yet in Lohfink's view, the Psalter was "also imbued by the spirituality that learned from the exile to see the entire people of Israel as the community of the 'poor of Yahweh,' persecuted and exploited by the peoples of the world, but rescued and protected by their God."[25] Finally, it was also clear in the Psalter "that the fissure goes through Israel itself: that the 'true Israel' of the 'poor' stands against the rich and powerful in Israel, who for their part also claim to have God on their side."[26] Lohfink argues that the piety of the poor in Pss 138; 140; 142; 143; 145; 146; 147; and 149, as well as in

---

22. W. Herrmann 1999, 76–77.

23. "In view of this, it is no wonder that we find in many places, especially in the later period, religious value being attributed to the words *'ebyon, dal,* and *'ani* (in particular *'anaw*), because these lexemes relate to YHWH and appear to be particularly the believers…. The group of people seen in the linguistic environment observed above are the pious ones who persistently remain in their faith and ask about their God, in their sanctuary and in daily life…. And from the social perspective, the boundaries may have been flexible, since the affiliation to the faith played the decisive role" (W. Herrmann 1999, 74–75).

24. Lohfink 1990a, 101; on this, see also Stolz 1983, 38: "According to the original cultic order, the 'wretched' and the disfranchised deserve special protection and can claim their rights (with the king) and expect their complaints to be heard (by God)." On the religious valuation of poverty in ancient Egypt, see, e.g., Brunner 1961, 319–44.

25. Lohfink 1990a, 101.

26. Ibid.

the Qumran texts, belongs to this last stage of Israel's various pieties of the poor.

6.1.2. Signs of Individuality: Further Interpretations of the Terminology relating to the Poor

Some models discussed above, especially that of Lohfink, take into account the critique by scholars who reject the hypothesis that the piety of the poor was formed in conjunction with an organized group, faction, or orientation of any type.

Mowinckel has already ruled out the role of any factional confrontations in the psalms of the poor.[27] According to Mowinckel, the topic of the "poor" in the profane realm refers to present suffering of the affected; in the religious realm it means the humble, who honor YHWH.

Ten years later, Mowinckel's pupil Harris Birkeland once again investigated the status of the poor in the Psalms: "The problem that this investigation intends to solve is, in short, as follows: Should ʿani and ʿanaw in the Psalms be regarded as an indication of a faction or not?"[28] He concludes that the terminology relating to the poor in the Psalms refers throughout to present poverty and immediate suffering.

In 1939, A. Kuschke investigated the hostile stance of the רשעים toward the ענוים and came to the conclusion that it had nothing to do with "a 'faction of the godless rich' and a 'faction of the pious poor' who would have engaged in class conflict against each other."[29] Rather, it concerned two "classes" or "types" that were "largely incompatible with each other in their outward conduct as well as in their social and religious attitude."[30] The רשעים were satisfied and self-righteous citizens who evaluated matters according to rational schemes of retributive justice; they considered poverty to be something derogatory. The ענוים, on the other hand, would have set their hope on YHWH's omnipotence and regarded their group as the true Israel.

---

27. Mowinckel (2014, 1:83–86, 120–25) explains that the opposition of the "poor" and "enemies" originally meant that these "poor ones" were the victims of magical manipulations by their enemies.

28. Birkeland 1933a, 31.

29. Kuschke 1939, 57.

30. Ibid.

Even if Hans-Joachim Kraus consistently speaks of a "group," his view is close to that of Mowinckel, who recognizes the individual in the terminology relating to the poor.[31] Therefore, Kraus defines the poor as those presently discriminated against and thus helpless in their struggle to survive. The poor one is one who is persecuted and without rights, one who seeks refuge in YHWH from his violent enemies and leaves his lost cause to God as the righteous judge. The poor person is one who relies on God's justice.[32]

For Erhard Gerstenberger, all speculation about the formation of economic and religious factions based on the terminology relating to the poor is meaningless, since the suppliant can theoretically be an oppressed poor person as well as a rich person in distress. The single condition of being poor is the religious motivation to take part in a ritual of supplication. He assumes that the terminology relating to the poor was a self-depiction originating in the supplication ritual. There are no criteria at all to restrict the supplication ceremony to a particular social class of the population. The decisive factor is the situation of distress.[33]

6.1.3. Evaluation and Conclusions

The overview of the most important positions and trends in previous research concerning the question of the "poverty" discussed in the Psalms allows us to identify several themes. For example, in the older works of Graetz, Rahlfs, W. W. Graf Baudissin, Causse, Kittel, Albert Gelin, and Gunkel, the psalms in question were said to reflect a type of piety of the poor for which a corresponding group of tradents could be assumed. On the other hand, Mowinckel, Birkeland, Kuschke, and Kraus maintain that the terminology relating to the poor has nothing to do with a group name but instead refers to the struggle for survival of a persecuted and helpless people.

Both perspectives can cite support for their arguments. For whatever reason, despite the abundance of material, the explanations of the evidence tend to be monolithic. Therefore, the relevant standpoint with regard to current research depends on either the selection of the psalms or the fact that in the psalms in question the viewpoint has gone through

---

31. Kraus 1978, 110.
32. Ibid., 109–10.
33. Gerstenberger 1980, 140–41.

some development.[34] Such developments lead to the perception of a shift in emphasis in the texts. In many cases in the previous research this kind of shift in emphasis has not been considered thoughtfully enough. The arguments made below attempt to avoid this error.

Furthermore, it is apparent that those who interpret the terminology relating to the poor as the name of a group may nevertheless also disagree about the social location of such a group, faction, or orientation.[35] The dispute centers on a discussion of the status of the "poor," and many questions arise when considering the issue of whether they really belonged to the economically impoverished lower class of Israelite society during that time period. For example, were they poor in absolute or relative terms? Were the authors in question motivated to call themselves poor mainly by religious reasons or by economic considerations? In regard to these questions, views are extremely divergent. This may be due in part to the same reasons for the divergences mentioned above, namely, that the breadth of the entire material on the subject of the poor has been focused partially and unfairly on efforts to establish a certain sociological categorization. Moreover, they are also dependent on assumptions about the prehistory and later development of the piety of the poor.[36] In this context, Gunkel

---

34. See the remarks by Lohfink, who seeks "[to] inquire about something like a second *Sitz im Leben* of the original categories of psalms" (Lohfink 1986, 174); see also Gerstenberger, who noted "how creative the processes of composition and of reinterpretation of the Psalms were until the late phase of the Hebrew Bible" (1995, 5–6); Hossfeld and Zenger 1993, 14–15; and Becker 1975, 85 (a "collective or collectivizing interpretation of psalms"). The fact that various developments play a role is frequently conceded by those who reject the faction theory.

35. E.g., in the view of Graetz and Kittel, social and spiritual poverty are inseparably interconnected. Whereas other researchers explicitly or implicitly assume that material poverty in the psalms of the poor has been elevated as an ideal and glorified as a particularly pious way of life (e.g., Causse 1922, 104–6), Rahlfs, Gelin, Lohfink, and W. Herrmann tend to assume that one considered oneself to be "poor" primarily for religious reasons, and that the ideal of piety in the psalms of the poor in question is not based on material poverty.

36. Thus, Rahlfs understands by *'anawim* "the resolute worshipers of Yahweh during the Exile" (Rahlfs 1892, 83) and suggests primarily religious contradictions. Causse (1922, 81–83, 104–6) believes that the poor people's movement was deeply rooted in the nomadic beginnings of Israel in opposition to Canaanite culture and thus should be understood as a protest and revolt against social egotism. According to Kittel (1929b, 702–3), the religious contradictions of the postexilic period were especially important in shaping the piety of the poor.

correctly points out the misguided nature of focusing on the individual: "To speak about the personal situation of the suppliant is inappropriate. At this point, the statements of the psalmist are quite vague and move in general suggestions and images which are not readily transparent."[37]

6.2. Methodological Approaches to the Psalms of the Poor

It may be posited that completely different testimonies of poverty and the piety of the poor were incorporated into the Psalter at different times.[38] Although in certain psalms poverty is meant to signify material poverty, we should not immediately conclude that the poor described in the Psalms generally belonged to the oppressed and impoverished lower class.[39] Nor

---

37. Gunkel 1933, 184. The uncertainty of the attribution of the relevant suppliants portrayed as poor to the lower class of Israelite society can be established with the following examples: Ps 9:10 [9 EV] ויהי יהוה משגב לדך משגב לעתות בצרה "The LORD is a stronghold for the oppressed, a stronghold in times of trouble"; Ps 9:13 [12 EV] כי־דרש דמים אותם זכר לא־שכח צעקת עניים "For he who avenges blood is mindful of them; he does not forget the cry of the afflicted." However, in our view, the expressions "in times of trouble" (לעתות בצרה), "blood" (דמים), and "cry" (צעקת) illustrate a strong and severe act of persecution by the enemies, who imply a mortal threat to the suppliant, rather than chronic socioeconomic plight. In the narrative passages of the Hebrew Bible that are contextually more clearly profiled than in the Psalms (see, e.g., Gen 4:10; 1 Sam 19:5; 1 Kgs 2:5–31; 21:19; and 2 Kgs 9:7), the lexeme "blood" (דם) in the negative sense is mainly associated with treacherous murder attempts. Here, the economic aspect plays hardly any role (the only clear exception is the story of Naboth's vineyard, although in this case it is clear that Naboth does not belong to the economically poor). Hossfeld claims to be able to find in Ps 9:10, 13 references to "social need and exploitation" (1993, 81). Hossfeld's conclusion that the negative connotation of the lexeme "blood" (דם) in the Psalms carries a prominent socioeconomic character is based primarily on the fact that this lexeme is sometimes associated with the terminology relating to the poor. However, his conclusion, which emphasizes the economic character of the terminology relating to the poor in the relevant psalms, is highly speculative.

38. On this, see, e.g., Hossfeld and Zenger 1993, 14–15 and Lohfink 1990a, 101.

39. Here Pss 41:2; 68:6, 11; 72:2, 4, 12, 13; 82:3; and 112:9 could be mentioned, where the theme is about the wretched and disfranchised as well as their protection. The two groups in Ps 68:6 (the fatherless and the widow; here the stranger is missing) are no more than the socioeconomically poor. Similarly, the fatherless in Ps 82:3 (here the widow and the stranger are missing) is nothing but an object of special care as a marginalized group. In sharp contrast, a special theological connotation of the three groups is found in Pss 94:6 and 146:9. In Ps 94 the widow, the stranger, and the

can it be assumed that a uniquely religious connotation is intended by the use of certain terminology relating to the poor.

With regard to the Hodayot, the following discussion will consider whether the similar or identical theologies and eschatological orientations of the piety of the poor also found their way into the Psalter.[40] That is to say, we will examine whether situations similar to those described in the Hodayot are also reflected in certain psalms or sections of psalms.[41] By doing so, we can identify tendencies in the so-called psalms of the poor, clarifying whether the terminology relating to the poor refers to people such as those who are disenfranchised and disadvantaged or whether it rather witnesses those who are aware of their closeness to God in a special way and who regard their "being poor" as an inner, spiritual attitude, for example, humility before God as well as perseverance against their enemies.

Answering these questions in a comparative study might lead to a new and important awareness with regard to the question of the sociological and religious classification of the so-called piety of the poor. In the following discussion, we will therefore examine those psalms of the poor that contain statements coinciding with texts in the Hodayot.[42] Such an examination suggests that psalms which reflect the ideas of an older cultic order (e.g., Pss 41; 68; 72; 82; and 112) or which consider Israel to be the community of the poor of God (e.g., Pss 9–10 and 74) are hardly relevant for our discussion. Psalms 12; 25; 34; 35; 37; 40; 62; 69; 73; 76; 94; 102; 109; 140; 146; and 149 in particular need to be discussed.[43] Some of them

---

fatherless are delineated as a core part of God's people (עַם: Ps 94:5) and possession (נַחֲלָתֹך: Ps 94:5). In Ps 146:9, the three groups are juxtaposed as opposing terms to the wicked (רְשָׁעִים). This qualitative heterogeneity leads to the conclusion that the two types of psalms presuppose different theological orientations.

40. For further discussion of the Hodayot, see ch. 7, below.

41. See ch. 7, below.

42. See ch. 7, below.

43. Bremer (2016, 411–29) claims that Pss 4; 9–10; 12; 14; 22; 25; 31; 34; 35; 37; 40; and 41 reflect a homogeneous theology of the poor as the Psalms of David, shaped and formed by the same *Trägerkreis*. His opinion is mainly based on a retrospective view from the final stage of the period of canonization of the entire Psalter (ibid., 411–37). However, Bremer's "canonical" approach unfairly homogenizes the uniqueness of the relevant psalms of the poor and accordingly generalizes the peculiarity of the postexilic theology of the poor. In our view, the piety reflected in Pss 4; 9–10; 14; 22; 31; and 41 indicates a disparate theological orientation in comparison to the other

will be investigated in more detail. First, Ps 34 will be analyzed based on the author's translation and will provide the starting point for further clarification.

6.3. Psalm 34

6.3.1. Translation

(1) a Of David,
     b when he feigned insanity before Abimelech,
     c and he sent him away and he left.
(2) a I will bless YHWH at all times,
     b his praise shall continually be on my mouth.
(3) a My soul makes its boast in YHWH,
     b the humble shall hear and rejoice.
(4) a Proclaim with me the greatness of YHWH,

---

aforementioned psalms of the poor. It would be more appropriate to clarify and differentiate depending on whether the terms "Israel" or "God's people" are in fact meant (literally) as Israel as a whole or only as the truly pious group within the larger society. It should also be more carefully considered whether the terminology relating to the poor is employed to indicate a certain theological ideal that can be identified with the persecuted righteous. Bremer's opinion derives from his highly arbitrary choice of criteria for analyzing the psalms of the poor (semantic, thematic, and sociological [see ibid., 317–34]; instead, why not anthropological, theological and philosophical criteria?) and from his questionable three-stage reconstruction of the socioeconomic situation of Judean society in Persian-era Palestine (ibid., 301–16). One should remember that not only the chronological order of the archaeological stratigraphy and topography of the finds, including coinage, pottery, and stamp impressions (see Stern 1982, 93–142, 196–237; Betlyon 1986, 633–42; Lipschits 2005, 192–206; Lipschits and Vanderhooft 2007, 75–94; and Fantalkin and Tal 2013, 133–96 with further bibliography), but also even the demography and the borders of Yehud (see Stern 1982, 237–55; Lipschits 2006, 19–52; Lipschits and Tal 2007, 33–52; Finkelstein 2010, 39–54; Faust 2003, 37–53; 2013, 119–25; J. Wright 2006, 67–89; Carter 1999, 190–213; Ben-Zvi 1997, 194–209; J. Kessler 2002, 90–96; Weinberg 1992, 43–48; Barstad 2003, 3–14; 2008, 90–159; Janssen 1956, 39–42; Y. Levin 2013, 4–53; Guillaume 2014, 227–30; and Fantalkin and Tal 2013, 135–98 with further bibliography) are not solidly established and are still intensely debated. In light of the current state of archaeological as well as biblical scholarship, Bremer's conclusions reflect a mixture of (unproven) textual and archaeological presuppositions. For the demographic and economic situation in the exilic as well as the postexilic Judean communities in Palestine, see §3.3, above.

	b	and let us exalt his name together.
(5)	a	I have sought YHWH and he has answered me,
	b	and he frees me from all my fears.
(6)	a	Fix your gaze on YHWH and be radiant,
	b	and let not your faces be ashamed.[44]
(7)	a	This poor man: he cried out, YHWH: he heard,
	b	and delivered him from all his troubles.
(8)	a	The angel of YHWH encamps
	b	around those who fear him, and rescues them.
(9)	a	Taste and see that YHWH is good.
	b	blessed is the man who takes refuge in him.
(10)	a	Fear YHWH, you his holy ones;
	b	those who fear him lack nothing.
(11)	a	Young lions[45] may go needy and hungry,
	b	but those who seek YHWH shall not lack any good thing.
(12)	a	Come, children, listen to me,
	b	I will teach you the fear of YHWH.
(13)	a	Who is the man that takes delight in life,
	b	that loves days in order to see goodness?[46]
(14)	a	Guard your tongue from evil,
	b	and your lips from speaking deceit.
(15)	a	Turn away from evil and do good,
	b	seek peace and pursue it.
(16)	a	The eyes of YHWH are on the upright,
	b	and his ears turn to their cry for help.
(17)	a	YHWH's face is set against those who do evil,
	b	to cut off the memory of them from the earth.
(18)	a	They[47] cry out and YHWH hears,

---

44. Since MT ("They fixed their gaze on him and were radiant, and their faces shall not be ashamed") is barely comprehensible within its broader context, a correction along the lines of LXX and Syr. is necessary.

45. The expression "young lions" is a metaphor (e.g., Ps 35:17; Nah 2:12–14; see also Pss 7:3; 22:14, 21–22). There is no need to emend MT along the lines of LXX ("rich").

46. There is a slight difference in syntax between MT and LXX, whereby LXX attests to a later simplification of the word order.

47. Here LXX, Syr. and Tg. add "the righteous" in order to avoid the misunderstanding that "the wicked" mentioned in v. 17 are the subject in v. 18. However, as the *lectio brevior*, MT is to be preferred.

        b   and rescues them from all their troubles.

(19)   a   YHWH is near to the broken-hearted,

        b   he helps those whose spirit is crushed.

(20)   a   Though many hardships beset the upright,

        b   YHWH brings rescue from them all.

(21)   a   He watches over all his bones,

        b   not one of them will be broken.

(22)   a   Evil shall slay the wicked,

        b   and those who hate the upright will be punished.

(23)   a   YHWH ransoms the lives of his servants,

        b   and there will be no punishment for those who seek refuge in him.

6.3.2. Textual Analysis

6.3.2.1. Observations on Motifs and Style

Terminology relating to the poor appears twice in Ps 34: "My soul makes its boast in YHWH, the humble [עֲנָוִים] shall hear and rejoice" (34:3); "This poor man [עָנִי], he called out and YHWH heard, and delivered him from all his troubles" (34:7).

First, we need to clarify who these poor people are; specifically, what the intention is of the author of this psalm in using the terminology relating to the poor. We need to determine whether he means they were weak in an economic sense or humble in a religious sense. Second, a discussion of the motifs and style in Ps 34 will allow us to identify similarities and allusions to pericopes of the Qumran texts that will be discussed in the next chapter.

The use of the image of the lion (כְּפִירִים) in verse 11 can be regarded as an indication that Ps 34 shows a parallel to Zeph 3 and 1QH^a 13.[48] Such a supposition is also applicable to the warning against evil and deceitful speech in verse 14.[49] Furthermore, the positive evaluation of the broken hearts and the crushed spirit in verse 19 (קָרוֹב יהוה לְנִשְׁבְּרֵי־לֵב וְאֶת־דַּכְּאֵי־רוּחַ יוֹשִׁיעַ) clearly reminds us of נְכֵה רוּחַ in Isa 66:2; נכאי רוח in 1QM 11:10; and לֵב נָמֵס in 1QM 11:9 (see also 1QM 14:7). The pronounced antithesis between the poor ("holy," "upright," etc.) and the evildoers in Ps 34 should

---

48. In Zeph 3:3 and in 1QH^a 13:13, 18–19, the afflicting opposite is characterized as אֲרָיוֹת; see also Pss 7:3; 10:8–9; and 22:14, 17, 22.

49. See Zeph 3:13; otherwise, see also Jer 9:7 and Ps 50:19.

be assessed with its contrast (שנאי צדיק יאשמו against לא יאשמו כל־החסים
בו), highlighted in verse 22b and verse 23b, which stands close to the
eschatological orientation in Isa 66 and Zeph 3 concerning the fate of the
poor on the one hand and that of the godless on the other.[50] Moreover, it
must be mentioned that verse 5 (דרשתי את־יהוה) and verse 11 (דרשי יהוה)
with their theme of "seek YHWH" (see also v. 15, בקש שלום) clearly allude
to Zeph 2:3 (בקש את יהוה, בקש צדק, בקש ענוה), where the correct path of
salvation is shown to the poor.

6.3.2.2. The Question of Unity in Psalm 34

The psalm consists of two main parts: verses 2–11 and verses 12–23. Moreover, it can be subdivided as follows:

1. Hymnic introduction with alternating self-appeal and sum-
    moning others to praise YHWH (vv. 2–4)
2. Proclamation of the grateful person about his destiny (v. 5)
3. Teaching and confession (vv. 6–11)
4. Introductory saying (v. 12)
5. Didactic question (v. 13) and answer as a reminder (vv. 14–15)
6. Sapiential teachings on the principle of retribution (vv.
    16–23)[51]

In terms of form criticism, the first part (vv. 2–11) can be categorized as
a "thanksgiving song of the individual," while the second part (vv. 12–23)
approaches a pedagogical wisdom psalm.[52]

---

50. For the Qumran texts, see similarly 1QM 1:11–12; 7:5–6 and CD-A 8:1–3. The
texts of 1QM 1:11–12; 7:5–6 will be mentioned again in §6.6, below.

51. On this, see also Gunkel 1892 [1986], 142–43.

52. Verse 23 completely deviates from the alphabetical acrostic and is therefore
evaluated as a secondary addition by many scholars; on the other hand, in terms of
content, it matches very well with the preceding verses. For Hossfeld and Zenger,
"Verse 23 may be traced to postexilic editing (23b refers linguistically to 22b, 9b, while
23a uses new words and has a different emphasis: 'the servants' are honorific for Israel
in regard to its mission to people)" (1993, 211). However, Hossfeld and Zenger do
not take into consideration the fact that this "honorific" could also have been claimed
by a certain orientation of piety that regarded itself as the only true "Israel." See ibid.,
210–11 for it being a pedagogical wisdom psalm.

Due to its ambivalent form, Ps 34 has posed enormous difficulties throughout the history of research with regard to its genre and thus also with regard to the unity of the text. Since Ps 34 has an acrostic structure, there can be no doubt that the final text can be ascribed to one and the same author.[53]

6.3.2.3. The Logic and Structure of the Final Text

There is ongoing disagreement over whether the final text of Ps 34 is a loose collection of individual sayings or whether an author's uniform and consistent development of thought is present. For Duhm, Ps 34 is a "mosaic."[54] Crüsemann is of the same opinion: "This psalm is not a song of thanksgiving, but it is also not a hymn and not a wisdom song. It completely defies classification into any normal categories. None of the identifiable formal elements characterizes its overall form."[55] On the other hand, Gunkel considers Ps 34 to be a clear example of the "complete" song of thanksgiving of the individual and thus implicitly assumes the uniformity of Ps 34.[56] In regard to its sociological setting or *Sitz im Leben* he writes, "Particularly for this category we are still able to determine the original place in the religious ceremony with absolute certainty. The psalm of thanksgiving is originally part of a thanksgiving offering."[57] Zenger has also recently argued for the uniformity of the final text of Ps 34, although he concludes that the text could be a dynamically structured mixed form comprised of heterogeneous elements.[58]

One may infer that, since nowhere in Ps 34 does the suppliant speak to YHWH, the present psalm does not address God but rather the author's fellow men.[59] Personal words of thanks addressed to YHWH do not play a role; instead, the narrative and didactic intent of the author is signifi-

---

53. Only the ו-line between v. 6 and v. 7 is missing.

54. Duhm 1922, 97.

55. Crüsemann 1969, 296.

56. Gunkel 1933, 265–66. Gunkel analyses the subject much more critically in his other work (1892 [1986], 142–44).

57. Gunkel 1933, 265–66.

58. Hossfeld and Zenger 1993, 210.

59. In view of the author's strong interest in the joy of עֲנָוִים (34:3) and his expectation that the עֲנָוִים would rejoice in the author's experience of salvation (v. 3), there can be no doubt that the author and the עֲנָוִים together constitute a community sharing the same destiny.

cant. That is to say, the statement of concern in the psalm does not go in a vertical direction, but remains concentrated on the horizontal plane. The author's didactic intent provides an inner logic to Ps 34 despite its mixed form and mosaic character.

There are numerous examples illustrating that the didactic and pedagogical intentions of the author characterize the entire text of Ps 34 across various genres: Verse 3 states that the poor (ענוים) will listen to the praise of the author for his experience of salvation and rejoice. In verse 4, the group of listeners (probably identical to the ענוים in the preceding verse) is asked to join in the praise of God. In verses 6–11, the announcement of redemption is incorporated with verse 5 and alternately continued in the form of encouraging appeals and references to the salvific actions of YHWH. The didactic introduction in 34:12 begins the second part, which follows the teaching of wisdom. The author, now clearly in the role of a reflective sage, first combines a didactic question (v. 13) with an admonition referred to as an answer (vv. 14–15). This is followed by remarks typical of wisdom literature on the principle of retribution (vv. 16–23). Thus, by explaining, exhorting, and teaching, the statements in Ps 34 reveal one common goal, namely, to counsel and assure its listeners, especially the ענוים to take to heart the message and teaching passed on to them and to rejoice (v. 3). On the whole, Ps 34 is structured like "a comprehensive … teaching for life ('from A to Z')."[60]

Apart from the author's didactic concern, which characterizes the entire psalm, a number of lexical and thematic links are present between the first part (34:2–11) and the second part (34:12–23) of the psalm. These links reveal a consistent line of thought in Ps 34. For example, the participial construction "those who seek YHWH" (דרשי יהוה) in verse 11 can be interpreted as a clear reflection of verse 5 (דרשתי את־יהוה) and thus as linked to the message of salvation there. The keyword "good, goodness" (טוב) in verse 11b corresponds with the statement of verse 9 about the nature of YHWH (כי־טוב יהוה) and is also found in verse 15. In addition, the verb "to seek" (דרש) in verse 11 is thematically similar to בקש in verse 15. Another link may be found in verse 5, corresponding topically and in part also lexically with verse 18 (see respectively נצל in the *hiphil* form with YHWH as the subject):[61]

_____

60. Hossfeld and Zenger 1993, 211.

61. On the *niphal* form of נצל appearing in the piety-of-the-poor-oriented redaction of the book of Jeremiah, see §4.3, above; see also Ps 34:20.

דרשתי את־יהוה וענני ומכל־מגורותי הצילני   34:5:
צעקו ויהוה שמע ומכל־צרותם הצילם   34:18:

Furthermore, the expression "the fear of YHWH" (יראת יהוה) in verse 12 refers lexically and thematically to the verbal expressions in verse 10 (יראו and ליראיו) and in verse 8 (ליראיו). The fear of YHWH is therefore one of the central theological topics in Ps 34 and connects its two parts. The motif of "hearing of YHWH" plays a major role in verse 7 (שמע) in the first part as well as in verse 16 (אזניו) and verse 18 (שמע) in the second. In addition, verse 2 and verse 14 set up a contrast: 34:2 refers to the speech appropriate for the pious (תהלתו בפי), while v. 14 warns against evil and deceptive words (לשונך מרע ושפתיך מדבר מרמה). Another link is found in the motif of "hiding in YHWH," which is used in verse 9 (יחסה־בו) as well as in verse 23 (כל־החסים בו). Finally, verse 7 and verse 19 are closely associated with the reference to YHWH's "help" (cf. הושיעו in v. 7 and יושיע in v. 19).

In conclusion, in light of its subject matter, one may agree with Joachim Becker that Ps 34, like other acrostic psalms, is a "composition from the desk of a scholar in the postexilic wisdom milieu."[62] However, the decisive point is that this composition and the mixed form of the psalm are characterized by the author's consistent line of thought. Certain phrases in the psalm, such as "to hide oneself in YHWH," "to seek YHWH," and "(not) to become ruined," which in the older lamentations and thanksgiving songs have a particular meaning determined by their *Sitz im Leben*, now act as an expression of an inner pious attitude to which the author is committed. Therefore, we can conclude that the author has before him not a cultic ceremony but rather a group of pious people close to him.

6.3.3. The Question of the Authorial Voice in Psalm 34[63]

A majority of researchers accept that עני in 34:7 should be regarded as the

---

62. Becker 1975, 77.

63. For our investigation, generally we must note that the "I" (or the "suppliant") speaking in the relevant psalms of the poor cannot be identified exclusively as a concrete individual (so also Becker 1975, 85; Lohfink 1986, 174; Gerstenberger 1995, 5–6; and Hossfeld and Zenger 1993, 14–15); every member of the community who could apply the statements in the psalms of the poor to themselves should be able to identify themselves with the "I." In the case of Ps 34, this means that the "I" stands for one who is teaching rather than one who is praying. Therefore, the "I" in Ps 34 is not only for

self-depiction of the speaker himself.[64] Hence, he is a "poor one." But what exactly does he say about himself? Does he consider himself to be poor from a socioeconomic point of view, and should his experience of salvation thus be interpreted as liberation from his economically miserable situation? The following observations speak against such an interpretation.

First, the relationship between זה and עני in verse 7 is not appositional, but thought to be demonstrative.[65] Diethelm Michel interprets verse 7 as follows: "This poor one: he cried, Yahweh: he answered."[66] According to Michel, the structure of the sentence in question in verse 7 should be seen syntactically as one "nominal clause after another nominal clause."[67] According to their nature, neither nominal clause describes a sequence of action; rather, they set the statements about their subjects in relation to each other.[68] The point in 34:7 is that both the subjects, namely, "this poor one" and "YHWH," are set in juxtaposition to each other. Therefore, even after being saved by YHWH, the suppliant remains a "poor one." We have before us an attitude or disposition.[69] This leads to the conclusion that, for the suppliant, being "poor" is not a temporal or changeable matter.

Second, concerning the strong interest of the suppliant in the joy of the עניים in verse 3, we noted above that the suppliant and the עניים together constitute a type of community sharing the same destiny.[70] This opens up the possibility of gathering more precise information regarding the socioeconomic situation of the group of addressees as well as that of the speaker.

---

the author himself, but the author might be using the "I" to portray all of the pious individuals close to him.

64. See, e.g., Kraus 1978, 419; and Hossfeld and Zenger 1993, 210.

65. Birkeland 1933a, 68; see also Kraus 1978, 419: "In verse 7, beginning with זה, the psalmist's destiny is referred to paradigmatically and demonstratively."

66. Michel 1960, 81. According to Michel, the translation "he was a poor one, he cried, YHWH answered" would be wrong, since this implies that the suppliant was poor before being rescued by YHWH but now (following God's salvation) he is not "poor" any longer.

67. Ibid., 185.

68. Ibid.

69. The terminology relating to the poor also functions in the Qumran texts not as a description of changing circumstances but rather as an indication of a permanent attitude or disposition. On this matter, see §7.1.2, below.

70. Thus, עניים and עני in Ps 34 are used contextually without any differentiation in meaning.

Here it is very revealing that the following statements characterize the group of listeners, who are identical with the ענוים:

1. The holy ones of YHWH (קדשיו, v. 10)
2. Those that seek YHWH (v. 11)
3. The sons (בנים, cf. v. 12)
4. Those that love life and wish to see good days (v. 13)
5. The righteous (צדיקים and צדיק, vv. 16, 20, 22)
6. Those that have a broken heart and crushed spirit (לנשברי לב ואת דכאי רוח, v. 19)
7. The servants of YHWH (עבדיו, v. 23)

The group of listeners indicated as ענוים is primarily seen here as a religious and wisdom-oriented group of people for whom economic factors do not play any role.[71] Nowhere is there a suggestion that the suppliant and his group of listeners were made poor through exploitation by an enemy; nor do they suffer from a lack of material possessions. The deprivation the speaker mentions in verse 5 and verse 7 should not be seen as a condition of misery caused by material poverty. The phrases "from all my fears" (מכל-מגורותי) and "from all his troubles" (מכל-צרותיו) refer more to threats by enemies than to chronic socioeconomic plight. The lexeme "fear" (מגורה) appears only three times in the entire Hebrew Bible (Ps 34:5; Prov 10:24; and Isa 66:4). In Prov 10:24 and Isa 66:4, מגורה points to a sudden disastrous turning point, which contextually does not suggest the idea of material poverty:

Prov 10:24: מגורת רשע היא תבואנו ותאות צדיקים יתן
What the wicked dread will come upon them, but the desire of the righteous will be granted.

Isa 66:4: גם-אני אבחר בתעלליהם ומגורתם אביא להם יען קראתי ואין עונה דברתי ולא שמעו ויעשו הרע בעיני ובאשר לא-חפצתי בחרו
I also will choose to mock them, and bring upon them what they fear; because, when I called, no one answered, when I spoke, they did not listen; but they did what was evil in my sight, and chose what did not please me.

---

71. Brueggemann and Bellinger 2014, 169–70.

The interest of the speaker as well as of his listeners in Ps 34 concentrates on success in life. The question after the corresponding behavior (v. 13) and subsequent deliberations do not allow us to conclude that here being "poor," "upright," or "servants" implies a life of material poverty. The following will clearly show just the opposite; in regard to the aforementioned observations, we can assume that here "poor" primarily indicates a religious and sapiential category.

Third, if we understand the terminology relating to the poor in 34:3 and verse 7 in socioeconomic terms and assume that it indicates material poverty, then such an interpretation is contradictory to verse 10b: "Those who fear him lack nothing" (כי־אין מחסור ליראיו). This point is reaffirmed by verse 11b: "Those who seek YHWH shall not lack any good thing" (ודרשי יהוה לא־יחסרו כל־טוב). In the opinion of the speaker, therefore, it is those who neither fear nor seek YHWH that will suffer "from lack of all goodness." Thus, we cannot infer from the terminology relating to the poor that the author and his addressees see themselves as impoverished and belonging to a lower class. The antonyms "poor" and "rich" do not play any role in Ps 34.[72]

The religious wisdom of the speaker is also an indicator of this. That the suppliant comes from a milieu of wisdom literature can be further established with reference to the following elements in Ps 34:

1. The fear of God as the basic tenet for a successful life (cf. vv. 8, 10, and 12 with Prov 1:7; 9:10; and 15:33)[73]
2. The ideal of a long and happy life (cf. v. 13 with Prov 3:13–18)

---

72. Many commentators (e.g., Duhm, Gunkel, Kraus, and Zenger) maintain, however, that in light of LXX the word "young lions" (כפירים) in v. 11 should be emended and translated rather as "rich." In their view, the term כפירים occurs without any reference to the previous verses and is therefore completely unsuitable within its broader context. From this point of view, the contradictory terms "poor-rich" in the material sense would be an important aspect in Ps 34. However, as already mentioned, the image of a lion is used frequently in the Hebrew Bible to indicate hostile and threatening behavior, as is the case in some psalms of the poor (e.g., Pss 22:14 and 35:17) and in prophetic writings (e.g., Ezek 22:25 and Zeph 3:3). This can also be seen in a few Qumran texts (e.g., 1QHᵃ 13:13, 18–19). Thus, the "young lion" motif occurring in v. 11 in no way compels us to assume any corruption of the text (so also Roberts 1973, 265–67); the reading of LXX is clearly the *lectio facilior*.

73. Brueggemann and Bellinger 2014, 169–70.

3. The religionness related to a cause-and-effect relationship based on rational schemes of retributive justice (vv. 13–23)
4. Admonition in the context of a didactic question-and-answer (vv. 13–15)

Finally, we cannot ignore the affinity of Ps 34 to other wisdom psalms such as Pss 25; 37; 62; and 73. These psalms are now widely recognized as containing a postexilic, so-called theologized wisdom; the contents they articulate apparently reflect the worldview of certain educated circles of the upper class or at least members of the middle class interested in religious wisdom and piety.[74]

6.4. Parallels to Psalm 34

6.4.1. Psalm 62

Some of the parallels between Ps 34 and Ps 62 are so conspicuous that we need to explore, from the viewpoint of Ps 62, the possibility of more precisely identifying the theological group responsible for the piety of the poor. We can recognize the following thematic and lexical similarities between Pss 34 and 62.

1. The sapiential character (the admonitions to believe in God in Ps 62:10–11; the statement of numbers in Ps 62:12)[75]
2. The principle of retributive justice (cf. Ps 34:13–23 with Ps 62:13)
3. The aversion to malice and deceitful conversation (cf. Ps 34:14 with Ps 62:5)
4. The didactic intent of the suppliant with regard to the audience (cf. Ps 34:12 with Ps 62:9), which is based on personal experience and individual piety (cf. Ps 34:5, 7 with Ps 62:1–8)[76]
5. Factional antagonism (cf. Ps 34:22–23 with Ps 62:4–5)

---

74. Gordis 1944, 161–63; Pleins 1987, 62–64; Albertz 1992, 545 n. 44; on the other hand, Kraus (1978, 419) interprets the עֲנָוִים as "despondent" and "people in need of help" and as such implicitly understood to be economically poor.

75. Hossfeld and Zenger 2000, 180.

76. See ibid.: "The confession of trust is spoken per se before others and is like a testimony. This is also evident from the direction of the speech: God is not addressed,

6. The motif of "taking refuge in God" (cf. Ps 62:8 [מחסי באלהים],
   9 with Ps 34:9 [יחסה־בו])
7. The motif of the "help/relief of YHWH" (cf. Ps 62:2, 3, 7
   [ישועתי] with Ps 34:7, 19)

Considering these parallels, the assumption is that Ps 34 and Ps 62 can be traced to the same group of authors or, at least, that they belong to a group of adherents with a similar theological and social background regardless of the fact that the terminology relating to the poor is not necessarily found in Ps 62.

In the past, various commentators have noted that the speaker or suppliant in Ps 62 is not just an ordinary believer of YHWH, but a person who is specially qualified.[77] Therefore, according to Duhm, the suppliant is a high priest, while Willy Staerk characterizes him as a "revered person in a leading position."[78] According to Weiser, the suppliant has become the leader of the community by virtue of "his calm disposition of mind," having "the correct standard" and dispensing "confident judgment."[79] Hans Schmidt believes that he is one who is suffering for being accused.[80]

---

but the text is of and about God.... The speaker of the psalm intends to pass on to others his own way of trust in God which he 'learned' in vv. 2–8 as a teaching of life."

77. Many scholars argue that there is a secondary textual expansion in Ps 62. For example, Balla describes Ps 62 as "the religion of the heart, which requires no mediation of the cult, no priest, no sacrifice, but communication of the pious soul with its God in a quiet chamber" (1912, 15). In order to uphold his assumption, Balla has to identify vv. 9–12 as secondary elements "which were added due to the mixture of styles out of completely different genres" (ibid., 16). On the other hand, Seybold (1996, 244) is of the opinion that Ps 62 reflects the arguments made by someone who is driven into a sanctuary of asylum with his persecutors. He classifies vv. 2–3, 6–7, and 13 as a secondary addition. As opposed to these positions, the consistent development of thought in Ps 62 should be highlighted. The psalm begins with the self-instruction of the author ("Be silent in God, my soul!" in v. 2). Following this, the circle of the author's audience is gradually broadened. In vv. 4–5 the author focuses on his enemies, and in vv. 9–12 he finally turns to the community of his audience. His thoughts are consistent from the beginning to the end, with an emphasis on trust in God over trust in other things. Therefore, Ps 62 should be regarded as a literary unity, and literary-critical operations are not necessary. For this approach, see, e.g., Kraus 1978, 598; see also Hossfeld and Zenger 2000, 180–82, who are more careful on this issue.

78. Duhm 1922, 243; Staerk 1911, 222.

79. Weiser 1966, 304.

80. See H. Schmidt 1934, 118; Kraus 1978, 596; and Beyerlin 1970, 28, who regard

In spite of many differences, all the efforts outlined here to determine the identity of the suppliant of Ps 62 move in a direction that understands the suppliant as an institutionally exceptional person. Therefore, the suppliant is not merely an ordinary person, but one who is aware of his obligations to a wider circle or one who has a public mission of particular significance. Like the suppliant in Ps 34, he is expected to communicate the piety that he pursues to the circle of his audience.[81] The suppliant's call to his community (hardly a community of common people) and his instructions (Ps 62:9) are clear evidence of his political influence and his religious authority in the community.[82]

But, on the other hand, the suppliant asserts that he is attacked and deceived (62:4, 5).[83] In his assertion of trust, the speaker describes God repeatedly as "my rock" (צורי), "my help" (ישועתי), and "my protection" (משגבי). By underlining all that he acknowledges here as assured by God, he indicates at the same time the gravity of his threatened and insecure situation. Such a situation—that an influential religious leader is threatened and persecuted—can only be explained by the fact that his religious authority and his public actions are appreciated and acknowledged only by a limited circle but resisted and rejected by others.[84] Assuming the pres-

---

Ps 62 as a ritual text for the accused at the sanctuary where he has found protection from his persecutors. In contrast, Hossfeld and Zenger oppose this hypothesis: "The outlined distinctiveness of the Psalms makes the theory that the psalm had been formed and used as a ritual text for sanctuary asylum quite improbable. The image of sanctuary asylum may have been employed here as a metaphor of protection and refuge which characterizes this psalm in general; however, it is simply an aspect of the mixture of metaphors in this psalm" (Hossfeld and Zenger 2000, 181).

81. Brueggemann and Bellinger 2014, 273–75.

82. Cf. Ps 40:10–11, which is similar.

83. The adversaries "rush" (Kraus 1978, 594–95) against the suppliant, who feels like a "collapsing wall." Here, the contrast between the helplessness of an individual and his numerous adversaries' chances of attack should be highlighted. For a different view, see Hossfeld and Zenger 2000, 183–84.

84. The somewhat odd עם in v. 9 can be explained well with this hypothesis. In LXX we read כל עדת עם. Regarding the animosities from the opponent group, we have to suppose that the suppliant was not in a position to influence the "entire community of people" with his didactic psalm. Therefore, by כל עדת עם what is meant is the circle reduced to the audience of the suppliant, the religiously qualified "true" Israel, a group that we can call, following Gunkel (1933, 181), "the distraught friends" ("die verzweifelten Freunde").

ence of an opposing faction, we must investigate what kind of group this opposing faction was.

The reference in 62:5 that the opposing faction "blesses" the speaker in public but "curses" (יקללו) him in secret is clear evidence that there is direct contact and there are regular encounters between the factions and their members.[85] Moreover, we may infer from the reference to בפיו יברכו ובקרבם יקללו that hostilities have not yet broken out openly. This could be an indication that the opposing faction acts cautiously and must exercise restraint in public, which may be due to the public standing or influence of the speaker and the social position of the circle that constitutes his audience.[86]

We may conclude, therefore, that this is a situation in the Persian period in which the confrontation between both factions does not yet imply a total break or an irreversible split in the community of YHWH.[87] Also, the speaker of the psalm does not yet respond with annihilation appeals directed at YHWH or with verdicts of total rejection.[88] We may further conclude from the nature of the discussion that a certain equal status prevailed; thus, we can understand from the behavior of the opposing faction that the speaker's circle is a group that is to be feared. Accordingly, we can assume that this is not a conflict between the upper and lower classes, where the distribution of power would be altogether unbalanced.

If we can infer from the reference to the activities of the adversaries in verse 4 (תהותתו and תרצחו) and in verse 5 that the conflict takes place within influential, power-conscious circles, that is, among members of the upper class, then according to the observations made so far the speaker and his audience must be in at least a similar socioeconomic or political position.[89] This can also be inferred from verse 11, where the suppliant's

---

85. Hossfeld and Zenger 2000, 182: "The description of the situation in v. 5cd also requires a background where the speaker of the psalm apparently lives 'peacefully' with his enemies."

86. This assessment does not contradict the view established in v. 4 that the opposing faction threatens the speaker frontally because on the side of the opposing faction there must have been a wide spectrum of attitudes of rejection and hostility, from covert distancing to open aggression.

87. Most researchers place Ps 62 in the postexilic period; see, e.g., Pohlmann 1989, 51; Albertz 1992, 547; and Seybold 1996, 244. On the split of the community, see Stolz 1983, 52; and Hossfeld and Zenger 2000, 182.

88. See, e.g., the suppliant in the so-called confessions in the book of Jeremiah.

89. Albertz 1992, 547.

admonitions to his followers presuppose that it is at least theoretically possible to pressure the others politically and economically.[90]

In principle, we can also assume a corresponding socioeconomic situation for the speaker of Ps 34 and his circle of followers.[91] The fact that in Ps 34 references to any open confrontation between the speaker and his adversaries as well as massive accusations are absent suggests that until then, although tensions existed between both sides and the speaker felt threatened, it had probably not come to an open break, to a split in the community of YHWH.[92] As mentioned above, the speaker and his audience may belong to a circle of religious, wisdom-oriented, and learned people; that is to say, as such they cannot be members of a lower class, but of an upper class. In regard to the socioeconomic structure of the late Persian and Hellenistic Judean community, we may assume with certainty a differentiation of the classes. Between the lay as well as the priestly aristocracy at the top of the community on the one hand and the impoverished lower class on the other, there must have been another intermediate social stratum. For example, the scribe (ספר) Ben Sira could not have belonged to the most privileged class of the Judean community but rather to an upper class or at least an upper middle class circle.[93] As Lenski remarks,

---

90. In contrast to Seybold 1996, 246, who is of the opinion that the admonitions are not aimed at the followers of the suppliant but rather at his persecutors. However, an admonishing statement of this nature does not fit well with what is said about the adversaries in vv. 4–5. Hossfeld and Zenger 2000, 182: "The essentially wisdom-oriented nature of the psalm and the social location reflected in v. 11 (the possibility to suppress others or to attain riches) suggest that the psalm is derived from the milieu of 'academic wisdom.'"

91. It is probable that Ps 34 is a postexilic composition. This is confirmed not only by close parallelisms with Ps 62 but also by its acrostic form, which became prevalent as an art form in the exilic/postexilic period (Kraus 1978, 418). A preexilic origin is also challenged by the fact that the lexemes דרש in v. 11 (with YHWH as the object) and בקש in v. 15 (with שלום as the object) are used with a religious connotation. The words obviously characterize a certain type of spiritual attitude and religious behavior (otherwise mainly in the sense of "looking for something" as a routine activity of daily life, e.g., in Gen 42:22 and Lev 10:16; see W. Herrmann 1999, 71–72). This type of religious usage of the terms is normally only the case in exilic or postexilic texts (on בקש, see, e.g., Exod 33:7; Deut 4:29; and Isa 45:19; 51:1; on דרש, see, e.g., Deut 4:29 and Isa 9:12).

92. Significantly, the crisis of the suppliant mentioned in v. 5 with מכל־מגורותי and with מכל־צרותיו in v. 7 is not associated with the wicked in vv. 17 and 22.

93. On this, see, e.g., Hengel 1988, 241–43.

in advanced agrarian societies there was a considerable number of people in occupations whose socioeconomic standing fell somewhere between the two extremes.[94] Furthermore, advanced agrarian societies reflect an increasing overlap in the statuses of different classes of people, especially regarding wealth and property.[95] The gradation of the classes seems to have developed gradually in the Judean communities in Palestine beginning in the mid-fifth century BCE, when the Judean socioeconomic structure was slowly beginning to be rebuilt from the simplified social hierarchy that is typical of a postcollapse society.[96]

This can only suggest a constellation of factions within the upper class in which one group presents itself as poor, holy, upright, and servants of YHWH while members of the other hostile faction are blamed as godless evildoers, as in Ps 34. The "poor and righteous" are clearly in the weaker position, as can be concluded from self-depictions especially in verse 19 לנשברי־לב ואת־דכאי־רוח and the references to frequent suffering in verse 20.

6.4.2. Psalm 25 and Psalm 40

Psalm 25 is also related to Ps 34 in several ways and should also be considered here. Psalm 25, like Ps 34, belongs to the group of acrostic psalms: "with regard to the acrostic, this psalm has a close relative in Ps 34 (one-line acrostic, missing *waw* verse, additional *pe* verse as a supplication of redemption for Israel, synonymous verse beginning in the *mem, ayin* and *pe* lines, central position of the *lamed* line)."[97] Besides this formal relationship, both psalms have in many ways some commonalities with regard to content: "Both psalms agree in their perception of God and in their ethical objectives."[98] As in Ps 34, the opposing faction in Ps 25 shows relatively pale contours; Ps 25:2, 19 speaks merely of the "enemies" of the suppliant. As in Ps 34, the suppliant considers himself to be with the group of the poor (25:9, 16); he trusts in YHWH, hopes in him and, as in Ps 34:8, 10, 12 regards the members of the group as those that fear YHWH (25:12).

The question of whether both psalms (25 and 34) should be regarded as "cornerstone psalms" within the literary block consisting of Pss 25–34,

---

94. Lenski, Nolan, and Lenski 1995, 216.
95. Ibid.
96. Tainter 1999, 1023–24.
97. Hossfeld and Zenger 1993, 161.
98. Ibid., 211.

which had its origin in postexilic editing ("supplication"–"thanksgiving") must remain unanswered here.[99] In any case, based on common formal and thematic features, we can safely assume that Pss 25 and 34 originated from the same theological circle of authors.

What is particularly interesting for our question is that "the social characterization of the poor goes into the background or is hardly tangible, whereas the religious description comes into the foreground."[100] Thus, in Ps 25 everything focuses on the suppliant's religious confession of sins (25:7, 11, 18). As a "poor man," he is a pious man who is worried about his own sins. This fervent confession of sins reminds us in many ways of the pessimistic anthropology in the Hodayot, where the suppliant admits his sinfulness before God (cf. Ps 25:7, 11, 18 with 1QH[a] 9:21–25).[101]

With regard to the theme of sin and the corresponding pessimistic anthropology, we must refer to another psalm of the poor, namely, Ps 40.[102] As in Ps 25:9, 16, the suppliant in Ps 40:18 considers himself to be poor and, as in Ps 25, he emphasizes his own sinfulness (Ps 40:13), which is once again comparable with certain statements in the Hodayot.[103] The suppliants in Pss 25 and 40 consider themselves to be sinners but do not cease at this negative assessment. The postulate of a special religious status emerges dialectically from the confession of being a sinner. Thus, the suppliant and the community associated with him wish to be seen as pious and as especially favored by God (see Pss 25:4–6, 9–10, 12–17, 20–21; 40:3–6, 8–12).

Apparently, this paradoxical juxtaposition of an awareness of futility with being the chosen is a fundamental characteristic of the suppli-

---

99. So also Hossfeld and Zenger 2000, 180.

100. Hossfeld and Zenger 1993, 161.

101. For a detailed discussion of the pessimistic anthropology in the Hodayot, see §7.1.1, below. A similarly pessimistic anthropology is also found in Ps 62:10; see Hossfeld and Zenger 2000, 186, who confirm here an "anthropological statement of nullity" ("*anthropologische Nichtigkeitsaussage*"). See also Koenen 1995, 84, who understands Ps 102:4, 12 as a "statement on human transience" ("*Aussage über die menschliche Vergänglichkeit*").

102. On vv. 14–18, see Ps 70.

103. Ps 40:12: "For evils have encompassed me without number; my iniquities have overtaken me, until I cannot see; they are more than the hairs of my head, and my heart fails me." 1QH[a] 9:21–22: "I am a creature of clay, fashioned with water, a foundation of shame and a source of impurity, an oven of iniquity and a building of sin, a spirit of error and depravity without knowledge" (trans. García Martínez and Tigchelaar 1997, 159).

ants' piety in Ps 25 as well as Ps 40 and is therefore constitutive of their theology.[104] The terminology relating to the poor in these psalms of the poor should be examined in relation to acknowledgement of one's own sinfulness.[105] This acknowledgement makes these pious people evaluate themselves as being "poor before God." At the same time, however, it is a religious privilege and a precondition for their special status before God. The enemies do not have this awareness of being poor and humble before God. In this regard, the poor man is distinctly different from his arrogant adversaries (cf. Ps 40:5).

However, despite the aforementioned parallelisms between Pss 25 and 40, we cannot disregard the fact that there are certain obvious differences between these two psalms of the poor with regard to content. Thus, for example, instead of the relatively bleak portrayal of the enemy in Ps 25, the confrontation in Ps 40 between the pious suppliant and his adversaries is depicted pointedly.[106] The enemies in Ps 40 behave much more aggressively against the suppliant than those in Ps 25. Their aversion to the suppliant is no longer on the emotional level (Ps 25:19), and Ps 40:15–16 might allude to concrete hostile actions.[107]

---

104. A possible preliminary phase of these theological reflections may be present in Pss 25 and 40 and might ultimately have resulted in the pessimistic anthropology in the Hodayot.

105. For the parallelism between "sinners" and "poor," see Ps 25:8–9.

106. Even though the adversaries' "deadly hatred" toward the suppliant is reported in Ps 25:19, a concrete violent act by the adversaries is not found anywhere in Ps 25. The suppliant's "fear," "distress" (v. 17), "affliction" and "troubles" (v. 18) are not explicitly associated with the adversaries.

107. "Let all those be put to shame and confusion who seek to snatch away my life; let those be turned back and brought to dishonor who desire my hurt. Let those be appalled because of their shame who say to me, 'Aha, Aha!'" (Ps 40:15–16). It is also intriguing that Ps 25 is colored by Deuteronomistic phrases and concepts that are absent in Ps 40, such as the "name theology" (Ps 25:11), the theme of inheriting the land (Ps 25:13), and the verb "to teach" (למד piel; Ps 25:4, 5, 9). For further details, see Marttila 2012, 73–75. However, as argued in ch. 4, above, the theological group that was responsible for the piety-of-the-poor-oriented redaction in the book of Jeremiah frequently directed severe criticism at Deuteronomistic theology while also employing Deuteronomistic phrases and themes. Thus, it is doubtful whether the seemingly Deuteronomistic features reflected in Ps 25 are truly Deuteronomistic. In our view, the Deuteronomistic spirit is not wholeheartedly embraced in Ps 25.

Furthermore, it is significant that in Ps 40:7, as in Isa 66:3, there is a strong critique of the sacrificial cult that is absent in Ps 25.[108] In light of this and the aforementioned intensification of the confrontation in Ps 40, we can assume that Ps 40 indicates a clear split in the Judean community (see Isa 66:3).[109] This change apparently indicates a diachronic evolution. Therefore, Ps 40 could reflect a historically later situation than that of Ps 25.

If we ask why the tension that was still latent in Ps 25 developed into an open confrontation within the community of YHWH and which events could have played a role in the latter, we must look particularly to Pss 37 and 73 for further clues.

6.4.3. Psalms 37 and 73

6.4.3.1. Psalm 37

There are clear parallels between Ps 37 and Pss 25; 34; 40; and 62:

1. The juxtaposition of "righteous against wicked" in Ps 37, which once again reflects factional antagonism within the community of YHWH (cf. vv. 1–2, 9–24 with Pss 25:2–3, 19; 34:11, 16–18, 22–23; 40:2, 5, 15–16; 62:4–5)
2. The emphatic promise of the possession of land to the pious in Ps 37:9, 11, 29 and the blessing of material prosperity for the children or descendants of the righteous in Ps 37:26, all of which remind us of the traditional sapiential concept of retributive justice according to the cause-and-effect relationship in Ps 25:13[110]

---

108. Ps 40:7 "Sacrifice and offering you do not desire, but you have given me an open ear. Burnt offering and sin offering you have not required."

109. Hossfeld and Zenger assume this as well: "In this form, [Ps 40] is well suited as a prayer of a local cult community in the countryside that performed its worship without the sacrificial cult. We could also suppose, based on the content of the psalm, that due to theological as well as political reasons, the local cult group increasingly opposed the claim to power by the priestly circle at the temple of Jerusalem.... This could ... not be regarded as a biographical individual statement, but as 'group awareness'" (1993, 252).

110. On the motif of "land possession of the righteous," see also Isa 60:21 and 1 En. 5.7. For the theme of retributive justice, see Hossfeld and Zenger 1993, 164–66.

3. The emphasis on the practice of righteous conversation (cf. v. 30 with Pss 34:14; 40:5; and 62:5)[111]

4. The suppliant's didactic involvement with his audience, which pertains to his personal experiences. These factors play an especially important role in verses 21–29 in the context of imparting insights of wisdom concerning the consequences of the צדיק and of the רשע

5. The ideal image of the suppliant as "the calm, silent one" (cf. v. 7 with Ps 62:2, 6) and "the humble, poor one" (cf. v. 11 with Ps 34:3, 7)

6. The acrostic form (cf. Pss 25 and 34)[112]

7. The verbal similarities between Ps 34:15 and Ps 37:27 (סור מרע ועשה טוב)

8. The emphasis on internalization of the torah in Ps 37:31 and Ps 40:9

Psalm 37 belongs form-critically to the genre of didactic poetry.[113] It consists of twenty-two individual verses that together constitute a self-contained logical unit and not a mere collection of verses. This is evident from the form of the acrostic. In addition to this, the psalm is characterized by three interconnected and closely related primary themes that motivate the suppliant:

1. The success of the wicked: "Do not worry about the success of the wicked" (vv. 1, 7)

2. Trust in God: "Trust, hope, await upon YHWH, the righteous will not be shamed, but will own the land" (vv. 3, 7, 19, 22, 34)

3. The fate of the wicked: "The wicked come to an evil end, only a short time; and then the wicked one is no longer there" (vv. 2, 10, 20)

---

111. These emphases seem to form a theological correspondence with the piety-of-the-poor-oriented redaction's repulsion against false prophecies (Jer 7:4 and 7:8 [דברי השקר]; Jer 20:6 [נבאת להם בשקר]); see ch. 4, above.

112. This is an important indication for dating the psalm to the postexilic period.

113. Kraus 1978, 439; Hossfeld and Zenger 1993, 229; Witte 2014, 49–50; Brueggemann and Bellinger 2014, 184.

In comparison to Pss 25; 34; and 62, the speaker in Ps 37 concentrates on the fact that the wicked and evil ones are (at least for a while) especially prosperous (cf. vv. 1, 7, 16, 20, 35).[114] In this regard he turns to the one who is enraged and agitated about the glaring socioeconomic condition of such contemporaries (see especially the second-person sg. form of address in vv. 4–6).[115] With "you" a group is meant that begins to doubt the validity of God's principle of retributive justice in light of the prosperity of the wicked. The speaker admonishes this group of people to trust in God (vv. 3, 6) to wait upon him (v. 7), and to hope in him (v. 9). With reference to the future perspective intended by God for them (e.g., "possession of the land"; vv. 9, 11, 22, 29, and 34) he encourages them, in contrast to the wicked, to conserve their manner and attitude as the "poor" (ענוים and עני, vv. 11, 14) and "righteous" (צדיק and צדיקים, vv. 16, 21, 29).

The fact that with the terminology relating to the poor (ענוים and עני, vv. 11, 14) the suppliant is in no way alluding to any economic adversity is evident in Ps 37, which uses ענוים synonymously with "the righteous" as the ideal of piety.[116] According to verses 21 and 26, the righteous are in a position to distribute alms and to help others (וצדיק חונן ונותן) and are so prosperous that they are well-fed even in times of famine (vv. 18–19). The children of the righteous never need to beg (v. 25) because there is enough money even for lending. They are a blessing to others and not a burden (v. 26).

Moreover, with regard to the question concerning the historical background of the speaker in Ps 37 and how poverty is understood, we need to consider the following:

First of all, it is apparent that the so-called concept of retributive justice is expressed more clearly in Ps 37 than in Pss 25; 34; and 62, and, significantly, its applicability is often emphasized (37:1–2, 9, 14–15, 25). We can infer from this that this concept was no longer accepted without

114. It is normally assumed that Ps 37 was conceived in the postexilic period (see, e.g., Kraus 1978, 439; Witte 2014, 43–48). According to Hossfeld and Zenger, the psalm comes close "to the teaching advocated by the friends of Job without the problematization of this position accomplished by Job's refutation. This dates the text to the fifth century" (1993, 229). On the prosperity of the wicked, see Brueggemann and Bellinger 2014, 183.

115. The expression קנא in v. 1 is mainly used in the Psalms and the wisdom literature in order to indicate the meaning "to be envious of the success of adversaries and rivals" (see Ps 73:3; Prov 3:31; 23:17; 24:1, 19; and Gen 26:14).

116. Birkeland 1933a, 88–89.

question by the audience of the author of this psalm; therefore, doubts are raised among the speaker's audience that he seeks to clarify. At the same time, it is obvious that in addition the speaker no longer adheres to this concept naively or optimistically. Of course, in Pss 25; 34; and 62 emphatic references are made to a cause-and-effect relationship, and there might be doubts about its functioning. But compared to these psalms, the formulations חרה and קנא in Ps 37:1 may indicate that, in the meantime, questioning among the audience has increased.[117]

In addition, it is striking that nowhere in Ps 37 can we find an indication that points to material poverty as the reason for the pious to be zealous; there are no references at all to needs of the poor such as hunger, nakedness, homelessness, or begging.[118] Apparently, it was not their own economic need that they had to overcome; it was a malaise of a different kind that they were unable to deal with, namely, that the wicked could resist and act against the will of God and yet prosper politically and economically. Their own concrete, material difficulties were not the actual reason for doubting YHWH's retributive justice, but the perception that wicked attitudes and actions have brought socioeconomic advantages to their adversaries.

What is the adversaries' situation that the speaker or the author of Ps 37 has in mind? From the perspective of the suppliant, the adversaries are unmistakably wicked (מרעים in v. 1) and are evildoers (עשי עולה in v. 1): they are full of guilt (v. 21); they mock and hate the followers of YHWH (v. 12). Moreover, they are their persecutors (v. 14) and even intend to kill the righteous (v. 32).[119] Based on these observations, if we compare Pss 25; 34; and 62 with Ps 37, we can assume a worsened stage of the conflict.[120]

---

117. Psalm 37 must be classified, therefore, not as "theologically and historically older" than Pss 25 and 34 (as assumed by Hossfeld and Zenger 1993, 230) but rather as more recent.

118. In contrast to Albertz (1992, 540), who classifies Ps 37 as important proof of the socioeconomic downfall of major sections of the lower class during the postexilic period. However, the references given by Albertz (Ps 37:7, 12, 14, 32) are so vague that we can hardly conclude economic suppression or exploitation. In our view, the references relate to a conflict between the two feuding groups within the Judean community that has become volatile.

119. It is interesting to note that in the psalms considered here, the adversaries are nowhere described as idol worshipers or followers of foreign gods. They can only be criticized for disregarding God (see, e.g., Ps 73:11).

120. As mentioned above, in Pss 25 and 34 there is no indication of direct or con-

Regardless of the different situations that they depict, a common element in the wisdom-oriented psalms considered so far is that the irritations, disadvantages, threats, and persecution described are not related to any form of involuntary material poverty. Rather, the suppliants feel threatened primarily on account of their perception that the godless or the wicked prosper and God's retributive justice no longer seems to be valid; thus, their own theological position and religious existence appear to be invalidated.

6.4.3.2. Psalm 73

Further references to a more precise location of the opposing faction (i.e., the so-called wicked) may be seen in Ps 73, in which the portrayal of the enemy reminds us clearly of Ps 37. As in Ps 37, the adversaries in Ps 73 seem to hold a particularly important social position and to be successful. Similarly, the speaker makes no secret here of the fact that he was driven to exasperation by the success of the wicked (Ps 73:2, 13–14).

Psalm 73, which is generally regarded as a didactic poem but is sometimes also categorized as a cultic psalm or royal psalm, is a text of eminently pedagogic character.[121] The basic elements forming the song of thanksgiving include the convergence of exhortation and liturgy, teaching (vv. 1–3) and prayer (vv. 18–20), accounts of experience (vv. 4–6, 13–17, 21–22), and confessions of trust (vv. 23–26) with personal observations. It has the form of an artistically structured poem. Considering the portrayal of the enemy, the description of the problem, and the didactic concept that presents an argument based on the personal experiences and the individual piety of the speaker, the entire expressive horizon of the psalm is certainly close to the postexilic psalms of the poor, although the speaker/suppliant calls neither himself a poor one nor God the "deliverer of the poor."[122]

---

crete confrontation between the suppliants (or their audiences) and their adversaries; likewise, in Ps 62 latent tensions might be playing a role.

121. As a didactic poem, see, e.g., Gunkel 1892 [1986], 312; Kraus 1978, 665; Seybold 1996, 281; Oeming and Vette 2010, 180; cultic psalm: Irsigler 1984, 366–68; royal psalm: Würthwein 1950, 542–44; and Ringgren 1953, 271. On its pedagogic character, see Kartje 2014, 103–112.

122. Irsigler 1984, 371; see also Seybold 1996, 282 and Hossfeld and Zenger 1993, 230. Here it is important that in Ps 73 and in Ps 37 a new form of wisdom theology is found. This type of theology can be described in the context of postexilic sapiential

For our investigation, verses 3–7 are of special interest:

(3)   For I was envious of the arrogant; I saw the prosperity
        [שלום] of the wicked [רשעים].
(4)   For they have no pain; their bodies are sound and sleek.
(5)   They are not in trouble as others are; they are not plagued like
        other people.
(6)   Therefore pride is their necklace; violence covers them like a
        garment.
(7)   Their eyes swell out with fatness; their hearts overflow with
        follies.

The "I" in Ps 73 is "one who is burdened by heavy sorrows" (vv. 14, 26) and someone who, most scholars agree, belongs to the leading circles in society.[123] What particularly saddens the supplicant and raises serious doubts about his confidence in YHWH is that he must regard himself as troubled and suffering (v. 14), while the wicked flourish and are as successful as ever (vv. 3–12). The assurance of innocence in verse 13 affirms that the supplicant belongs to the צדיקים. Why must the righteous suffer while the godless fare so well? That is the decisive question.[124]

It is evident from the didactic intent of the psalm that it cannot be a psalm of individual thanksgiving.[125] Throughout the psalm it is obvious that the speaker or the supplicant is aware of his responsibility to his particular religious community.[126]

---

theology as a specific form of "theologized wisdom" (on this, see Hossfeld and Zenger 2000, 335).

123. Kraus 1978, 666. Würthwein (1950, 542–44) and Ringgren (1953, 271) even consider the king as a possible speaker. Albertz refers to the "solidary part of the aristocracy" (1992, 545). Despite all their differences, most attempts to determine the person of the supplicant in Ps 73 more closely result in classifying the supplicant as a particularly qualified person liturgically and institutionally.

124. "It is intellectual and religious suffering related to his view of life as well as his worldview, it is suffering related to his concept of God, that is to say, concerning his God" (Hossfeld and Zenger 2000, 335–36).

125. As proposed by Birkeland 1933a, 92.

126. See Irsigler 1984, 1–2, 366–71, who classifies Ps 73 as a monologue of a "Hebraic Pascal" declaring his confession before and for a religious community. Irsigler perceives here the speaker responsible for a religious community.

Considering the almost identical perspectives in Ps 37 and Ps 73 and the closely associated statements about the wicked, we can assume the same constellation for both psalms: the speaker, who belongs to the upper class as well as to the religious community he represents, is in a situation of confrontation with other leading, influential, and power- ful circles because, by virtue of his theology concerning YHWH's will, he has to reject the practices of the opposing circle, practices which are despicable and unprincipled but which ensure success and power. Psalm 37 and Ps 73 may represent chronologically a middle stage between the earlier psalms of the poor (e.g., Pss 25; 34; 62) and the later ones (e.g., Pss 12; 35; 40; 69; 76). Characteristic features of this stage of the psalms of the poor are aspects such as the aggravated images of conflict (compared to Pss 25; 34; and 62) and the speaker's intensified awareness of rivalry vis-à-vis his adversaries.[127]

The expressions חרה and קנא in Ps 37:1 (see also Ps 73:3) indicate a higher degree of envy in regard to the socioeconomic success of the enemies compared to other earlier and later psalms of the poor. Such an awareness of rivalry did not yet characterize the early psalms of the poor. Obviously, the socioeconomic prosperity of the adversaries was then within certain limits; the power and property distribution between both sides remained somewhat balanced. In the later psalms of the poor, such a feeling of rivalry no longer played a role because, meanwhile, the superior- ity of the adversaries was such that there was no question of any "rivalry" at all.

6.4.4. Psalms 12; 35; 40; 69; 76; 94; 102; 109; 140; 146; and 149: Images of Enemies

In contrast to the psalms examined so far (Pss 25; 34; 37; 62; and 73), a clear escalation of aggressive postures among the adversaries can be observed in the following psalms of the poor: Pss 12; 35; 69; 76; 94; 102; 109; 140; 146; and 149 (as well as in Ps 40, which has already been discussed), although

---

127. However, in comparison to Ps 37, Ps 73 offers an eschatological outlook in vv. 24–26, which points to the removal of the souls of the pious from the underworld into the heavenly world of light. Similar images can be found in 1 Enoch (on the details, see Kaiser 2013, 377–80; Witte 2014, 108–9). The psalm could not then have originated before the middle of the third century BCE. Nonetheless, it cannot be ruled out that the verses in question are a secondary supplement.

the main aim of the accusations remains the same (it is neither about idol worshipers nor about heathens).[128] This will be discussed in detail in the following section. Moreover, we will also investigate to what extent commonalities as well as divergences are present within these psalms of the poor, including for comparison those we considered earlier. It may be possible to show more clearly that different phases of confrontation are reflected in the psalms of the poor. By taking everything into consideration, a more explicit profile of the piety articulated in these psalms of the poor as well as that of their adversaries may be revealed.

In these later psalms of the poor, the adversaries of the respective suppliants are represented as enemies (אויב, Pss 35:19; 69:5, 19; 102:9; צוררי, Ps 69:20) and as wicked (רשע, Pss 12:9; 94:3; 109:2; 140:5, 9); there is also mention of haters (שונא, Pss 35:19; 69:5, 15). Such a portrayal of enemies also appears in the earlier psalms of the poor ("enemies" in Ps 25:2, 19; "wicked" in Ps 34:22; "haters" in Ps 25:19 and 34:22) but in a clearly less aggressive context.[129]

In addition to this, several epithets for the enemies, such as robbers (גוזל Ps 35:10; thematically also Ps 69:5), condemners (משפטי Ps 109:31) and persecutors (רודף Pss 35:3; 69:27; 109:16; thematically also Ps 40:15) appear, but only in the later psalms of the poor. Here, the enemies are described as frightening snakes (נחש Ps 140:4) and vipers (עכשוב Ps 140:4). The adversaries tell lies or speak deceitfully in the earlier (Pss 34:14; 62:5) and later psalms of the poor (Pss 12:3–5; 40:5; 94:4; 109:2–3; cf. Zeph 3:13), but they fight (לחם Ps 35:1; thematically also Pss 76:4, 6; 94:5; 140:3; 149:6–9) with the "poor one" and even seek to eliminate him (מבקשי נפשי Pss 35:4; 40:15; thematically also Ps 94:6, 21) in the

---

128. Regardless of how Ps 76 is dated, the eschatological portion in v. 10 seems to be a postexilic addition. Psalm 146 is a hymn that speaks about YHWH in the third person. The somewhat obscure pictures of the enemy and of conflict in this psalm probably result from its literary genre. Ps 146 should be attributed to a late time period (the late postexilic period) because of "its form-critical development, its apparent use of earlier material and the lateness of its language, viz. ש "who" (vv 3, 5), עשתנות "thoughts" (v 4), שבר "hope" (v 5), and זקף "raise" (v 8)." (Allen 1983, 302). Hossfeld and Zenger regard this psalm as "a scribal work by the final redactors of the Psalter" (2011, 612; see also Hossfeld and Zenger 2008, 815). Psalm 37 seems to portray the enemies quite aggressively (vv. 12, 14, 32). This psalm appears to have been formed after the first phase of conflict, but before the climax phase of the conflict (the eschatological expectations are still absent).

129. Cf., e.g., Ps 25:2 with Ps 35:19–21; cf. also Pss 69:5 and 102:9.

later psalms of the poor. They are described in the later psalms of the poor as those that lay snares (פח Ps 140:6) and condemn innocent blood (ודם נקי ירשיעו Ps 94:21; lexematically and thematically also Jer 7:6 and 22:3).[130] Here, the adversaries are considered arrogant (גאים Pss 94:2; 140:6), ostentatious (המגדילים Ps 35:26), and powerful (חזק Ps 35:10; עצם Ps 69:5). They plan harm (חשבי רעתי Ps 35:4; thematically also Ps 40:15) and are glad about it (שמחי רעתי Ps 35:26; thematically also Ps 40:16).

Taking all the above views into consideration, the confrontation here may be the same as that in the somewhat older psalms, but the progression in the portrayal of the aggressive enemy indicates an advanced stage of conflict. In other words, the adversaries in Pss 12; 35; 40; 69; 76; 94; 102; 109; 140; and 149 are basically the same as those in Pss 25; 34; 37; 62; and 73 but are perceived as more threatening and more aggressive. The texts examined above can be arranged chronologically in different stages. First, Stage 1 is represented by texts such as Pss 25; 34; 62 in which a cause-and-effect in terms of retributive justice is regarded as valid. In these early psalms of the poor, the power and position between the suppliants and their enemies seem to be balanced.[131]

The late Persian period may be classified as Stage 2, and examples of this stage may be found in texts such as Pss 37 and 73 in which, compared to other earlier and later psalms of the poor, a higher degree of envy by the suppliants regarding the socioeconomic success of the enemies is expressed.[132] Such a consciousness of rivalry does not appear in the early or late psalms of the poor.

Texts such as Pss 12; 35; 40; 69; 76; 94; 102; 109; 140; 146; and 149 seem to have been formed and shaped in Stage 3, which can be found in the late Persian period or throughout the Hellenistic period. In these late psalms of the poor a clear escalation of aggressive postures between the adversaries is reflected. In this stage, complete splits within the Judean community can be observed.[133]

In this context, Ps 109 is an example of the escalation of the conflict between both sides in this advanced stage that has now triggered in the suppliant forceful aggression and a strong urge for vengeance against his

---

130. On this, see also §4.3, above.
131. For details, see §§6.4.3.1 and 6.4.3.2, above.
132. For details, see §§6.4.3.1 and 6.4.3.2, above.
133. For details, see §6.6, below.

enemies (Ps 109:6–20).[134] These commonalities in the later psalms of the poor (Pss 12; 35; 40; 69; 76; 94; 102; 109; 140; and 149) with regard to the portrayal of one's enemies can hardly be a coincidence. The largely consistent profile of the portrayal of the enemy in the psalms of the poor discussed here is a clear indication that the respective authors as well as the groups behind them find themselves in the same or at least a similar constellation of conflict and feel vulnerable to the same circles of enemies.[135] Furthermore, we must observe that here, despite their misdeeds, the enemies of the suppliants are nowhere accused of idol worship. It is also significant that they are not directly called the "rich" (e.g., עשיר) although they are identifiable implicitly and explicitly as politically powerful and economically wealthy compared to the poor; rather, they should be primarily seen as violent and as persecuting.

6.5. Observations on the Piety of the Poor in the Psalms of the Poor[136]

6.5.1. The Suppliant and His Community

The assumption that both the suppliants and their communities share the same destiny in their confrontation with their Judean adversaries is explicitly confirmed, for example, by the references in Pss 34:3; 35:27; and 69:33.[137] According to Pohlmann, in Ps 69:7 the suppliant is "apparently

---

134. According to Tucker, in Ps 109 "the identity of powerlessness equates with shame, consequently creating within the psalmist the desire for a reversal" (2014, 74–75). Tucker claims that the suppliant of Ps 109 seeks to construct a negative image of the Persian Empire while concurrently deconstructing the imperial ideology and its significance (ibid). However, in our view the conflict and tension delineated in Ps 109 are rather witnesses for an internal Judean schism.

135. For similar descriptions of the enemy in other types of psalms, see Ro 2002, 165. Even though these images of enemies are associated with a fixed style, it is apparent in the psalms investigated that, in contrast to the earlier psalms of the poor, their authors preferred more aggressive images of their enemies in order to characterize their situations of conflict. Since Pss 9/10; 14; and 86 indicate a different kind of piety of the poor, where the whole of Israel is regarded as "God's poor," they will not be investigated in the present study.

136. Pss 12; 25; 34; 35; 37; 40; 62; 69; 73; 76; 94; 102; 109; 140; 146; and 149.

137. The lexeme כל in Ps 76:10 refers, in our view, to the postexilic development of group awareness among the "poor." Ps 35:27 does not explicitly say that the followers of the suppliant are the poor; however, we can infer this from the fact that the suppliant regards himself as a "poor one" (Ps 35:10).

the representative of a group."[138] Albertz is of the same view with regard to Pss 35; 69; 109; and 140. These psalms describe "individual lamentations" in which the individuals and the groups assure each other of their certainty of salvation despite all oppression (Pss 35:9–10; 69:7, 33–37; 70:5; 109:30–31). Through the salvation of the individual, all of his followers would have a reason for jubilation (Ps 35:27–28). Furthermore, on the basis of the group's theological certainty that YHWH will take up their cause, the individual is assured of being heard (Ps 140:13).[139]

Regarding the relationship between the suppliant and his audience in Pss 35; 69; 109; and 140, it must be mentioned that some recent researchers assume that these psalms were used in the postexilic period as liturgical forms for the communities.[140] It is probable that the psalms of the poor reflect not only individual animosities in the context of concrete situations but also collective situations of continuously threatened conflict. The psalms are intended to be taken up publicly in an "act of worship." Observations on Pss 34; 37; 62; and 73 have followed the same trend, so that we can assume here a type of community sharing the same destiny. The didactic concerns of the speakers imply that their texts were conceived by like-minded communities and had lasting value within such frameworks, especially as guidance in conflict situations.

Whether we can also categorize Ps 102 in the same way is not entirely clear. The suppliant of Ps 102 complains about being derided (v. 9), about God's anger at him (v. 11), and, not least, about his own pain and sickness (vv. 4–6). By and large, verses 2–12, both in their form and content (vv. 2–3 form an invocation with an introductory plea for hearing; vv. 4–12 form a complaint), are like an individual psalm of complaint. However, what follows in verses 13–23 is entirely different. Here, a group ("your servants," v. 15; cf. v. 29) articulates the expectation of the future glorification of Zion. The differences between both units in terms of content and style suggests that the second section (vv. 13–29 as well as v. 1) represents a later supplement to the individual psalm of complaint in verses 2–12 and was added during the postexilic period with the aim of reworking verses 2–12 into a collective hymnic statement that was probably conceived for worship gatherings of the "ser-

---

138. Pohlmann 1989, 54.
139. Albertz 1992, 572–73.
140. Kraus 1978, 1104–6; Lohfink 1990a, 106–7; and Hossfeld and Zenger 2000, 180, 266–67, 335.

vants of YHWH."[141] Thus, for the final form of the psalm we can assume a second *Sitz im Leben*.[142] Since it is not our concern here to reconstruct the original (possibly preexilic) form by means of literary or redaction criticism, the final composition of Ps 102 can be safely classified as a late-postexilic liturgical text. The psalm was originally written in reference to the critical situation of an individual (vv. 2–12) who was surrounded by "enemies" (v. 9). However, the text was later expanded and applied to a group of "servants of YHWH" in order to announce the end of such threats and suffering in a hymnic form praising YHWH (vv. 13–29). It can be concluded that the above-mentioned psalms of the poor, at least at the level of their final composition, presuppose communities that share the same destiny as the suppliants.

6.5.2. The Piety of the Poor and Their Theological Perspective

The view that the factional antagonism we have examined has primarily religious and not socioeconomic causes is supported by several further observations on the piety of the poor in Pss 12; 25; 34; 35; 37; 40; 62; 69; 73; 76; 94; 102; 109; 140; 146; and 149. In the first place, these psalms converge insofar as none of them contain aspects of a salvation-history-oriented theology.[143] Nowhere is there any reference to traditions

---

141. See, e.g., Birkeland 1933a, 47; Seybold 1996, 398–400; Hossfeld and Zenger 2008, 39–42. For a different position, see Körting 2006, 43, who argues for the inseparability of the two parts. See also Oeming and Vette 2016, 80.

142. See on this Lohfink 1986, 174; see also Hossfeld and Zenger 1993, 14–15. According to Steck, Ps 102 is "a uniform text in which an exemplary suppliant pleads for rescue from premature death.... The psalm is based on the ideas of late wisdom literature and employs characteristics of late prophetic and eschatological expectation as a theological argument. It was probably created only editorially for its literary place in the Psalter and emerged perhaps in the second half of the third century or at the beginning of the second century BCE" (Steck 1990, 372).

143. See also Rahlfs (1892, 29), who concluded, due to the lexical as well as syntactic similarities and their "originality," that the group of psalms he selected (Pss 22; 25; 31; 34; 35; 38; 40; 69; 102 and 109) originated from one and the same author. It is intriguing that Rahlfs's psalms are not completely but largely identical with the aforementioned psalms. With regard to the differences observed above between individual psalms that might be interrelated with the changed situations of the community of the poor, it could be concluded that different authors were responsible for this group of psalms. However, the authors seem to belong to the same orientation of piety but to have been active at different points in time.

or motifs of salvation history. Apparently, references to a past salvation history are of no value for this type of piety. The hope of this theological orientation is focused on the future eschatological act of salvation by God (Pss 12:6; 35:9–10; 40:18; 69:28–30, 33–34; 76:9–10; 94:1–2, 13, 16; 102:14, 17; 109:22, 26–27, 31; 140:8, 11–13; 149:4; see also Pss 9:13, 17, 19; 10:12, 17–18).[144] There appears to be textual evidence of the development of a type of piety in which a theology that regarded the God of Israel as controlling and guiding history was viewed as problematic in light of contemporary circumstances. It was more important that God, as the eschatological agent, would ultimately assert his order and bring the truly pious, namely, the poor, to their well-earned destiny as the "true" Israel.[145] Thus, the eschatological concepts of certain psalms of the poor coincide with future expectations in late prophetic texts, in which no longer the entire community of Israel,[146] but only the "poor" as the "truly pious," the "righteous" and the "servants," can survive divine judgment.[147]

YHWH will arise on behalf of the oppressed righteous, appear in glory, and intervene to save them.[148] At the same time, he will bring an end to the wicked within the Judean community, who will be "put to

---

144. E.g., characteristic are the intensified eschatological traits in Pss 12:6; 76:9–10; 94:16, which clearly allude to Zeph 3:8, since here also YHWH's act of "arising" (קום) is explicitly connected with the salvation of the poor. However, what is also significant is that in Pss 25; 34; 37; 62; and 73 the future restoration of YHWH's retributive justice is in the foreground. On the eschatological character of these references, see Gunkel 1933, 330–32; Pohlmann 1989, 54–55; Albertz 1992, 571–72; Lohfink, 1990a, 107. Due to the literary genre, the eschatological expressions and ideas in these texts remain unaccomplished. With regard to the literary forms of prayer, the authors must have had to avoid detailed explanations and descriptions of their eschatology.

145. Michel 1979, 75–76.

146. This dualistic eschatology seems to have competed with the theology articulating the salvific function of the righteous reflected in Gen 18:22b–33a. On this issue, see §5.5, above.

147. For the poor, see Isa 66:2 and Zeph 2:3; 3:12; for the truly pious, see, e.g., Pss 12:2 and 149:1, 5, 9; see also Isa 66:2. For the righteous, see, e.g., Pss 35:27; 69:29; and 140:14; see also Zeph 3:13. For the servants, see, e.g., Pss 35:27; 69:18, 37; and 102:15, 29; see also Isa 66:14.

148. On behalf of the oppressed righteous, see Pss 12:6; 35:2; 76:10; and 102:14; see also Zeph 3:8. For appearing in glory, see Ps 102:17; see also Isa 66:5. On intervention, see Pss 35:3, 9; 40:6, 17–18; 69:30; 109:26–31; and 140:8; see also Isa 66:10–11, 14 and Zeph 3:14–15.

shame."[149] The suppliants or speakers may hope for salvation by seeking YHWH, praising him, fearing him, and waiting upon him, while their enemies have disqualified themselves through lying, negative conversation, and acts of violence.[150]

The eschatological character of Ps 149 cannot be ignored.[151] This psalm "becomes as a whole the eschatological *tehilla* in the assembly of the *hăsîdîm* (v. 1b). Accordingly, v. 5 reads: 'Let the *hăsîdîm* exult in glory, let them sing for joy on their couches.' In v. 4 the older term *'anāwîm* is used in the same sense, as is *'ammô* 'his people,' which refers here to the minority of the true Israel."[152] What is remarkable is the statement concerning the poor in Ps 149, as it "appears again exactly where it always stands in the texts from Qumran, namely, in the context of the statement of salvation."[153]

Second, a common aspect of the psalms of the poor considered here is that matters concerning the Jerusalem temple, cult, and sacrifices play hardly any role. In Ps 73:17, מקדשי אל could have meant areas of the sanctuary, but this is not entirely certain.[154] The use of דרש with YHWH

---

149. For ending the wicked, see esp. Pss 12:4; 35:1, 4–5; 40:15–16; 69:28–29; 109:28; and 140:11; see also Isa 66:14 and Zeph 3:8, 11. "Put to shame" (יבשו), as in Pss 35:4, 26; 40:15–16; 69:7; and 109:28; also in Isa 66:5 and Zeph 3:11.

150. Seeking YHWH, see Ps 69:33; see also Zeph 2:3. Praising, see, e.g., Pss 35:27 and 69:31; see also Isa 66:10 and Zeph 3:14. Fearing, see Pss 76:8 and 102:16; see also Isa 66:2. Waiting, see Pss 40:2 and 69:7; see also Zeph 3:8. For enemies disqualifying themselves through lying and negative conversation, see, e.g., Pss 12:3–4; 35:20; 69:11–12; and 140:4; see also Isa 66:5 and Zeph 3:13; by acts of violence, see, e.g., Pss 12:2; 35:19; 69:5, 20; 102:9; 109:2–3; and 140:5, 9; see also Isa 66:5 and Zeph 3:3.

151. C. Levin 1993, 378; Oeming and Vette 2016, 253.

152. C. Levin 1993, 377–78; see also Lohfink 1990a, 122; W. Herrmann 1999, 77; Oeming and Vette 2016, 253.

153. Lohfink 1990a, 122. The close parallelisms between Ps 149 and the relevant Qumran texts suggest that the theological and spiritual "ancestors" of the Qumran community shared the concept of the piety of the poor in the Hebrew Bible investigated so far.

154. See, e.g., the view of R. Kittel 1929a, 270–71: "By itself *miqdash* means the outer sanctuary, especially the place of worship. Therefore, the entrance of the temple would have been meant here. But it may not be just the act of entering. It could rather express a prayerful way of approaching God together with the innermost contemplation of divine counsel and the disclosure of one's own thoughts. Thus, essentially, those scholars are right who, based on the plural that otherwise does not occur, think of the same meaning as Wis 2:22 μυστήρια θεου: the secrets, the hidden counsel, the revelation of God." There are also "occasional indications that individual psalm writers know the idea of mystically contemplating God. Therefore, here too this type of

as an object in Ps 34:5, 11 need not be the technical term for a visit to the sanctuary, as can be seen from a glance at the concordance.[155]

Moreover, the reference to the "hut" (סכו) and "dwelling place" (מעונתו) of God in Ps 76:3 cannot be seen as an indication of a special interest in the Jerusalem temple, since the terms "hut" (סך) and "dwelling place" (מעון or מענה) can also be used to mean a "den" or "lair" (see, e.g., Job 38:40).[156] With regard to the obviously unofficial character of the terms in question, we can consider Zenger's view of translating both terms not as "hut/tent" and "home/dwelling" but rather as "den" (*Versteck*) and "lair" (*Lagerplatz*).[157] The choice of words can be explained by the fact that reverence is probably denied not to Zion as an abode of YHWH but to the temple. This interpretation demonstrates a clear dissociation of certain circles from the temple. For example, Albertz notes that there are several references in the psalms of the poor indicating that during postexilic times religious groups conducted their own acts of worship outside the temple in Jerusalem, perhaps in their houses or in synagogues.[158] Frank Lothar Hossfeld and Zenger's view on Ps 12 follows the same line of thought; they recognize in Ps 12 a liturgy that took place "as a community or group liturgy outside the temple in Jerusalem or somewhere in the countryside."[159]

In Pss 40:7 and 69:32 there is even a critical reevaluation of the significance of sacrifices. Some scholars seem to have gathered from Ps 69:10 that the suppliant, who clearly acts as the representative of a group (v. 7), is "an enthusiast of the temple."[160] However, we cannot conclude with certainty that the enmity ascribed to him is associated with the fact that this "enthusiast" belonged to the group of those "who rushed instantly to the temple construction after their homecoming from exile."[161] The self-characterization of the suppliant as an enthusiast could also have meant

---

observation of mysticism should be considered—the deepening into the 'holy', pious world of God" (R. Kittel 1929a, 270–71). See also Buber 1952, 50: "It is not the temple in Jerusalem that is meant ... but rather the holy mysteries of God"; amended by Kraus 1978, 670.

155. Kraus (1978, 419) sees it as a technical term. See, e.g., Ezek 20:1 and 14:2–3; see also W. Herrmann 1999, 73.

156. Hossfeld and Zenger 2000, 385.

157. Ibid.

158. Albertz 1992, 572–73.

159. Hossfeld and Zenger 1993, 93.

160. Kraus 1978, 643.

161. So Kraus 1978, 643 with regard to v. 10.

that with regard to the temple and temple cult he had special demands and claims over which he was victimized by the opposing side.[162] In such a case, the critical attitude in Ps 69:32 would not be a contradiction to the suppliant's enthusiasm for the temple in Ps 69:10. Otherwise, we would have to correlate the divergence between verse 10 and verse 32 with later editorial corrections in an older version of the psalm. In any case, in the present version of the psalm with the clear statements of verse 32, a cult-critical form of piety is articulated rather than a cult-focused perspective.[163]

On the whole, then, we can observe in the final forms of the psalms of the poor discussed here (cf. also Jer 7:1–12; 20:7–13) a reserved, if not critical, attitude toward the temple in Jerusalem.[164] From this it follows that one cannot assume the official temple cult of Jerusalem as the *Sitz im Leben* for these texts. Rather, this group of psalms seems to be used as a community liturgy for those who, as the poor, found themselves in a situation of threatened conflict. At the same time, the existence of these psalms of the poor is a strong indication that their authors were in a critical confrontation with the contemporary temple leadership and, consequently, that the enemies—who are always portrayed in these texts as menacing—were likely to have been found within the circles of the temple priesthood.

In this regard, a conspicuous convergence can be seen between these psalms of the poor and some texts from Qumran (e.g., 1QpHab 8:8–11; 9:9–10), since in the latter it is often the postexilic priesthood in Jerusa-

---

162. So Weiser 1966, 336; on Ps 69, see also Pohlmann 1989, 54–55; Oeming and Vette 2010, 155.

163. It is also possible that the criticism is aimed at a particular understanding of cult and sacrifice. According to Hossfeld and Zenger 2000, 273–74, "two postexilic contexts, which propagate the prophetic criticism against the temple cult, can be considered, depending on whether the psalm is associated with the early postexilic dispute over the construction of the temple or with protest from some circles that obviously occurred after the establishment of the temple as well as the sacrificial cult.... If we notice the parallelisms, which associate vv. 6–14ab with the book of Jeremiah, the criticism of the temple by Jeremiah, and the description of the negative consequences that this criticism has for Jeremiah (see esp. Jer 7:1–11 and 26:1–19 and Jer 12:6; 15:15), then the second alternative is more probable.... But then our psalm belongs to the fierce confrontations between both competing positions in the postexilic community, which may be regarded—somewhat roughly—as a conflict between a hierocratic position on the one hand and a prophetic position on the other, or between salvation presentists on the one hand and eschatologists on the other." On this, see also §4.3, above.

164. On this issue, see also §4.3, above.

lem from which the circles of the poor distance themselves and to whose sanctions they find themselves exposed.[165] The fact that more concrete references to the opposing faction are absent in the psalms of the poor is probably because the traditional literary forms of speech and prayer, which had to be taken into account for supplemental formulations as well as rewordings, are incorporated into the psalms of the poor.

Third, not all of the psalms of the poor take on a sapiential character, something that is particularly evident in Pss 12; 25; 34; 37; 62; and 73.[166] However, we can observe that, as in the case of the aforementioned psalms (such as Ps 35:27 and 40:10–11), the respective speakers or suppliants are represented or identifiable as such institutionally important persons that they are in a position to influence their group or community. Their actions are a cause for the opposing faction to act against them so as to subdue them (see, e.g., Pss 35:15–16; 40:15–16). This observation leads to the conclusion that these psalms of the poor must have their origin in a social milieu in which material as well as religious resources were such that those belonging to it could dare to confront the adversaries and to do so in such a manner that the adversaries saw in the actions of these groups a serious threat to their own position. This makes it clear that the piety of the poor cannot be seen as something that concerned only those that belonged to an impoverished and less influential lower class.

In the psalms of the poor, there is no indication that the suppliants and their audience were not in a position to gather the necessary means to secure their existence or that they suffered from a lack of basic material necessities, such as food, clothing, or shelter. Likewise, there are hardly any indications that the group in question suffered from bondage or forced labor. Apart from the actual terminology relating to the poor, there is no other reason to assume that the suppliants and their audience suffered from material poverty and that this is the reason for their lamentations. Furthermore, in his attempt to explain this remarkable finding by assuming that the psalms of the poor do not originate from the affected people themselves, Albertz observes that "the image of the pious poor man, who is usually depicted only as the victim of the wicked, is less sharp. The reason for this is probably that the majority of these descriptions do not

---

165. On this, see §7.2, below.

166. Seybold speaks of Ps 12 as a "text influenced by wisdom literature" (1996, 62); see also Oeming and Vette 2000, 100.

come from the persons concerned but from the perspective of the pious upper class."[167]

For the authors and suppliants of these psalms, what they regarded as their "poverty" was not actually material poverty. Throughout the psalms of the poor discussed here, "to be poor" is a characteristic attitude toward YHWH, a religious approach to life. The deficits they lament are not of a material nature. For example, the suppliant of Ps 102 complains about an insult (v. 9), about God's furious anger (v. 11), and about inner pain and sickness (vv. 4–6), but nowhere is a dearth of material goods mentioned.

The findings in the remaining psalms are similar. The suppliants complain about their "adversaries" (e.g., Pss 12:9; 25:2, 19; 34:22; 35:19; 69:5, 19; 102:9; 109:2; 140:5, 9), "sins" (e.g., Pss 25:7, 11, 18; 40:13), "distress" and "anxieties" (e.g., Pss 25:17, 22; 34:7, 18; 37:39) but not about any lack of material goods. Of course, the authors of some psalms of the poor observe and make accusations about the unjust treatments of the opposing faction toward socially marginalized groups such as the widow, the stranger, and the fatherless (Ps 94:6; see also Ps 146:9; Jer 7:6; 22:3). However, it is clear that the authors describe the unfair sufferings of such disadvantaged groups not as the afflicted, but as the observer.

Fourth, the authors of these psalms of the poor do not attempt to describe poverty with reference to concrete circumstances. Instead, here the terminology relating to the poor tends to occur in statements about volatile situations of interpersonal conflict.[168] In such statements, the terminology of poverty is especially significant, since it reveals the kinds of relationships those involved in the conflicts have, not only with other parties but also with God.

The terminology relating to the poor is closely connected with the triad constellation being presented, namely, "the oppressed suppliant— the adversaries oppressing the suppliant—the rescuing God." Every time a term relating to the poor appears as a self-depiction of the suppliant or of his community, the adversaries' acts of persecution and the corresponding deliverance by God are described simultaneously.[169]

---

167. Albertz 1994, 500.

168. For the similar interpersonal constellations of conflict in the Hodayot, see §7.1.2, below.

169. However, the terminology relating to the poor is used many times even without direct reference to the act of rescue by God or persecution by adversaries (see, e.g., עֲנָוִים in Pss 34:3; 37:11; and 69:33); here they indicate the followers of the suppliant.

In Pss 12:6; 25:16; 34:7; 35:10a; 40:18; 69:30; 76:10; 102:1; 140:13, among others, the poverty terminology is found in the triad constellation (suppliant, persecuting adversaries, God as deliverer).[170] As these examples affirm, what is deemed to be "poor" and what is meant by the "poor one" or "poverty" depend on a complex set of relationships that are often expressed as a triad. Here, the poor one is one who understands himself as being helpless and unwillingly delivered to his adversaries. At the same time, he also considers himself to be poor because he totally depends on God alone and in this regard differs from his adversaries.[171] On the one hand, the terminology relating to the poor within the framework of such a triad (suppliant, persecuting adversaries, and God the deliverer) highlights the qualitative difference between the suppliant(s) and the adversaries, as well as the contrast between the respective relationships and attitudes of both groups to God. Thus, it is clear that the "wicked" are wicked not only because of their actions against the pious, but also because of their attitude toward God. This reinforces the observation that "to be poor" is a conscious and constantly cultivated attitude of piety before God, regardless of any material inadequacies.

Below, we will see with regard to the pessimistic anthropology of the Hodayot that the terminology relating to the poor used there involves an interplay between "lowliness" and "elevation" and that "being poor before God" is superior to "being poor before one's adversaries."[172] This appears to be similar to some psalms of the poor (e.g., Pss 25 and 40). Of course, we cannot assume exactly the same concept of lowliness as that found in the Hodayot for our group of psalms of the poor. However, the soul-searching confessions of sin (e.g., Pss 25:7, 11, 18; 40:13), which have parallels with the pessimistic anthropology of the Hodayot, suggest a similar orientation.[173] The confessions of sin in Pss 25 and 40 are not merely confessions of sin, but function concurrently as a characteristic of piety which differentiates the righteous from their adversaries, who cultivate violent acts without acknowledging their sin (e.g., Pss 25:18–19; 40:13–16). The

---

Very often both aspects (the threat or persecution by adversaries and the act of rescue by God) are inseparably fused into one sentence in the psalms of the poor.

170. For a similar pattern and constellation in the Hodayot, see §7.1, below.

171. On the details, see ch. 7, below.

172. See §7.1, below.

173. On the details, see §7.1.1, below.

speakers can be identified as "the suffering righteous."[174] Here we may assume that the suppliant's understanding of poverty is based on a dialectic between an admitted sinfulness and lowliness as well as a distinct awareness of being the chosen.[175]

However, we cannot disregard the fact that what is characteristic in other postexilic psalms of the poor, in contrast to the Hodayot, is normally just the antithesis of righteous-wicked.[176] On the other hand, we should not overvalue this difference. In both cases, the pattern of orientation, which is a characteristic way of thinking in wisdom literature, namely, "pride goes before a fall" and YHWH's antipathy to everything "high" and presumptuous, was decisive.[177] Accordingly, the elevation of the humiliated and suffering righteous should be seen as the central subject in the psalms of the poor as well as in the confessions of Jeremiah and in the Hodayot.[178]

We thus arrive at the following conclusions concerning the intended meaning of the terminology relating to the poor in the relevant psalms.

(1) The terminology relating to the poor typically uses a triad constellation, namely, God the deliverer—the oppressed suppliant as the suffering righteous—the adversaries oppressing the suppliant.

(2) Being "poor before God" is placed above being "poor before one's adversaries." Before God, the terminology relating to the poor serves as an acknowledgement of one's own lowliness and sinfulness.

(3) With regard to adversaries, the psalms underline the contrast between one's own lowliness and the threatening superiority of the godless adversaries in order to emphasize before God the helplessness of the suffering righteous.

(4) In the case of the "suffering righteous," material poverty does not play any role in the aforementioned psalms of the poor, in the confessions

---

174. On the motif of the suffering righteous from the postexilic period up to the extrabiblical Qumran texts, see, e.g., Ruppert 1972, 39, 182–86.

175. On the details, see §7.1.1, below.

176. For a detailed discussion of the pessimistic anthropology in the Hodayot, *see* §7.1.1, below. For the antithesis between righteous-wicked, see, e.g., Pss 12:2; 34:16, 20, 22; 35:27; 37:6, 16–17, 21–22, 29–40; and 73:13; see also Jer 12:1–3).

177. See, e.g., Gen 11:1–9; Isa 2:12–17; 10:33–34; 14:12–15; Ezek 17:24; 21:31; and Job 22:29.

178. For the suffering righteous, see, e.g., Prov 24:16; for a detailed discussion, see Ruppert 1972, 184–88. As a central subject, see, e.g., Pss 12; 25; 34; 37; 40; 69; 73; and 140. For the confessions of Jeremiah, see Jer 12:1–3 and 20:7–13. For the Hodayot, see 1QH[a] 10:20–30; 11:37–12:4; and 13:13–18.

of Jeremiah, or in the relevant Hodayot.[179] The manner in which the terminology relating to the poor is used indicates that it does not refer to an
economic situation of deficiency threatening one's own existence.

(5) Thus, the terminology relating to the poor serves as a key expression in a dialectic theology of humility and election according to which
the elect are restored by God while their adversaries are rejected. This
eschatologically oriented theology of humility and election is often critical
of the temple and sacrifices.

Despite the main theological aspects characterizing the relevant
psalms of the poor outlined above, we cannot infer that these psalms
are traceable to a single author. Rather, we may assume that the circle of
authors behind these texts belonged to the same religious faction during
the postexilic period. There are a number of indications that this group,
despite its self-depiction as being poor, cannot be equated with the socioeconomically impoverished lower class. On the contrary, it comprises
theologically well-educated individuals. The speakers are conspicuously
didactic and exhortative toward their communities. The thoughts of the
speakers are deeply anchored to an ethos of theologized wisdom. We can
assume that a particular theological circle in the postexilic period pur-
sued this piety of the poor. The socioeconomic as well as the theological
capacities of the circle were considerable. Therefore, this circle attracted
the serious attention of and disapproval from its adversaries. At the same
time, the opposing group regarded the actions of this theological circle as
a serious threat to its own position. Consequently, this implies a certain
degree of socioeconomic prosperity and power in the theological circle.[180]
The concerns of this theological circle were alienation and persecution by
adversaries, the invalidity of God's retributive justice, God's wrath, their
own sin, and inner pain and sickness.[181]

---

179. On this issue, see §7.1.1 below.

180. See, e.g., Ps 34:10.

181. For persecution by adversaries, see, e.g., Pss 34:22; 35:4, 7, 11, 12; 37:12, 14;
40:15–16; 62:4, 5; and 140:5, 9. For retributive justice, see, e.g., Pss 37:1, 7; and 73:3, 12.
For God's wrath, see, e.g., Ps 102:11. For sin, see, e.g., Pss 25:7, 11, 18; and 40:13. For
inner pain and sickness, see, e.g., Ps 102:4–6.

6.6. The Historical Stages of Conflict and
Theological Reflection in the Psalms of the Poor

In the foregoing discussion, with reference to the intensification of the aggressive images of the enemy, it was concluded that the psalms of the poor reflect a historical development in the conflict and can be arranged according to various stages of the conflict. Something similar is also apparent with regard to the future expectations articulated in these psalms, since a clear shift in tone is perceptible in the wide spectrum of such expectations.

Thus, for example, there are statements—such as in Pss 34:13–23; 37:1–2, 9, 14–15; and 62:13—that only reflect hope for a speedy implementation of retributive justice. Yet there are also statements in which eschatologically oriented expectations play an important role.[182] Several examples follow:

Psalm 12:6: "Because of the oppression of the poor, because of the groaning of the needy, now will I arise," says YHWH, "I will place them in the safety for which they long."[183]

Psalm 35:9: Then my soul will rejoice in YHWH, exult in his salvation.

---

182. Albertz (1992, 572–76) is of the opinion that the eschatology in the psalms of the poor (see Pss 9:13, 19; 10:17–18; 35:9–10; and 69:33–34) had its origin in the postexilic socioeconomic chasm between the poor and the rich. The poor "had no claim to deliverance except the fact that Yahweh, the God of liberation, would be denying himself if in the long term he kept on overlooking the crying of the poor, so time and again they anticipated his ultimate mercy on the oppressed in eschatological songs of praise" (519–20). On the other hand, we may concur with the objection of Preuss: "Even a reference to social tensions and stratifications within Israel, which gave rise to eschatological expectations (Eifler), cannot explain why such eschatologies did not also originate in Israel's environment in view of the similar problems and troubles" (1978, 9). For Albertz (1992, 569–76), the eschatology in the biblical Psalms is mainly the product of economically impoverished circles within the lower stratum. However, why should the possibility be ruled out at the outset that certain circles of the postexilic upper stratum or middle stratum, due to their situations of status inconsistency (see §2.3, above) or due to their spiritual-religious orientation in the face of the injustice of their adversaries, hoped for an eschatological future, that is, the expectation of a final action by YHWH to set everything in order and to eliminate the miserable situation? For this interpretation, see the comments of Meeks 1993, 347 on the origin of religious convictions (here: apocalyptic beliefs).

183. This and the following biblical texts are author's translations.

Psalm 69:35–36: Let heaven and earth acclaim him, the oceans and all that moves in them! For God will save Zion, and build the towns of Judah.

Psalm 76:9–10: From the heavens you caused judgment to be heard, the earth stays silent with dread when God stands up to give judgment, to save all the poor of the earth.

Psalm 102:14: You should arise and take pity on Zion, since the time has come to show her mercy. The right time has come.

Psalm 102:17: When YHWH builds Zion, he will be seen in his glory."

Psalm 109:26–27: Help me, YHWH, my God, save me since you love me, and let them know that this is your hand at work, that you yourself have done it, YHWH.

Psalm 140:8: Day of the battle (יום נשק).[184]

Psalm 140:11: Let the burning coals fall down on them! Let them be thrown into deep pits, no more to rise!

Psalm 149:9: To carry out on them the judgment written. That is honor for all his Hasidim.

Components of apocalyptic notions also emerge.[185] In spite of all the individual differences, especially between Ps 34:13–23 and the other points of view, we can summarize the following important commonalities:

Future expectations are conceived dualistically throughout, which results from the aforementioned strained relationships. The poor hope that YHWH will justly repay the wicked and evil, while God will not abandon those that abide with him as the poor.

Of course, the author responsible for Ps 34 does not seem to know of any eschatological future vision. Nevertheless, in our view, it is not a great

---

184. The expression "day of the battle" (יום נשק) in Ps 140:8 reminds us of the similar eschatological motif in the Qumran texts (e.g., 1QHᵃ 7:20 and 1QM 1:11–12; 7:5–6) and in the book of Zephaniah (e.g., Zeph 2:2–3 and 3:11, 16).

185. Cf. מספר חיים in Ps 69:29 with בספר in Dan 12:1 and הספר in Dan 12:4; see also Ps 40:8.

step, after several disappointing experiences, to move from a hope for speedy implementation of YHWH's retributive justice to a hope (which ultimately included apocalyptic concepts) for a still dualistically conceived but now final eschatological action by YHWH.[186]

We cannot assume a development that was carried out systematically or deliberately. Here, Otto Plöger's view of the development from eschatology to apocalypse is illuminating for our investigation:

> This line is not without its breaks; connecting pieces must be drawn up hypothetically by trial and error. Moreover, it is not a straight and consistent line. At times, it takes a few altogether backward steps or remains at a point on reaching it. Above all, the misconception must be ruled out that we are dealing with a line that is primarily characterized by a forward-moving development, which would have deliberately left behind the stages of development it had overcome. Elements repeatedly emerge of the older restorative eschatology, which expects a definitive formation of historical circumstances; that is to say, a completion of this earthly world with Israel as its focus. But increasingly these elements are being interpreted by more modern ideas as being characterized by the end of the present world as well as by the emergence of a new aeon that appears to be reserved for Israel alone or for what is gradually perceived as Israel.[187]

Thus, the psalms of the poor in question can be arranged diachronically, at least hypothetically, in terms of their future expectations. In this regard,

---

186. The question of the origins of Jewish apocalypticism (i.e., in wisdom or prophecy) cannot be discussed in detail here (on this, see, e.g., Albertz 1992, 634–36). However, it can be assumed that the prophetic-eschatological group and the wisdom-oriented circle no longer opposed or confronted each other but instead came together or at least significantly influenced each other. This transition seems to have taken place at a certain point in the postexilic period (probably before the completion of the final form of the book of Daniel, namely, prior to 164 BCE; on the dating of the final form of the book of Daniel, see Kaiser 1994, 171). Thus, in view of the final text of the book of Daniel, the apparently different future expectations of the psalms of the poor discussed above can be traced back to the same circle of authors. Hypothetically, one could postulate a line of development from the wisdom psalms (e.g., Pss 25; 34; 37; 62; and 73) to the eschatological psalms of the poor (e.g., Pss 12; 35; 40; 69; 76; 94; 102; 140; and 149). A typically apocalyptic text, 1 Enoch (5:7), shares the motif of "possession of land by the pious" with a wisdom psalm (Ps 37:11) as well as with a prophetic-eschatological text (Isa 60:21); on this, see Uhlig 1984, 514.

187. Plöger 1968, 131–32.

it is interesting and hardly accidental that eschatological elements surface in such psalms, in which the conflict between the two sides is sharply reflected. This clearly applies to Pss 12; 35; 40; 69; 76; 94; 102; 109; 140; and 149. Therefore, a correlation exists between the aggravation of the conflict and the emergence of eschatological expectations. Accordingly, on the basis of these observations, the material examined so far can be arranged as follows: Pss 25; 34; and 62 reflect an earlier stage of the conflict (Stage 1); Pss 37 and 73 might have been conceived somewhat later (Stage 2); and Pss 12; 35; 40; 69; 76; 94; 102; 109; 140; 146; 149 and Jer 7:1–12; 11:18–12:6; 15:10–21; 17:12–18; 18:19–23; 20:7–13 are of more recent date (Stage 3).[188]

There is no doubt that between the psalms of the poor and the Qumran texts that we will investigate in the next chapter there are commonalities and clear parallelisms. Despite the divergences we have also observed, the findings so far support, on the whole, the premise of the initial question of our investigations. Up to the present, the meaning of the terminology relating to the poor in the psalms has been debated. Now we may assume a largely consistent theological horizon for the problem, which in turn suggests a specific point of origin for the psalms of the poor.

In light of their particular characteristics, these psalms can be associated with an orientation of piety in the Persian and Hellenistic period, which, with its religious convictions, came into confrontation with other groups within the Judean community. These pious people signal such confrontation by using terminology relating to the poor. What is important for the suppliants in these psalms is that they present themselves, in contrast to their enemies, as exclusively dependent on the help and support of YHWH.

For the members of this orientation of piety, the terminology relating to the poor is a type of honorific or trademark by which they wish to indicate, from their point of view, their special status before God and before the world. Unlike the opposing group—the political leaders of Jerusalem and the temple leadership—the pious circle, as poor ones, adhere truly and exclusively to YHWH. They are the true righteous ones and the servants of YHWH. Only the pursuit of such an attitude of humility and self-abasement will find divine recognition.

---

188. Some portions of the prose texts in the book of Jeremiah (Jer 7:1–12; 22:1–5; 26:2–6; 32:40–41) seem to derive from this stage of development in the piety of the poor. On this, see also §4.4, above.

Their situation of suffering does not result from the fact that the opposing side was aiming to exploit and suppress them economically, that is, to drive them to impoverishment.[189] The reason for the hostilities was rather that the pious rejected their adversaries' theological standpoint and the way of life derived from it. The adversaries saw in this an attack on their own positions and a hindrance to their own political growth and economic prosperity as well as to the methods being used to achieve these goals. In conclusion, the psalms of the poor cannot be ascribed to lower-class circles (e.g., impoverished hired workers, small farmers, shepherds, destitute servants, or people deprived of their rights) but rather to circles of people who possessed a notable level of material capacities.[190]

The theological group that gave written expression to the theology of the poor considered itself to be in conflict with Jerusalem's political elites, particularly the temple leadership. In this regard, it stood very close to groups whose conflicts are described similarly in certain Qumran texts.[191] As Lenski notes, the exercise of power and privilege by elites tends to evoke diverse reactions from other classes of society.[192] In particular, members of the priestly class often react with a religious claim that their basis of power is independent of the ruling elite.[193] As already mentioned in chapter 2, a priestly class such as the Levites (Ezra 2:40; 3:9–12; 6:16; 8:30; Neh 3:17; 7:43; 8:11; 10:28) or the forerunner of the group that was later called Hasidim (1 Macc 2:42; 7:13; 2 Macc 14:6) is an ideal candidate for the aforementioned authorial group. Levites and Hasidim were not part of the upper class, since they were priests who were ranked lower than the כהנים

---

189. The fact that some psalms refer to practices of economic exploitation and suppression by adversaries (e.g., Pss 37:7–8; 62:11; and 73:6–7, 12) need not necessarily mean that the suppliants themselves were affected by these practices. It could be due to the fact that the suppliants observed such practices and criticized them with these remarks.

190. Of course, this notion does not mean that the lower strata were not able to orally form some parts of the psalms of the poor. It is possible that some psalms of the poor were shaped orally among the very poor and were theologized and written down by a wealthier theological group. At this point, it must be highlighted that my hypothesis regarding the authorship of the psalms of the poor is mainly based on the issues of literacy and not on the issues of intellectual or spiritual capability. For a detailed discussion of these matters, see ch. 2, above, and ch. 8, below.

191. On this, see §7.2, below.

192. Lenski 1966, 63–64.

193. Ibid., 67.

(Ezra 2:36; 3:2; 6:9; Neh 3:22; 5:12; 7:64; 12:41). They seem to have suffered from status inconsistency.[194] In the Judeo-Christian tradition, the priestly class frequently resisted oppressive and unjust rule, defending the rights of the underclass.[195] It is also worth noting that lower-ranking priests such as Levites were frequently engaged in hostile situations with the higher-ranking כהנים.[196]

6.7. On the History of the Piety of the Poor
in the Postexilic Judean Communities

Investigation of Isa 66 suggests that a certain dispute existed within the postexilic communities.[197] According to Isa 66:1–5, YHWH is clearly on the side of the "poor" and of "those that tremble at his word" (v. 2) and is against those whose cult practices he rejects and whom he will bring to justice (vv. 3–4).[198] Isaiah 66 thus reflects an internal Judean conflict between one group with an eschatological orientation and another with a temple- and cultic orientation.[199]

It is not clear exactly which historical circumstances led to the conflict described in Isa 66, but it seems likely that the conflict had a long prehistory. Was the seed already sown when, after the catastrophe of 587 BCE, diverging theological reflections on coping with it emerged? At this point we need only to recall the different positions regarding the reconstruction

---

194. Status inconsistency indicates a social phenomenon that becomes apparent when a person's resources are not ranked consistently according to different social class systems. For details on this social phenomenon, see ch. 1, above. The lower-ranking priests such as Levites and Hasidim, in sharp contrast to their high position within the educational and occupational class systems, did not enjoy a high rank within the political and cultic class systems. With this theory of status inconsistency, the active participation of Levites and Hasidim in writing and following the theology of the poor can be persuasively argued. For further discussion, see ch. 1, above.

195. Lenski 1966, 263.

196. Pohlmann 2004, 486–98.

197. On the details, see Ro 2002, 35–75.

198. For further discussion, see ibid., 46–63.

199. Ibid., 61–63. Likewise, according to Berges, the group mentioned in Isa 66:2, 5 stands "in sharp contrast to the 'brothers who hate you' (66:5), probably to those that believed to find their safety in the temple and in ritual observance" (1999, 173). Isaiah 66:1–4 refers to "a relativization of the temple cult" (ibid., 172); on the critical attitudes to cult and sacrifice in Ps 69:31–32, see Berges 2000, 175.

of the temple and related discussions about the appropriateness of prophecies of salvation.[200] However, the question is also whether the positions reflected in Isa 66 were in fact in total disagreement with each other theologically.[201] In Isa 66, the temple- and cultic orientation on the one hand and eschatologically oriented piety on the other hand are in confrontation. This might be due to the fact that the theological conflict in Isa 66 is intrinsically connected with fluctuations in the social structures of power and order (66:5). In other words, such fluctuations were decisive for unilaterally intensifying the confrontation and for taking a certain theological position. There is insufficient evidence for an exact dating of the conflict described in Isa 66.[202] At this point we cannot say any more about it than that it likely dates from the late Persian to the early Hellenistic period. Nevertheless, it is possible to propose a hypothetical relative chronology for the religious conflict discussed in Isa 66 and for the other religious confrontations occurring during the late postexilic period.

In Isa 66:5, the "poor" (v. 2) are still willing to acknowledge their adversaries as their "brothers." It is obvious that "both groups still belong to the same community."[203] If we compare the situation discussed here with the constellation of factions in the confessions of Jeremiah, it may be supposed that the confessions reflect a later stage in the conflict, since they only deal with outright rejection and dismissal.[204] Therefore, we can agree with Pohlmann in "classifying the confrontation found in the confessions as a continuation and intensification of a long-running dispute."[205] The confessions make it quite clear that compared to Isa 66, the tensions between the suppliant (and the orientation represented by him) and the opposing faction have worsened to the extent that we must assume an irreversible split within the Persia-era Judean communities.[206]

---

200. See Jer 5:12; 7:4; 8:11; and 14:13; for the salvific prophetic position, Hag 2:9.

201. On this, see, e.g., the comments in Plöger 1968, 135.

202. Following Vermeylen (1978, 492–94), we could date v. 5 and vv. 14–15, which are particularly significant for our discussion, to the fourth century. Berges (1998, 482–84, 530) considers the turn of the fifth to the fourth century BCE. Steck (1991, 229–42) tentatively dates the composition of Isa 63:7–66:24 to around 300 BCE.

203. So Westermann 1981, 330.

204. As in Isa 66, the adversaries of the suppliant in the confessions belong to leading circles at the temple in Jerusalem.

205. Pohlmann 1989, 74.

206. See the radical desires of the suppliant for destruction in, e.g., Jer 12:3b ("set them apart for the day of slaughter"); 17:18; 18:21–23; and 20:11–12.

As the foregoing investigations were able to show, such developments are also reflected in the so-called psalms of the poor.[207] Thus, with regard to Pss 25; 34; and 62 we can assume a situation in the postexilic period in which the confrontation between both factions does not yet imply a total break or an irreversible split. Moreover, here the speaker in the psalm does not yet react with consistent appeals for YHWH to destroy the enemy.[208] Moreover, we may suppose from the nature of the confrontation that a certain "equal ranking" of the factions existed. The situation in Pss 37 and 73 is different when compared to Pss 25; 34; and 62; here there are some indications pointing to the fact that the conflict has intensified. Finally, we can infer from Pss 12; 35; 40; 69; 76; 94; 102; 109; 140; and 149 that the conflict deteriorated further. We can observe here that eschatological expectations corresponding to the threatening situation became more and more evident. Therefore, a gradual development over a considerable period of time that ultimately resulted in the total segregation of the opposing groups is apparent in the texts concerning the piety of the poor.

The religious differences worsened further during the Hellenistic period as the theocratic and temple-oriented circles of the priestly aristocracy in Jerusalem gradually succumbed to Hellenistic assimilation.[209]

---

207. In some of these psalms, as assumed for the so-called confessions of Jeremiah, confrontations between a suppliant of the piety of the poor and representatives of the temple cult might have been incorporated; on Ps 40, see Hossfeld and Zenger, who associate the psalms with groups that "conducted their worship without the sacrificial cult" and "increasingly (for theological and political reasons) opposed the power claim of the priestly hierarchy at the temple" (1993, 252). As discussed above in ch. 4, a critical and negative perception of the priestly circle at the temple of Jerusalem is found not only in the psalms of the poor, but also in Jeremiah's confessions as well as in some portions of the prose sermons in the book of Jeremiah, a representative example of which is Jer 7:1–12. The aforementioned texts seem to derive from the same theological group that is based on the theology of the poor in the postexilic period. Analysis of Jer 7:1–12 indicates that this theological group also raised an opposing voice against the theology of the Deuteronomistic editors; for a detailed discussion, see §4.3, above.

208. See, e.g., the suppliant in the so-called confessions of Jeremiah.

209. Hengel 1988, 322. As a reason for this, Plöger assumes "an indifferent attitude toward the eschatology in the priestly hierarchy of Jerusalem" (1968, 58). "There must be a certain emptiness and aimlessness, because one expected nothing more from religion. They lost the elements that could have given fresh impetus to their religious life. Thus, in the circle of the higher priesthood one became susceptible to

The eschatologically oriented piety of the poor had to deal with the fact that, in view of the increasing political as well as economic prosperity of the opposing side, the validity of YHWH's retributive justice no longer appeared comprehensible (see, e.g., Ps 37:1, 7, 8 and Jer 12:1–4).[210] Added to this were the disadvantages, insults, and persecutions enacted by the theocratically oriented lay and priestly aristocracies (see, e.g., Isa 66:5; Pss 35:10; 69:5, 12–13; 102:9).

During the Hellenistic period of the fourth–third centuries BCE, in which the texts embodying the piety of the poor in the book of Zephaniah were composed, the break between the different currents was so far-reaching that the eschatologically oriented circles assumed and propagated the belief that the representatives of the temple, including the ruling class prevailing in Jerusalem, had as a whole fallen out from YHWH's plan of salvation because of their haughty, aggressive, and ruthless behavior (Zeph 2:1–3; 3:11–13).[211]

The piety of the poor repeatedly reminds us of the Qumran-Essenes, particularly because of their often recognizable aversion to or reservations against certain circles connected to the temple.[212] It is relevant to note here a structural parallelism to the piety of the poor and to recognize a spiritual/theological as well as historical connection. Consequently, not only do the so-called Hasidim belong to the past history of the Qumran-Essene movement, but this past history can be traced back further (e.g., the term חסידים in Ps 149:1, 5, 9).[213] The piety of the poor articulated in the biblical

---

what was luring externally within the scope of one's own view. It is not by chance that, particularly in this circle, attempts at hellenization during the first decades of Seleucid rule fell on fertile ground. The gradual receding of eschatological expectation, which was seen as obsolete, contributed significantly to the secularization of certain influential groups within the priesthood" (ibid.). The full-scale Hellenization of Palestine by the Seleucids seems to have occurred after circa 200 BCE (for archaeological evidence, see Wol. Thiel 2007, 364–81).

210. On the general economic situation of the postexilic period in Palestine, see, e.g., Hengel 1988, 32–107; Kippenberg 1978, 55–75; and Albertz 1992, 536–41.

211. For further discussion, see Ro 2002, 76–112.

212. On the aversion of the Qumran community/Essenes to certain circles responsible for the temple, see ch. 7 below.

213. According to Hengel (1988, 323 n. 448), we should assume for Ps 149 "a formation in the 'prechassidic' circles in the third century BCE." See also Nõmmik (1999, 526–27), who associates the texts on justice in the psalms (composed between the fourth and third centuries BCE) with the prehistory of the Hasidim.

texts examined above can be regarded as a type of precursor movement for these pious people of the Maccabean period (1 Macc 2:42; 7:13–14; 2 Macc 14:6).[214]

Let us inquire further about why this precise terminology relating to the poor was used prominently as a means of self-definition and as an indication of lowliness. At this point, we can consider the following: if all power and wealth were gradually concentrated in the hands of the opposing side, and real piety to YHWH was absent due to their practices, it was unavoidable for the piety-of-the-poor faction to distinguish itself from the opposing group in terms of their different attitude to YHWH, with the righteous on one side and the wicked on the other. It was also necessary to publicly clarify their own position that they did not approve of their adversaries' practices and their greed for possessions (see, e.g., Pss 37:1, 7–8; 62:11; 73:6–7) and therefore defined themselves as the poor. Thus, with the terminology relating to the poor as a self-definition, they demonstrated before the world and before God that they, unlike their economically and politically prospering adversaries, did not seek to enhance their own social position. Therefore, their self-definition as poor was the religious trademark of these (certainly not impoverished) pious people as well as a sign of their lowliness and of the theology of humility.[215]

---

214. For a more detailed discussion of the possible authorial group for the piety of the poor related to the Hasidim, see §6.6 above.

215. Considering Bammel (1959), we can also assume that, e.g., the double form עָנִי וְאֶבְיוֹן, a frequent expression in the Psalms for the attitude of the suppliant toward God, originally signified that the suppliant is submissive to God (עָנִי) and thus approaches God as a petitioner (אֶבְיוֹן). Also for Israel's neighbors, the self-depiction poor is affirmed in prayers without indicating material poverty. For Egypt, see, e.g., Brunner and Beyerlin 1975, 59 n. 123: "In the language of piety, the term 'poor' does not solely refer to material need. Praying means śnmḥ, i.e., 'to make oneself poor,' to be humble before God." See also ibid., 64 n. 148; furthermore, see Kaiser 1991, 880 for the text of Simut, also known as Kiki (ca. 1250 BCE), who designates the goddess Mut as the inheritor of his wealth: "I am a weak man of her place, a poor one and a pilgrim of her city; I have disposed of my possessions in favor of her power." See also the comment by Lambert (1960, 18 n. 1) that the Babylonian King Nabopolassar was able to regard himself as poor.

6.8. Conclusion

The following attributes of the psalms of the poor have gradually emerged from the investigation thus far: (1) the terminology relating to the poor is used as a self-depiction by the respective authors or their followers; (2) the terminology relating to the poor—including the stranger (גר), the widow (אלמנה), and the fatherless (יתום)—is employed as a synonym of the persecuted righteous; (3) references to an internal Judean conflict are present; and (4) eschatological positions (which may be considered the most recent material in the Psalter) can be identified.

The reason and the initial point at issue for the present investigation was the controversial discussion over (1) what is meant by "poverty" as thematized in numerous texts of the Hebrew Bible, especially in a number of psalms; (2) whether and to what extent there are references in these texts to a certain type of piety of the poor; and (3) how these references can be understood from a theological and sociological perspective.

The main concern was to examine the assumption—which has been strongly advocated in relatively recent research—that the relevant texts of the Psalter testify to a piety of the poor and are closely associated with a movement of the poor. Some scholars even argue that the adherents of this piety belonged to a totally impoverished and downtrodden lower stratum and a lower-class conventicle. Regarding the situation of the Qumran-Essenes and their piety of the poor, it is striking that a large, influential, and materially well-off community was able to describe itself as a "community of the poor."[216] The terminology relating to the poor functions mainly as a self-depiction of the Qumran community to emphasize its own sinfulness and lowliness.[217]

What is characteristic of the use of terminology relating to the poor in some psalms of the poor is that the terms are set within an eschatological horizon of expectation. The consciously assumed humility circumscribed with traditional attributes was regarded as the precondition for the pious to overcome eschatological crisis. According to the piety-of-the-poor-movement, election and elevation are assured by God to the humble and the low. Therefore, the members of this theological orientation considered themselves to be the poor.

---

216. On this matter, see §7.2, below.
217. For details, see §7.1.1, below.

The psalms of the poor investigated in this chapter present a type of piety that is very similar to the theology portrayed in some relevant Qumran texts in the next chapter.[218] The circumstances reflected in, for example, Isa 66:1–17 are comparable to the situation of the Qumran texts.[219] The texts clearly indicate situations of theological confrontation with the temple leadership. The piety of the poor, obedience to the law, and eschatological movements in confrontation with the temple leadership are found in Isa 66:1–17 as well as in certain Qumran texts. In Isa 66:1–17 there is a critical rejection of the temple and an aversion to circles officially responsible for the temple because of their incorrect cult practices.

Isaiah 66:1–17 sheds light on the theological dispute between the two internal Judean groups. The text reflects a stage of conflict in which one faction called the "poor" and "those that tremble at YHWH's word" (Isa 66:2) was pushed into ignominy. The members of this faction hoped that YHWH would finally affirm their theological position at the eschatological judgment. They also believed that the opposing faction, that is, those who "believed to find their safety in the temple and in the observation of rituals," would be punished at the judgment. [220]

With reference to the theological background of the conflict between both sides, we can be sure about Isa 66:1–17 that the use of terminology relating to the poor (עני) in Isa 66:2 does not indicate economic poverty; עני in Isa 66:2, along with "contrite spirit" (נכה רוח), is a purely theological category.[221]

Investigations of the Psalter have shown that in a considerable number of psalms the terminology relating to the poor plays a role as a self-depiction in the context of conflict situations. In some of these psalms of the poor, even eschatological positions are identifiable (e.g., Pss 12; 35; 40; 69; 76; 94; 102; 109; 140; and 149). Despite their self-depiction as the poor, the group of people behind the relevant psalms of the poor cannot be equated with the socioeconomically impoverished lower classes. Rather, they are theologically well-trained intellectuals with a particular interest in sapiential topics. The real problem for them was not material poverty

---

218. Furthermore, see, e.g., Isa 66:1–11; Jer 7:1–12; 11:18–12:6; 15:10–21; 17:12–18; 18:19–23; 20:7–13; 22:1–5; 26:2–6; 32:40–41; Zeph 2:1–3; 3:11–13.

219. See ch. 7, below.

220. Berges 1999, 173.

221. For further discsussion, see Ro 2002, 58–59, 62–63.

but rejection and persecution by their adversaries (e.g., Pss 34:22; 35:4, 7, 11, 12; 37:12, 14; 40:15–16; 62:4–5; 140:5, 9), the invalidity of God's retributive justice (e.g., Pss 37:1, 7; 73:3, 12), the wrath of God (e.g., Ps 102:11), one's own sin (e.g., Pss 25:7, 11, 18; 40:13) and inner pain and sickness (e.g., Ps 102:4–6).

We may assume that a postexilic group composed these psalms of the poor. The members of the group oriented themselves around a piety of humility and lowliness using terminology related to the poor. They were confronted with rejection and hostility from religiously and politically powerful groups in the Judean community, especially the leading circles of the temple in Jerusalem. As the conflict worsened and intensified, the piety-of-the-poor group began to adopt an increasingly eschatological orientation. In this respect, the groups behind the relevant psalms of the poor are very close to those circles whose conflicts are reflected in Isa 66 as well as in the relevant Qumran texts.

The foregoing investigations lead to the following conclusions. Regarding the texts discussed, we must be very wary of the notion that the terminology of the poor employed in the relevant texts refers to material poverty. Rather, it seems to point to a consciously postured attitude of humility and a theologically reflected consciousness of lowliness towards YHWH.

It is remarkable that terminology relating to the poor is used as a self-depiction in both the prophetic literature and the Psalms, that is, in different sections of the Hebrew Bible. It is also worth noting that terminology relating to the poor was employed over a long period of time, up to the period of the Qumran-Essenes.[222] This can only be explained by concluding that the piety articulated in the texts investigated had great significance within the Judean communities for a long period of time. There must have been theologically reflective individuals who sought to offer proper answers to their communities using the language of poverty in didactic psalms (e.g., Pss 34; 37; and 73) and liturgical texts (e.g., Pss 12; 25; 35; 40; 69; 76; 102; 109; 140; 146; and 149). They also composed eschatologically charged texts in the Psalms as well as in the prophetic literature. These postexilic theologians actively participated in the editorial process of the book of Jeremiah and stood in sharp confrontation to Deuteronomistic theology.[223]

---

222. On the terminology relating to the poor in the Hodayot, see §7.1, below.

223. On the criticism by the piety-of-the-poor-oriented redaction in the book of Jeremiah toward the Deuteronomistic theology, see §4.3, above.

Finally, we must point out that the texts investigated here cannot be evaluated as evidence of any particular admiration of poverty in the material sense.[224] For the authors of these texts, material poverty was not a precondition of piety and did not ensure a special relationship with God. For them, it was only decisive that one regard oneself as poor before God and therefore as totally dependent on God.[225] In other words, they believed that one should act with an awareness of one's humility and lowliness before God.

---

224. Cf. in contrast Hengel (1988, 100), who avers that "the Chassidic-apocalyptic circles were clearly committed to condemning wealth and highly evaluating poverty in terms of religion, which found its perfect expression in the Qumran community and in its self-depiction 'the poor' (אביונים)."

225. We may recall Luther's "Wir sein pettler. Hoc est verum" (1967, 318); here, too, "beggars" is not used in the sense of the material poor.

7
THE PIETY OF THE POOR IN THE QUMRAN COMMUNITY

7.1. Poverty Terminology in the Hodayot: Defining the Problem

The previous chapter analyzed the meanings and connotations of some terms related to poverty in Yehud that were used as self-designations by religious groups. These terms for poverty seem to have played a special role in the self-understanding of certain religious groups in the Judean communities of Persian- and Hellenistic-era Palestine. The concerns of the previous chapter continue in this chapter. What is the theological substance of the piety of the poor in certain psalms, and how is it related to the conception of poverty in the Dead Sea Scrolls? These are the questions to which this chapter is devoted. Therefore, attention should now be paid to how this piety of the poor articulated in some Psalms and prophetic texts was transmitted and taken up by subsequent generations.

Accordingly, this chapter is concerned with the problem of poverty terms in the Qumran-Essene community. We will provide several arguments indicating that the language of poverty in the literature from Qumran carries eschatological connotations. The relevant Qumran texts seem to imply situations of theological confrontation with the temple leadership. The self-expressions of being poor in the relevant Qumran texts can be characterized by a tripartite constellation of "the redemptive God—the oppressed suppliant—the adversaries intimidating the suppliant." Toward God, the poverty terminology functions as an expression of the suppliant's own sinfulness and lowliness; in relation to adversaries, it highlights the threatening superiority of godless adversaries in order to develop a discourse of divine intervention for the suppliant. According to the piety of the Qumran community, election and elevation are assured by God to the humble and the lowly. The language of poverty seems to presuppose such a conceptual assumption.

Certain texts from Qumran seem to be profoundly influenced by the so-called piety of the poor. The Qumran community understood itself as a "community of the poor" (עדת האביונים).[1] In light of this, it might be possible to gain a new perspective on the development of the piety of the poor presented in the Dead Sea Scrolls as well as to illuminate specific criteria for evaluating relevant texts from the Hebrew Bible.

To this end, a range of Qumran texts will be presented and evaluated below. For this purpose, the collection of thanksgiving songs called the Hodayot, in which poverty terminology is used significantly more frequently than in other texts from Qumran, must first be considered.[2] The following terms relating to poverty occur in the Hodayot:[3]

אביון	1QH[a] 10:32; 11:25; 13:16, 18, 22
ענו	1QH[a] 6:3; 13:21; 23:14
ענוה	1QH[a] 4:22
עני	1QH[a] 9:36; 10:34; 13:13–14
רש	1QH[a] 10:34; 13:14, 20
יתום	1QH[a] 13:20
פתיים	1QH[a] 10:9
נמהרים	1QH[a] 9:35; 10:9; 13:21

The passages listed above will be examined by asking whether or not the terms for poverty connote "material poverty." In other words, we should try to understand whether the author of the relevant texts in each case addresses life-threatening circumstances related to a lack of material goods or other situations of socioeconomic misery, or whether the terms for poverty should be understood in a religious context.[4] This problem

---

1. 4Q171 2:10; 3:10; see also 1QpHab 12:3.
2. For the history of research on the Hodayot, see, e.g., Hughes 2006, 1–33.
3. Lohfink 1990a, 42.
4. The question of whether the text of the Hodayot derived from one author or several authors should be left open here. On this issue, see, e.g., Segal 1951, 135; Schubert 1952, 23; Molin 1954, 103; and Harkins 2012, 449–67. Harkins argues that "the vivid and dramatic language in the Teacher Hymns should not be understood as evidence of a real person's experience but rather as a marker of a textualized self, a rhetorical persona that seeks to describe phenomenal, extraordinary experiences through an imaginal body. This view goes against a long-held scholarly view that has hypothesized that these compositions can be traced back to the experiences of the founder of the community, the Teacher of Righteousness. The Teacher Hymns Hypothesis has

can be summarized in the following question: Were the relevant terms selected and used as words of self-description that reflected socioeconomic marginalization (*paupertas*) or a certain religious piety or attitude (e.g., "humility in front of God," *humilitas*)?

If the relevant terms contain clearly negative connotations, then the first interpretation can be regarded as more accurate. A clearly positive connotation would be an indication that the author consciously and carefully selected the terms for self-description. If it turns out that the relevant terms connote both positive and negative attributes in their surrounding contexts, then an examination is warranted of whether the negative meanings are connected with circumstances related to material poverty or are instead associated with other disadvantages with which the author is confronted.

As an example, 1QH[a] 13:5–19 will be examined and evaluated:[5]

1QH[a] 13:5–19[6]

(5) I give you thanks, Lord, because you did not desert me when I stayed among a for[eign] people [… and not] according to my guilt (6) did you judge me, nor did you abandon me to the plottings of my inclination but you saved my life from the pit. You gave [...] among (7) lions, appointed for the sons of guilt, lions which grind the bones of strong men, and drink the bl[ood] of heroes. You made my (8) lodging with many fishermen, those who spread the net upon the surface of the water, those who go hunting the sons of injustice. And there you established me for the judgment, (9) and strengthened in my heart the foundation of truth. The covenant, therefore, for those searching for it. You closed the mouth of the lion cubs, whose (10) teeth are like a sword, whose fangs are like a sharpened spear. Vipers' venom is all their scheming to snatch away. They lay in wait, but did not (11) open their mouths against me. For you, my God, hid me from the sons of Adam, concealed your law in [me, un] til the moment of (12) revealing your salvation to me. For in the distress of my soul you did not desert me, you heard my call in the bitterness of my soul, (13) you paid attention to the outcry of my pain in my com-

---

never been the consensus view among Scrolls scholars, yet it has unduly influenced the popular understanding of these texts" (464).

5. On the literary structure and theological interpretation of the text, see, e.g., Harkins 2013, 2018–55; García Martínez and Tigchelaar 1997, 171; Lichtenberger 1980, 61–65; B. Kittel 1981, 80–97; Lohfink 1990a, 63–77; Nitzan 1994, 349; Morawe 1960, 111–35; Jeremias 1963, 218–26; and Schultz 1974, 60–66.

6. Translation follows García Martínez and Tigchelaar 1997, 171.

plaint and saved my soul of the poor man [נפשי עני][7] in the lair of lions, who sharpen their tongue like swords. (14) And you, my God, you closed their teeth so they would not rip up my soul of the poor and wretched [נפשי עני ורש];[8] their tongue has been drawn in (15) like a sword into the scabbard, so that it would not [dest]roy the soul of your servant [עבדכה]. And to show your greatness /through me/ before the sons of Adam, you did wonders (16) with the poor [באביון], you placed him [like g]old in the cruci[ble] to be worked by fire, and like purified silver in the furnace of the smiths to be refined seven times. (17) The wicked [רשעי] of the nations hustle me with their trials, and the whole day they crush my soul. (18) But you, my God, have changed the storm to a calm and have freed the soul of the poor [נפש אביון] like […] prey from the power of (19) lions.

In this segment of the text, the suppliant describes himself relatively frequently as "a poor one." He uses the terms עני, רש, and אביון in lines 13, 14, 16, and 18, all of which are in the masculine singular form. Therefore, the terms clearly refer to the one who composed this text.[9] Furthermore, terms for poverty like ענוים "the poor people" (1QH[a] 6:3; 13:21; and 23:14), נמהרים "the trembling" (1QH[a] 9:35; 10:9; and 13:21), and פתיים "the simple-minded" (1QH[a] 10:9) always emerge in the plural form and must have accordingly meant the suppliant's addressees. Based on this, one can assume that the terms characterize the suppliant's supporters who turn to his messages and teachings (see esp. 1QH[a] 9:35; 10:9).

Further examination reveals that the suppliant's typical self-designation אביון is also often used as a designation for the congregation.[10] Likewise, the lexeme עני, with which the suppliant characterizes himself in 1QH[a] 13:13–14, is used to designate the supporters in 1QH[a] 9:36. This circumstance is most likely connected with the fact that the "I" who expresses the prayer in the Hodayot is not so much biographical as typical or exemplary. Each member of the community could apply the statements found in the Hodayot to himself or herself. The religious experiences described

---

7. García Martínez and Tigchelaar (1997, 170) read נפש{י} (my soul) instead of נפש (soul).

8. Here again we follow the reading of García Martínez and Tigchelaar (see n. 7 above).

9. The self-designation of the praying individual as poor is found also in 1QH[a] 10:32; 10:34 (עני); 11:25 (אביון); and 13:20 (יתום רש).

10. 1QH[a] 13:22; 4Q171 2:10; 3:10; 1QpHab 12:3.

could easily be related to each member of the community. Despite their first-person style, the songs might reflect the self-understanding of the entire community.

Thus, the following analysis is based on the assumption that the "I" in the Hodayot includes a collective sense, meaning that the self-conscious-ness of the whole Qumran community is reflected therein. We can subse-quently conclude that the topic of poverty in the Hodayot is by no means a special idea or the particular thought of an individual, but a collective worldview that the whole community shared.[11] This methodological pre-supposition is also valid for the analysis of other texts from Qumran. Thus, the literary-critical and redaction-critical questions related to the relevant Qumran texts will not be intensively examined in this analysis.

The terms for poverty are mainly used in 1QH[a] 13:5–19 in connec-tion with statements about God's saving actions (ותצל, 1QH[a] 13:13; סגרתה, 1QH[a] 13:14; הגבירכה and הפלתה, 1QH[a] 13:15–16; פלטתה, 1QH[a] 13:18) toward the suppliant (lines 13, 14, 16, 18). The suppliant is in a situation of distress. In other words, as in the relevant psalms of the poor discussed in the previous chapter, the terms for poverty stand in a three-point con-stellation: the saving actions of God—the suppliant in the situations of distress—the suppliant's enemy.[12] Whenever one of the poverty terms emerges as a self-designation of the suppliant, the oppressing actions of the enemies and the following actions of salvation of God are reported at the same time. The following are three examples of this from the Hodayot:

1QH[a] 13:13
You have saved
(ותצל—1. God's deliverance)

---

11. Harkins 2012, 464–67. In this context, Harkins's conclusion is intrigu-ing: "This essay has asked whether the Teacher of the Teacher Hymns is a historical Teacher-figure. My conclusion to this question, first asked more than fifty years ago by Sukenik, is that this is not a historical person. The vivid and dramatic references to the speaker's experiences in the Teacher Hymns do not point to a historical flesh and blood Teacher but rather construct an imaginal body that assists the reader in entering into the world of the Hodayot" (467).

12. See §6.5.2, above. See also Harkins 2013, 2054: "The enemies are likened to monstrous beasts and lions with swords for teeth. He describes his foes by the ferocity of their savage mouths, lips, and tongue, which point to the viciousness of their mali-cious words. This text underscores both the severity of the speaker's ordeal and the extraordinariness of divine deliverance."

my soul of the poor man

(נפשי עני—2. The supplant as a poor one)

in the lair of lions, who sharpen their tongue like swords.

(אריות אשר שננו כחרב לשונם—3. Persecution by adversaries)

1QH^a 13:14

And you, my God, you closed their teeth,

(סגרתה בעד שניהם—1. God's deliverance)

so they would not rip up

(יטרפו—2. Persecution by adversaries)

my soul of the poor and wretched.

(נפשי עני ורש—3. The suppliant as a poor one)

1QH^a 13:18–19

And the soul of the poor

(נפש אביון—1. The suppliant as a poor one)

you have freed

(פלטתה—2. God's deliverance)

like […] prey from the power of lions.

(מכה אריות—3. Persecution by adversaries)

The main concern of the aforementioned texts is not an objective description or illustration of concrete situations of poverty. It is not concerned with poor people or material poverty. In its core message, the relationship of the suppliant to God and to his or her enemies is of central interest. The significance of terms like "poor" and "poverty" can thus not be understood without consideration of these double relationships.

The poor seem to be helpless and powerless over their adversaries, yet at the same time the suppliant describes himself as poor because he experiences divine salvation as one who is helpless and powerless. For this, one can refer to 1QH^a 10:31–36, where the same three terms for "poor" (עני, רש, and אביון) appear as in 1QH^a 13:5–19 and where they are used just as in 1QH^a 13:5–19, always in connection with the verbs פדה ("to redeem"; see 1QH^a 10:32) and עזר ("to help"; see 1QH^a 10:34), which describe God's deliverance.

1QH[a] 10:32–33[13]
You have freed
(פדיתה—1. God's deliverance)
the life of the poor person
(נפש אביון—2. The supplant as a poor one)
which they thought to finish off by pouring out his blood.
(חשבו להתם דמו לשפוך—3. Persecution by adversaries)

1QH[a] 10:34–35[14]
But you, my God, have freed
(עזרתה—1. God's deliverance)
the soul of the poor and needy
(נפש עני ורש—2. the supplant as a poor one)
from the hand of someone stronger than him
(מיד חזק ממנו—3. Persecution by adversaries)

Thus, the question arises as to whether the self-designation "poor" puts its priority on the relationship of the supplant toward God and therefore expresses a special self-assessment before God. If there is such a priority, then it may be termed a status that derives from the will of God. It would then be an appropriate form of existence before God. On the other hand, the self-designation could result from the fact that the threat and pursuit by adversaries led the supplant to a situation of poverty, so that the supplant used the self-designation "poor" as an appeal before God. In this case, the terms related to poverty would mean a form of existence that derives from economic suppression and material deficiency caused by one's enemies.

In other words, it remains to be clarified whether more emphasis is placed on the aspect of "poor in relation to God" (see, e.g., 1QH[a] 13:21–22) or on the aspect of "poor in relation to one's adversaries" (see, e.g., 1QH[a] 11:25). In order to clarify this question, we must investigate the unique anthropology of the Hodayot.[15]

---

13. Translation follows García Martínez and Tigchelaar 1997, 163.
14. Translation follows ibid.
15. On this, see, e.g., Lichtenberger 1980, 176–230; J. Maier 1960, 67.

7.1.1. The Anthropology of the Hodayot: Further Self-Designations

The basic anthropological concept of the suppliant can be recognized in the following texts:[16]

> 1QH[a] 9:21–25[17]
> Although I am a creature of clay [יצר החמר], fashioned with water, a foundation of shame and a source of impurity, an oven of iniquity and a building of sin, a spirit of error and depravity without knowledge, terrified by your just judgments. What can I say which is not known? Or declare which has not been told? Everything has been engraved before you with the stylus of remembrance for all the incessant periods and the cycles of the number of everlasting years in all their predetermined times, and they will not be hidden, and will not be lacking from before you. How will a man count his sin? How will he defend his iniquities?

> 1QH[a] 11:23–25[18]
> But I, a creature of clay [יצר החמר], what am I? Mixed with water, as whom shall I be considered? What is my strength? For I find myself at the boundary of wickedness and share the lot of the scoundrels. The soul of a poor person [נפש אביון] lives amongst great turmoil, and the calamities of hardship are with my footsteps.

> 1QH[a] 12:29[19]
> What is flesh compared to this? What creature of clay [יצר חמר] can do wonders?

> 1QH[a] 19:3[20]
> I give you thanks, my God, because you have done wonders with dust; with the creature of mud [וביצר חמר] you have acted in a very, very powerful way.

> 1QH[a] 20:24–26[21]
> And I, from dust [I] have been gathered, [and from clay (ומחמר)] I have

---

16. For a similar anthropology in the relevant psalms of the poor, see §6.4.2.
17. Translation follows García Martínez and Tigchelaar 1997, 159–61.
18. Translation follows ibid., 167.
19. Translation follows ibid., 169–71.
20. Translation follows ibid., 189.
21. Translation follows ibid., 193.

been [fo]rmed to be a source of impurity, and of vile filth, a pile of dust, mixed with [water,...] a lodging of darkness.

The metaphorical self-depiction in these passages, namely, of being a "form made of clay" (יצר החמר)—which is characteristic of the pessimistic anthropology of the suppliant—has its origin in the potter's language.[22] Beginning in Jeremiah (Jer 18:2–7) and Deutero-Isaiah (Isa 45:9 and 64:7), the noun and the verb יצר were used to signify the sovereignty of God. The noun יצר "form" implies that man without God's discretion is nothing but clay or dust (1QS 11:22). Therefore, the expression יצר החמר articulates the frailty and nothingness of human existence, inasmuch as God's power and glory is the measure.[23]

As the juxtaposition of יצר החמר and נפש אביון in 1QH[a] 11:23–25 (see above) clearly shows, the anthropological self-depiction of the suppliant as a form of clay closely conforms with the self-depiction of being poor. Both of these are the outcome of a strangely pessimistic image of humanity as understood by the Qumran community: the suppliant in 1QH[a] 9:21–23 considers himself to be a form of clay (יצר החמר) and one that is kneaded with water, an epitome of shame and source of impurity, a smelting furnace of guilt and an edifice of sin, an erring spirit and one that is distorted without discernment, and frightened by God's righteous judgments.

At the same time, the admission of one's own sinfulness is closely associated with the self-depictions as a "form made of clay" and "poor." By confessing to being poor as well as low, wretched, and sinful creatures, the suppliant and his followers set themselves apart from their adversaries and thereby justify their special religious status before God.[24] Naturally, they may regard themselves as those especially favored and chosen by God, and as the true Israel, chosen even from their mothers' wombs. For example, 1QH[a] 17:29–31 states:[25]

For you have known[26] me since my father, from the womb [..., ... of] my mother you have rendered good to me, from the breasts of her who

---

22. J. Maier 1960, 65–66 (on 1QH[a] 9:21).

23. Ibid., 66.

24. On 1QH[a] 11:21 ("formed of dust"), see ibid., 79: "The chosen one was created by God as futile and susceptible, like the ungodly, but for a different purpose."

25. Translation follows García Martínez and Tigchelaar 1997, 185.

26. According to Jer 1:5, know = choose; see J. Maier 1960, 102.

conceived me your compassion has been upon me, on the lap of my
wet-nurse [...] from my youth you have shown yourself to me in the
intelligence of your judgment.

And in 1QHᵃ 4:21–22:[27]

However, I have understood that [you smoothen] the path of the one
whom you choose [בחרתה] and by the insight [of your knowledge you
pre]vent him from sinning against you, you [re]store his humility [ענותו]
through your punishment, and by [...] you [...] his heart.

According to Johann Maier, these reflections lead to the conclusion that
the poor one entrusts his legitimacy to God, knowing well at the same
time that he, as a futile and sinful creature, has no claim on God's benevo-
lence and that his right may only be restored through the restoration of
God's honor.[28] The poor one completely submits to the will of God, contrary to his adversaries, namely, the wicked who boastfully control the law
and wealth. This notion of poverty thus became a religious conviction,
regardless of the material condition of the individual, as also in the case of
the rich, whose attitude to God and their neighbor is condemned but not
their possessions.[29]

If we wish to understand what is intended in the Hodayot by the use
of the terminology relating to the poor as the preferred self-depiction,
we must consider the paradoxical juxtaposition of radical nothingness
or awareness of being low against the assured awareness of being chosen.
Here, what is fundamental and characteristic is obviously the scheme of
"lowness—elevation," that is, the one who is most humble is most elevated.[30] The mirror image of this is "pride goes before a fall," which is typical
thinking of wisdom literature.[31] This might account for the basic pattern
of piety articulated in the Hodayot.

---

27. Translation follows García Martínez and Tigchelaar 1997, 149.
28. J. Maier 1960, 84.
29. Ibid.
30. Ibid., 85.
31. See, e.g., Prov 16:18; 17:19; 18:12; and 29:23. For references to YHWH's antipathy to highly placed and overbearing individuals, see, e.g., Gen 11:1–9; Isa 2:12–17;
10:33–34; 14:12–15; Ezek 17:24; 21:31; Job 22:29; and Sir 10:12–14. On the motifs of
elevation and humiliation in Qumran texts, see, e.g., 1QM 14:11–15; for these motifs

In conclusion, we must note that in the Qumran community, the suppliant's perception of poverty and the piety of the poor is based on a dialectical relationship between a clear consciousness of sinfulness and lowness on the one hand and a distinct awareness of being chosen on the other. From the manner in which the author responsible for the Hodayot in question describes his perception of poverty, we can unequivocally conclude that he is concerned with a basic existential question, namely, what type of existence is worthy before God?[32] This leads to the conclusion that the aspect of being poor before God is more deeply rooted in the piety of the poor in the Hodayot than that of being poor before one's adversaries. Therefore, the terminology relating to the poor primarily emphasizes the suppliant's relationship to God. The view that "poor" means a form of existence that is forced upon them by their adversaries and that deprives them of material possessions is not in the foreground.[33]

It is therefore methodologically inadmissible to limit the semantic scope of the terminology relating to the poor solely to the socioeconomic, material sense of poverty. If we wish to speak about the frequent usage of the terminology concerning the piety of the poor in the Hodayot, then we mean by this a consciously assumed posture of humility and not the piety of people threatened by material poverty. According to Maier, we cannot speak of "one group of the 'poor' in the sense of an organization, but, probably, of a religious movement that later clearly differs from Sadduceeism and Pharisaism, primarily due to its image of humanity (I, 26.35) and eschatology."[34]

7.1.2. Poverty Terminology Describing a Situation of Persecution and Crisis

We have already noted above that the use of the terminology relating to the poor is not restricted to describing the suppliant's relationship to God,

---

in the New Testament, see, e.g., Matt 23:12 and Luke 1:51–53; 14:11; 18:14; see also the topic of the first and the last in Matt 19:30 and passim.

32. See Lange 1995, 226: "The doxology of lowness contraposes the human, who is wretched and wicked from the beginning, to the almighty God, the creator before whom the order of being and history is determined on the heavenly tablets, in order to describe God's righteousness and greatness with praise."

33. See also 1QM 11:7–14, where the poor are portrayed not as victims of their adversaries but rather as God's troops battling against enemies.

34. J. Maier 1960, 85.

but that we can also observe political and social aspects, where one side feels disadvantaged, oppressed, and threatened by the other. Therefore, we must clarify to what extent the terminology relating to the poor can provide information about the type of material needs or social disadvantages the suppliant might have experienced. As is evident from the Qumran-Essene texts, the suppliant and his followers or his community find themselves confronted with a hostile presence or atmosphere.[35] Regardless of one's views regarding the origins of the Qumran-Essene community, it is indisputable that its relationship with the temple in Jerusalem was strained and essentially polemical.[36] Another hostile situation possibly existed with a leader who was regarded as a "man of lies."[37] The real threat and situation of persecution against the Essene community probably emerged mainly from the official temple leadership in Jerusalem. Space does not permit a full discussion of the contentions and tensions with other groups and orientations of piety.[38]

In the various descriptions of persecution and crisis in which the speaker in the Hodayot found himself, the contrast between the suppliant and his adversaries is very striking. In 1QH^a 10:31–36, the adversaries, with their attacks against the suppliant, are seen as "violent people" (1QH^a 10:21; עריצים) and as the "strong" and "powerful" (1QH^a 10:35), from

---

35. Here, the widely accepted hypothesis that the Qumran community was identical with Essenes (or at least a subgroup of Essenes) is assumed. For detailed arguments in favor of this hypothesis, see Stegemann 1999, 116–21, 194–226 and VanderKam 1998, 92–119.

36. On the origins of the community, see, e.g., Lichtenberger and Lange 1997, 66, who argue that "the teacher of righteousness did not appear as the founder of the community, but came as high priest driven by Jonathan into an existing community and claimed there the leadership (see CD I)." On the events that followed, see, e.g., the deliberations of Stegemann (1999, 206). On their relationship with the temple, see Lichtenberger and Lange 1997, 66.

37. The appearance of the teacher of righteousness led to a split in the community: some members of the original community followed him, while those who did not were termed "liars" (Lichtenberger and Lange 1997, 66; for further discussion, see Hengel 1988, 407–9).

38. On many of the distresses of the author and various names for the enemies in the Hodayot and in the Habakkuk commentaries, see Ruppert 1972, 15–225; Brownlee 1982, 1–37; P. Davies 1986, 361–68; van der Woude 1982, 349–59; 1996, 375–84; and Lim 1993, 415–25.

whose hands God has rescued "the soul of the poor [אביון], the wretched [עני], and the needy [רש]."[39]

In 1QHª 13:5–19, the suppliant compares his adversaries to lions, from whom God rescued "the soul of the poor and the needy" (= עני, line 13; רש, line 14), the "soul of the poor" (= אביון, lines 16, 18), and his "servant" (= עבדכה, line 15); for God is with the "orphaned, the needy, the humble [ענוים]" and the "poor seeking mercy" (lines 20–22).[40] Here, too, "there is no suggestion that the 'poverty of persecution' is equated with material poverty."[41]

It is obvious that for the suppliant the emphasis is on the contrast between high and low, powerful and powerless. In sharp contrast to the humble suppliant, whom God supports, the adversaries' attitude demonstrates arrogance toward God. This hostile situation is motivated by theological differences; it results from contradicting positions challenging each other's orthodoxy and does not seem to be about material possessions. Thus, we must completely agree with Lohfink that "the material aspect is simply not the leading viewpoint."[42]

This can also be understood from the fact that "the described plight of the suppliant is often not a temporal distress" but rather "a portrayal of the eschatological horror which occasionally also goes into describing the eschatological world catastrophe."[43] The affliction of the suppliant or his followers is regarded as part of the eschatological horror that needs to be overcome—something that is possible through the power of God alone.[44] It is also an unavoidable transitional phase of lowliness that is to be followed by exaltation. In this theological context, poverty can be understood as a posture of religionness. Being poor in the Hodayot means an attribute

---

39. Here, everything is concentrated on the suppliant being pushed out of the community by the persecution of others. There is "as good as no indication that things such as low economic status, material misery and physical needs are important for the suppliant" (Lohfink 1990a, 59). The suppliant stands here, "as presumed by many who find here a self-description of the 'teacher of righteousness,' against the high priest and the high council" (ibid.).

40. On the enemy in the image of a lion, see, e.g., Pss 17:12; 22:14; 34:11; 35:17; and 57:5. In Ezek 22:25 and Zeph. 3:3 the image of a lion characterizes the debased and oppressive upper class.

41. Lohfink 1990a, 73 on 1QHª 13:5–19.

42. Ibid. on 1QHª 13:5–19.

43. J. Maier 1960, 71.

44. Ibid., 86.

of lowness, awareness of one's own futility and man's powerlessness, associated with the confession of sins. In other words, the awareness of one's own futility and the confession of one's own sins are the preconditions for the mercy of God who forgives sins, gives power, purifies the human heart, and ultimately brings about the eschatological redemption. Such poverty is, in its essence, not a condition, but rather an attitude.[45]

In 1QH[a] 10:20–30, in regard to the portrayal of the plight of the suppliant, it is "clear how various eschatological and mythological archetypes emerge from the chaotic struggle."[46] According to 1QH[a] 13:5–19, the suppliant's persecution is, after all, "a persecution of cosmic dimensions."[47] "After repeated recognition of the futility of humanity," 1QH[a] 11:24–36 describes "the eschatological horror which the pious one overcomes, not through one's own strength ... but only by virtue of being chosen and strengthened by God."[48]

7.2. The Subject of the Poor in Other Qumran Texts[49]

The terminology relating to the poor as a self-depiction of the community, poverty as an attribute of lowness, confession of one's own futility and powerlessness as an attitude of religionness, and the eschatological expectation that is characteristic of this attitude play an important role in other Qumran texts as well.[50]

---

45. Ibid., 86–87.

46. On 1QH[a] 10:20–30, see Lohfink 1990a, 49. The quotation is from ibid., 51.

47. Ibid., 75.

48. J. Maier 1960, 79; on 1QH[a] 11:24–36, see also Lohfink 1990a, 92–94.

49. By other Qumran texts I mean the nonbiblical manuscripts from Qumran apart from the Hodayot; this concerns mainly the relevant portions of 1QS, 1Q28b, CD-A, 1QM, 1QpHab, and 4Q171.

50. אביון and אביונים appear clearly in the Qumran texts at least twenty-two times (Ro 2002, 25). In CD-A 6:21, אביון (along with עני and גר) is not used in the sense of self-description. In its context it concerns the instruction "to keep away from the sons of the wicked," to forsake "unclean" and "unlawful" possessions, and to fulfill one's obligations to the socially weak. On the Qumran-Essene notions of ritual purity and on the associated outcome, i.e., the strict distinction between pure and impure possessions, see Paschen 1970, 85–109; see also Lohfink 1990a, 28–31. See the references in CD-A 6:16–17 to the "poor of his people," "widows," and "fatherless" (clearly a reference to Isa 10:2). Accordingly, possession itself is not regarded as wicked (see J. Maier 1960, 51; see also Paschen 1970, 106–9; and Lohfink 1990a, 30–31). The same applies to CD-A 14:14 as to CD-A 6:16–17.

In 1QpHab 12:2–6, the אביונים are portrayed as those oppressed by the godless priests; that is to say, the former are identified implicitly with the followers of the teacher of righteousness.[51] Here, אביונים as a self-description of the Qumran-Essenes parallels other labels such as "the council of the community" (עצת היחד), "the simple ones of Judah" (פתאי יהודה), and "the doers of the law" (עושה התורה).

In the context of obedience to the law, the term "simple one" is a positive label.[52] "Doers of the law" is a fixed phrase that probably came about at the time of the Hasidim.[53]

The expression was familiar among circles with an eschatological orientation, possibly targeted against the Pharisees (Matt 23:3). 1QpHab 12:10 mentions that the "wicked priest" in the "cities of Judah" stole the "possessions of the poor [אביונים]." Here it is unclear whether "the poor" means the socioeconomically weak or rather the "doers of law" settled in the "cleansed" cities.[54]

In 4Q171, a pesher on Ps 37, the "community of the poor" is mentioned twice.[55] In 4Q171 2:9, first Ps 37:11 is quoted: "And the poor [ענוים] shall possess the land and enjoy peace in plenty."[56] This is followed by the marker פשרו על and the interpretation of the quoted text: "Its interpretation concerns the congregation of the poor [עדת האביונים] who will tough out the period of distress and will be rescued from all the snares of Belial. Afterwards, all who shall po[sse]ss the land will

---

51. By "the godless priests" probably the ruling high priests in Jerusalem are meant; for arguments about the identification of the godless priests in 1QpHab, see Brownlee 1982, 1–37; P. Davies 1986, 361–68; García Martínez 1988, 113–28; van der Woude 1982, 349–59; 1996, 375–84; and Lim 1993, 415–25. Lohse (1971, 296) notes that the oppressed are specifically recognized as the followers of the teacher of righteousness.

52. J. Maier 1960, 150: "The attitude of 'simplicity' is the uncompromised obedience which rejected the Pharisaic interpretation of laws (also possibilities of evasion! cf. Dam. I, 19). Cf. the pious in 1 Macc 2:37 who in their simplicity would rather let themselves ... be slaughtered on a Sabbath day than break a Sabbath." On the other hand, we cannot overlook the fact that פותה in 1Q28a I 19 and פתי in CD-A 13:6; 15:15 appears exceptionally in an explicitly negative connotation, i.e., in the sense of "foolish" (Lohse 1971, 49, 93, 99; see also García Martínez and Tigchelaar 1997, 101, 563, 571, who translates the word as "simpleton").

53. As assumed by J. Maier 1960, 146.

54. On אביון in the sense of socioeconomically weak, see Ro 2002, 25; on the other hand, J. Maier (1960, 151) assumes the latter.

55. On this, see Stegemann 1963, 235–70.

56. Translation follows García Martínez and Tigchelaar 1997, 343.

enjoy and grow fat with everything enjoy[able to] the flesh."[57] Here, as in
4Q171 3:10, עדת האביונים undoubtedly indicates the community of the
Qumran-Essenes under the leadership of the "teacher of righteousness."[58]
They find themselves persecuted by the "godless priest" (4Q171 4:8–9)
but in the end will witness the "judgment over godlessness" (4Q171 4:11;
משפט רשעה).

As in the Hodayot and the relevant psalms of the poor, in 1QpHab
and 4Q171 the use of terminology relating to the poor is closely linked to
the aforementioned three-point constellation of the redemptive God—the
desperate suppliant—the adversaries intimidating the suppliant. Moreover, for 4Q171, we must note the unequivocally eschatological perspective (2:8–12).[59]

In the so-called War Scroll (1QM), the eschatological orientation of
the poor is more clearly explained.[60] In 1QM 13:13–14, the terminology
relating to the poor is seen to exhibit a specifically eschatological perspective, stating that God's powerful hand is on the side of the poor.[61] The
notion that the terminology relating to the poor at Qumran indicates a
qualification or distinction in the spiritual sense is further supported by
the phrase עני רוח, which occurs frequently in Qumran texts.[62] In 1QM
14:6–7, the sons of light are called עניי רוח (cf. Isa 66:2):[63]

Those with knocking knees he gives strength to stand upright, and vigor
of loins to broken backs. By the poor in spirit [עניי רוח] [...] a hard heart.

---

57. Translation follows García Martínez and Tigchelaar 1997, 343. On 4Q171
2:9–12, see C. Levin 1993, 379: "According to this Midrash the Qumran-Essenes considered themselves to be the direct successors of the *Anawim* and Hasidim."

58. 4Q171 3:15–19.

59. On 1QH[a] 13:5–19, see §7.1.2, above.

60. A pre-Essene work that was transmitted, revised, and extended by the Essenes;
on this, see Stegemann 1999, 145–47. For eschatological orientation, see, e.g., 1QM
11:13–15: "For you shall deliver the enemies of all lands into the hands of the poor
[אביונים], and into the hand of those that are bent into the dust in order to humiliate
the powerful ones of the peoples, to render recompense to the wicked on their heads,
to prove the court of your truth as just to all sons of men, to make you an eternal name
among the people of ... the wars, and to reveal yourself great and holy before the eyes
of the remainder of the peoples." (author's translation).

61. "Who is like you in power, O God of Israel? And your powerful hand is with
the poor [אביונים]." (author's translation).

62. On this, see, e.g., Lohfink 1990a, 35–37.

63. Translation follows García Martínez and Tigchelaar 1997, 135–37.

By the perfect ones of the path [תמימי דרך] all the wicked peoples shall be destroyed.

The עניי רוח are regarded in this case as synonymous with the perfect ones of the path (תמימי דרך). Material and economic aspects hardly play a role. In the phrase עניי רוח, the spiritual dimension of poverty is obvious. Furthermore, here the spiritual dimension of the poor that is mostly suggested only implicitly in the Hodayot is mentioned explicitly.[64]

Similarly, 1QS 3:8 states, "And by the spirit of uprightness and of humility [וברוח יושר וענותה] his sin is atoned. And by the compliance of his soul [ובענות נפשו] with all the laws of God his flesh is cleansed."[65] Moreover, it is remarkable here that for רוח the expression נפש "soul" is also used. These expressions clearly relate to a spiritual attitude.[66] Furthermore, in 1QS 4:3, רוח ענוה stands parallel to "patience, generous compassion, and eternal goodness."

The eschatological and spiritual side of the perception of poverty is mentioned particularly in 1QM 11:7–11:

And through your anointed, the seers of the rules, you have declared to us the times of the wars of your hands to glorify you [להכבד][67] to

---

64. The term רוח in combination with a word for poor appears in a fragment of the Hodayot: "[... those who l]ove compassion, the poor in spirit [וענוי רוח], those refined by poverty [ענוי]" (1QHᵃ 6:3–4; translation follows García Martínez and Tigchelaar 1997, 153). The text is very mutilated, but the parallel expressions might be sufficient as evidence of a purely spiritual meaning to this doubtful expression without any reference to economic poverty. Lohfink 1990a, 35: "The central meaning of the expressions is undoubtedly moved by the words 'spirit' and 'soul' into the area of inner attitude." Lohfink also states: "With all the emphasis on the fact that the 'poor in spirit' are people, inwardly accepting that before God they are small, bent, and broken, we must see in a semantic continuity that this attitude developed from experience. For the sake of the Torah, they actually do belong to the humiliated, outcast, robbed, and insignificant" (36).

65. Translation follows García Martínez and Tigchelaar 1997, 75.

66. As opposed to J. Maier 1960, 63, who argues that the lexical association in question עני רוח means "the willingness to be poor." His view ignores the Qumran community's pessimistic image of humankind described above, which forms an important background to the piety of the poor at Qumran.

67. García Martínez and Tigchelaar (1997, 130–31) consider the reading להכבד to be secondary. In their opinion, להלחם "to fight" is the original reading here. However, this position is not employed in the present study. For the rationale, see below.

our enemies, to fell the multitudes of Belial, the seven futile peoples, through the hand of the poor of your redemption [ביד אביוני פדותכה] ... and a melting heart [ולב נמס] comes to the gate of hope.... But those of shattered spirit [ונכאי רוח] you shall ignite like a torch of fire in straw that consumes the iniquity and stops not till the guilt is purged. (author's translation)

The synonymous use of אביוני פדותכה, לב נמס, and נכאי רוח indicates that a spiritual attitude is meant; this attitude is in the context of an eschatological viewpoint and stems from the notion of active participation of the poor in the eschatological drama.

With regard to the previous investigation of the use of terminology relating to the poor in Qumran literature, we can conclude that this pious community did not depict itself as being poor or a community of the poor in respect to a status of material poverty. Lohfink concludes in his analysis of the Hodayot: "It is very apparent that poverty never appears to be specifically the lack of earthly possessions, and that, as opposed to the 'poor,' a group of the 'rich' never appears."[68]

This also corresponds with what is otherwise quite well known about the Qumran-Essene community, namely, that its members could not have belonged to an impoverished or economically exploited lower class. According to Hartmut Stegemann, it is certain that

This type of a community of property placed the Essenes in an economically better position than the rest of the Jewish population of Palestine. The Essenes were materially not poor, but relatively rich! The reason for this relative wealth was the principle behind the domestic economy which the Essene community of property followed, because the demands of ritual purity and holiness largely restricted importing goods. For example, the Essene craftsman bought his bread from the Essene baker, trusting that his flour came from the harvest of an Essene farmer who, in turn, would have dutifully paid the tithe on his harvest to the Essene community. What Pharisees and other Jews paid to the temple in Jerusalem, the Essenes were able to keep for their own needs.... The profits which the Essenes earned, thanks to their type of community property, were so large that they were the only Jewish organization of their time which was able to afford to include nonmembers in their system of charity. Therefore, this must be particularly emphasized here, because, in

68. Lohfink 1990a, 99.

many writings, often the erroneous impression is created that the Essenes' renunciation of property had driven them into personal poverty and asceticism, if not even to death by starvation. Exactly the opposite is true. Particularly because of their type of community of property, there was no organized group in ancient Judaism which would have been as wealthy as that of the Essenes.[69]

The archaeological evidence, including the highly developed water system and enormous library at Khirbet Qumran, clearly indicates the Qumran community's substantial economic means.[70] The Qumran community's leading members came from the upper stratum of retainers, priests, and scribes in Jerusalem during the Hasmonean period.[71] The lack of decoration and ornamentation in the building complex at Khirbet Qumran was due to religious rather than to economic reasons.[72]

In the pertinent research, it has been long recognized that the piety of the poor of the Qumran-Essene community did not emerge from a vacuum but had a long prehistory.[73] The clear presence of the phenomenon in both the Qumran-Essene writings and in the Hebrew Bible point in that direction. The pessimistic anthropology and triad constellation (the suppliant, the persecuting adversaries, and God the deliverer) in the Hodayot as well as in the relevant psalms of the poor have already been discussed.[74] Moreover, Isa 66:1–5 and 1QM 11:8–10 constitute further examples of such references.[75]

Furthermore, the dependence on the book of Jeremiah is well established in some Qumran texts, especially in the Hodayot.[76] It is particu-

---

69. Stegemann 1999, 257–58.

70. Stegemann and Stegemann 1999, 160.

71. Ibid.

72. Ibid., 162.

73. "The self-depiction of the suppliant and the labeling of the true community of God by the word for 'poor' ... is nowhere introduced or even substantiated. It occurs rather as self-evident and seems to have been a spiritual inheritance" (Lohfink 1990a, 99). On the prehistory, see J. Maier 1960, 83–85.

74. See §§6.4.2 and 6.5.2, above.

75. Cf. עני (Isa 66:2, cf. פדותכה אביוני in 1QM 11:9), נכה רוח (Isa 66:2, cf. נכאי רוח in 1QM 11:10), and יכבד (Isa 66:5, cf. 1QM 11:8). On this, see J. Maier's observations (1960, 86). Maier also argues that עני ונכה רוח "'nyy rwh in 1QM XIV,7 ... can be easily explained" in light of Isa 66:2 (85).

76. See, e.g., 1QHª 7:15–16 (cf. Jer 10:23); 7:20 (cf. Jer 12:3); 7:24 (cf. Jer 10:23b); 10:14 (cf. Jer 15:10); 10:29 (cf. Jer 18:22); 10:32 (cf. Jer 20:13); 13:7–8 (cf. Jer 16:16);

larly notable that the Hodayot often follow the so-called confessions in the book of Jeremiah.[77] Because the allusions can be proved predominantly for passages that are traced to the "teacher of righteousness," Christian Wolff infers even that "the confessions of Jeremiah were familiar to this man who was from the Hasidic movement."[78] The clear correspondence between Jer 12:3b ("Set them apart for the day of slaughter") and 1QH[a] 7:20 ("But the wicked you have created for [the time] of your wrath, from the womb you have predestined them for the day of slaughter") can only be explained by assuming that the author of 1QH[a] 7:20 had Jer 12:3 in mind, here taking up the cause of the Qumran community.[79]

In recent years, many scholars have examined the prehistory and origins of the Qumran community.[80] According to Émile Puech, the Qumran community may have been not a marginal Essene group but the center of the Essene movement where the Essene way of life evolved.[81] The Hasidim were the spiritual and theological ancestors of the Qumran community.[82] Blenkinsopp argues that there is a historical link between the forerunner group of the Qumran community and the self-segregating diaspora community of the Persian period.[83] Alexei Sivertsev also notes similarities between the social structure of the Ezra-Nehemiah movement (see esp. Neh 8–10) and that of the Qumran community.[84] Based on the aforementioned observations, it would not be implausible to suggest that the origins

---

13:22–23 (cf. Jer 15:10); 16:24 (cf. Jer 17:6); 16:30–31 (cf. Jer 20:9); 17:30 (cf. Jer 1:5); 1QS 2:8 (cf. Jer 18:23).

77. See also Wolff 1976, 124–126. For the piety-of-the-poor-oriented redaction articulated through the confessions of Jeremiah, see ch. 4, above.

78. Wolff 1976, 129.

79. Translation follows García Martínez and Tigchelaar 1997, 155. For the biblical texts that are used in the Hodayot, see Holm-Nielsen 1960, 354–59.

80. See, e.g., Dimant 2016, 7–14; 2014, 238–46; Wassén 2016, 127–150; Crawford 2012, 13–29; Collins 2010, 34–39; Blenkinsopp 2007, 388–93; Hempel 2005, 249–55; Elgvin 2005, 273–79; Puech 2005, 298–302; Boccaccini 2005, 303–9; Campbell 1995, 143–56; Murphy-O'Connor 1974, 215–44.

81. Puech 2005, 302.

82. Ibid.

83. Blenkinsopp 2007, 393. Blenkinsopp concludes that "the *bene haggola* was a self-segregating group that constituted itself as a distinct *qahal*" (394).

84. Sivertsev 2005, 61–72, 77. The sectarian character of the Ezra-Nehemiah movement can be regarded as a forerunner to the sectarianism of the Qumran-Essene texts (Blenkinsopp 2007, 395). On the sectarianism of the Qumran community, see also Jassen 2009, 12–44.

of the piety of the poor in the Qumran community should be sought in the internal Judean sectarianism found throughout the Persian period.

7.3. Conclusion

The observations can be summarized as follows. First, the terms relating to the poor in the Qumran texts primarily function as a self-depiction of the Qumran community. They refer either to the suppliant himself or to his followers and ultimately reflect the collective self-awareness of the entire community.

Second, the self-depictions of being poor in the Hodayot as well as in 1QpHab and 4Q171 are closely related to the aforementioned three-point constellation of the redemptive God—the oppressed suppliant—the adversaries intimidating the suppliant. Toward God, the terminology relating to the poor serves to indicate one's own sinful nature and lowness; in regard to the adversaries, it emphasizes the contrast between one's own baseness and the threatening superiority of the godless adversaries in order to stress one's own need for help from God. In this situation, the evaluation as poor before God is placed above the evaluation as poor vis-à-vis one's adversaries.

Third, nowhere in the texts are there statements objectively defining or explaining the nature of this poverty. As to how the terminology relating to the poor is used, we can clearly see that it does not have to do with a state of economic impoverishment.[85] Moreover, in the Qumran texts, there is hardly any mention of economically distressing situations such as hunger, forced labor, or lack of material possessions.[86] The community faced multiple hostile elements, particularly a conflict with the temple leadership of Jerusalem. Based on this, we may conclude that a real threat to the Qumran-Essene community might have been present in this sphere.

Fourth, the terms relating to the poor often reflect an eschatological perspective; for example, 1QM 11:7–14 presumes an active participation of the poor in the eschatological drama.[87] The deliberately assumed position of humility is the means by which the pious one overcomes the eschatological horror—not through his own strength, but only by virtue of being the chosen one with the strength bestowed on the humble and the

---

85. On the very rare usage in the material sense, see Ro 2002, 25.
86. For exceptions, see ibid.
87. Ibid., 23–29.

lowly by God. Therein a spiritual attitude is affirmed, for example, by the synonymous use of אביוני פדותכה, לב נמס, and נכאי רוח in 1QM 11:7–10.

Fifth, the Essenes' obvious position as a wealthy religious group also underlines the fact that poverty in the material sense is not an essential element in the piety of the poor.

Finally, the theological and lexical correspondences between the Hebrew Bible and the Qumran texts could indicate that the piety of the poor in the Qumran community, which characterizes the foundational spirit of the Qumran-Essenes, had a long prehistory.[88] Therefore, it is necessary to investigate these correspondences and allusions. In particular, biblical texts composed in the Persian and Hellenistic periods would be most meaningful for determining the extent to which similar ideals of piety are articulated in the Qumran texts. Moreover, the texts of the Persian and Hellenistic periods could be instrumental in clarifying whether and in what way the findings in the Qumran texts regarding the community of the poor can contribute to a better understanding of similar concepts in the Hebrew Bible and their historical context.[89]

---

88. See the above-mentioned references in n. 76. Furthermore, cf. the pessimistic anthropology and triad constellation (suppliant, persecuting adversaries, God as deliverer) in the Hodayot as well as in the relevant psalms of the poor (see §§6.4.2 and 6.5.2, above).

89. So already Rofé 1985, 205–17. See also Hengel, who assumes that the Essenes originated from the Hasidim (1988, 319–21) and that the Hasidim had a long prehistory stretching backward from the time of crisis (between ca. 175 and 170 BCE) well into the third century or perhaps even to the Persian period (321); so also C. Levin 1993, 372–74.

8

Epilogue

In our view, the Judean communities in Persian- and Hellenistic-era Palestine can be characterized by the term "coexistence." The descendants of the דלת הארץ, the lay returnees, the priestly returnees and the Samaritans coexisted, influenced each other and formed the Pentateuch together. Dualistic eschatology and cultic cosmology coexisted side by side. Deuteronomistic theology and the piety of the poor coexisted and responded intertextually. Thus, we can say that the Judean communities in Persian- and Hellenistic-era Palestine are filled with a wide spectrum of intriguing topics such as contradiction, literacy, conflict, compromise, poverty, law, and the question of divine justice to name a few.

Based on the investigation so far, it can be concluded that among the major socioeconomic models, the foreign tributary mode of production is the most suitable model for Yehud.[1] The basic features of the tributary mode of production can be summarized with the following three points.[2] First, there is no fully developed private ownership of land, which ultimately belongs to the state. Therefore, the ruler lays claim to the entire territory and there is no clear distinction between tax and rent. Second, the foundation of the system is a number of self-sufficient village communities. The people in the communities work the land in an autonomous fashion but are forced to deliver surpluses to state agents in the form of taxes and rents.[3] Third, the central government plays a commanding role.

---

1. See §3.7, above.

2. Grabbe 2004, 191–92; Houston 2008, 36.

3. It is probable that small peasants had to deliver a certain amount of produce regularly (annually) regardless of the size of the harvest. Sometimes this was not surplus but essential sustenance for the family that was handed over, leaving them short and having to sell family members as indentured servants or do whatever they could to make ends meet. On this, see §§2.3 and 3.7, above.

The main exploiting class, which depends on the labor of the peasants, is the state bureaucracy. The main difference between the tributary mode of production and the ancient class society is pinpointed in the question of whether the people of the exploiting class acted as agents of the state (tributary mode of production) or independently (ancient class society). However, the agent of the state on the one hand and the independent exploiter on the other are not completely exclusive of each other, but sometimes overlap. They are proportional concepts. For example, in the time of Nehemiah, it goes without saying that the direct beneficiaries of the peasants' surpluses came from various socioeconomic backgrounds.[4] However, ultimate authority was located in the Persian central government, for which "money for the king's tribute" (כסף למדת המלך) is explicitly mentioned in Neh 5:4. Furthermore, the tributary mode of production corresponds in many respects to Lenski's sociological model of an agrarian society.[5]

In our view, Lenski's model provides a useful framework for explaining socioeconomic structures, social inequality, and theological developments in the Judean communities in Persian- and Hellenistic-era Palestine.[6] In recent years, Lenski's theories have frequently been applied to the Hebrew Bible.[7] Lenski states that technology, population, and organization are particularly important factors for determining social stratification, which is multidimensional. However, the development of technology is the most influential single determinant of variations in the distributive system, since modification of technology changes not only the level of productivity and the size of the economic surplus, but also basic demographic, political, and productive patterns of organization.[8] According to Lenski, agrarian societies are based on the stage of technology whose requisite criteria includes the appearance of the plow in the case of a simple agrarian society and the use of iron in the case of an advanced agrarian society.[9]

On the other hand, the investigation thus far indicates that even though Lenski's general descriptions offer a useful tool for analyzing ancient Judean society, his model must be adjusted and adapted to the

---

4. See Neh 5:7 (את־החרים ואת־הסגנים).
5. Houston 2008, 36–37.
6. Lenski 1966, 192–95; Lenski, Nolan, and Lenski 1995, 175–222.
7. For the relevant bibliography, see Cook 2012, 41–42.
8. Lenski 1966, 90.
9. Lenski, Nolan, and Lenski 1995, 175–77, 188–91.

Judean communities in Persian- and Hellenistic-era Palestine. First, Lenski's concept of private ownership in agrarian societies should be more accurately defined and explained based on Levantine socioeconomic and ideological circumstances. Lenski claims that, "the proprietary theory of the state ... dominated the thinking of most men of power in virtually all agrarian societies."[10] According to this theory, the state is a piece of property that its owner can utilize for his or her own benefits. Lenski continues:

> It seems far more important to recognize that all agrarian rulers enjoyed significant proprietary rights in virtually all of the land in their domains.... If this is true, then agrarian rulers are owners, or part owners, not only of their royal estates and other lands which they lease, assign, or grant as fiefs, but also of all the lands from which they, by right, exact taxes or tribute—especially when they are free to use these revenues for private purposes.[11]

But Lenski's model cannot persuasively explain how royal ownership coexisted with and related to local possession in Levantine agrarian societies.[12]

Second, Lenski does not give a clear explanation of the religious and ideological mechanism through which "the proprietary theory of the state" was validated and legitimated for the rulers of Levantine agrarian societies. It should be carefully considered that according to ancient Levantine concepts, the land was given by the divinity that the society worshiped (Exod 3:8; Lev 20:24; Deut 6:23) and the rulers were the representatives or principal servants of the divinity.[13] Recent discussions related to the plenitude of land and the shortage of labor also miss this crucial point of ancient religionness in which divinity is related to land as giver and grantor.[14] Again, in Yehud *homo economicus* was tightly integrated with *homo religiosus*. The mechanisms and dynamics of mutual relationships between the socioeconomic and religious dimensions should not be ignored.

Third, it should be taken into account that most agrarian societies in the Levantine area were only a small portion of larger agrarian empires. The Judean communities in Persian- and Hellenistic-era Palestine did not stand and fall alone, but were tiny segments of the Persian Empire or of the

---

10. Lenski 1966, 214.
11. Lenski 1966, 215–16.
12. See §§3.6 and 3.7, above.
13. Horsley and Tiller 2002, 91.
14. See §3.7, above.

Greek Empire. The ruling classes of the Judean communities were simultaneously leaders of the dependent agrarian societies and subordinates of the greater empires. Therefore, the overall socioeconomic and religious systems of the Judean communities within the structures of the Persian Empire or the Greek Empire were significantly more complicated than Lenski's agrarian society theory assumes.[15] Consequently, it seems to be more appropriate to look at Judean communities in the Persian and Hellenistic periods on two different levels, namely, on both a macro- and a microlevel. On the macrolevel, in the context of the Persian and Greek Empires as a whole, the general theoretical framework of Lenski's advanced agrarian society should be employed, but on the microlevel, in the context of the Judean communities in Persian- and Hellenistic-era Palestine, more particular theories beyond Lenski's general model are required. In our view, the Judean communities in Persian- and Hellenistic-era can be analyzed most effectively and appropriately as a postcollapse society and a citizen-temple community for the Judeans in Palestine.[16] The models of postcollapse society and citizen-temple community can be simultaneously employed for Judean communities for a limited time period. However, the postcollapse society model is more suitable for analyzing Judean society from the Babylonian exile until the establishment of the Second Temple, while the citizen-temple community model is more useful for explaining the socioeconomic structures of Judean communities after the completion of the Second Temple. In our view, it seems that features of the post-

---

15. Horsley and Tiller claim that it is necessary to integrate Lenski's priestly class into the ruling class in the case of high-priestly families and into the retainer class in the case of ordinary priests and scribes/sages (Horsley and Tiller 2002, 100) since Lenski was mistakenly and anachronistically making the Western differentiation between church and state, spiritual power and temporal power, and religious and political institutions (ibid., 89). However, the Judean priesthood and its power dynamics in the Persian as well as the Hellenistic periods seems to have played highly distinguished roles in societies with limited literacy by composing and editing considerable portions of the religious documents which became the heart of the Hebrew Bible.

Van der Toorn properly indicates that in Mesopotamian and Egyptian parallels, the Levitical scribes served a decisive function in the study, preservation, transmission, and creation of sacred texts (van der Toorn 2007, 51–108). Regarding the formation history of the Hebrew Bible, in our view it is worth viewing the priestly class as an independent and separate class within postexilic Judean societies.

16. As a postcollapse society, see §5.4, above. As a citizen-temple community, see §3.3, above.

collapse society and the citizen-temple community served to transform, in their own ways, the distributive systems of advanced agrarian Judean communities and to amplify status inconsistency within the communities.

In other words, the Judean communities in Persian- and Hellenistic-era Palestine should be investigated and analyzed with a hybrid combination of the aforementioned sociological models (tributary mode of production, advanced agrarian society, postcollapse society, and citizen-temple community). The key characteristics of the province of Yehud can be summarized as follows:

1. The overwhelming majority of the population were simple peasant farmers, and urban dwellers were a small minority.
2. The residents of urban centers usually dominated Judean communities politically, economically, religiously, and culturally. This phenomenon derives from the fact that both economic privilege and political authority were focused in the urban areas.
3. Literacy and education were typical tools of social control. They served to widen the traditional division between the ruling classes and the ruled people by introducing a major cultural and intellectual distinction between the literate minority and the illiterate majority. This aspect of Yehud has been demonstrated in relation to the formation of the piety of the poor in chapter 2 ("Literacy and the Socioeconomic Context of the Judean Postexilic Communities") as well as in chapter 6 ("The Psalms of the Poor").
4. Power, wealth, privilege, and honor were distributed extremely unequally between the urban minority and the rural majority.[17]

---

17. Guillaume claims that "biblical farmers never were passive victims, neither to natural, economic or political factors" (2014, 57). In his view, the bargaining power of small farmers was mainly located in "the simple fact that, in the ancient world, land was plentiful while farmers were in chronic shortage" (59). Furthermore, Guillaume argues that "the constraints imposed by constant rivalry and conflict of interests between the crown, the elite and the producers are basic to changes in any society" (66) and concludes that "no one party can dispense with the others, and the most exposed party in the triad was not necessarily the peasants" (ibid.). His model sounds like the equilibrium theory that assumes the symbiotic relationship between the peasant and the landlord, between the rich and the poor (Boer 2013, 111; 2015, 12, 32–33).

5. The socioeconomic structure of Yehud resembled a tree with roots spreading in every direction. The socioeconomic center of the Persian Empire was the royal capital, ruled by the Persian king and the most superior members of the governing class. Surrounding the national center were provincial or local capitals ruled by royal officials and intermediate members of the governing class. Each of these local centers was surrounded by smaller towns controlled by lower-ranking members of the governing class. Finally, each of these towns was surrounded by small villages. Jerusalem in the Persian and Hellenistic eras can be viewed as a local capital surrounded by towns and villages.

6. The main source of wealth was the agricultural production of the rural peasants, whose economic surplus was seized and largely redistributed to the governing class in the urban area. Fundamentally, there were three types of exchange in Yehud: reciprocity, redistribution, and market exchange.[18]

7. In particular, concerning the Judean society of Palestine in the sixth–fifth centuries BCE, due to the Babylonian exile and the various factors accompanying the catastrophe (e.g. destruction of infrastructures, war dead and wounded, lack of necessities) the population had been reduced and the socioeconomic foundation was weak in comparison to the

---

According to Guillaume, the rich and the poor in Israelite history needed each other. If the poor became poorer, so did the rich. In this socioeconomic environment, debt functioned as a benevolent method to support the poor small farmers rather than to exploit them. However, due to the lack of solid and compelling evidence I am still skeptical about Guillaume's assumption that the balance of power between the crown, the elite, and the small farmers was a universal phenomenon throughout Israelite history. For details on this issue and other limitations of Guillaume's hypothesis, see ch. 2 as well as §§3.6 and 3.7, above.

18. Polanyi 2001, 49–70. Polanyi adds to these three categories "the principle of householding" which is composed of production for one's own use (55). However, householding can be subsumed within the category of reciprocity, since it should be viewed as a form of family reciprocity (Stegemann and Stegemann 1999, 34). Polanyi's thesis has been influential in biblical studies (see Boer 2015, 23–28 with further bibliography). In spite of some limitations and problems that Polanyi's theoretical framework implies, his work is insightful in many respects for an analysis of Judean communities in the Persian and Hellenistic periods.

preceding monarchic period. Territorial and political fragmentation can also be observed.[19] The discussion of the theological concept of punitive justice in chapter 5 pursues the
trajectory of conceptual transformation in which the material
circumstances of Yehud as a postcollapse society had a profound impact on the formation of a perspective concerning
divine punitive justice.

8. On the other hand, especially from the fifth century BCE on,
there was another tendency for socioeconomic dynamics in
Yehud, in which an economic framework was centered on
the temple economy in Jerusalem.[20] Social, political, and economic power was seated in the Second Temple in Jerusalem.
Membership in this emergent citizen-temple community was
limited to the priesthood and temple functionaries and members of agnatic collectives that were loyal to YHWH. Yehud
consisted of plural entities: a politically as well as geographically defined province on the one hand and the citizen-temple
community on the other, which can be identified with the
golah community of the Babylonian exile.

9. These diverse entities were not so much geographically and
physically divided, as mentally and psychically separated, for
the members of the respective entities had to inhabit the same
territory. This socioeconomic component is addressed in
chapter 3 ("The Portrayal of Judean Communities in Persian
Era Palestine: Through the Lens of the Covenant Code").[21]

It is beyond question that the socioeconomic structure of Yehud had a
profound influence on the production and development of theological
thought and concepts and, of course, vice versa. Relentless materiality
and relentless spirituality are inseparably integrated in the religionness
of Judean communities in the Persian and Hellenistic periods, and here
homo religiosus cannot be separated from *homo economicus*. The piety of

---

19. See, e.g., Tainter 1999, 1021–26; Donner 1995, 387; Faust 2003, 37–53; 2013,
119–25; J. Wright 2006, 67–89; Carter 1999, 190–213; and J. Kessler 2002, 90–96.

20. Weinberg 1992, 34–48.

21. In our view, the sociopolitical competitions and collaborations among these
diverse entities were the main forces that gave birth to the biblical law codes such as
CC, DC, and HC.

the poor in the Psalms as well as in the Hodayot eloquently illustrates this dialectical relationship between socioeconomic structure on the one hand and theological concepts on the other. The piety of the poor was formed and shaped within the socioeconomic framework in which the hybrid dynamics between the postcollapse society and the citizen-temple community served to radicalize status inconsistency.[22] At the same time, the piety of the poor had an enormous impact in Yehud on questions regarding the validity and legitimacy of the relevant socioeconomic pattern.[23] In this sense, the piety of the poor is a clear example of the dynamic dialectics between *homo economicus* and *homo religiosus*.

This study has sought to contribute to a better understanding of the Judean communities in Persian- and Hellenistic-era Palestine as reflected in the Hebrew Bible (and in the case of ch. 7 partially thereafter). The postexilic period, especially the Persian era, was a decisive time period during which such parts of the Hebrew Bible as the Pentateuch and the prophetic books achieved their present shape. Therefore, it is a critically important task in the field of Hebrew Bible studies to clarify the socioeconomic structure and the theological profile of the Judean-Samaritan communities in Persian-era Palestine.[24] Employing philological, historical, and sociological approaches, this study has concluded that the socioeconomic structure of Judean society in Persian- and Hellenistic-era Palestine can be best understood on the macrolevel as an advanced agrarian society that, on the microlevel, also exhibits the characteristics of a postcollapse society and a citizen-temple community.[25]

---

22. See §§2.3 and 6.6, above.

23. See §§6.6 and 6.7, above.

24. For various phases of the relationship between Judean and Samaritan communities, see Hensel 2016, 163–281. According to Hensel, there was no rivalry between the provinces of Yehud and Samaria before the third century BCE (ibid). Samaritan-Judean relations between the sixth and second centuries BCE can be characterized as peaceful coexistence between both communities. Diverse interactions between both communities on Mt. Gerizim and in Jerusalem took place until the Hasmonean period. The common Pentateuch (*gemeinsame Pentateuch*) is an outcome of these interactions. The Pentateuch is the two cult communities' compromise document (ibid, 170–94). For a survey of related discussions, see Pummer 2007, 237–69; Nihan 2007b, 187–223.

25. For critical adjustments and adaptations to Lenski's concepts regarding advanced agrarian societies, see the previous section of this chapter. As already stated in ch. 1, this study does not blindly follow Weinberg's concept of the citizen-temple

As constituents of an advanced agrarian society, the Judean communities in Persian- and Hellenistic-era Palestine were economically almost exclusively based on agriculture. Over 90 percent of community members were involved in agriculture, and most of their economic surplus was derived from farming.[26] Most members of the Judean communities in Persian- and Hellenistic-era Palestine belonged to the lower socioeconomic stratum, while only a small percentage of people could be placed in the upper and middle strata. Lenski indicates that the governing class in an agrarian society rarely contained more than 2 percent of the population.[27] According to Karl Christ, a socioeconomic middle stratum was present in ancient agrarian societies.[28] Géza Alföldy criticizes Christ's concept, claiming that ancient societies, including the Roman Empire, were fundamentally based on a socioeconomic dichotomy composed of upper and lower strata without a middle stratum.[29] Of course, there was nothing in ancient agrarian societies that was equivalent to the middle class

community. Weinberg claims that the population of the citizen-temple community rapidly increased to roughly 150,000 after 458/457 BCE and that this number amounted to 70 percent of the people residing in Yehud (1992, 43). Weinberg is often criticized because of his somewhat exaggerated population numbers for Yehud (Carter 1999, 297–99). According to more recent research, the population residing in Yehud during the Persian period amounted to roughly 30,000 (Lipschits 2003, 360–64 and Grabbe 2004, 200–202). Despite such shortcomings, Weinberg's citizen-temple community theory is still useful for examining postexilic Judean communities. A citizen-temple community seems to have taken form gradually in Palestine after the completion of the Second Temple. It was a community shaped entirely of returnees from the Babylonian exile and was separate from the Persian imperial administration. A large number of returnees from the Babylonian exile did not have vested rights to land in Palestine. Socioeconomic power in Palestine at this time was held by the descendants of the Judeans who were not exiled. The descendants of those who remained in Palestine were outside the framework of the citizen-temple community. The בית אבות was a social body founded in response to the particular religious and socioeconomic circumstances of the returnees from the Babylonian exile. I argued in ch. 6 that the histories of the formation of CC, HC, and DC, as well as their interconnected relationships, can be more persuasively explained by this line of thought. Christ's early acceptance of the concept of the citizen-temple community is both selective and critical.

of modern industrial societies.[30] However, when explaining the socioeconomic class structure of postexilic Judean communities, Alföldy's perspective exposes its limitations. For example, one cannot dismiss the possibility that Levites, temple singers, gatekeepers, scribes, and so on (Ezra 2:70;
Neh 7:72) belonged to neither the uppermost nor the lowest stratum of
postexilic Judean society.

As already stated above, concerning the socioeconomic structures
of postexilic Judean communities, a gradation of the classes should be
assumed.[31] For example, the scribe (ספר) Ben Sira clearly preaches a
middle stratum ethic.[32] The gradation of the classes seems to have developed gradually in the Judean communities in Palestine beginning in the
fifth century BCE, when the socioeconomic structure of Yehud began to
be restored from the simplified social hierarchy that is typical of a postcollapse society.[33] Even though the features of this ancient middle stratum must have been essentially different from the modern industrial
middle class, it seems reasonable or even necessary to assume that there
was such a socioeconomically ambivalent stratum in postexilic Judean
society that was superior to the poor masses but had to serve and defer to
the ruling aristocracy, as Ben Sira and his disciples did. Perhaps the size
of this ancient middle stratum was significantly smaller than the size of
the modern industrial middle class. However, their social tasks and ser-
vices seem to have played qualitatively crucial roles in postexilic Judean
society.

The upper stratum was composed of higher-ranking priests, who took
the leadership of the temple in Jerusalem, and nobles.[34] Relevant texts
from the book of Nehemiah (Neh 2:16, 5:7, 6:17, 7:5, 13:17) as well as

---

30. Meeks 1983, 54–55.

31. See §6.4.1, above.

32. See Horsley and Tiller 2002, 85–86: "Although these functions are explicitly understood as service of the ruling aristocracy, Ben Sira's instruction [for other
sages] displays both a clear sense of the sages' sense of superiority to the peasantry
and urban artisans and a special concern for the sages' role in protecting the poor
and exploited.... Ben Sira displays a similar ambivalence toward, as well as social-
political distance from, the ruling aristocracy that he and others served with their
wisdom.... Yet despite this emphasis on subservience and deference to their superiors
and patrons, Ben Sira also cautions his disciples about the potential dangers involved
in dealing with the powerful (13.9)."

33. Tainter 1999, 1023–24.

34. See, e.g., Grabbe 2004, 172–73 and Gerstenberger 2005, 88–96.

the Elephantine papyri attest to nobles and priests having a position of leadership in the Judean society of Persian-era Palestine.[35] In short, leaders (שרים), priests (כהנים), nobles (חרים), and officials (סגנים) made up the upper stratum of Judean society in this era. In our view, this upper stratum included wealthy individuals descended from the Judeans who had not been exiled.[36]

The middle stratum was composed of lower-ranking personnel of the temple in Jerusalem, such as Levites (לוים), temple singers (משררים), and gatekeepers (שערים).[37] It can also be assumed that most of the scribes (ספרים) were included in the middle stratum of postexilic Judean society.[38] The scribes were employed for administrative duties, while the scribes of the temple in Jerusalem were also involved in writing and editing the religious documents that became the core of the Hebrew Bible. Often, Levites and other lower-ranking priests took on the duties of the scribes of the temple in Jerusalem.[39]

In our view, the following groups made up the lower stratum of postexilic Judean society: the עם (people), אביון (poor), עני (poor), דל (poor), מוך (low, poor), גר (stranger), שכיר (hired servants), עבד (male servants), אמה (female servants), אלמנה (widow), and יתום (fatherless, orphan).[40]

Normally, economic surplus in an advanced agrarian society is distributed among the ruling class, governing class, and the subservient

---

35. Grabbe 2004, 172.
36. See §3.6, above.
37. Grabbe 2004, 226–30.
38. Ibid., 152–54.
39. Ibid., 152–53. For the status of the Levitical scribes in the Second Temple period, see van der Toorn 2007, 104–8. According to van der Toorn, a Levitical scribe was a kind of civil servant belonging to the middle stratum (105). For the positions and functions of the preexilic scribes, see Fox 2000, 101–5.
40. People: Neh 5:1; poor (אביון): Exod 23:6, 11; Deut 15:4, 7, 9, 11; 24:14; (עני): Exod 22:24; Lev 19:10; 23:22; Deut 15:11; 24:12, 14, 15; (דל): Exod 23:3; Lev 19:15; (מוך): Lev 25:25, 35, 39, 47; stranger: Exod 22:20; 23:9, 12; Lev 17:8, 10, 12, 13, 15; 18:26; 19:10, 33, 34; 20:2; 22:18; 23:22; 24:16, 22; 25:23, 35, 47; Deut 14:21, 29; 16:11, 14; 23:8; 24:14, 17, 19, 20, 21; 26:11, 12, 13; hired servants: Exod 22:14; Lev 19:13; 22:10; 25:6, 40, 50, 53; Deut 15:18; 24:14; male servants: Exod 21:2, 5, 6, 7, 20, 26, 27, 32; Lev 25:6, 39, 42, 44, 55; 26:13; Deut 12:12, 18; 13:6, 11; 15:15, 17; 16:11, 12, 14; 23:16; 24:18, 22; female servants: Exod 21:7, 20, 26, 27, 32; 23:12; Lev 25:6, 44; Deut 12:12, 18; 15:17; 16:11, 14; widow: Exod 22:21, 23; Lev 21:14; 22:13; Deut 14:29; 16:11, 14; 24:17, 19, 20, 21; 26:12, 13; orphan: Exod 22:21, 23; Deut 14:29; 16:11, 14; 24:17, 19, 20, 21; 26:12, 13.

retainer class.[41] As a result, ancient agrarian societies are constructed like a tree or plant that spreads its roots in every direction.[42] A system is created whereby economic surplus is transferred in stages to arrive in the hands of city-dwellers, the final consumers. However, there were small farming villages populated by a few hundred villagers that produced the surplus maintaining this system.[43]

In our view, three religious subgroups of the Judean communities in Persian-era Palestine were present in this type of socioeconomic structure.[44] They contributed in their own ways to the formation of the Hebrew Bible while mutually influencing each other. In particular, these three subgroups gave shape to CC, HC, and DC. The most fertile and most significant land was already possessed by the descendants of the דלת הארץ.[45] Competition and conflict among the three subgroups was closely connected to the completion of the Pentateuch.[46] In our view, CC reflects the concepts of the descendants of those who remained, including Samaritans in Palestine during the exilic period, while DC attempts to maximize the social profits of the nonpriestly returnees. The priestly returnees unquestionably formed HC. These three subgroups dominated Judean society around 500 BCE and competed with each other to make their law codes the Judean social norm. In contrast to the returnees from the Babylonian exile, those who attempted to make CC the social norm of Judean society already held land in Persian-era Palestine. From a socioeconomic standpoint, the exile was for them a period of socioeconomic upheaval in which improving one's status was made possible by the acquisition of the most fertile arable land. Members of the former upper stratum of Judean society were taken to the Babylonian Empire as captives, and the preexilic order of land rights held by that upper stratum was shaken to its roots. In an advanced agrarian society, in which agriculture was the primary source of economic value, this situation provided an incredible opportunity for those who remained in Palestine to acquire fertile land. Accordingly, the end of the Babylonian exile could not, for them, be thought of as the starting point for the formation of a

41. Lenski, Nolan, and Lenski 1995, 195–97.
42. Ibid., 196.
43. Lenski 1966, 206.
44. See §3.6, above.
45. D. Smith 1991, 96; and Oswald 1998, 160.
46. See §3.6, above.

new Judean society.[47] Unlike DC and HC, CC does not refer to a desire or ambition for a new ideal society.

As previously mentioned, the differences and contradictions between the three law codes and their relationships within the Pentateuch seem to have been deeply influenced by the political and economic dynamics within which the aforementioned three groups of postexilic Judean society related to each other.[48] CC, HC, and DC were generated in the historical context of the return from the Babylonian exile and reflect different ideal futures for Judean society as planned and imagined from the perspective of each subgroup.[49]

The Judeans in Persian-era Palestine were under political pressure from the Persian Empire to create their own law code for governing and managing their daily lives.[50] However, none of the subgroups of Judean society around 500 BCE had enough power to force their law codes on the other subgroups. Thus, in order to acquire the consensus of the entire Judean society, the three contradictory law codes had to be juxtaposed into a document of consensus, the Proto-Pentateuch.[51] This study has reached the conclusion that the formation of the Pentateuch is not merely a mediation between the theology of lay returnees, represented by DC, and the theology of priestly returnees, as reflected in HC. It is also the product of cooperation with the theology upon which CC is based, that of the Judeans and the Samaritans who were not exiled. Up to now, research on the Hebrew Bible has not directed enough attention to the voices of these Judeans and of the Samaritans who remained and of their descendants. Future research should thus give due attention to the theological legacy of the Judeans and of the Samaritans who remained and of their descendants, not only in their relation to the Pentateuch but also in their relation to the prophetic books and the Writings.

The postexilic Judean community quickly transformed into a postcollapse society.[52] Later in the Persian period, after the construction of the

---

47. See §3.6, above.
48. See §3.6, above.
49. See §3.6, above.
50. See §3.6, above.
51. See §3.6, above.
52. According to Tainter (1999, 1021–26), the following features are representative of a postcollapse society: depopulation, disruption of the social order, simplification of the political and societal hierarchy, territorial and political fragmentation, and

Second Temple, the citizen-temple community gradually began to develop within the framework of an advanced agrarian society.[53] During this historical process, those who had been exiled to Babylon as captives experienced particularly extreme status inconsistency, which played a key role in shaping the theology of postexilic Judean society.

Among the aforementioned three subgroups of Judean society in Persian-era Palestine, those who returned from the Babylonian exile belonging to the priestly class deserve special consideration. They played a crucial role in copying, preserving, writing, and editing the religious documents of postexilic Judean society. Of course, it cannot be said that the members of the priestly class bore exclusive responsibility for handing down religious traditions in the postexilic period, but they were without doubt the most important class with respect to the formation of the Hebrew Bible. As the socioeconomic structure of the citizen-temple community achieved stability, the priestly class gradually began to divide into two socioeconomically heterogeneous groups, namely, higher-ranking priests and lower-ranking priests.[54] The theology of the poor, which left its mark in a number of psalms and prophetic texts, seems to be closely connected to this priestly division during the postexilic period.

In postexilic Judean society, the following nine advanced agrarian social classes were present: a ruling class, a governing class, a retainer class, a priestly class, a peasant class, a merchant class, an artisan class, an unclean and degraded class, and an expendable class. According to Lenski, members of the priestly class within a largely illiterate advanced agrarian society played a crucial role for all of society through their expertise in literacy.[55] The higher-ranking priests of postexilic Judean society—those who controlled the temple in Jerusalem—accepted the preexisting order and supported the ruling and governing classes or joined them, thereby helping to perpetuate the inequality of the social structure.[56] On the other

---

regional differentiation. These features are phenomena that can easily be assumed to have in fact occurred in the postexilic Judean community. For details, see §5.4, above.

53. However, it is probable that for a considerably large portion of the Persian era, Judean society still demonstrated some of general features of a postcollapse society (Faust 2007, 49–50). On this issue, see §5.4, above.

54. Grabbe 2004, 224–30. It is possible that the aforementioned restorative and conservative tendency in the P material derives from the hands of higher-ranking priests.

55. Lenski 1966, 260.

56. Ibid.

hand, the Levites and the forerunners of Hasidim, who had gradually fallen
to the status of lower-ranking priests in their struggle with the higher-
ranking priests for power and authority, rallied against the tyranny and
dishonesty of the ruling and governing classes, including higher-ranking
priests who legitimated and validated the status quo.[57] The lower-ranking
priests developed a theology of the poor that, at least indirectly, reflected
their socially disadvantaged position.[58]

These authors of the theology of the poor were excluded by the
power-wielding higher-ranking priests and felt their rights had been for-
feited. In this way, the theology of the poor seems to derive from the
hands of the lower-ranking priests. As discussed above, one can conclude that the theological perspectives reflected in Pss 12; 25; 34; 35; 37;
40; 62; 69; 73; 76; 94; 102; 109; 140; 146; and 149 indicate a homogenous
orientation and direction.[59]

It is worth noting that a theological perspective based on salvation
history is almost completely absent in all the psalms of the poor.[60] There
are hardly any elements that employ historical salvific motifs or traditions. This suggests that referring to past salvation history carried hardly
any theological meaning or value for the religious group that produced
these psalms. Conversely, the eschatological concepts belonging to the
psalms of the poor (Pss 12:6; 35:9–10; 40:18; 69:28–30, 33–34; 76:9–10;
102:14, 17; 109:22, 26–27, 31; 140:8, 11–13; 149:4) are consistent with
the expectations for the future and the eschatological hopes of postexilic
prophetic literature. The lower-ranking priests who composed the theology of the poor may have also given birth to the dualistic eschatology (see
Mal 3 and Isa 66) discussed in chapter 5. This dualistic eschatology was a
new concept concerning divine punitive justice, that is, the idea that God
gives the righteous and the wicked different rewards within one single
community, established in order to supplement the theological weaknesses of the transgenerational or collective concept of divine punitive

---

57. For a discussion of the Hasidim, see §2.3, above. In postexilic Judean society,
the Levites and the Hasidim were very closely interconnected and as a social body
both groups were almost identical (Albertz 1992, 598–620).

58. See §6.5.2, above.

59. See §§6.5 and 6.6, above.

60. See §6.5.2, above.

justice originating from the priestly worldview (Group 1: Exod 20:5b–6; Num 15–16; Deut 13:12–16; Josh 7; 2 Sam 21; Amos 8:1–2).[61]

It also attempted to improve the individualistic concept of punitive justice (Group 2: Deut 24:16; Jer 31:29–30; Ezek 14:12–20; Ezek 18) based on the principle that appeared during the Babylonian exile: individual retribution in accordance with deeds. In other words, the dualistic eschatology was created to compensate for the limitations of an individualistic theology wherein rewards are thought to be returned to an individual. As such, this dualistic eschatology competed with the theology emphasizing the salvific function of the righteous found in Gen 18:22b–33a (Group 3: Mal 3; Isa 66 versus Gen 18:22b–33a).[62]

At this point, the mutual relationship between Gen 18:22b–33a, on the one hand, and the psalms of the poor, on the other, should be briefly discussed. Perhaps we can hear the voice of the postexilic author in Gen 18:22b–33a who could not agree with the dualistic eschatology of the theology of the poor. The writers of Gen 18:22b–33a believed that treating the righteous and the wicked in the same way—that is, killing both the righteous and wicked together—was illegitimate and unjust, even if it was a divine act. This theological concept is thought to presuppose the individualization of postexilic Judean society.[63] However, the author of Gen 18:22b–33a went a step further than individualization. Even if almost all of society was considered to be corrupt and wicked, there had to be at least a small minority of righteous people; and if that were the case, then forgiveness and patience toward the entire society for the sake of the righteous minority would be more desirable than the annihilation of the evil majority.

The deepest theological concern of Gen 18:22b–33a is the salvific function of the righteous minority in a sinful society. The chief theological interest has moved from the judgment of the wicked to the salvation of the righteous. In contrast to Gen 18:22b–33a, Ezek 14:12–20 and Ezek 18 do not show any interest at all in the concept of a righteous few exercising a salvific effect on a corrupted community. It was far more important for the writers of Ezek 18 that the wicked and the righteous met an end that reflected their actions and attitudes. However, the appropriate functioning of the principle of individual retribution is no longer a real problem for the

---

61. See §5.4, above.
62. See §5.5, above.
63. See §5.3, above.

writers of Gen 18:22b–33a. The protection of the righteous few lay in the heart of the author of Gen 18:22b–33. Perhaps here can be seen a feature of the Judean community as a postcollapse society. In other words, the socioeconomic and demographic circumstances, declining population, shrinking economy, and weakening political power had a glaring impact on the theological concepts of this time period. Amid the socioeconomic situation of a weakened and fragile Judean society suffering from the declining population and shrinking economy of Persian-era Palestine, the author of Gen 18:22b–33a referred to the new theology appropriate for these circumstances as the salvation of the righteous, not the judgment of the wicked. In Marxist terms, the theology of Gen 18:22b–33a can be understood as a case where the base determines the superstructure.

The ideas of sin and punishment in preexilic Judean society were established through religious commandments and ritual rules. These ideas provided the Judean people with clear criteria for who belonged and who did not belong to this sacred cosmos. It was believed that this cosmic order, created by God, could be made to endure by the removal and purging of sin, wickedness, and unrighteousness through the performance of religious rituals. According to this preexilic idea, the cosmos can be maintained by confining the sphere of sin. In the preexilic period, religious regulations and ethical commands offered the necessary standards to certify the position of the insiders of this almost faultless and impeccable cosmos. This priestly idea of a flawless cosmos was closely connected to a sacrificial cultic system, which was, by definition, community-oriented and transgenerational.[64]

Within this ritual worldview, a family, community, city, or even a nation was taken as a single homogenous unit. However, as a result of the disastrous Babylonian exile in the sixth century BCE, the religionness of ancient Judeans within the stability of their flawless cosmos and their faultless social order was completely shattered. The Judeans who survived the national disaster fell into deep despair amid the chaos that surrounded them.[65] After the temple in Jerusalem was destroyed, where could one dedicate sacrifices, or perform rituals for God's grace and atonement for one's sin and guilt? Prior to the completion of the Second Temple, this was the fundamental theological problem facing Judeans during and after the Babylonian exile.

---

64. See §5.3, above.

65. See §5.4, above.

The author of Ezek 18:14–20 placed an emphasis on the idea of individual retribution, since the communal foundation of religious rituals and the collective order of the divine cosmos had been undermined by the destruction of the temple.[66] After the Babylonian exile, the possibility of collective and transgenerational retribution had disappeared, since there was no longer a communal foundation of Judean religionness for a community, a city, or even a nation. Therefore, without cult the only theological choice that was available for the exilic/early postexilic Judeans was to develop the religious principle of individual retribution so that they did not lose their spiritual orientation entirely (Ezek 14:12–20; 18).

However, postexilic Judeans gradually became aware of the latent difficulties in this theological concept.[67] This individual approach eliminated the historical salvific aspect of YHWH, who was supposed to be governing the nation's fate and future, and closed the theological way toward the macrocosmic worldview that emerges from the relationship between YHWH and his people. God was reduced to existing for the sake of resolving the minute problems of individuals, and the great theological dimension of salvation history was largely lost. And so it is no wonder that the theological group that composed the theology of the poor in postexilic Judean society gradually developed a dualistic eschatology—that is, an eschatology that supposed a dualistic resolution in which the righteous are saved and the wicked are destroyed.[68] This theological group made an effort to grasp a hope for God's legitimate justice in an outrageous world where the order and principle of divine retribution seemed to be broken.

For this theological group that composed the piety of the poor, not all of the Judeans could avoid a purifying, eschatological judgment. The only ones who could endure judgment were the "truly pious" (see esp. Pss 12:2; 149:1, 5, 9; cf. Isa 66:2), the "poor" (Isa 66:2; Zeph 2:3; 3:12), the "righteous" (see esp. Pss 35:27; 69:29; 140:14; cf. Zeph 3:13), and the "servants" (see esp. Pss 35:27; 69:18, 37; 102:15, 29; cf. Isa 66:14).[69]

One aspect of the psalms of the poor observed in this study is their neglect or even disregard of the priesthood and the temple in Jerusalem

---

66. See §5.4, above.
67. See §5.4, above.
68. See §5.4, above.
69. See §6.5.2, above.

itself.[70] For example, in most of these psalms, offerings and rites at the temple are not mentioned at all. It is possible to recognize a critical disinterest toward the temple in the aforementioned psalms of the poor. Significantly, this kind of antitemple attitude is also found in the book of Jeremiah. In particular, the piety-of-the-poor-oriented redaction in the book of Jeremiah, including Jer 7:1–12, clearly indicates this theological orientation. For example, the author of Jer 7:1–12 severely criticizes the theological profile of 2 Kgs 18–19 concerning the temple of Jerusalem.[71] The author of Jer 7:1–12 asserts that the prophecy related to the inviolability of the temple in Jerusalem is simply "deceptive words" (דברי השקר, Jer 7:4).

Deuteronomistic editors demonstrate a strong theological concern for the temple of Jerusalem as well as for the Davidic dynasty. They highly esteem the salvific value of the temple of Jerusalem (1 Kgs 8:33–50) and the Davidic dynasty (1 Kgs 11:12–13, 32–39). For the author of Jer 7:1–12, the temple in Jerusalem is no such theological center and has no soteriological effect. These passages conjure up associations with the aforementioned attitude of the psalms of the poor.[72] In our view, it seems probable that the author of Jer 7:1–12 belonged to the same theological group as the authors of the psalms of the poor.[73]

This can also be recognized from the theological nuances of the three groups, the stranger (גר), the widow (אלמנה), and the fatherless (יתום), all of whom appear in Jer 7:6.[74] The theological connotation behind these three groups as given by the book of Deuteronomy is that they are nothing more than the socially disadvantaged whose lives must be protected. However, as previously discussed, the three groups found in Jer 7:6 and 22:3 connote, like the poor (נפש אביון) in Jer 20:13, an image of the sinless yet persecuted righteous.[75] It is clear that the group of texts known as the confessions of Jeremiah (Jer 11:18–12:6; 16:10–21; 17:12–18; 18:19–23; 20:1–13) are surprisingly similar in theological structure and worldview to a selection of the prose texts in the book of Jeremiah (Jer 7:1–12 among others).[76] We can conclude that these texts do not derive from the prophet

70. See §6.5.2, above.
71. See §4.3, above.
72. See §6.5.2, above.
73. See §4.2, above.
74. See §4.3, above.
75. Cf. also the three groups as the persecuted righteous in Pss 94:6 and 146:9.
76. For details, see §4.2, above.

Jeremiah; rather, they were inserted during the postexilic period by an editor adhering to the piety of the poor.[77]

These editors of the piety of the poor were antagonistic to the editors influenced by Deuteronomistic theology. This is evident in the clear editorial differences between the Deuteronomistic editors and the editors of the theology of the poor in the book of Jeremiah. As discussed above, the editors of the theology of the poor who composed Jer 7:1–12 display a strong antagonism toward the temple in Jerusalem. For these editors, the temple was no more than a "den of thieves" (המערת פרצים, Jer 7:11), and the theological expectations that the Deuteronomistic editors had regarding the temple were vain and empty.[78]

One more significant matter that we need to remember is that the aforementioned authors of the theology of the poor belonged to a socio-economically competent group.[79] Many of them were deeply influenced by wisdom literature. Of course, not all of the psalms of the poor display the theological features of wisdom literature. However, elements of wisdom literature are apparent in many psalms of the poor, such as Pss 12; 25; 34; 37; 40; 62; 69; 73; and 104. A theological pattern based in wisdom literature appears throughout the aforementioned psalms of the poor, Jeremiah's confessions (e.g., Jer 12:1–3, 20:1–13), and the Hodayot (1QH[a] 10:20–30; 11:37–12:4; 13:13–18). This is because of YHWH's hatred toward all brazenly proud people: "Pride goes before a fall."[80] This theological motif is of key importance for understanding the piety of the poor.[81] Accordingly, the elevation of the righteous from suffering and persecution (e.g., Prov 24:16) is the central theological theme of the psalms of the poor, Jeremiah's confessions, and the Hodayot. These elements of wisdom literature demonstrate that the authors of these texts received a high level of theological education whose curriculum included theologized sapiential literature.[82]

In the psalms of the poor that we have examined, in particular in Pss 35:27; 40:10–11, the suppliants seem to be in a position, as important and

---

77. See §4.4, above.

78. See §4.3, above.

79. See §6.5.2, above.

80. Cf. Gen 11:1–9; Isa 2:12–17; 10:33–34; 14:12–15; Ezek 17:24; 21:31; and Job 22:29.

81. See §6.5.2, above.

82. See §6.5.2, above.

authoritative figures, to deeply influence the members of their communities. The influential and authoritative position of the suppliants explains why the adversary group desperately wanted to overthrow the suppliants (Pss 35:15–16; 40:15–16). The adversary group pays considerable attention to the suppliants in order to subdue them (see, e.g., Pss 35:15–16; 40:15–16). It can be concluded that the adversaries noticed in the groups of suppliants a serious potential to threaten their own position. This clearly indicates that the theology of the poor was not composed by the economically exploited and completely impoverished lower stratum. Based on the texts of the psalms of the poor, one can assume the existence of an organized religious community independent and separate from the priesthood and the temple of Jerusalem. However, from the adversaries' perspective, this poor community was a capable opponent that they could not ignore or neglect due to its sociopolitical influence and religious authority. The poor in the relevant psalms were a theological rival threatening their adversaries' position.[83]

Of course, the aforementioned observations do not exclude the possibility that some portion of the psalms of the poor may have been germinated verbally by people from the lower stratum of Judean society in the Persian period. While such a scenario cannot simply be taken for granted due to a lack of evidence (i.e., written documents), it is not impossible that considerable elements of the piety of the poor were initially created verbally by the lower stratum of Judean society, and that a theological group belonging to the wealthier stratum was then inspired to further elaborate and theologize the piety of the poor.[84] At this point, I would like to emphasize once again that the aforementioned hypothesis concerning the authorship of the psalms of the poor is closely connected to the issue of literacy in postexilic Judean society. Yet the supposed incapability of the lower stratum to produce such texts is only limited on the level of the written compositions and not to the basic concepts that underlie them. Therefore, it cannot be ruled out that a lower stratum was involved in developing a piety of the poor in its original verbal and nonliterary form in postexilic Judean society. It should be underscored that the aforementioned theory concerning the authorship of the psalms of the poor should not be mis-

83. See §6.5.2, above.
84. See §2.4, above.

understood as diminishing or downplaying the intellectual competence or spiritual capacity of the lower stratum of society.[85]

It is also worth noting that descriptions of the poor in the relevant psalms are inseparably interconnected with the tripartite constellation in which the enemy persecuting the suppliant—the persecuted suppliant—the saving God are present. In other words, the terminology of poverty in the psalms of the poor is almost always accompanied by both the oppressing actions of adversaries and the saving actions of God.[86] Here, as in the Hodayot, the poor are those who are conscious of their own powerlessness. The poor are also aware of how they are in the miserable state of being overwhelmed by a powerful and arrogant enemy. At the same time, they have made a decision to be completely dependent on God because they have confidence and trust in God alone.[87] The poor distinguish themselves from their adversaries by recognizing their own sinfulness and viciousness as well as by locating their hope and reliance only in God.

A dialectic between an admitted sinfulness and lowliness on the one hand and a distinct awareness of being the chosen on the other is an indispensable element of the religionness of these theological groups that composed the texts based on the piety of the poor.

The poverty in the psalms of the poor is not a temporary or provisional state imposed by material deficiency. Rather, it signals a permanent disposition before God that should be consciously chosen no matter what the circumstances. For those who took this theological position, the use of poverty terminology functioned as a kind of honorific trademark. Through this trademark, the poor sought to indicate their special status before God and the world. Using the theology of the poor to set up a contrast with their adversaries—that is, the higher-ranking priests and political leaders who governed the temple in Jerusalem—the poor sought to make it known to God and to the world that they were the truly righteous and pious who faithfully relied on YHWH alone.[88]

The psalms of the poor (Pss 12; 25; 34; 35; 37; 40; 62; 69; 73; 76; 94; 102; 109; 140; 146; 149), Isa 66, the texts of the piety-of-the-poor-oriented redaction in the book of Jeremiah (e.g., Jer 7:1–12; 11:18–12:6; 15:10–21; 17:12–18; 18:19–23; 20:1–13), and the Hodayot seem to have been formed

---

85. For a detailed discussion on this issue, see §2.4, above.
86. See §6.5.2, above.
87. For details, see ch. 7, above.
88. See §6.6, above.

by a group of authors who were deeply influenced by the theology of the poor. These texts are related to the historical circumstances surrounding postexilic Judean communities that continued for several centuries. The aforementioned texts seem to be situated theologically and ideologically within a common linear genealogy.

Once again, the phenomenon of status inconsistency provides a possible answer to why the theology of the poor was generated by a select group of people who cannot be located in the lower stratum of postexilic Judean society. As discussed above, the authors of the psalms of the poor were probably the Levites and the forerunners of Hasidim, who fell to a lower priestly rank in their conflict with the higher-ranking priests administering the temple of Jerusalem.[89] The Levites and the forerunners of Hasidim seem to have received a thorough theological education that a majority of postexilic Judeans could not afford. Therefore, they were able to achieve a high degree of literacy and thus held a high position within the educational class system of postexilic Judean society. Even in the occupational class system, being a priest must have been highly esteemed in a citizen-temple community such as postexilic Yehud. Their tasks as priests included labor that dealt with the creation and preservation of sacred texts.

However, according to Num 18:3, as lower-ranking priests, Levites could not approach either the utensils of the sanctuary or the altar, as they were not the higher-ranking Aaronite priests.[90] Only the higher-ranking priests could approach the sanctuary and altar to perform the various sacrificial rites and cultic rituals reflected in Lev 1–16. It is ambiguous whether Nehemiah promoted the status of the Levites at the expense of the higher ranking priests.[91] The cultic duty of the lower-ranking priests, including Levites and Hasidim, was restricted to aiding the higher-ranking priests as they performed the various rites and rituals (Num 18:3; Ezek 44:11–13). In short, in sharp contrast to their high positions within the educational and occupational class systems, the lower-ranking priests did not have a high status within the political, ritual, and cultic class systems.

---

89. For details, see §2.3, above.

90. For a discussion on the priesthood in ancient Judean society, including the relationship between "Aaronites" and "Zadokites," see Cody 1969, 146–92; Spencer 1992, 1–6; Blenkinsopp 1998, 25–43; Nurmela 1998, 51–175; Schaper 2000, 79–302; and Grabbe 2004, 225–30.

91. Grabbe 2004, 229–30.

With this phenomenon of status inconsistency as a motivator, it is no surprise that a group from this ambivalent priestly class actively engaged in the writing and composition of the theology of the poor. As previously argued, if the terminology of poverty is excluded from the psalms of the poor, there is hardly anything left to support the hypothesis that the suppliants were suffering from material deficiency or socioeconomic poverty.[92] Regardless of the use of the terminology of the poor, it is difficult to explain the absence of concrete expressions delineating material misery. In this study, an answer to this inexplicable phenomenon was given by supposing that the psalms of the poor were not written by people from the oppressed lower stratum.[93] The lack of descriptions related to material poverty demonstrates that the writers of these texts were not members of the economically exploited lower stratum, but rather members of the upper and middle strata. On the other hand, the fact that the authors of the theology of the poor referred to themselves as poor reveals that they pitied the miserable lives of the impoverished lower stratum. They also accuse their adversary faction of economic exploitation and suppression to the lower stratum not as the afflicted, but as the observers (e.g., Pss 37:7–8; 62:11; 73:6–7, 12; 94:6; 146:9). In the hearts of the authors, an intention to sympathize with the economically poor must have existed.[94] At this point, however, we must ask why these authors sympathized with the socioeconomic position of the impoverished lower stratum and identified themselves with the economically poor. To answer this question, the status inconsistency of the lower-ranking priests could offer a helpful clue. I hope future research on the Hebrew Bible will pay more attention to this intriguing and significant social phenomenon.

Having said this, we should remember at the same time that status inconsistency cannot explain all the essential aspects of the piety of the poor. On the one hand (external motivation), the piety of the poor is a textual product of *homo economicus*, since this theological orientation derived at least partly from status inconsistency, a phenomenon that presupposes a social circumstance suffused with *homo economicus*. In such a social circumstance, the authors of the psalms of the poor apparently attempted to maximize their social honor and religious as well as political legitimacy within Judean communities in the Persian and Hellenistic peri-

---

92. See §§2.3 and 6.5.2, above.
93. See §§2.3 and 6.5.2, above.
94. See §2.3, above.

ods. In this sense, the relevant authors seem to have behaved as rational maximizers of profit and utility.

On the other hand (internal motivation), the piety of the poor demonstrates the opposite side of human nature. In the piety of the poor, poverty indicates an attitude of humility and self-denial in which the suppliants' own sinful nature and lowliness are portrayed and sometimes even emphasized in a strangely pessimistic manner. The suppliants in the piety of the poor are fundamentally flawed. They suffer and become frustrated as a result of conflicting desires, and they search for meaning and the sacred, frequently at the cost of their own comfort and well-being. The suppliants' struggles to view and recognize themselves before the Divine are so fundamental and so radical that in this milieu the suppliants seem not to mind irrationally minimizing their own self-interest. Thus, the piety of the poor serves as evidence that a particular religionness had interacted so dynamically with other religionness as well as with the existing socio-economic and cultic hierarchy in Judean communities in the Persian and Hellenistic periods that the "poor" in this religionness may not be naively understood as materially insufficient or marginalized but as a redefined form of piety. In the piety of the poor, the external and internal motivations were inseparably intertwined. Both aspects were merged and fused as essential elements of this form of piety.

Based on the analysis presented above, it is clear that the material situation and political as well as economic circumstances in the Judean communities of Persian- and Hellenistic-era Palestine significantly influenced the theological concepts and ideas that were born in and emerged from the relevant communities. On the other hand, it is also true that in response these theological concepts and ideas exerted their own deep influence on the material, political, and economic circumstances of postexilic Judean society. Again, *homo religiosus* and *homo economicus* are Janusian facets of Yehud's religionness. Neither relentless materiality nor relentless spirituality would be the ultimate message of the Hebrew Bible. "*Die Wahrheit liegt immer in der Mitte* [the truth lies always in the middle]" (Adolph Freiherr von Knigge).

Bibliography

Achenbach, Reinhard. 2009. "Das sogenannte Königsgesetz in Deuteronomium 17,14–20." *ZABR* 15:216–33.

———. 2011. "*gêr—nåkhrî—tôshav—zâr*: Legal and Sacral Distinctions Regarding Foreigners in the Pentateuch." Pages 29–51 in *The Foreigner and the Law: Perspectives from the Hebrew Bible and the Ancient Near East*. Edited by Reinhard Achenbach, Rainer Albertz, and Jakob Wöhrle. BZABR 16. Wiesbaden: Harrassowitz.

Ahuis, Ferdinand. 1982. *Der klagende Gerichtsprophet: Studien zur Klage in der Überlieferung von den alttestamentlichen Gerichtspropheten.* CThM.BW 12. Stuttgart: Calwer.

Albertz, Rainer. 1989. "Die Intentionen und die Träger des Deuteronomistischen Geschichtswerks." Pages 37–53 in *Schöpfung und Befreiung: Für Claus Westermann zum 80. Geburtstag.* Edited by R. Albertz, Friedemann W. Golka, and Jürgen Kegler. Stuttgart: Calwer.

———. 1992. *Religionsgeschichte Israels in alttestamentlicher Zeit.* 2 vols. GAT 8.1–2. Göttingen: Vandenhoeck & Ruprecht.

———. 1994. *A History of Israelite Religion in the Old Testament Period.* Translated by John Bowden. 2 vols. OTL. Louisville: Westminster John Knox.

———. 2001. *Die Exilszeit: 6. Jahrhundert v. Chr.* BiE 7. Stuttgart: Kohlhammer.

———. 2003. "The Thwarted Restoration." Pages 1–17 in *Yahwism after the Exile: Perspectives on Israelite Religion in the Persian Period; Papers Read at the First Meeting of the European Association for Biblical Studies, Utrecht, 6–9 August 2000.* Edited by Rainer Albertz and Bob Becking. STAR 5. Assen: Van Gorcum.

———. 2011. "From Aliens to Proselytes: Non-Priestly and Priestly Legislation Concerning Strangers." Pages 53–70 in *The Foreigner and the Law: Perspectives from the Hebrew Bible and the Ancient Near East.*

Edited by Reinhard Achenbach, Rainer Albertz, and Jakob Wöhrle. BZABR 16. Wiesbaden: Harrassowitz.

———. 2015. *Exodus 19–40.* ZBK 2.2. Zurich: TVZ.

Alföldy, Géza. 1986. *Die römische Gesellschaft: Ausgewählte Beiträge.* Heidelberger althistorische Beiträge und epigraphische Studien 1. Stuttgart: Steiner.

Allen, Leslie. 1983. *Psalms 101–150.* WBC 21. Waco, TX: Word.

Anderson, Gary A. 1992. "The Interpretation of the Purification Offering (חטאת) in the Temple Scroll (11QTemple) and Rabbinic Literature." *JBL* 111:17–35.

Archer, Léonie. 1990. *Her Price Is Beyond Rubies: Jewish Women in Graeco-Roman Palestine.* JSOTSup 60. Sheffield: JSOT Press.

Ashley, Timothy. 1993. *The Book of Numbers.* NICOT. Grand Rapids: Eerdmans.

Ausloos, Hans. 2014. "What Happened to the Proto-Deuteronomist? The Epilogue to the 'Book of the Covenant' (Exod 23,20–33) as a Test Case." Pages 17–29 in *A Pillar of Cloud to Guide: Text-Critical, Redactional, and Linguistic Perspectives on the Old Testament in Honour of Marc Vervenne.* Edited by Hans Ausloos and Bénédicte Lemmelijn. BETL 269. Leuven: Peeters.

Avigad, Nahman. 1976. *Bullae and Seals from a Post-Exilic Judean Archive.* Qedem 4. Jerusalem: Hebrew University of Jerusalem.

Avioz, Michael. 2014. "The Purification of the Levites according to Josephus." *ETL* 90:441–51.

Awabdy, Mark. 2014. *Immigrants and Innovative Law: Deuteronomy's Theological and Social Vision for the* גר. FAT 2/67. Tübingen: Mohr Siebeck.

Backhaus, Franz-Josef, and Ivo Meyer. 2016. "Das Buch Jeremia." Pages 553–82 in *Einleitung in das Alte Testament.* Edited by Erich Zenger et al. 9th ed. Stuttgart: Kohlhammer.

Bailey, K. 1986. "Micro-Macro Analysis of Status Inconsistency: Toward a Holistic Model." Pages 118–29 in *Status Inconsistency in Modern Societies: Proceedings of a Conference on "New Differentiations of Status Structures? On the Viability of the Concept of Status Inconsistency in Contemporary Society," Duisburg, F.R.G., May 7–9, 1985.* Edited by Hermann Strasser and Roger Hodge. Sozialwissenschaftliche Schriften 33. Duisburg: Sozialwissenschaftlichen Kooperative.

Bak, Dong Hyun. 1990. *Klagender Gott—Klagende Menschen: Studien zur Klage im Jeremiabuch.* BZAW 193. Berlin: de Gruyter.

Baker, David L. 2009. *Tight Fists or Open Hands: Wealth and Poverty in Old Testament Law*. Grand Rapids: Eerdmans.

Balla, Emil. 1912. *Das Ich der Psalmen*. FRLANT 16. Göttingen: Vandenhoeck & Reprecht.

Bammel, Ernst. 1959. "πτωχός." *TWNT* 6:888–915.

Banaji, Jairus. 2010. *Theory as History: Essays on Modes of Production and Exploitation*. Historical Materialism 25. Leiden: Brill.

Barnett, Bernice McNair. 2004. "Introduction: The Life, Career, and Social Thought of Gerhard Lenski—Scholar, Teacher, Mentor, Leader." *Sociological Theory* 22:163–93.

Barstad, Hans M. 2003. "After the 'Myth of the Empty Land': Major Challenges in the Study of Neo-Babylonian Judah." Pages 3–20 in *Judah and the Judeans in the Neo-Babylonian Period*. Edited by Oded Lipschits and Joseph Blenkinsopp. Winona Lake, IN: Eisenbrauns.

———. 2008. *History and the Hebrew Bible: Studies in Ancient Israelite and Ancient Near Eastern Historiography*. FAT 61. Tübingen: Mohr Siebeck.

Baudissin, W. W. Graf. 1912. "Die alttestamentliche Religion und die Armen." *Preußischen Jahrbüche* 149:193–231.

Baumgartner, Walter. 1917. *Die Klagegedichte des Jeremia*. BZAW 32. Giessen: Töpelmann.

Becker, Joachim. 1975. *Wege der Psalmenexegese*. SBS 78. Stuttgart: Katholisches Bibelwerk.

Becking, Bob. 2006. "We All Returned as One: Critical Notes on the Myth of the Mass Return." Pages 3–18 in *Judah and the Judeans in the Persian Period*. Edited by Oded Lipschits and Manfred Oeming. Winona Lake, IN: Eisenbrauns.

Bedford, Peter. 2001. *Temple Restoration in Early Achaemenid Judah*. JSJSup 65. Leiden: Brill.

Ben Zvi, Ehud. 1991. *A Historical-Critical Study of the Book of Zephaniah*. BZAW 198. Berlin: de Gruyter.

———. 1992. "The Dialog Between Abraham and YHWH in Genesis 18:23–32: A Historical-Critical Analysis." *JSOT* 53:27–46.

———. 1997. "The Urban Center of Jerusalem and the Development of the Literature of the Hebrew Bible." Pages 194–209 in *Urbanism in Antiquity: from Mesopotamia to Crete*. Edited by Walter E. Aufrecht, Steven W. Gauley, and Neil A Mirau. JSOTSup 244. Sheffield: Sheffield Academic.

Bendor, Shunya. 1996. *The Social Structure of Ancient Israel: The Institution of the Family from the Settlement to the End of the Monarchy*. JBS 7. Jerusalem: Simor.

Berges, Ulrich. 1998. *Das Buch Jesaja: Komposition und Endgestalt*. HBS16. Freiburg: Herder.

———. 1999. "Die Armen im Buch Jesaja: Ein Beitrag zur Literaturgeschichte des AT." *Bib* 80:153–77.

———. 2000. "Die Knechte im Psalter: Ein Beitrag zu seiner Kompositionsgeschichte." *Bib* 81:153–78.

———. 2002. *Klagelieder*. Freiburg: Herder.

Bergey, Ronald L. 1988. "Postexilic Hebrew Linguistic Developments in Esther: A Diachronic Approach." *JETS* 31:161–68.

Berner, Christoph. 2012. "Wie Laien zu Leviten wurden: Zum Ort der Korachbearbeitung innerhalb der Redaktionsgeschichte von Num 16–17." *BN* 152:3–28.

Berquist, Jon. 1995. *Judaism in Persia's Shadow: A Social and Historical Approach*. Minneapolis: Fortress.

Betlyon, John. 1986. "The Provincial Government of Persian Period Judea and the Yehud Coins." *JBL* 105:633–42.

Bettenzoli, Giuseppe. 1984. "Deuteronomium und Heiligkeitsgesetz." *VT* 34:385–98.

Beyerlin, Walter. 1970. *Die Rettung der Bedrängten in den Feindpsalmen der Einzelnen auf institutionelle Zusammenhänge untersucht*. FRLANT 99. Göttingen: Vandenhoeck & Ruprecht.

Bezzel, Hannes. 2007. *Die Konfessionen Jeremias: Eine redaktionsgeschichtliche Studie*. BZAW 378. Berlin: de Gruyter.

Biddle, Mark. 2003. *Deuteronomy*. SHBC. Macon, GA: Smyth & Helwys.

Binns, Leonard. 1927. *The Book of Numbers: With Introduction and Notes*. London: Methuen.

Birkeland, Harris. 1933a. *Ānî and ānāw in den Psalmen*. SNVAO.HF 2. Oslo: Dybwad.

———. 1933b. *Die Feinde des Individuums in der israelitischen Psalmenliteratur: Ein Beitrag zur Kenntnis der semitischen Literatur- und Religionsgeschichte*. Oslo: Grøndahl.

Blenkinsopp, Joseph. 1982. "Abraham and the Righteous of Sodom." *JJS* 33:119–32.

———. 1991. "Temple and Society in Achaemenid Judah." Pages 22–53 in *Second Temple Studies 1: Persian Period*. Edited by Philip R. Davies. JSOTSup 117. Sheffield: Sheffield Academic.

———. 1996. *A History of Prophecy in Israel.* 2nd ed. Louisville: Westminster John Knox.

———. 1998. "The Judean Priesthood during the Neo-Babylonian and Achaemenid Periods: A Hypothetical Reconstruction." *CBQ* 60:25–43.

———. 2001a. "The Social Roles of Prophets in Early Achaemenid Judah." *JSOT* 93:39–58.

———. 2001b. "Was the Pentateuch the Civic and Religious Constitution of the Jewish Ethnos in the Persian Period?" Pages 41–62 in *Persia and Torah: The Theory of Imperial Authorization of the Pentateuch.* Edited by James W. Watts. SymS 17. Atlanta: Society of Biblical Literature.

———. 2007. "The Development of Jewish Sectarianism from Nehemiah to the Hasidim." Pages 385–404 in *Judah and the Judeans in the Fourth Century B.C.E.* Edited by Oded Lipschits, Gary N. Knoppers, and Rainer Albertz. Winona Lake, IN: Eisenbrauns.

Blum, Erhard. 1984. *Die Komposition der Vätergeschichte.* WMANT 57. Neukirchen-Vluyn: Neukirchener Verlag.

———. 1990. *Studien zur Komposition des Pentateuch.* BZAW 189. Berlin: de Gruyter.

———. 1996. "Das sog. 'Privilegrecht' in Exodus 34:11–26: Ein Fixpunkt der Komposition des Exodusbuches?" Pages 347–66 in *Studies in the Book of Exodus: Redaction, Reception, Interpretation.* Edited by Marc Vervenne. BETL 126. Leuven: Leuven University Press.

———. 2002. "Die literarische Verbindung von Erzvätern und Exodus. Ein Gespräch mit neueren Endredaktionshypothesen." Pages 119–56 in *Abschied vom Jahwisten: Die Komposition des Hexateuch in der jüngsten Diskussion.* Edited by Jan Christian Gertz, Konrad Schmid, and Markus Witte. BZAW 315. Berlin: de Gruyter.

———. 2006. "The Literary Connection between the Books of Genesis and Exodus and the End of the Book of Joshua." Pages 89–106 in *A Farewell to the Yahwist? The Composition of the Pentateuch in Recent European Interpretation.* Edited by Thomas B. Dozeman and Konrad Schmid. SymS 34. Atlanta: Society of Biblical Literature.

———. 2011. "Pentateuch–Hexateuch–Enneateuch? Or: How Can One Recognize a Literary Work in the Hebrew Bible?" Pages 43–71 in *Pentateuch, Hexateuch, or Enneateuch? Identifying Literary Works in Genesis through Kings.* Edited by Thomas B. Dozeman, Thomas Römer, and Konrad Schmid. AIL 8. Atlanta: Society of Biblical Literature.

Boccaccini, Gabriele. 2005. "Qumran: The Headquarters of the Essenes or a Marginal Splinter Group." Pages 303–9 in *Enoch and Qumran Ori-*

gins: New Light on a Forgotten Connection. Edited by Gabriele Boccac-cini. Grand Rapids: Eerdmans.

Bodi, Daniel. 1991. *The Book of Ezekiel and the Poem of Erra.* OBO 104. Fribourg: Universitätsverlag; Göttingen: Vandenhoeck & Ruprecht.

Boecker, Hans Jochen. 1984. *Recht und Gesetz im Alten Testament und im Alten Orient.* NStB 10. Neukirchen-Vluyn: Neukirchener Verlag.

———. 1985. *Klagelieder.* Zurich: Theologischer Verlag.

Boer, Roland. 2003. *Marxist Criticism of the Bible.* London: T&T Clark.

———. 2013. Review of *Land, Credit and Crisis: Agrarian Finance in the Hebrew Bible,* by Philippe Guillaume. *BCT* 9:109–12.

———. 2015. *The Sacred Economy of Ancient Israel.* LAI. Louisville: West-minster John Knox.

Bornschier, V. 1986. "Social Structure and Status Inconsistency: A Research Note." Pages 204–20 in *Status Inconsistency in Modern Societies: Pro-ceedings of a Conference on "New Differentiations of Status Structures? On the Viability of the Concept of Status Inconsistency in Contemporary Society," Duisburg, F.R.G., May 7–9, 1985.* Edited by Hermann Stras-ser and Roger Hodge. Sozialwissenschaftliche Schriften 33. Duisburg: Sozialwissenschaftlichen Kooperative.

Brecht, Bertolt. 1988. *Werke: Große kommentierte Berliner und Frankfurter Ausgabe.* Vol. 11. Frankfurt: Suhrkamp.

Bremer, Johannes. 2016. *Wo Gott sich auf die Armen einlässt: Der sozio-ökonomische Hintergrund der achämenidischen Provinz Yehud und seine Implikationen für die Armentheologie des Psalters.* BBB 174. Göt-tingen: V&R Unipress.

Brett, Mark. 2013. Review of *Land, Credit and Crisis: Agrarian Finance in the Hebrew Bible,* by Philippe Guillaume. *BCT* 9:113–15.

Bright, John. 1965. *Jeremiah.* AB 21. Garden City, NY: Doubleday.

Broshi, Magen, and Israel Finkelstein. 1992. "The Population of Palestine in Iron Age II." *BASOR* 287:47–60.

Brownlee, William H. 1982. "The Wicked Priest, the Man of Lies and the Righteous Teacher: The Problem of Identity." *JQR* 73:1–37.

Brueggemann, Walter. 2010. *Genesis.* IBC. Louisville: Westminster John Knox.

———. 2016. "On Reading Mistakenly … and Otherwise: A Response to Roland Boer, *The Sacred Economy of Ancient Israel.*" *HBT* 38:173–184.

Brueggemann, Walter, and William H. Bellinger. 2014. *Psalms.* NCBiC. New York: Cambridge University Press.

Brunner, Hellmut. 1961. "Die religiöse Wertung der Armut im Alten Ägypten." *Saec* 12:319–44.

Brunner, Hellmut, and Walter Beyerlin. 1975. *Religionsgeschichtliches Textbuch zum Alten Testament.* GAT 1. Göttingen: Vandenhoeck & Ruprecht.

Buber, Martin. 1952. *Recht und Unrecht: Deutung einiger Psalmen.* Sammlung Klosterberg, Europäische Reihe. Basel: Schwabe.

Budd, Philip. 1984. *Numbers.* WBC 5. Waco, TX: Word Books.

Bultmann, Christoph. 1992. *Der Fremde im antiken Juda: Eine Untersuchung zum sozialen Typenbegriff "ger" und seinem Bedeutungswandel in der alttestamentlichen Gesetzgebung.* Göttingen: Vandenhoeck & Ruprecht.

Campbell, J. G. 1995. "Essene-Qumran Origins in Exile: A Scriptural Basis?" *JJS* 46:143–56.

Carr, David. 2001. "Method in Determination of Direction of Dependence: An Empirical Test of Criteria Applied to Exodus 34:11–26 and Its Parallels." Pages 107–40 in *Gottes Volk am Sinai: Untersuchungen zu Ex 32–34 und Dtn 9–10.* Edited by Matthias Köckert and Erhard Blum. VWGTh 18. Gütersloh: Gütersloher Verlagshaus.

Carroll, Robert. 1986. *Jeremiah: A Commentary.* OTL. London: SCM.

Carter, Charles. 1999. *The Emergence of Yehud in the Persian Period: A Social and Demographic Study.* JSOTSup 294. Sheffield: Sheffield Academic.

Cataldo, Jeremiah. 2003. "Persian Policy and the Yehud Community During Nehemiah." *JSOT* 28:240–52.

Causse, Antonin. 1922. *Les "pauvres" d'Israël.* EHPhR 3. Strasbourg: Istra.

Chaney, Marvin. 1986. "Systematic Study of the Israelite Monarchy." *Semeia* 37:53–76.

———. 1993. "Bitter Bounty: The Dynamics of Political Economy Critiqued by the Eighth-Century Prophets." Pages 250–63 in *The Bible and Liberation: Political and Social Hermeneutics.* Edited by Norman Gottwald and Richard Horsley. Bible and Liberation. Maryknoll, NY: Orbis Books.

———. 2016. "Some Choreographic Notes on the Dance of Theory with Data: A Response to Roland Boer, *The Sacred Economy of Ancient Israel.*" *HBT* 38:137–144.

Childs, Brevard. 1974. *The Book of Exodus: A Critical, Theological Commentary.* OTL. Philadelphia: Westminster.

Chirichigno, Gregory. 1993. *Debt-Slavery in Israel and the Ancient Near East*. JSOTSup 141. Sheffield: JSOT Press.

Christ, Karl. 1980. "Grundfragen der römischen Sozialstruktur." Pages 197–228 in *Studien zur antiken Sozialgeschichte: Festschrift Friedrich Vittinghoff*. Edited by Werner Eck, Hartmut Galsterer, and Hartmut Wolff. KHAb 28. Vienna: Böhlau.

Cody, Aelred. 1969. *A History of Old Testament Priesthood*. AnBib 35. Rome: Pontifical Biblical Institute.

Collins, John J. 2010. *Beyond the Qumran Community: The Sectarian Movement of the Dead Sea Scrolls*. Grand Rapids: Eerdmans.

Cook, Stephen. 2012. "The Levites and Sociocultural Change in Ancient Judah: Insights from Gerhard Lenski's Social Theory." Pages 41–58 in *Social Theory and the Study of Israelite Religion*. Edited by Saul M. Olyan. RBS 71. Atlanta: Society of Biblical Literature.

Coote, Robert. 1981. *Amos among the Prophets: Composition and Theology*. Philadelphia: Fortress.

Crawford, Sidnie White. 2012. "The Identification and History of the Qumran Community in American Scholarship." Pages 11–29 in *The Dead Sea Scrolls in Scholarly Perspective: A History of Its Research*. Edited by Devorah Dimant. STDJ 99. Leiden: Brill.

Crüsemann, Frank. 1969. *Studien zur Formgeschichte von Hymnus und Danklied in Israel*. WMANT 32. Neukirchen-Vluyn: Neukirchener Verlag.

———. 1992. *Die Tora: Theologie und Sozialgeschichte des alttestamentlichen Gesetzes*. Munich: Kaiser.

Davies, Eryl. 1995. *Numbers*. NCB. Grand Rapids: Eerdmans.

Davies, Philip R. 1986. "Qumran Beginnings." Pages 361–68 in *Society of Biblical Literature 1986 Seminar Papers*. Edited by Kent H. Richards. SBLSP 25. Atlanta: Scholars Press.

———. 2007. "The Trouble with Benjamin." Pages 93–112 in *Reflection and Refraction: Studies in Biblical Historiography in Honour of A. Graeme Auld*. Edited by Robert Rezetko, Timothy H Lim, and W. Brian Aucker. VTSup 113. Leiden: Brill.

Dearman, John Andrew. 1988. *Property Rights in the Eighth-Century Prophets: The Conflict and Its Background*. SBLDS 106. Atlanta: Scholars Press.

Deist, Ferdinand. 2000. *The Material Culture of the Bible: An Introduction*. Sheffield: Sheffield Academic.

Dimant, Devorah. 2014. *History, Ideology and Bible Interpretation in the Dead Sea Scrolls: Collected Studies.* FAT 90. Tübingen: Mohr Siebeck.

———. 2016. "The Library of Qumran in Recent Scholarship." Pages 5–14 in *The Dead Sea Scrolls at Qumran and the Concept of a Library.* Edited by Sidnie White Crawford and Cecilia Wassen. STDJ 116. Leiden: Brill.

Domeris, William. 2007. *Touching the Heart of God: The Social Construction of Poverty among Biblical Peasants.* LHBOTS 466. London: T&T Clark.

Donner, Herbert. 1995. *Geschichte des Volkes Israel und seiner Nachbarn in Grundzügen.* GAT 4. Göttingen: Vandenhoeck & Ruprecht.

Douglas, Mary. 2002. "Responding to Ezra: The Priests and the Foreign Wives." *BibInt* 10:1–23.

Dozeman, Thomas B. 2009. *Commentary on Exodus.* ECC. Grand Rapids: Eerdmans.

Duhm, Bernhard. 1901. *Das Buch Jeremia.* KHC 11. Tübingen: Mohr.

———. 1922. *Die Psalmen.* 2nd ed. KHC 14. Tübingen: Mohr.

Dunn, Stephen. 2012. *The Fall and Rise of the Asiatic Mode of Production.* Routledge Revivals. London: Routledge.

Dyck, Jonathan. 1998. *The Theocratic Ideology of the Chronicler.* BibInt 33. Leiden: Brill.

Ebach, Ruth. 2014. *Das Fremde und das Eigene: Die Fremddendarstellungen des Deuteronomiums im Kontext israelitischer Identitätskonstruktionen.* BZAW 471. Berlin: de Gruyter.

Edelman, Diana. 2005. *The Origins of the "Second" Temple: Persian Imperial Policy and the Rebuilding of Jerusalem.* BibleWorld. London: Equinox.

———. 2007. "Settlement Patterns in Persian-Era Yehud." Pages 52–64 in *A Time of Change: Judah and Its Neighbours in the Persian and Early Hellenistic Periods.* Edited by Yigal Levin. London: T&T Clark.

Eissfeldt, Otto. 1965. *The Old Testament, An Introduction: Including the Apocrypha and Pseudepigrapha, and also the Works of Similar Type from Qumran; The History of the Formation of the Old Testament.* Translated by Peter Ackroyd. Oxford: Blackwell.

Elgvin, Torlief. 2005. "The Yaḥad Is More Than Qumran." Pages 273–79 in *Enoch and Qumran Origins: New Light on a Forgotten Connection.* Edited by Gabriele Boccaccini. Grand Rapids: Eerdmans.

Eliade, Mircea. 1959. *The Sacred and the Profane: The Nature of Religion.* Translated by Willard R. Trask. New York: Brace & Company.

Epsztein, Léon. 1986. *Social Justice in the Ancient Near East and the People of the Bible.* London: SCM.

Fager, Jeffrey. 1993. *Land Tenure and the Biblical Jubilee: Uncovering Hebrew Ethics through the Sociology of Knowledge*. JSOTSup 155. Sheffield: JSOT Press.

Faigenbaum-Golovin, Shira, Arie Shaus, Barak Sober, David Levin, Nadav Na'aman, Benjamin Sass, Eli Turkel, Eli Piasetzky, and Israel Finkelstein. 2016. "Algorithmic Handwriting Analysis of Judah's Military Correspondence Sheds Light on Composition of Biblical Texts." *PNAS* 113.17:1–6.

Fantalkin, Alexander, and Oren Tal. 2013. "Judah and Its Neighbors in the Fourth Century BCE: A Time of Major Transformations." Pages 135–98 in *From Judah to Judaea: Socio-economic Structures and Processes in the Persian Period*. Edited by Johannes Unsok Ro. HBM 43. Sheffield: Sheffield Phoenix.

FAO, IFAD, UNICEF, WFP, and WHO. 2017. *The State of Food Security and Nutrition in the World 2017: Building Resilience for Peace and Food Security*. Rome: FAO. http://www.fao.org/3/a-I7695e.pdf.

Faught, Jim. 1986. "The Relevance of Status Groups for a Theory of Status Inconsistency." Pages 592–605 in *Status Inconsistency in Modern Societies: Proceedings of a Conference on "New Differentiations of Status Structures? On the Viability of the Concept of Status Inconsistency in Contemporary Society," Duisburg, F.R.G., May 7–9, 1985*. Edited by Hermann Strasser and Roger Hodge. Sozialwissenschaftliche Schriften 33. Duisburg: Sozialwissenschaftlichen Kooperative.

Faust, Avraham. 2003. "Judah in the Sixth Century B.C.E.: A Rural Perspective." *PEQ* 135:37–53.

———. 2005. "The Settlement of Jerusalem's Western Hill and the City's Status in Iron Age II Revisited." *ZDPV* 121:97–118.

———. 2007. "Settlement Dynamics and Demographic Fluctuations in Judah from the Late Iron Age to the Hellenistic Period and the Archaeology of Persian-Period Yehud." Pages 23–51 in *A Time of Change: Judah and Its Neighbours in the Persian and Early Hellenistic Periods*. Edited by Yigal Levin. LSTS 65. London: T&T Clark.

———. 2013. "Social, Cultural and Demographic Changes in Judah during the Transition from the Iron Age to the Persian Period and the Nature of the Society during the Persian Period." Pages 106–32 in *From Judah to Judaea: Socio-economic Structures and Processes in the Persian Period*. Edited by Johannes Unsok Ro. HBM 43. Sheffield: Sheffield Phoenix.

Feder, Yitzhaq. 2013. "The Aniconic Tradition, Deuteronomy 4, and the Politics of Israelite Identity." *JBL* 132:251–74.

Finkelstein, Israel. 2010. "The Territorial Extent and Demography of Yehud/Judea in the Persian and Early Hellenistic Periods." *RB* 117:39–54.

———. 2015. "Migration of Israelites into Judah after 720 BCE: An Answer and an Update." *ZAW* 127:188–206.

Finkelstein, Israel, and Neil Silberman. 2001. *The Bible Unearthed: Archaeology's New Vision of Ancient Israel and the Origin of Its Sacred Texts.* New York: Free Press.

Fischer, Georg. 2005a. *Jeremia 1–25.* HThKAT. Freiburg: Herder.

———. 2005b. *Jeremia 26–52.* HThKAT. Freiburg: Herder.

———. 2007. *Jeremia: Der Stand der theologischen Diskussion.* Darmstadt: Wissenschaftliche Buchgesellschaft.

Fleischer, Gunther. 1989. *Von Menschenverkäufern, Baschankühen und Rechtsverkehrern.* AM.T 74. Frankfurt: Athenäum.

Flury-Schölch, André. 2007. *Abrahams Segen und die Völker: Synchrone und diachrone Untersuchungen zu Gen 12, 1–3 unter besonderer Berücksichtigung der intertextuellen Beziehungen zu Gen 18; 22; 26; 28; Sir 44; Jer 4 und Ps 72.* FB 115. Würzburg: Echter.

Fohrer, Georg. 1967. *Studien zur alttestamentlichen Prophetie (1949–1965).* BZAW 99. Berlin: de Gruyter.

Fox, Nili. 2000. *In the Service of the King: Officialdom in Ancient Israel and Judah.* Cincinatti: Hebrew Union College Press.

Frei, Peter. 2001. "Persian Imperial Authorization: A Summary." Pages 5–40 in *Persia and Torah: The Theory of Imperial Authorization of the Pentateuch.* Edited by James W. Watts. SymS 17. Atlanta: Society of Biblical Literature.

Fried, Lisbeth. 2006. "The ʿam hāʾāreṣ in Ezra 4:4 and Persian Imperial Administration." Pages 123–45 in *Judah and the Judeans in the Persian Period.* Edited by Oded Lipschits and Manfred Oeming. Winona Lake, IN: Eisenbrauns.

———. 2007. "From Xeno-Philia to -Phobia: Jewish Encounters with the Other." Pages 179–204 in *A Time of Change: Judah and its Neighbours in the Persian and Early Hellenistic Periods.* Edited by Yigal Levin. LSTS 65. London: T&T Clark.

Fuerstenberg, Friedrich. 1993. "Evaluation Norms in Industrial Organisations as Sources of Status Inconsistency." Pages 270–82 in *Change and Strain in Social Hierarchies: Theory and Method in the Study of*

Status Inconsistency. Edited by Robert W. Hodge and Hermann Strasser. Delhi: Ajanta.

García Martínez, Florentino. 1988. "Qumran Origins and Early History: A Groningen Hypothesis." *FO* 25:113–36.

García Martínez, Florentino, and Eibert J. C. Tigchelaar. 1997. *The Dead Sea Scrolls Study Edition*. Vol. 1: *1Q1–4Q273*. Leiden: Brill.

Garnsey, Peter, Keith Hopkins, and C. R. Whittaker. 1983. *Trade in the Ancient Economy*. Berkeley: University of California Press.

Gelin, Albert. 1953. *Les Pauvres de Yahvé*. TeDi 14. Paris: Cerf.

Gerstenberger, Erhard. 1980. *Der bittende Mensch: Bittritual u. Klagelied d. Einzelnen im Alten Testament*. WMANT 51. Neukirchen-Vluyn: Neukirchener Verlag.

———. 1995. "Der Psalter als Buch und als Sammlung." Pages 3–13 in *Neue Wege der Psalmenforschung: Für Walter Beyerlin*. Edited by Klaus Seybold and Erich Zenger. HBS 1. Freiburg: Herder.

———. 2003. Review of *Die sogenannte 'Armenfrömmigkeit' im nachexilischen Israel*, by Johannes Unsok Ro. *RBL*: http://tinyurl.com/ SBL2635a.

———. 2005. *Israel in der Perserzeit: 5. und 4. Jahrhundert v. Chr.* BiE 8. Stuttgart: Kohlhammer.

Gertz, Jan Christian. 2000. *Tradition und Redaktion in der Exoduserzählung: Untersuchungen zur Endredaktion des Pentateuch*. FRLANT 186. Göttingen: Vandenhoeck & Reprecht.

———. 2006. "The Transition between the Books of Genesis and Exodus." Pages 73–87 in *A Farewell to the Yahwist? The Composition of the Pentateuch in Recent European Interpretation*. Edited by Thomas B. Dozeman and Konrad Schmid. SymS 34. Atlanta: Society of Biblical Literature.

———. 2009. "Tora und Vordere Propheten." Pages 193–311 in *Grundinformation Altes Testament*. Edited by Jan Gertz. 3rd ed. UTB 2745. Göttingen: Vandenhoeck & Ruprecht.

Gitler, Haim, and Oren Tal. 2006. *The Coinage of Philistia of the Fifth and Fourth Centuries BC: A Study of the Earliest Coins of Palestine*. Collezioni Numismatiche 6. New York: Amphora Books/Kreindler.

Goffman, Irwin. 1957. "Status Consistency and Preference for Change in Power Distribution." *ASR* 22:275–81.

Goodman, Martin D. 1994. "Texts, Scribes and Power in Roman Judaea." Pages 99–108 in *Literacy and Power in the Ancient World*. Edited by

Alan K. Bowman and Greg Woolf. Cambridge: Cambridge University Press.

Gordis, Robert. 1944. "The Social Background of Wisdom Literature." *HUCA* 18:77–118.

Gorringe, Timothy. 1994. *Capital and the Kingdom: Theological Ethics and Economic Order*. London: SPCK.

Gottwald, Norman. 1980. *The Tribes of Yahweh: A Sociology of the Religion of Liberated Israel, 1250–1050 B.C.E.* London: SCM.

———. 1993. "Social Class as an Analytic and Hermeneutical Category in Biblical Studies." *JBL* 112:3–22.

———. 2001. *The Politics of Ancient Israel*. LAI. Louisville: Westminster John Knox.

Grabbe, Lester. 1998. *Leading Captivity Captive: 'The Exile' as History and Ideology*. JSOTSup 278. Sheffield: Sheffield Academic Press.

———. 2004. *A History of the Jews and Judaism in the Second Temple Period I: Yehud—A History of the Persian Province of Judah*. LSTS 47.1. London: T&T Clark.

———. 2015. "The Reality of the Return: The Biblical Picture Versus Historical Reconstruction." Pages 292–307 in *Exile and Return: The Babylonian Context*. Edited by Jonathan Stökl and Caroline Waerzeggers. BZAW 478. Berlin: de Gruyter.

Graetz, Hirsch. 1882. *Kritischer Kommentar zu den Psalmen nebst Text und Uebersetzung I*. Breslau: Schottlaender.

Grimshaw, Allen. 1986. "Talk: A Neglected Behavioral Indicator of Status Inconsistency?" Pages 307–20 in *Status Inconsistency in Modern Societies: Proceedings of a Conference on "New Differentiations of Status Structures? On the Viability of the Concept of Status Inconsistency in Contemporary Society," Duisburg, F.R.G., May 7–9, 1985*. Edited by Hermann Strasser and Roger Hodge. Sozialwissenschaftliche Schriften 33. Duisburg: Sozialwissenschaftlichen Kooperative.

Grol, Harm van. 2011. "Three Hasidisms and Their Militant Ideologies: 1 and 2 Maccabees, Psalms 144 and 149." Pages 93–115 in *Between Evidence and Ideology: Essays on the History of Ancient Israel Read at the Joint Meeting of the Society for Old Testament Study and the Oud Testamentisch Werkgezelschap, Lincoln, July 2009*. Edited by Bob Becking and Lester Grabbe. OTS 59. Leiden: Brill.

Grünwaldt, Klaus. 1999. *Das Heiligkeitsgesetz Leviticus 17–26: Ursprüngliche Gestalt, Tradition und Theologie*. BZAW 271. Berlin: de Gruyter.

Guillaume, Phillippe. 2008. "Jerusalem 720–705 BCE. No Flood of Israelite Refugees." *SJOT* 22:195–211.

———. 2014. *Land, Credit and Crisis: Agrarian Finance in the Hebrew Bible.* BibleWorld. London: Routledge.

Gunkel, Hermann. 1892 [1986]. *Die Psalmen.* 6th ed. HKAT. Göttingen: Vandonhoeck & Ruprecht.

———. 1922. *Genesis übersetzt und erklärt.* HKAT. Göttingen: Vandenhoeck & Ruprecht.

———. 1933. *Einleitung in die Psalmen: Die Gattungen der religiosen Lyrik Israels.* 4th ed. HKAT. Göttingen, Vandonhoeck & Ruprecht.

Gutierrez, Gustavo. 1988. *A Theology of Liberation: History, Politics, and Salvation.* Translated by Caridad Inda and John Eagleson. Maryknoll, NY: Orbis Books.

Halbe, Jörn. 1975. *Das Privilegrecht Jahwes: Ex 34,10–26 Gestalt und Wesen, Herkunft und Wirken in vordeuteronomischer Zeit.* FRLANT 114. Göttingen: Vandenhoeck & Reprecht.

Hamilton, Jeffries. 1992. *Social Justice and Deuteronomy: The Case of Deuteronomy 15.* SBLDS 136. Atlanta: Scholars Press.

Hankins, Davis. 2016. "Introduction to Reviews of Roland Boer, *The Sacred Economy of Ancient Israel.*" *HBT* 38:133–36.

Hanson, Ann Ellis. 1991. "Ancient Illiteracy." Pages 159–98 in *Literacy in the Roman World.* Edited by John H. Humphrey. JRASup 3. Ann Arbor, MI: Journal of Roman Archaeology.

Hardmeier, Christof. 1990. *Prophetie im Streit vor dem Untergang Judas: Erzählkommunikative Studien zur Entstehungssituation der Jesaja- und Jeremiaerzählungen in II Reg 18–20 und Jer 37–40.* BZAW 187. Berlin: de Gruyter.

———. 1991. "Die Propheten Micha und Jesaja im Spiegel von Jeremia XXVI und 2 Regnum XVIII–XX: Zur Prophetie-Rezeption in der nachjoschijanischen Zeit." Pages 172–89 in *Congress Volume: Leuven 1989.* Edited by John Emerton. VTSup 43. Leiden: Brill.

Harkins, Angela. 2012. "Who is the Teacher of the Teacher Hymns? Re-Examining the Teacher Hymns Hypothesis Fifty Years Later." Pages 449–67 in *A Teacher for All Generations: Essays in Honor of James C. VanderKam.* Edited by Eric Mason and Samuel Thomas. JSJSup 153. Leiden: Brill.

———. 2013. "Thanksgiving Hymns (Hodayot)." Pages 2018–94 in *Outside the Bible: Ancient Jewish Writings Related to Scripture.* Edited by Louis

Feldman, James Kugel, and Lawrence Schiffman. Philadelphia: Jewish Publication Society.

Harris, William V. 1989. *Ancient Literacy.* Cambridge: Harvard University Press.

Hartman, Moshe. 1986. "Possible Extensions of the Status Inconsistency Concept: A General Outline." Pages 537–51 in *Status Inconsistency in Modern Societies: Proceedings of a Conference on "New Differentiations of Status Structures? On the Viability of the Concept of Status Inconsistency in Contemporary Society," Duisburg, F.R.G., May 7–9, 1985.* Edited by Hermann Strasser and Roger Hodge. Sozialwissenschaftliche Schriften 33. Duisburg: Sozialwissenschaftlichen Kooperative.

Hempel, Charlotte. 2005. "The Groningen Hypothesis: Strengths and Weaknesses." Pages 249–55 in *Enoch and Qumran Origins: New Light on a Forgotten Connection.* Edited by Gabriele Boccaccini. Grand Rapids: Eerdmans.

Hengel, Martin. 1988. *Judentum und Hellenismus: Studien zu ihrer Begegnung unter besonderer Berücksichtigung Palästinas bis zur Mitte des 2. Jh.s. v. Chr.* WUNT 10. Tübingen: Mohr.

Hensel, Benedikt. 2016. *Juda und Samaria.* FAT 110. Tübingen: Mohr Siebeck.

Herr, Larry G. 1997. "The Iron Age II Period." *BA* 60:114–51, 154–83.

Herrmann, Siegfried. 1990. *Jeremia: Der Prophet und das Buch.* EdF 271. Darmstadt: Wissenschaftliche Buchgesellschaft.

Herrmann, Wolfram. 1999. "Die Armen, die Gott suchen." Pages 68–77 in *Gedenkt an das Wort: Festschrift für Werner Vogler zum 65. Geburtstag.* Edited by Christoph Kähler, Martina Böhm, and Christfried Böttrich. Leipzig: Evangelische Verlagsanstalt.

Hjelm, Ingrid. 2004. "What Do Samaritans and Jews Have in Common? Recent Trends in Samaritan Studies." *CurBR* 3:9–59.

Hoglund, Kenneth. 1992. *Achaemenid Imperial Administration in Syria-Palestine and the Missions of Ezra and Nehemiah.* SBLDS 125. Atlanta: Scholars Press.

Holladay, William L. 1986. *Jeremiah 1: A Commentary on the Book of the Prophet Jeremiah Chapters 1–25.* Hermeneia. Philadelphia: Fortress.

Holm-Nielsen, Svend. 1960. *Hodayot: Psalms from Qumran.* ATDan 2. Aarhus: Universitetsforlaget.

Hölscher, Gustav. 1922. "Komposition und Ursprung des Deuteronomiums." *ZAW* 40:161–255.

Horsley, Richard A. 1991. "Empire, Temple and Community—But No Bourgeoisie! A Response to Blenkinsopp and Petersen." Pages 163–74 in *Second Temple Studies 1: Persian Period*. Edited by Philip R. Davies. JSOTSup 117. Sheffield: Sheffield Academic.

Horsley, Richard A., and Patrick Tiller. 2002. "Ben Sira and the Sociology of the Second Temple." Pages 74–107 in *Second Temple Studies III: Studies in Politics, Class and Material Culture*. Edited by Philip R. Davies and John M. Halligan. JSOTSup 340. New York: Sheffield Academic.

Hortmann, W. 1986. "Status Inconsistency and Literature: No Man Is a Hero to the Inconsistency Theorist." Pages 52–67 in *Status Inconsistency in Modern Societies: Proceedings of a Conference on "New Differentiations of Status Structures? On the Viability of the Concept of Status Inconsistency in Contemporary Society," Duisburg, F.R.G., May 7–9, 1985*. Edited by Hermann Strasser and Roger Hodge. Sozialwissenschaftliche Schriften 33. Duisburg: Sozialwissenschaftlichen Kooperative.

Hossfeld, Frank Lothar. 1982. *Der Dekalog: Seine späten Fassungen, die originale Komposition und seine Vorstufen*. OBO 45. Fribourg: Presses Universitaires; Göttingen: Vandenhoeck & Ruprecht.

Hossfeld, Frank Lothar, and Erich Zenger. 1993. *Die Psalmen I: Psalm 1–50*. NEchtB 29. Würzburg: Echter.

———. 2000. *Psalmen 51–100*. HThKAT. Freiburg: Herder.

———. 2008. *Psalmen 101–150*. HThKAT. Freiburg: Herder.

———. 2011. *Psalms 3: A Commentary on Psalms 101–150*. Translated by Linda Maloney. Hermeneia. Minneapolis: Fortress.

Houston, Walter J. 2008. *Contending for Justice: Ideologies and Theologies of Social Justice in the Old Testament*. Revised ed. LHBOTS 428. London: T&T Clark.

———. 2013. Review of *Land, Credit and Crisis: Agrarian Finance in the Hebrew Bible*, by Philippe Guillaume. *VT* 63:170.

Houten, Christiana van. 1991. *The Alien in Israelite Law*. JSOTSup 107. Sheffield: JSOT Press.

Houtman, Cornelis. 1997. *Das Bundesbuch: Ein Kommentar*. DMOA 24. Leiden: Brill.

Hübner, Ulrich. 1994. "Die Münzprägungen Palästinas in alttestamentlicher Zeit." *Trumah* 4:119–45.

———. 2014. "The Development of Monetary Systems in Palestine during the Achaemenid and Hellenistic Eras." Pages 159–83 in *Money as God? The Monetization of the Market and Its Impact on Religion, Politics,*

Law, and Ethics. Edited by Jürgen von Hagen and Michael Welker. Cambridge: Cambridge University Press.

Hudson, Michael, and Baruch A. Levine, eds. 1996. *Privatization in the Ancient Near East and Classical World: A Colloquium Held at New York University, November 17–18, 1994.* Peabody Museum Bulletin 5. Cambridge: Peabody Museum of Archaeology and Ethnology.

———. 1999. *Urbanization and Land Ownership in the Ancient Near East: A Colloquium Held at New York University, November 1996, and the Oriental Institute, St. Petersburg, Russia, May 1997.* Peabody Museum Bulletin 7. Cambridge: Peabody Museum of Archaeology and Ethnology.

Hughes, Julie A. 2006. *Scriptural Allusions and Exegesis in the Hodayot.* STDJ 59. Leiden: Brill.

Hurvitz, Avi. 1997. "The Historical Quest for 'Ancient Israel' and the Linguistic Evidence of the Hebrew Bible: Some Methodological Observations." *VT* 47:301–15.

———. 2000. "Can Biblical Texts Be Dated Linguistically? Chronological Perspectives in the Historical Study of Biblical Hebrew." Pages 143–60 in *Congress Volume: Oslo 1998.* Edited by André Lemaire and Magne Sæbø. VTSup 80. Leiden: Brill.

Hyatt, J. Philip. 1980. *Exodus.* Rev. ed. NCB. Grand Rapids: Eerdmans.

———. 1984. "The Deuteronomic Edition of Jeremiah." Pages 247–67 in *A Prophet to the Nations: Essays in Jeremiah Studies.* Edited by Leo G. Perdue and Brian W. Kovacs. Winona Lake, IN: Eisenbrauns.

Irsigler, Hubert. 1984. *Psalm 73: Monolog eines Weisen: Text, Programm, Struktur.* ATSAT 20. St. Ottilien: EOS Verlag.

Ittmann, Norbert. 1981. *Die Konfessionen Jeremias: Ihre Bedeutung für die Verkündigung des Propheten.* WMANT 54. Neukirchen-Vluyn: Neukirchener Verlag.

Jackson, Elton F. 1962. "Status Inconsistency and Symptoms of Stress." *ASR* 27:469–80.

Janssen, Eno. 1956. *Juda in der Exilszeit: Ein Beitrag zur Frage der Entstehung des Judentums.* FRLANT 51. Göttingen: Vandenhoeck & Ruprecht.

Janzen, David. 2002a. *Witch-hunts, Purity and Social Boundaries: The Expulsion of the Foreign Women in Ezra 9–10.* JSOTSup 350. London: Sheffield Academic Press.

———. 2002b. "Politics, Settlement, and Temple Community in Persian-Period Yehud." *CBQ* 64:490–510.

Jaruzelska, Izabela. 1998. *Amos and the Officialdom in the Kingdom of Israel: The Socio-economic Position of the Officials in the Light of the Biblical, the Epigraphic and Archaeological Evidence.* Seria Socjologia 25. Poznań: Adam Mickiewicz University Press.

Jassen, Alex P. 2009. "The Dead Sea Scrolls and Violence: Sectarian Formation and Eschatological Imagination." *BibInt* 17:13–44.

Jeon, Jaeyoung. 2015. "The Zadokites in the Wilderness: The Rebellion of Korach (Num 16) and the Zadokite Redaction." *ZAW* 127:381–411.

Jeremias, Gert. 1963. *Der Lehrer der Gerechtigkeit.* SUNT 2. Göttingen: Vandenhoeck & Ruprecht.

Jones, Douglas R. 1992. *Jeremiah.* NCB. Grand Rapids: Eerdmans.

Kaiser, Otto. 1984. *Einleitung in das Alte Testament: Eine Einführung in ihre Ergebnisse und Probleme.* Gütersloh: Gütersloher Verlagshaus Mohn.

———. 1991. *Texte aus der Umwelt des Alten Testaments II, Lieferung 6: Lieder und Gebete.* Gütersloh: Gütersloher Verlagshaus Mohn.

———. 1992a. *Grundriß der Einleitung in die kanonischen und deuterokanonischen Schriften des Alten Testaments I: Die erzählenden Werke.* Gütersloh: Gütersloher Verlagshaus Mohn.

———. 1992b. *Klagelieder.* ATD 16/2. Göttingen: Vandenhoeck & Ruprecht.

———. 1994. *Grundriß der Einleitung in die kanonischen und deuterokanonischen Schriften des Alten Testaments II: Die prophetischen Werke.* Gütersloh: Gütersloher Verlagshaus Mohn.

———. 2013. *Der eine Gott Israels und die Mächte der Welt: Der Weg Gottes im Alten Testament vom Herrn seines Volkes zum Herrn der ganzen Welt.* FRLANT 249. Göttingen: Vandenhoeck & Ruprecht.

Kartje, John. 2014. *Wisdom Epistemology in the Psalter: A Study of Psalms 1, 73, 90, and 107.* BZAW 472. Berlin: de Gruyter.

Kellenberger, Edgar. 2008. "Schöpfung und Chaos: Bemerkungen zu Num 16,30 und weiteren alttestamentlichen Stellen." *TZ* 64:1–12.

Keown, Gerald L., Glenn W. Barker, David A. Hubbard, Bruce M. Metzger, Pamela J. Scalise, and Thomas G. Smothers. 1995. *Jeremiah 26–52.* WBC 27. Dallas: Word Books.

Kessler, John. 2002. *The Book of Haggai: Prophecy and Society in Early Persian Yehud.* VTSup 91. Leiden: Brill.

Kessler, Rainer. 1992. *Staat und Gesellschaft im vorexilischen Juda: Vom 8. Jahrhundert bis zum Exil.* VTSup 47. Leiden: Brill.

Kilian, Rudolf. 1966. *Die vorpriesterlichen Abrahams-Überlieferungen: Literarkritisch und traditionsgeschichtlich untersucht.* BBB 24. Bonn: Hanstein.

Kimberly, James. 1986. "The Social Psychology of Status Inconsistency: Status Structures and Psychological Processes." Pages 83–102 in *Status Inconsistency in Modern Societies: Proceedings of a Conference on "New Differentiations of Status Structures? On the Viability of the Concept of Status Inconsistency in Contemporary Society,"* Duisburg, F.R.G., May 7–9, 1985. Edited by Hermann Strasser and Roger Hodge. Sozialwissenschaftliche Schriften 33. Duisburg: Sozialwissenschaftlichen Kooperative.

Kippenberg, Hans G. 1977. "Die Typik antiker Entwicklung." Pages 9–61 in *Seminar: Die Entstehung der antiken Klassengesellschaft.* Edited by Hans G. Kippenberg. STW 130. Frankfurt am Main: Suhrkamp.

———. 1978. *Religion und Klassenbildung im antiken Judäa: Eine religionssoziologische Studie zum Verhältnis von Tradition und gesellschaftlicher Entwicklung.* SUNT 14. Göttingen: Vandenhoeck & Ruprecht.

Kittel, Bonnie. 1981. *The Hymns of Qumran: Translation and Commentary.* SBLDS 50. Chico, CA: Scholars Press.

Kittel, Rudolf. 1929a. *Die Psalmen.* 6th ed. KAT 13. Leipzig: Scholl.

———. 1929b. *Geschichte des Volkes Israel III: Die Zeit der Wegführung nach Babel und die Aufrichtung der neuen Gemeinde.* Stuttgart: Kohlhammer.

Kletter, Raz. 1998. *Economic Keystones: The Weight System of the Kingdom of Judah.* JSOTSup 276. Sheffield: Sheffield Academic.

Knauf, Ernst Axel. 1994. *Die Umwelt des Alten Testament.* NSKAT 29. Stuttgart: Katholisches Bibelwerk.

———. 2006. "Bethel: The Israelite Impact on Judean Language and Literature." Pages 291–349 in *Judah and the Judeans in the Persian Period.* Edited by Oded Lipschits and Manfred Oeming. Winona Lake, IN: Eisenbrauns.

Knight, Douglas A. 2009. "Traditio-Historical Criticism: The Development of the Covenant Code." Pages 97–116 in *Method Matters: Essays on the Interpretation of the Hebrew Bible in Honor of David L. Petersen.* Edited by Joel LeMon and Kent H. Richards. RBS 56. Atlanta: Society of Biblical Literature.

Knowles, Melody D. 2008. "Pilgrimage to Jerusalem in the Persian Period." Pages 7–24 in *Approaching Yehud: New Approaches to the Study of the*

Persian Period. Edited by Jon L. Berquist. SemeiaSt 50. Atlanta: Society of Biblical Literature.

Köckert, Matthias. 2006. "Die Geschichte der Abrahamüberlieferung." Pages 103–28 in *Congress Volume: Leiden 2004.* Edited by André Lemaire. VTSup 109. Leiden: Brill.

Koenen, Klaus. 1995. *Jahwe wird kommen, zu herrschen über die Erde: Ps 90–110 als Komposition.* BBB 101. Weinheim: Athenäum.

Körting, Corinna. 2006. *Zion in den Psalmen.* FAT 48. Tübingen: Mohr Siebeck.

Kratz, Reinhard G. 2000. *Die Komposition der erzählenden Bücher des Alten Testaments: Grundwissen der Bibelkritik.* UTB 2157. Göttingen: Vandenhoeck & Ruprecht.

———. 2015. *Historical and Biblical Israel: The History, Tradition, and Archives of Israel and Judah.* Translated by Paul Kurtz. Oxford: Oxford University Press.

Kraus, Hans-Joachim. 1978. *Psalmen.* 5th ed. BKAT 15. Neukirchen-Vluyn: Neukirchener Verlag.

Kreckel, Reinhard. 1993. "Status Inconsistency and Status Deficiency in Meritocratic Society." Pages 248–69 in *Change and Strain in Social Hierarchies: Theory and Method in the Study of Status Inconsistency.* Edited by Robert W. Hodge and Hermann Strasser. Delhi: Ajanta.

Kugler, Robert A. 1999. "The Deuteronomists and the Latter Prophets." Pages 127–44 in *Those Elusive Deuteronomists: The Phenomenon of Pan-Deuteronomism.* Edited by Linda S. Schearing and Steven L. McKenzie. JSOTSup 268. Sheffield: Sheffield Academic.

Kupfer, Christian. 2012. *Mit Israel auf dem Weg durch die Wüste: Eine leserorientierte Exegese der Rebellionstexte in Exodus 15:22–17:7 und Numeri 11:1–20:13.* OTS 61. Leiden: Brill.

Kuschke, A. 1939. "Arm und reich im Alten Testament mit besonderer Berücksichtigung der nachexilischen Zeit." *ZAW* 57:31–57.

Lambert, Wilfred G. 1960. *Babylonian Wisdom Literature.* Oxford: Clarendon.

Lang, Bernhard, ed. 1985a. *Anthropological Approaches to the Old Testament.* IRT 8. London: SPCK.

———. 1985b. "The Social Organization of Peasant Poverty in Biblical Israel." Pages 83–99 in *Anthropological Approaches to the Old Testament.* IRT 8. London: SPCK.

Lang, Bernhard, and Helmer Ringgren. 1986. "נכר." *ThWAT* 5:454–63

Lange, Armin. 1995. *Weisheit und Prädestination: Weisheitliche Urordnung und Prädestination in den Textfunden von Qumran.* STDJ 18. Leiden: Brill.

Lemche, Niels Peter. 1985. *Early Israel: Anthropological and Historical Studies on the Israelite Society before the Monarchy.* Translated by Frederick H. Cryer. VTSup 37. Leiden: Brill.

———. 1994. "Kings and Clients: On Loyalty between the Ruler and the Ruled in Ancient 'Israel.'" *Semeia* 66:119–32.

———. 1996. "From Patronage Society to Patronage Society." Pages 106–20 in *The Origins of the Ancient Israelite States.* Edited by Volkmar Fritz and Philip R. Davies. JSOTSup 228. Sheffield: Sheffield Academic.

Lenski, Gerhard E. 1954. "Status Crystallisation: A Non-vertical Dimension of Social Status." *ASR* 19:405–13.

———. 1966. *Power and Privilege: A Theory of Social Stratification.* New York: McGraw-Hill.

———. 1967. "Status Inconsistency and the Vote: A Four Nation Test." *ASR* 32:298–301.

Lenski, Gerhard E., Patrick Nolan, and Jean Lenski. 1995. *Human Societies: An Introduction to Macrosociology.* 7th ed. New York: McGraw-Hill.

Levin, Christoph. 1993. "Das Gebetbuch der Gerechten: Literargeschichtliche Beobachtungen am Psalter." *ZTK* 90:355–81.

———. 2000. "Das Deuteronomium und der Jahwist." Pages 121–36 in *Liebe und Gebot: Studien zum Deuteronomium; Festschrift zum 70. Geburtstag von Lothar Perlitt.* Edited by Reinhard G. Kratz and Hermann Spieckermann. FRLANT 190. Göttingen: Vandenhoeck & Ruprecht.

———. 2001. "Gerechtigkeit Gottes in der Genesis." Pages 347–57 in *Studies in the Book of Genesis: Literature, Redaction and History.* Edited by André Wénin. BETL 155. Leuven: Leuven University Press.

Levin, Yigal. 2003. "Who Was the Chronicler's Audience? A Hint From His Genealogies." *JBL* 122:229–45.

———. 2004. "From Lists to History: Chronological Aspects of the Chronicler's Genealogies." *JBL* 123:601–636.

———. 2013. "Judea, Samaria and Idumea: Three Models of Ethnicity and Administration in the Persian Period." Pages 4–53 in *From Judah to Judaea: Socio-economic Structures and Processes in the Persian Period.* Edited by Johannes Unsok Ro. HBM 43. Sheffield: Sheffield Phoenix.

Levine, Baruch A. 1993. *Numbers 1–20: A New Translation with Introduction and Commentary.* AB 4. New York: Doubleday.

Levinson, Bernard M. 1997. *Deuteronomy and the Hermeneutics of Legal Innovation*. Oxford: Oxford University Press.

———. 2004. "Is the Covenant Code an Exilic Composition?" Pages 272–325 in *In Search of Pre-exilic Israel*. Edited by John Day. JSOTSup 406. London: T&T Clark.

———. 2008. *Legal Revision and Religious Renewal in Ancient Israel*. Cambridge: Cambridge University Press.

Lichtenberger, Hermann. 1980. *Studien zum Menschenbild in Texten der Qumrangemeinde*. SUNT 15. Göttingen: Vandenhoeck & Ruprecht.

Lichtenberger, Hermann, and Armin Lange. 1997. "Qumran." *TRE* 28:45–79.

Lim, Timothy H. 1993. "The Wicked Priests of the Groningen Hypothesis." *JBL* 112:415–25.

Lindars, Barnabas. 1965. "Ezekiel and Individual Responsibility." *VT* 15:452–67.

Lipschits, Oded. 2003. "Demographic Changes in Judah between the Seventh and the Fifth Centuries B.C.E." Pages 323–76 in *Judah and the Judeans in the Neo-Babylonian Period*. Edited by Oded Lipschits and Joseph Blenkinsopp. Winona Lake, IN: Eisenbrauns.

———. 2005. *The Fall and Rise of Jerusalem: Judah under Babylonian Rule*. Winona Lake, IN: Eisenbrauns.

———. 2006. "Achaemenid Imperial Policy, Settlement Processes in Palestine, and the Status of Jerusalem in the Middle of the Fifth Century BCE." Pages 19–52 in *Judah and the Judeans in the Persian Period*. Edited by Edited by Oded Lipschits and Manfred Oeming. Winona Lake, IN: Eisenbrauns.

Lipschits, Oded, and Oren Tal. 2007. "The Settlement Archaeology of the Province of Judah: A Case Study." Pages 33–52 in *Judah and the Judeans in the Fourth Century B.C.E.* Edited by Oded Lipschits, Gary N. Knoppers, Rainer Albertz. Winona Lake, IN: Eisenbrauns.

Lipschits, Oded, and David Vanderhooft. 2007. "Yehud Stamp Impressions in the Fourth Century B.C.E.: A Time of Administrative Consolidation?" Pages 75–94 in *Judah and the Judeans in the Fourth Century B.C.E.* Edited by Oded Lipschits, Gary N. Knoppers, and Rainer Albertz. Winona Lake, IN: Eisenbrauns.

Lipton, Diana. 2012. "The Limits of Intercession: Abraham Reads Ezekiel at Sodom and Gomorrah." Pages 25–42 in *Universalism and Particularism at Sodom and Gomorrah: Essays in Memory of Ron Pirson*. Edited by Diana Lipton. AIL 11. Atlanta: Society of Biblical Literature.

Liverani, Mario. 2005. *Israel's History and the History of Israel*. Translated by Chiara Peri and Philip R. Davies. BibleWorld. London: Equinox.

Lohfink, Norbert. 1986. "Von der 'Anawim-Partei' zur 'Kirche der Armen': Die bibelwissenschaftliche Ahnentafel eines Hauptbegriffs der 'Theologie der Befreiung.'" *Bib* 67:153–75.

———. 1990a. *Lobgesänge der Armen: Studien zum Magnifikat, den Hodajot von Qumran und einigen späten Psalmen*. SBS 143. Stuttgart: Katholisches Bibelwerk.

———. 1990b. "Das deuteronomische Gesetz in der Endgestalt: Entwurf einer Gesellschaft ohne marginale Gruppen." *BN* 51:25–40.

Lohse, Eduard. 1971. *Die Texte Aus Qumran: Hebräisch und Deutsch: Mit masoretischer Punktation, Übersetzung, Einführung und Anmerkungen*. Munich: Kösel.

Lundbom, Jack. 1999. *Jeremiah 1–20: A New Translation with Introduction and Commentary*. AB 21A. New York: Doubleday.

Luther, Martin. 1967. *Werke: Kritische Gesamtausgabe; Tischreden (Weimarer Ausgabe) V (Tischreden aus den Jahren 1540–1544)*. Weimar: Böhlaus Nachfolger.

Machinist, Peter. 1994. "The First Coins of Judah and Samaria. Numismatics and History in the Achaemenid and Early Hellenistic Periods." Pages 365–80 in *Continuity and Change: Proceedings of the Last Achaemenid History Workshop, April 6–8, 1990, Ann Arbor, Michigan*. Edited by Heleen Sancisi-Weerdenburg, Amélie Kuhrt, and Margaret Cool Root. AchH 8. Leiden: Nederlands Instituut voor het Nabije Oosten.

Maier, Christl. 2002. *Jeremia als Lehrer der Tora: Soziale Gebote des Deuteronomiums in Fortschreibungen des Jeremiabuches*. FRLANT 196. Göttingen: Vandenhoeck & Ruprecht.

Maier, Johann. 1960. *Die Texte vom Toten Meer*. Munich: Reinhardt.

Malchow, Bruce V. 1996. *Social Justice in the Hebrew Bible: What Is New and What Is Old*. Collegeville, MN: Liturgical Press.

Marshall, Jay W. 1993. *Israel and the Book of the Covenant: An Anthropological Approach to Biblical Law*. SBLDS 140. Atlanta: Scholars Press.

Markl, Dominik, and Alexander Ezechukwu. 2015. "'For You Know the Soul of a Stranger' (Exod 23:9): The Role of the Joseph Story in the Legal Hermeneutics of the Pentateuch." *ZABR* 21:215–32.

Marttila, Marko. 2012. "The Deuteronomistic Heritage in the Psalms." *JSOT* 37:67–91.

Matthews, I. G. 1939. *Ezekiel: An American Commentary on the Old Testament*. Philadelphia: American Baptist Publication Society.

Matties, Gordon H. 1990. *Ezekiel 18 and the Rhetoric of Moral Discourse.* SBLDS 126. Atlanta: Scholars Press.

McKane, William. 1986. *A Critical and Exegetical Commentary on Jeremiah I: Introduction and Commentary on Jeremiah 1–26.* ICC. Edinburgh: T&T Clark.

———. 1996. *A Critical and Exegetical Commentary on Jeremiah II: Jeremiah 27–52.* ICC. Edinburgh: T&T Clark.

McKenzie, John L. 1974. *A Theology of the Old Testament.* Garden City, NY: Doubleday.

McNutt, Paula. 1999. *Reconstructing the Society of Ancient Israel.* London: SPCK.

Meeks, Wayne. 1983. *The First Urban Christians: The Social World of the Apostle Paul.* New Haven: Yale University Press.

———. 1993. *Urchristentum und Stadtkultur: Die soziale Welt der paulinischen Gemeinden.* Translated by Sieglinde Denzel and Susanne Naumann. Gütersloh: Kaiser.

Melotti, Umberto. 1977. *Marx and the Third World.* Translated by Pat Ransford. London: Macmillan.

Meshorer, Yaʿakov. 1998. *Ancient Means of Exchange, Weights and Coins.* Haifa: University of Haifa.

———. 2001. *A Treasury of Jewish Coins: From Persian Period to Bar Kokhba.* Jerusalem: Yad ben-Zvi Press.

Meshorer, Yaʿakov, Wolfgang Bijovsky, David Hendin, and Andrew Meadows. 2013. *Coins of the Holy Land I: The Abraham and Marian Sofaer Collection at the American Numismatic Society and the Israel Museum.* New York: American Numismatic Society.

Meulemann, Heiner. 1993. "Status Inconsistency and Social Biography: A Research Perspective for the Analysis of the Multidimensionality of Modern Social Structures." Pages 283–98 in *Change and Strain in Social Hierarchies: Theory and Method in the Study of Status Inconsistency.* Edited by Robert W. Hodge and Hermann Strasser. Delhi: Ajanta.

Michel, Diethelm. 1960. *Tempora und Satzstellung in den Psalmen.* AET 1. Bonn: Bouvier.

———. 1979. "Armut II, Altes Testament." *TRE* 4:72–76.

Mildenberg, Leo. 1996. "*Yĕhūd und šmryn*: Über das Geld der persischen Provinzen Juda und Samaria im 4. Jahrhundert." Pages 1:119–46 in *Geschichte—Tradition—Reflexion: Festschrift Martin Hengel zum 70.*

Geburtstag. Edited by Hubert Cancik, Hermann Lichtenberger, and Peter Schäfer. Tübingen: Mohr Siebeck.

———. 1998. "Yehud: A Preliminary Study of the Provincial Coinage of Judaea." Pages 67–76 in *Vestigia Leonis: Studien zur antiken Numismatik Israels, Palästinas und der östlichen Mittelmeerwelt*. Edited by Ulrich Hübner and Ernst Axel Knauf. NTOA 36. Fribourg: Presses Universitaires; Göttingen: Vandenhoeck & Ruprecht.

Milgrom, Jacob. 1990. *Numbers: The Traditional Hebrew Text with the New JPS Translation*. JPSTC. Philadelphia: Jewish Publication Society.

Millard, Matthias. 1994. *Die Komposition des Psalters: Ein formgeschichtlicher Ansatz*. FAT 9. Tübingen: Mohr.

Mirguet, Françoise. 2008. "Numbers 16: The Significance of Place—An Analysis of Spatial Markers." *JSOT* 32:311–30.

Molin, Georg. 1954. *Die Söhne des Lichts: Zeit und Stellung der Handschriften vom Toten Meer*. Vienna: Herold.

Morawe, Günter. 1960. *Aufbau und Abgrenzung der Loblieder von Qumran: Studien zur gattungsgeschichtlichen Einordnung der Hodajoth*. ThA 16. Berlin: Evangelische Verlagsanstalt.

Mosala, Itumeleng. 1989. *Biblical Hermeneutics and Black Theology in South Africa*. Grand Rapids: Eerdmans.

Moster, David Z. 2014. "The Levite of Judges 17–18." *JBL* 133:729–37.

———. 2015. "The Levite of Judges 19–21." *JBL* 134:721–30.

Mowinckel, Sigmund. 1914. *Zur Komposition des Buches Jeremia*. Kristiania: Dybwad.

———. 1964. *Studien zu dem Buche Ezra-Nehemia I*. Oslo: Universitetsforlaget.

———. 2014. *Psalm Studies*. Translated by Mark E. Biddle. 2 vols. History of Biblical Studies 2–3. Atlanta: SBL Press.

Murphy-O'Connor, Jerome. 1974. "The Essenes and Their History." *RB* 81:215–44.

Myers, Jacob M. 1965. *Ezra-Nehemiah*. AB 14. Garden City, NY: Doubleday.

Na'aman, Nadav. 2014. "Dismissing the Myth of a Flood of Israelite Refugees in the Late Eighth Century BCE." *ZAW* 126:1–14.

Nam, Roger S. 2012. *Portrayals of Economic Exchange in the Book of Kings*. BibInt 112. Leiden: Brill.

———. 2016. Review of *Social and Economic Life in Second Temple Judea*, by Samuel L. Adams, *The Sacred Economy*, by Roland Boer and *The*

City on a Hill: A Tradition-Historical Study of the Wealth of Nations Tradition, by Michael Chan. *CBQ* 78:339–45.

Namiki, Koichi. 2001. *Hebraizumuno Ningenkankaku* [Japanese]. Tokyo: Shinkyo.

———. 2014. *Kyuyakuseishono Suimyaku* [Japanese]. Tokyo: Nihon-kirisu-tokyodan-shupankyoku.

Nicholson, Ernest W. 1965. "The Meaning of the Expression עם הארץ in the Old Testament." *JSS* 10:59–66.

———. 1970. *Preaching to the Exiles: A Study of the Prose Tradition in the Book of Jeremiah*. Oxford: Blackwell.

———. 1977. "The Decalogue as the Direct Address of God." *VT* 27:422–33.

———. 2006. " 'Do Not Dare to Set a Foreigner Over You': The King in Deuteronomy and 'The Great King.' " *ZAW* 118:46–61.

Niesiolowski-Spano, Lukasz. 2017 "How Did 'Minimalists' Change Recent Biblical Scholarship?" Paper read at the European Association of Biblical Studies Annual Meeting/Society of Biblical Literature International Meeting, Berlin, 7–11 August 2017.

Nihan, Christophe. 2007a. *From Priestly Torah to Pentateuch*. FAT 2/25. Tübingen: Mohr Siebeck.

———. 2007b. "The Torah between Samaria and Judah: Shechem and Gerizim in Deuteronomy and Joshua." Pages 187–223 in *The Pentateuch as Torah: New Models for Understanding Its Promulgation and Acceptance*. Edited by Gary N. Knoppers and Bernard M. Levinson. Winona Lake, IN: Eisenbrauns.

———. 2011. "Resident Aliens and Natives in the Holiness Legislation." Pages 111–34 in *The Foreigner and the Law: Perspectives from the Hebrew Bible and the Ancient Near East*. Edited by Reinhard Achenbach, Rainer Albertz, and Jakob Wöhrle. BZABR 16. Wiesbaden: Harrassowitz.

Nitzan, Bilhah. 1994. *Qumran Prayer and Religious Poetry*. STDJ 12. Leiden: Brill.

Nodet, Étienne. 2007. "Asidaioi and Essenes." Pages 63–88 in *Flores Florentino: Dead Sea Scrolls and Other Early Jewish Studies in Honour of Florentino Garcia Martinez*. Edited by Anthony Hilhorst, Émile Puech, and Eibert J C Tigchelaar. JSJSup 122. Leiden: Brill.

Nõmmik, Urmas. 1999. "Die Gerechtigkeitsbearbeitungen in den Psalmen: Eine Hypothese von Christoph Levin formgeschichtlich und kolometrisch überprüft." *UF* 31:443–535.

——. 2012. "Remembering a Memorable Conversation: Genesis 18:22b–33 and the Righteous in the Persian Period." Pages 195–208 in *Remembering and Forgetting in Early Second Temple Judah*. Edited by Ehud Ben Zvi and Christoph Levin. FAT 85. Tübingen: Mohr Siebeck.

Noort, Edward. 2004. "For the Sake of Righteousness. Abraham's Negotiations with YHWH as Prologue to the Sodom Narrative: Genesis 18:16–33." Pages 3–15 in *Sodom's Sin: Genesis 18–19 and Its Interpretations*. Edited by Edward Noort and Eibert J. C. Tigchelaar. TBN 7. Leiden: Brill.

Noth, Martin. 1966. *Exodus: A Commentary*. Translated by John Bowden. OTL. London: SCM.

——. 1972. *A History of Pentateuchal Traditions*. Translated by Bernhard Anderson. Englewood Cliffs, NJ: Prentice-Hall.

Nurmela, Risto. 1998. *The Levites: Their Emergence as a Second-Class Priesthood*. SFSHJ 193. Atlanta: Scholars Press.

Nurmi, Janne J. 2004. *Die Ethik unter dem Druck des Alltags: Die Impulse der gesellschaftlichen Änderungen und Situation zu der sozialkritischen Prophetie in Juda im 8. Jh. v. Chr.* Åbo: Åbo Akademis Förlag.

Oeming, Manfred, and Joachim Vette. 2000. *Das Buch der Psalmen. Psalm 1–41*. NSKAT. Stuttgart: Verlag Katholisches Bibelwerk.

——. 2010. *Das Buch der Psalmen. Psalm 42–89*. NSKAT. Stuttgart: Verlag Katholisches Bibelwerk.

——. 2016. *Das Buch der Psalmen. Psalm 90–151*. NSKAT. Stuttgart: Verlag Katholisches Bibelwerk.

Olyan, Saul M. 2004. "Purity Ideology in Ezra-Nehemiah as a Tool to Reconstitute the Community." *JSJ* 35:1–16.

——, ed. 2012. *Social Theory and the Study of Israelite Religion: Essays in Retrospect and Prospect*. RBS 71. Atlanta: Society of Biblical Literature.

Osumi, Yuichi. 1991. *Die Kompositionsgeschichte des Bundesbuches Exodus 20,22b–23,33*. OBO 105. Fribourg: Presses Universitaires; Göttingen: Vandenhoeck & Ruprecht.

Oswald, Wolfgang. 1998. *Israel am Gottesberg: Eine Untersuchung zur Literargeschichte der vorderen Sinaiperikope Ex 19–24 und deren historischen Hintergrund*. OBO 159. Fribourg: Presses Universitaires; Göttingen: Vandenhoeck & Ruprecht.

——. 2012. "Die Exodus-Gottesberg-Erzählung als Gründungsurkunde der judäischen Bürgergemeinde." Pages 35–51 in *Law and Narrative in the Bible and in Neighbouring Ancient Cultures*. Edited by Klaus-Peter

Adam, Friedrich Avemarie, Nili Wazana, and Dorit Felsch. FAT 2/54. Tübingen: Mohr Siebeck.

———. 2014. "Lawgiving at the Mountain of God (Exodus 19–24)." Pages 169–92 in *The Book of Exodus: Composition, Reception, and Interpretation*. Edited by Thomas Dozeman, Craig A. Evans, and Joel N. Lohr. VTSup 164. Leiden: Brill.

Oswalt, John. 1981. "Recent Studies in Old Testament Eschatology and Apocalyptic." *JETS* 24:289–301.

Otto, Eckart. 1988. *Wandel der Rechtsbegründungen in der Gesellschaftsgeschichte des antiken Israel: Eine Rechtsgeschichte des 'Bundesbuches' Ex XX 22–XXIII 13*. StudBib 3. Leiden: Brill.

———. 1993. "Vom Bundesbuch zum Deuteronomium: Die deuteronomische Redaktion in Dtn 12–26." Pages 260–78 in *Biblische Theologie und gesellschaftlicher Wandel: Festschrift Norbert Lohfink*. Edited by Georg Braulik, Walter Gross, and Sean E. McEvenue. Freiburg: Herder.

———. 1994a. *Theologische Ethik des Alten Testaments*. ThW 3.2. Stuttgart: Kohlhammer.

———. 1994b. "Aspects of Legal Reforms and Reformulations in Ancient Cuneiform and Israelite Law." Pages 160–96 in *Theory and Method in Biblical and Cuneiform Law: Revision, Interpolation and Development*. Edited by Bernard M. Levinson. JSOTSup 181. Sheffield: Sheffield Academic.

———. 2000. *Das Deuteronomium im Pentateuch und Hexateuch: Studien zur Literaturgeschichte von Pentateuch und Hexateuch im Lichte des Deuteronomiumrahmens*. FAT 30. Tübingen: Mohr Siebeck.

———. 2007. "Scribal Scholarship in the Formation of Torah and Prophets: A Postexilic Scribal Debate between Priestly Scholarship and Literary Prophecy—The Example of the Book of Jeremiah and Its Relation to the Pentateuch." Pages 171–84 in *The Pentateuch as Torah: New Models for Understanding Its Promulgation and Acceptance*. Edited by Gary N. Knoppers and Bernard M. Levinson. Winona Lake, IN: Eisenbrauns.

———. 2010. "Das Bundesbuch und der 'Kodex' Hammurapi: das biblische Recht zwischen positiver und subversiver Rezeption von Keilschriftrecht." *ZABR* 16:1–26.

———. 2012. *Deuteronomium 1–11, Zweiter Teilband: 4,44–11,32*. HThKAT. Freiburg: Herder.

Paschen, Wilfried. 1970. *Rein und Unrein: Untersuchung zur biblischen Wortgeschichte*. SANT 24. Munich: Kösel-Verlag.

Patrick, Dale. 1977. "The Covenant Code Source." *VT* 27:145–57.

Pattison, Robert. 1982. *On Literacy: The Politics of the Word from Homer to the Age of Rock*. New York: Oxford University Press.

Paul, Shalom. 1970. *Studies in the Book of the Covenant in the Light of Cuneiform and Biblical Law*. VTSup 18. Leiden: Brill.

Pearce, Laurie. 2015. "Identifying Judeans and Judean Identity in the Babylonian Evidence." Pages 7–32 in *Exile and Return: The Babylonian Context*. Edited by Jonathan Stökl and Caroline Waerzeggers. BZAW 478. Berlin: de Gruyter.

Perlitt, Lothar. 1969. *Bundestheologie im Alten Testament*. WMANT 36. Neukirchen-Vluyn: Neukirchener.

Phillips, Anthony. 1984. "A Fresh Look at the Sinai Pericope: Part 1." *VT* 34:39–52.

Pleins, J. David. 1987. "Poverty in the Social World of the Wise." *JSOT* 37:61–78.

———. 2001. *The Social Visions of the Hebrew Bible*. Louisville: Westminster John Knox.

Plöger, Otto. 1968. *Theokratie und Eschatologie*. 3rd ed. WMANT 2. Neukirchen-Vluyn: Neukirchner.

Pohlmann, Karl-Friedrich. 1978. *Studien zum Jeremiabuch: Ein Beitrag zur Frage nach der Entstehung des Jeremiabuches*. FRLANT 118. Göttingen: Vandenhoeck & Ruprecht.

———. 1989. *Die Ferne Gottes: Studien zum Jeremiabuch, Beiträge zu den "Konfessionen" im Jeremiabuch und ein Versuch zur Frage nach den Anfängen der Jeremiatradition*. BZAW 179. Berlin: de Gruyter.

———. 2004. "Esra als Identifikationsfigur im Frühjudentum: Beobachtungen und Erwägungen zu Esr 9." Pages 486–98 in *Das Manna fällt auch heute noch: Beiträge zur Geschichte und Theologie des Alten, Ersten Testaments; Festschrift für Erich Zenger*. Edited by Frank-Lothar Hossfeld and Ludger Schwienhorst-Schönberger. HBS. Freiburg: Herder.

Polanyi, Karl. 2001. *The Great Transformation: The Political and Economic Origins of Our Time*. Boston: Beacon Press.

Preuss, Horst Dietrich. 1978. "Jahweglaube als Zukunftserwartung." Pages 293–305 in *Eschatologie im Alten Testament*. Edited by Horst Dietrich Preuss. WdF 480. Darmstadt: Wissenschaftliche Buchgesellschaft.

Puech, Émile. 2005. "The Essenes and Qumran, the Teacher and the Wicked Priest, the Origins." Pages 298–302 in *Enoch and Qumran Origins: New Light on a Forgotten Connection*. Edited by Gabriele Boccaccini. Grand Rapids: Eerdmans.

Pummer, Reinhard. 2007. "The Samaritans and Their Pentateuch." Pages 237–69 in *The Pentateuch as Torah: New Models of Understanding Its Promulgation and Acceptance*. Edited by Gary N. Knoppers and Bernard M. Levinson. Winona Lake, IN: Eisenbrauns.

Pury, Albert de. 2006. "The Jacob Story and the Beginning of the Formation of the Pentateuch." Pages 51–73 in *A Farewell to the Yahwist? The Composition of the Pentateuch in Recent European Interpretation*. Edited by Thomas B. Dozeman and Konrad Schmid. SymS 34. Atlanta: Society of Biblical Literature.

Rad, Gerhard von. 1936. "Die Konfessionen Jeremias." *EvT* 3:265–76.

———. 1965. *The Theology of Israel's Prophetic Traditions*. Volume 2 of *Old Testament Theology*. Translated by D. M. G. Stalker. Edinburgh: Oliver & Boyd.

———. 1976. *Das erste Buch Mose: Genesis übersetzt und erklärt*. 10th ed. ATD 2.4. Göttingen: Vandenhoeck & Ruprecht.

Rahlfs, Alfred. 1892. *ʿAni und ʿanaw in den Psalmen*. Göttingen: Dieterich.

Randall, Susan C., and Hermann Strasser. 1976. *Status Inconsistency Reconsidered: Theoretical Problems and Neglected Consequences*. Wien: Institute for Advanced Studies.

Rappaport, Uriel. 1984. "Numismatics." *CHJ* 1:25–59.

Reeder, Caryn A. 2007. "Malachi 3:24 and the Eschatological Restoration of the 'Family.'" *CBQ* 69:695–709.

Reindl, J. 1984. "לחץ." *ThWAT* 4:547–52.

Rendsburg, Gary A. 2002. "Some False Leads in the Identification of Late Biblical Hebrew Texts: The Cases of Genesis 24 and 1 Samuel 2:27–36." *JBL* 121:23–46.

Rendtorff, Rolf. 1963. *Die Gesetze in der Priesterschrift: Eine gattungsgeschichtliche Untersuchung*. FRLANT 62. Göttingen: Vandenhoeck & Ruprecht.

———. 1990. *The Problem of the Process of Transmission in the Pentateuch*. Translated by John J. Scullion. JSOTSup 89. Sheffield: JSOT Press, 1990.

Ringgren, Helmer. 1953. "Einige Bemerkungen zum 73. Psalm." *VT* 3:265–72.

Ro, Johannes Unsok. 2002. *Die sogenannte "Armenfrömmigkeit" im nachexilischen Israel*. BZAW 322. Berlin: de Gruyter.

———. 2008. "Socio-economic Context of Post-Exilic Community and Literacy." *ZAW* 120:597–611.

——. 2011. "The Theological Concept of YHWH's Punitive Justice in the Hebrew Bible: Historical Development in the Context of the Judean Community in the Persian Period." *VT* 61:406–25.

——, ed. 2013. *From Judah to Judaea: Socio-economic Structures and Processes in the Persian Period.* HBM 43. Sheffield: Sheffield Phoenix.

——. 2014. "The Portrayal of Judean Communities in Persian Era Palestine through the Lens of the Covenant Code." *Semitica* 56:249–89.

Roberts, J. J. M. 1973. "The Young Lions of Psalm 34,11." *Bib* 54:265–67.

Robinson, H. Wheeler. 1980. *Corporate Personality in Ancient Israel.* Revised ed. Philadelphia: Fortress.

Rofé, Alexander. 1985. "Isaiah 66,1–4, Judean Sects in the Persian Period as Viewed by Trito Isaiah." Pages 205–17 in *Biblical and Related Studies Presented to Samuel Iwry.* Edited by Ann Kort and Scott Morschauser. Winona Lake, IN: Eisenbrauns.

Rollston, Christopher. 2010. *Writing and Literacy in the World of Ancient Israel: Epigraphic Evidence from the Iron Age.* ABS 11. Atlanta: Society of Biblical Literature.

Rom-Shiloni, Dalit. 2013. *Exclusive Inclusivity: Identity Conflicts Between the Exiles and the People Who Remained (Sixth–Fifth Centuries BCE).* LHBOTS 543. London: T&T Clark.

Römer, Thomas. 1999. "How Did Jeremiah Become a Convert to Deuteronomistic Ideology?" Pages 189–99 in *Those Elusive Deuteronomists: The Phenomenon of Pan-Deuteronomism.* Edited by Linda S. Schearing and Steven L. McKenzie. JSOTSup 268. Sheffield: Sheffield Academic.

——. 2000. "Is There a Deuteronomistic Redaction in the Book of Jeremiah?" Pages 399–421 in *Israel Constructs Its History: Deuteronomistic Historiography in Recent Research.* Edited by Albert de Pury, Thomas Römer, and Jean-Daniel Macchi. JSOTSup 306. Sheffield: Sheffield Academic.

——. 2002. "Das Buch Numeri und das Ende des Jahwisten: Anfragen zur 'Quellenscheidung' im vierten Buch des Pentateuch" Pages 215–31 in *Abschied vom Jahwisten: Die Komposition des Hexateuch in der jüngsten Diskussion.* Edited by Jan Christian Gertz, Konrad Schmid, and Markus Witte. BZAW 315. Berlin: de Gruyter.

——. 2005. *The So-Called Deuteronomistic History: A Sociological, Historical and Literary Introduction.* London: T&T Clark.

——. 2006a. "Entstehungsphasen des 'deuteronomistischen Geschichtswerkes.'" Pages 45–70 in *Die deuteronomistischen Geschichtswerke: Redaktions- und religionsgeschichtliche Perspektiven zur*

"Deuteronomismus"-Diskussion in Tora und Vorderen Propheten. Edited by Markus Witte, Konrad Schmid, Doris Prechel, and Jan Christian Gertz. BZAW 365. Berlin: de Gruyter.

———. 2006b. "The Elusive Yahwist: A Short History of Research." Pages 9–27 in *A Farewell to the Yahwist? The Composition of the Pentateuch in Recent European Interpretation.* Edited by Thomas B. Dozeman and Konrad Schmid. SymS 34. Atlanta: Society of Biblical Literature.

———. 2009a. "Provisorische Überlegungen zur Entstehung von Exodus 18–24." Pages 128–54 in *"Gerechtigkeit und Recht zu üben" (Gen 18,19): Studien zur altorientalischen und biblischen Rechtsgeschichte, zur Religionsgeschichte Israels und zur Religionssoziologie; Festschrift für Eckart Otto zum 65. Geburtstag.* Edited by Reinhard Achenbach and Martin Arneth. BZABR 13. Wiesbaden: Harrassowitz.

———. 2009b. "The Formation of the Book of Jeremiah as a Supplement to the So-called Deuteronomistic History." Pages 168–83 in *The Production of Prophecy: Constructing Prophecy and Prophets in Yehud.* Edited by Diana Edelman and Ehud Ben Zvi. BibleWorld. London: Equinox.

———. 2013. *Dark God: Cruelty, Sex, and Violence in the Old Testament.* New York: Paulist Press.

———. 2014. "Der Pentateuch." Pages 53–166 in Walter Dietrich, Hans-Peter Mathys, Thomas Römer, and Rudolf Smend, *Die Entstehung des Alten Testaments.* ThW 1. Stuttgart: Kohlhammer.

———. 2015. "Joschija, Moses und Abraham als Erben Davids: Der Umgang mit der davidischen Dynastie in der persischen Zeit." Pages 85–101 in *A King Like All the Nations? Kingdoms of Israel and Judah in the Bible and History; An International Conference at Charles University Prague, April 2014.* Edited by Manfred Oeming and Petr Sláma. BVB 28. Berlin: LIT.

Rose, Martin. 1975. *Der Ausschließlichkeitsanspruch Jahwes: Deuteronomische Schultheologie und die Volksfrömmigkeit in der späten Königszeit.* BWANT 106. Stuttgart: Kohlhammer.

Rückl, Jan. 2016. *A Sure House: Studies on the Dynastic Promise to David in the Books of Samuel and Kings.* OBO 281. Fribourg: Presses Universitaires; Göttingen: Vandenhoeck & Ruprecht.

Rudolph, Wilhelm. 1968. *Jeremia.* 3rd ed. HAT 12. Tübingen: Mohr.

Rüpke, Jörg. 2007. *Historische Religionswissenschaft: Eine Einführung.* Religionswissenschaft heute 5. Stuttgart: Kohlhammer.

Ruppert, Lothar. 1972. *Der leidende Gerechte: Eine motivgeschichtliche Untersuchung zum Alten Testament Und zwischentestamentlichen Judentum.* FB 5. Würzberg: Echter.

———. 2002. *Genesis: Ein kritischer und theologischer Kommentar 2 (Gen 11,27–25,18).* FB 98. Würzberg: Echter.

Ruwe, Andreas. 1999. *'Heiligkeitsgesetz' und 'Priesterschrift': Literaturgeschichtliche und rechtssystematische Untersuchungen zu Leviticus 17,1–26,2.* FAT 26. Tübingen: Mohr Siebeck.

Samuel, Harald. 2014. *Von Priestern zum Patriarchen: Levi und die Leviten im Alten Testament.* BZAW 448. Berlin: de Gruyter.

Sandoval, Timothy J. 2006. *The Discourse of Wealth and Poverty in the Book of Proverbs.* BibInt 77. Leiden: Brill.

Sarna, Nahum M. 1989. *Genesis: The Traditional Hebrew Text with New JPS Translation.* JPSTC. Philadelphia: Jewish Publication Society.

Schäfer-Lichtenberger, C., and L. Schottroff. 2009. "Schulden." Pages 509–15 in *Sozialgeschichtliches Wörterbuch zur Bibel.* Edited by Frank Crüsemann et al. Gütersloh: Gütersloher Verlagshaus.

Schaper, Joachim. 2000. *Priester und Leviten im achämenidischen Juda: Studien zur Kult- und Sozialgeschichte Israels in persischer Zeit.* FAT 31. Tübingen: Mohr Siebeck.

———. 2005. "Exilic and Postexilic Prophecy and the Orality/Literacy Problem." *VT* 55:324–42.

Schmid, Hans Heinrich. 1976. *Der sogenannte Jahwist: Beobachtungen und Fragen zur Pentateuchforschung.* Zurich: TVZ.

Schmid, Konrad. 1996. *Buchgestalten des Jeremiabuches: Untersuchungen zur Redaktions- und Rezeptionsgeschichte von Jer 30–33 im Kontext des Buches.* WMANT 72. Neukirchen-Vluyn: Neukirchener Verlag.

———. 1999. *Erzväter und Exodus: Untersuchungen zur doppelten Begründung der Ursprünge Israels innerhalb der Geschichtsbücher des Alten Testaments.* WMANT 81. Neukirchen-Vluyn: Neukirchener Verlag.

———. 2006. "The So-Called Yahwist and the Literary Gap between Genesis and Exodus." Pages 29–50 in *A Farewell to the Yahwist? The Composition of the Pentateuch in Recent European Interpretation.* Edited by Thomas B. Dozeman and Konrad Schmid. SymS 34. Atlanta: Society of Biblical Literature.

Schmidt, Hans. 1934. *Die Psalmen.* HAT 15. Tübingen: Mohr.

Schmidt, Ludwig. 1976. *"De Deo": Studien zur Literarkritik und Theologie des Buches Jona, des Gesprächs zwischen Abraham und Jahwe in Gen 18, 22ff. u. von Hi 1.* BZAW 143. Berlin: de Gruyter.

Schmidt, Werner H. 2008. *Das Buch Jeremia: Kapitel 1–20.* ATD 20. Göttingen: Vandenhoeck & Ruprecht.

Schniedewind, William M. 2000. "Orality and Literacy in Ancient Israel." *RelSRev* 26:327–32.

———. 2005. *How the Bible Became a Book: The Textualization of Ancient Israel.* Cambridge: Cambridge University Press.

Scholl, Reinhard. 2000. *Die Elenden in Gottes Thronrat: Stilistisch-kompositorische Untersuchungen zu Jesaja 24–27.* BZAW 274. Berlin: de Gruyter.

Schubert, K. 1952. "Die jüdischen und judenchristlichen Sekten im Lichte der Handschriftenfunde von En Feshka." *ZKT* 74:1–62.

Schultz, Paul. 1974. *Der Autoritätsanspruch des Lehrers der Gerechtigkeit in Qumran.* Meisenheim am Glan: Hain.

Schwienhorst-Schönberger, Ludger. 1990. *Das Bundesbuch (Ex 20,22–23,33): Studien zu seiner Entstehung und Theologie.* BZAW 188. Berlin: de Gruyter.

Seebass, Horst. 2003. *Numeri, 2. Teilband: Numeri 10,11–22,1.* BKAT 4.2. Neukirchen-Vluyn: Neukirchener Verlag.

Segal, David R., and David Knoke. 1980. "The Impact of Social Stratification, Social Mobility, and Status Inconsistency on the German Political Party Infrastructure." Pages 149–66 in *Political Sociology: Readings in Research and Theory.* Edited by George A. Kourvetaris and Betty A. Dobratz. New Brunswick, NJ: Transaction Books.

Segal, M. H. 1951. "The Habakkuk 'Commentary' and the Damascus Fragments." *JBL* 70:131–47.

Seidl, Theodor. 1995. "Jeremias Tempelrede: Polemik gegen die joschijanische Reform? Die Paralleltraditionen Jer 7 und 26 auf ihre Effizienz für das Deuteronomismusproblem in Jeremia befragt." Pages 141–79 in *Jeremia und die "deuteronomistische Bewegung."* Edited by Walter Gross. BBB 98. Weinheim: Athenäum.

Seybold, Klaus. 1996. *Die Psalmen.* HAT 15. Tübingen: Mohr.

Sharp, Carolyn J. 2003. *Prophecy and Ideology in Jeremiah: Struggles for Authority in the Deutero-Jeremianic Prose.* London: T&T Clark.

Silver, Morris. 1983. *Prophets and Markets: The Political Economy of Ancient Israel.* Social Dimensions of Economics. Boston: Kluwer-Nijhoff.

Silverman, J. 2013. Review of *From Judah to Judea: Socio-economic Structures and Processes in the Persian Period,* ed. by Johannes Unsok Ro. *RBL:* http://tinyurl.com/SBL2635b.

Simkins, Ronald. 1999. "Patronage and the Political Economy of Ancient Israel." *Semeia* 87:123–44.

———. 2004. "Family in the Political Economy of Monarchic Israel." *BCT* 1:1–17.

Singh, Samrendra. 1986. "Status Inconsistency and Psychological Stress in a Non-Western Society: The Case of India." Pages 368–81 in *Status Inconsistency in Modern Societies: Proceedings of a Conference on "New Differentiations of Status Structures? On the Viability of the Concept of Status Inconsistency in Contemporary Society," Duisburg, F.R.G., May 7–9, 1985*. Edited by Hermann Strasser and Roger Hodge. Sozialwissenschaftliche Schriften 33. Duisburg: Sozialwissenschaftlichen Kooperative.

Sivertsev, Alexei. 2005. "Sects and Households: Social Structure of the Proto-Sectarian Movement of Nehemiah 10 and the Dead Sea Sect." *CBQ* 67:59–78.

Ska, Jean-Louis. 2008. "Genesis 2–3." Pages 1–27 in *Beyond Eden: The Biblical Story of Paradise (Genesis 2–3) and Its Reception History*. Edited by Konrad Schmid and Christoph Riedweg. FAT 2/34. Tübingen: Mohr Siebeck.

———. 2009. *The Exegesis of the Pentateuch: Exegetical Studies and Basic Questions*. FAT 66. Tübingen: Mohr Siebeck.

Skehan, Patrick W. 1987. *The Wisdom of Ben Sira: A New Translation with Notes*. AB 39. New York: Doubleday.

Skinner, John. 1930. *A Critical and Exegetical Commentary on Genesis*. ICC. Edinburgh: T&T Clark.

Slomczynski, Kazimierz M., and Bogdan W. Mach. 1997. "Dissolution of the Socialist Working Class in Poland, Hungary, and the Czech Republic: A Myth or Reality?" *Sisyphus* 10:93–117.

Smith, Daniel L. 1991. "The Politics of Ezra: Sociological Indicators of Postexilic Judaean Society." Pages 73–97 in *Second Temple Studies 1: Persian Period*. Edited by Philip R. Davies. JSOTSup 117. Sheffield: Sheffield Academic.

Smith, Morton. 1987. *Palestinian Parties and Politics that Shaped the Old Testament*. London: SCM.

Sneed, Mark R. 1999. *Concepts of Class in Ancient Israel*. SFSHJ 201. Atlanta: Scholars Press.

Soggin, J. Alberto. 1994. "Abraham hadert mit Gott: Beobachtungen zu Genesis 18,16–32." Pages 214–18 in *Wer ist wie du, Herr, unter den Göttern? Studien zur Theologie und Religionsgeschichte Israels: Fest-*

schrift für Otto Kaiser. Edited by Ingo Kottsieper et al. Göttingen: Vandenhoeck & Ruprecht.

Spencer, John. 1992. "Aaron." *ABD* 1:1–6.

Stackert, Jeffrey. 2007. *Rewriting the Torah: Literary Revision in Deuteronomy and the Holiness Legislation*. FAT 52. Tübingen: Mohr Siebeck.

Staerk, Willy. 1911. *Lyrik: Psalmen, Hoheslied und Verwandtes*. SAT 3.1. Göttingen: Vandenhoeck & Ruprecht.

Steck, Odil. 1982. *Wahrnehmungen Gottes im Alten Testament: Gesammelte Studien*. TB 70. Munich: Kaiser.

———. 1990. "Zu Eigenart und Herkunft von Ps 102." *ZAW* 102:357–72.

———. 1991. *Studien zu Tritojesaja*. BZAW 203. Berlin: de Gruyter.

Ste. Croix, G. E. M. 1981. *The Class Struggle in the Ancient Greek World: From the Archaic Age to the Arab Conquests*. Ithaca, NY: Cornell University Press.

Stegemann, Ekkehard, and Wolfgang Stegemann. 1999. *The Jesus Movement: A Social History of Its First Century*. Translated by O. Dean. Minneapolis: Fortress.

Stegemann, Hartmut. 1963. "Der Pešer Psalm 37 aus Höhle 4 von Qumran (4QpPs 37)." *RevQ* 4:235–70.

———. 1999. *Die Essener, Qumran, Johannes der Täufer und Jesus: Ein Sachbuch*. Freiburg: Herder.

Stern, Ephraim. 1982. *Material Culture of the Land of the Bible in the Persian Period, 538–332 B.C.* Warminster: Aris & Phillips.

———. 2001. *Archaeology of the Land of the Bible II: The Assyrian, Babylonian, and Persian Periods (732–332 B.C.E.)*. ABRL. New York: Doubleday.

———. 2006. "The Religious Revolution in Persian-Period Judah." Pages 199–205 in *Judah and the Judeans in the Persian Period*. Edited by Oded Lipschits and Manfred Oeming. Winona Lake, IN: Eisenbrauns.

Stevens, Marty E. 2006. *Temples, Tithes and Taxes: The Temple and the Economic Life of Ancient Israel*. Peabody, MA: Hendrickson.

Stipp, Hermann-Josef. 1995a. *Das masoretische und das alexandrinische Sondergut des Jeremiabuches: Textgeschichtlicher Rang, Eigenarten, Triebkräfte*. Göttingen: Vandenhoeck & Ruprecht.

———. 1995b. "Probleme des redaktionsgeschichtlichen Modells der Entstehung des Jeremiabuches." Pages 225–62 in *Jeremia und die "deuteronomistische Bewegung."* Edited by Walter Gross. BBB 98. Weinheim: Athenäum.

———. 2009. "Sprachliche Kennzeichen jeremianischer Autorschaft." Pages 148–186 in *Prophecy in the Book of Jeremiah*. Edited by Hans M. Barstad and Reinhard G. Kratz. BZAW 388. Berlin: de Gruyter.

———. 2013. *Alttestamentliche Studien: Arbeiten zu Priesterschrift, Deuteronomistischem Geschichtswerk und Prophetie*. BZAW 442. Berlin: de Gruyter.

———. 2015. *Studien zum Jeremiabuch: Text und Redaktion*. FAT 96. Tübingen: Mohr Siebeck.

Stolz, Fritz. 1983. *Psalmen im nachkultischen Raum*. ThSt 129. Zurich: TVZ.

Strasser, Hermann, and Robert W. Hodge. 1993. "Issues and Ideas in the Study of Status Inconsistency." Pages 3–36 in *Change and Strain in Social Hierarchies: Theory and Method in the Study of Status Inconsistency*. Edited by Robert W. Hodge and Hermann Strasser. Delhi: Ajanta.

Stryker, Sheldon. 1993. "Status Inconsistency From an Interactionist Perspective: A Theoretical Elaboration." Pages 70–82 in *Change and Strain in Social Hierarchies: Theory and Method in the Study of Status Inconsistency*. Edited by Robert W. Hodge and Hermann Strasser. Delhi: Ajanta.

Stulman, Louis. 1986. *The Prose Sermons of the Book of Jeremiah: A Redescription of the Correspondences with Deuteronomistic Literature in the Light of Recent Text-critical Research*. SBLDS 83. Atlanta: Scholars Press.

Sturdy, John. 1976. *Numbers*. CBC. Cambridge: Cambridge University Press.

Tainter, Joseph. 1988. *The Collapse of Complex Societies*. New Studies in Archaeology. New York: Cambridge University Press.

———. 1999. "Post-Collapse Societies." Pages 988–1039 in *Companion Encyclopedia of Archaeology II*. Edited by Graeme Barker. London: Routledge.

Thiel, Winfried. 1973. *Die deuteronomistische Redaktion von Jeremia 1–25*. WMANT 41. Neukirchen-Vluyn: Neukirchener Verlag.

———. 1981. *Die deuteronomistische Redaktion von Jeremia 26–45: Mit einer Gesamtbeurteilung der deuteronomistischen Redaktion des Buches Jeremia*. WMANT 52. Neukirchen-Vluyn: Neukirchener Verlag.

Thiel, Wolfgang M. 2007. *Untersuchungen zum hellenistischen Siedlungswesen in Palästina und Transjordanien*. Munich: Verlag Dr. Hut.

Tillich, Paul. 1951. *Systematic Theology: Reason and Revelation; Being and God*. Chicago: University of Chicago Press.

Toorn, Karel van der. 1996. *Family Religion in Babylonia, Syria and Israel: Continuity and Change in the Forms of Religious Life*. SHANE 7. Leiden: Brill.

———. 2007. *Scribal Culture and the Making of the Hebrew Bible*. Cambridge: Harvard University Press.

Tucker, W. Dennis, Jr. 2014. *Constructing and Deconstructing Power in Psalms 107–150*. AIL 19. Atlanta: SBL Press.

Uhlig, Siegbert. 1984. *Das Äthiopische Henochbuch*. JSHRZ 5.6. Gütersloh: Mohn.

UIS (UNESCO Institute for Statistics). 2017. "Literacy Rates Continue to Rise from One Generation to the Next." Fact Sheet No. 45. https://tinyurl.com/SBL2635k.

Van Seters, John. 1975. *Abraham in History and Tradition*. New Haven: Yale University Press.

———. 1994. *The Life of Moses: The Yahwist as Historian in Exodus–Numbers*. Louisville: Westminster John Knox.

———. 1999. "Is There Evidence of a Dtr Redaction in the Sinai Pericope (Exodus 19–24, 32–34)?" Pages 160–70 in *Those Elusive Deuteronomists: The Phenomenon of Pan-Deuteronomism*. Edited by Linda S. Schearing and Steven L. McKenzie. JSOTSup 268. Sheffield: Sheffield Academic.

———. 2003. *A Law Book for the Diaspora: Revision in the Study of the Covenant Code*. New York: Oxford University Press.

———. 2007. "Revision in the Study of the Covenant Code and a Response to My Critics." *SJOT* 21:5–28.

VanderKam, James C. 1998. *Einführung in die Qumranforschung: Geschichte und Bedeutung der Schriften vom Toten Meer*. Translated by Markus Müller. UTB. Göttingen: Vandenhoeck & Ruprecht.

Vermeylen, Jacques. 1978. *Du prophète Isaïe à l'apocalyptique: Isaïe, I–XXXV, miroir d'un demi-millénaire d'expérience religieuse en Israël*. EBib. Paris: Lecoffre.

Vielhauer, Roman. 2013. "Sodom and Gomorrah: From the Bible to Qumran." Pages 147–69 in *Rewriting and Interpreting the Hebrew Bible: The Biblical Patriarchs in the Light of the Dead Sea Scrolls*. Edited by Devorah Dimant and Reinhold G. Kratz. BZAW 439. Berlin: de Gruyter.

Volz, Paul. 1928. *Der Prophet Jeremia übersetzt und erklärt.* 2nd ed. KAT 10. Leipzig: Scholl.

Wanke, Gunther. 1995. *Jeremia 1.* ZBK 20.1. Zurich: TVZ.

———. 2003. *Jeremia 2.* ZBK 20.2. Zurich: TVZ.

Washington, Harold C. 1994. *Wealth and Poverty in the Instruction of Amenemope and the Hebrew Proverbs.* SBLDS 142. Atlanta: Scholars Press.

Wassén, Cecilia. 2016. "The Importance of Marriage in the Construction of a Sectarian Identity." Pages 127–150 in *Social Memory and Social Identity in the Study of Early Judaism and Early Christianity.* Edited by S. Byrskog, Raimo Hakola, and Jutta Jokiranta. NTOA 116. Göttingen: Vandenhoeck & Ruprecht.

Weber, Max. 1947. *The Theory of Social and Economic Organization.* Translated by Alexander M. Henderson and Talcott Parsons. New York: Free Press.

———. 1949. *The Methodology of the Social Sciences.* Translated by Edward Shils and Henry Finch. Glencoe, IL: Free Press.

———. 1957. *From Max Weber: Essays in Sociology.* Translated by Hans Gerth and C. Wright Mills. London: Routledge & Kegan Paul.

Weinberg, Joel. 1992. *The Citizen-Temple Community.* Translated by Daniel L. Smith-Christopher. JSOTSup 151. Sheffield: JSOT Press.

Weinfeld, Moshe. 1972. *Deuteronomy and the Deuteronomic School.* Oxford: Clarendon.

———. 1995. *Social Justice in Ancient Israel and in the Ancient Near East.* Jerusalem: Magnes Press.

Weippert, Helga. 1973. *Die Prosareden des Jeremiabuches.* BZAW 132. Berlin: de Gruyter.

Weiser, Artur. 1956. *Das Buch des Propheten Jeremia.* 2nd ed. ATD 20–21. Göttingen: Vandenhoeck & Ruprecht.

———. 1966. *Die Psalmen.* 7th ed. ATD 14–15. Göttingen: Vandenhoeck & Ruprecht.

Wellhausen, Julius. 1957. *Prolegomena to the History of Ancient Israel.* Translated by John S. Black and Allan Menzies. New York: Meridian.

———. 1963. *Die Composition des Hexateuchs und der historischen Bücher des Alten Testaments.* 4th ed. Berlin: de Gruyter.

Wells, Bruce. 2015. "The Interpretation of Legal Traditions in Ancient Israel." *HBAI* 4.3:234–66.

Wenham, Gordon. 1994. *Genesis 16–50.* WBC 2. Dallas: Word Books.

Westermann, Claus. 1981. *Das Buch Jesaja, Kap. 40–66*. ATD 19. Göttingen: Vandenhoeck & Ruprecht.

———. 1985. *Genesis 12–36: A Continental Commentary*. Translated by John J. Scullion. Minneapolis: Fortress.

———. 1990. *Die Klagelieder: Forschungsgeschichte und Auslegung*. Neukirchen-Vluyn: Neukirchener Verlag.

Weyde, K. W. 2015. "The Priests and the Descendants of Levi in the Book of Malachi." *AcT* 35:238–53.

Whitney, D. Charles. 1980. "Status Inconsistency and Attention to Public Affairs in Mass Media." *Journalism Quarterly* 57:138–41.

Whybray, Roger N. 1990. *Wealth and Poverty in the Book of Proverbs*. JSOTSup 99. Sheffield: Sheffield Academic.

Willi-Plein, Ina. 2007. "Palast, Gotteshaus oder Räuberhöhle: Erwägungen zum Tempelwort des Jeremia." Pages 163–82 in *Mein Haus wird ein Bethaus für alle Völker genannt werden (Jes 56,7): Judentum seit der Zeit des Zweiten Tempels in Geschichte, Literatur und Kult; Festschrift für Thomas Willi zum 65. Geburtstag*. Edited by Julia Männchen. Neukirchen-Vluyn: Neukirchener Verlag.

Winkler, Mathias. 2014. "Der Levit als totaler Stellvertreter: Theologische Vorstellungen zum Levitentum im Ausgang von Num 3–4." *BN* 162:3–22.

Wissmann, Felipe Blanco. 2011. "'He Did What Was Right': Criteria of Judgment and Deuteronomism in the Book of Kings." Pages 241–59 in *Pentateuch, Hexateuch, or Enneateuch? Identifying Literary Works in Genesis through Kings*. Edited by Thomas B. Dozeman, Konrad Schmid, and Thomas Römer. AIL 8. Atlanta: Society of Biblical Literature.

Witte, Markus. 2014. *Von Ewigkeit zu Ewigkeit: Weisheit und Geschichte in den Psalmen*. BThSt 146. Neukirchen-Vluyn: Neukirchener Verlag.

Wolf, Eric R. 1966. *Peasants*. Englewood Cliffs, NJ: Prentice-Hall.

Wolff, Christian. 1976. *Jeremia im Frühjudentum und Urchristentum*. TU 118. Berlin: Akademie-Verlag.

Woude, A. S. van der. 1982. "Wicked Priest or Wicked Priests?" *JJS* 33:349–59.

———. 1996. "Once Again: The Wicked Priests in the Habakuk Pesher from Cave 1 of Qumran." *RevQ* 17:375–84.

Wright, David P. 2009a. *Inventing God's Law: How the Covenant Code of the Bible Used and Revised the Laws of Hammurabi*. New York: Oxford University Press.

——. 2009b. "Chiasmus in the Covenant Code Reconsidered: The Final Apodictic Laws." Pages 171–81 in *"Gerechtigkeit und Recht zu üben"* *(Gen 18,19): Studien zur altorientalischen und biblischen Rechtsgeschichte, zur Religionsgeschichte Israels und zur Religionssoziologie; Festschrift für Eckart Otto zum 65. Geburtstag.* Edited by Reinhard Achenbach and Martin Arneth. BZABR 13. Wiesbaden: Harrassowitz.

——. 2014. "The Origin, Development, and Context of the Covenant Code (Exodus 20:23–23:19)." Pages 220–44 in *The Book of Exodus: Composition, Reception, and Interpretation.* Edited by Thomas B. Dozeman, Craig A. Evans, and Joel N. Lohr. VTSup 164. Leiden: Brill.

——. 2016. "Law and Creation in the Priestly-Holiness Writings of the Pentateuch." Pages 71–101 in *Laws of Heaven, Laws of Nature: Legal Interpretations of Cosmic Phenomena in the Ancient World.* Edited by Konrad Schmid and Christoph Uehlinger. OBO 276. Fribourg: Presses Universitaire; Göttingen: Vandenhoeck & Ruprecht.

Wright, John W. 2006. "Remapping Yehud: The Borders of Yehud and the Genealogies of Chronicles." Pages 67–89 in *Judah and the Judeans in the Persian Period.* Edited by Oded Lipschits and Manfred Oeming. Winona Lake, IN: Eisenbrauns.

Wuench, Hans-Georg. 2014. "The Stranger in God's Land—Foreigner, Stranger, Guest: What Can We Learn from Israel's Attitude Towards Strangers?" *OTE* 27:1129–54.

Würthwein, Ernst. 1950. "Erwägungen zu Ps 73." Page 532–49 in *Festschrift Alfred Bertholet: Zum 80. Geburtstag gewidmet von Kollegen und Freunden.* Edited by Walter Baumgärtner and Otto Wilhelm Hermann Leonhard Eissfeldt. Tübingen: Mohr.

——. 1988. *Der Text des Alten Testaments: Eine Einführung in die Biblia Hebraica.* Stuttgart: Deutsche Bibelgesellschaft.

Young, Ian M. 1998. "Israelite Literacy: Interpreting the Evidence. Part I." *VT* 48:239–53.

Zaborowski, Wojciech. 1986. "Normative Equilibrium Between Investments and Rewards: A New Look at Status Inconsistency." Pages 262–74 in *Status Inconsistency in Modern Societies: Proceedings of a Conference on "New Differentiations of Status Structures? On the Viability of the Concept of Status Inconsistency in Contemporary Society,"* *Duisburg, F.R.G., May 7–9, 1985.* Edited by Hermann Strasser and Roger Hodge. Sozialwissenschaftliche Schriften 33. Duisburg: Sozialwissenschaftlichen Kooperative.

Zadok, Ran. 2002. *The Earliest Diaspora: Israelites and Judeans in Pre-Hellenistic Mesopotamia*. Tel Aviv: Tel Aviv University.

Zehnder, Markus P. 2005. *Umgang mit Fremden in Israel und Assyrien: Ein Beitrag zur Anthropologie des "Fremden" im Licht antiker Quellen.* BWANT 168. Stuttgart: Kohlhammer.

Zenger, Erich. 1971. *Die Sinaitheophanie: Untersuchungen zum jahwistischen und elohistischen Geschichtswerk.* FB 3. Würzburg: Echter.

———. 2000. "Psalmenforschung nach Hermann Gunkel und Sigmund Mowinckel." Pages 399–435 in *Congress Volume: Oslo 1998. Congress Volume: Oslo 1998.* Edited by André Lemaire and Magne Sæbø. VTSup 80. Leiden: Brill.

Zenger, Erich, et al. 2016. *Einleitung in das Alte Testament.* 9th ed. KStTh 1.1. Stuttgart: Kohlhammer.

Zwickel, Wolfgang. 2010. "Warum waren die Orte in der Königszeit so klein?" *Welt und Umwelt der Bibel* 56:72–75.

———. 2015. *Studien zur Geschichte Israels.* Stuttgart: Verlag Katholisches Bibelwerk.

Zwickel, Wolfgang, et al. 2013. *Herders Neuer Bibelatlas.* Freiburg: Herder.

ANCIENT SOURCES INDEX

Modern Authors Index

CPSIA information can be obtained
at www.ICGtesting.com
Printed in the USA
FFOW02n1118190518
46676897-48759FF